BRIDGING NEOLIBERALISM AND HINDU NATIONALISM

The Role of Education in Bringing about Contemporary India

Marie Lall and Kusha Anand

BRISTOL
UNIVERSITY
PRESS

First published in Great Britain in 2022 by

Bristol University Press
University of Bristol
1–9 Old Park Hill
Bristol
BS2 8BB
UK
t: +44 (0)117 374 6645
e: bup-info@bristol.ac.uk

Details of international sales and distribution partners are available at bristoluniversitypress.co.uk

© Bristol University Press 2022

British Library Cataloguing in Publication Data
A catalogue record for this book is available from the British Library

ISBN 978-1-5292-2321-7 hardcover
ISBN 978-1-5292-2322-4 paperback
ISBN 978-1-5292-2323-1 ePub
ISBN 978-1-5292-2324-8 ePdf

The right of Marie Lall and Kusha Anand to be identified as authors of this work has been asserted
by them in accordance with the Copyright, Designs and Patents Act 1988.

Cover design: Nicky Borowiec
Image credit: Anadolu/Hindustan Times
Bristol University Press use environmentally responsible print partners.
Printed in Great Britain by CMP, Poole

'Patriotism cannot be our final spiritual shelter; my refuge is humanity. I will not buy glass for the price of diamonds, and I will never allow patriotism to triumph over humanity as long as I live.'
Rabindranath Tagore (1908)

For Kian Anand Mann, born at the same time as this book, and the next Indian generation he belongs to — may they become proud of their country

Contents

List of Abbreviations

AAP	Aam Aadmi Party
AASU	All Assam Students' Union
ABVP	Akhil Bharartiya Vidyarthi Parishad
AGP	Asom Gana Parishad
AJP	Assam Jatiya Parishad
ASA	Ambedkar Studies Association
ASER	Annual Status of Education Report
BJP	Bharatiya Janata Party
BoP	Balance of Payments
CBSE	Central Board of Secondary Education
CAA	Citizenship Amendment Act
CCA	Child-Centred Approach
DGs	Disadvantaged Groups
DMC	Delhi Minority Commission
DPEP	District Primary Education Programme
EAS	Employment Assurance Scheme
EMC	Entrepreneurial Mindset Curriculum
EMI	English Medium Instruction
EWSs	Economically Weaker Sections
FDI	Foreign Direct Investment
GDP	Gross Domestic Product
GIA	Group of Intellectuals and Academicians
GoI	Government of India
HE	Higher Education
HEFA	Higher Education Financing Agency
HEIs	Higher Education Institutions
HRW	Human Rights Watch
ICHR	Indian Council of Historical Research
IIMs	Indian Institutes of Management
IITs	Indian Institutes of Technology
IMDT	Illegal Migrants (Determination by Tribunals) Act
IMF	International Monetary Fund
INIs	Institutes of National Importance

JMI	Jamia Millia Islamia
JNU	Jawaharlal Nehru University
JNUTA	JNU Teachers' Association
MHRD	Ministry of Human Resource Development
MT	Mother Tongue
NCERT	National Council of Educational Research and Training
NCF	National Curriculum Framework
NDA	National Democratic Alliance
NEP	National Education Policy
NER	Net Enrolment Ratio
NETF	National Educational Technology Forum
NGOs	Non-Governmental Organisations
NRC	National Register of Citizens
NRIs	Non-Resident Indians
NSSO	National Sample Survey Organisation
NTFIT	National Task Force on Information Technology
OBCs	Other Backward Classes
PBAS	Performance Based Appraisal System
PM	Prime Minister
POTA	Prevention of Terrorism Act, 2002
PPPs	Public–Private Partnerships
RSS	Rashtriya Swayamsevak Sangh
RTE	Right to Education
SCs	Scheduled Castes
SDG	Sustainable Development Goal
SEQI	School Education Quality Index
SSA	Sarva Shiksha Abhiyan
STs	Scheduled Tribes
TDP	Telugu Desam Party
TFI	Teach for India
TISS	Tata Institute of Social Sciences
UDISE	Unified District Information System for Education
UGC	University Grants Commission
UPA	United Progressive Alliance
VHP	Vishva Hindu Parishad

Preface

Thirty years ago I arrived in India for the first time. I landed in Bombay on a hot monsoon morning in August, on Ganesh Chaturthi. I had never been to India, yet setting foot on the tarmac felt like coming home. Until that moment I knew I wanted to be an academic, but I had wondered what direction my research would take. When I stepped onto Indian soil, I knew India would be my life. Just over a year later I started my PhD at the London School of Economics on India, and shortly afterwards moved to Delhi. Five years after that first step in Mumbai's hot dawn rain I was married into a Delhi family. I was 25.

My PhD in international political economy set out to explore how India's Diaspora had or had not contributed to the economic reforms after 1991. I realized quickly that what I was exploring had nothing to do with economics, little with foreign policy, and everything to do with identity. My PhD explored what I termed the Nehruvian doctrine that regulated India's relationship with its Diaspora. Since India's national identity was based on shared history and not on ethnicity, religion, or language, Indians abroad could not be Indian. Nehru's vision was that India would only remain united if its identity was inclusive of all its citizens, forgoing any communal and religious definitions. It also allowed women like me who were marrying into Indian families to become a 'person of Indian origin'. This is in the Constitution.

As I lived in India until the late 1990s the economic reforms opened up India in front of my eyes. No one had to wait years for a new car any more. I still remember when India only had one TV channel; but soon this grew to dozens, with everyone glued to *The Bold and the Beautiful* on Star TV. Neoliberalism was on the march – not many of us knew this or even understood the ramifications. I was a witness both to the growth of the new middle classes and to the change of identity discourse as the Bharatiya Janata Party (BJP) won its first elections, and later, after another poll, formed its first government in 1998 – with the soon to follow nuclear tests.

My husband and I were on our way to London to complete our degrees when the BJP reformed the curriculum and rewrote the history textbooks. My interest in how identity was constructed through education led me to spend the next few years working on this issue as I was building an academic career at the IoE.

Over the years I began to explore other countries, with research in Pakistan and Myanmar; mostly on education issues, but also on broader political issues. Yet India was a constant in my life. At one point, Professor Subrata Mitra brought together a group of colleagues to look at citizenship in Europe and Asia – and India in particular. At that time India's citizenship was divorced from the identity changes that had taken place through education; ten years of Congress government had done little to reverse the changes made by the BJP; the communal direction seemed to have stalled – temporarily.

Modi's election win in 2014 did not come as a surprise; only the scale of the win was astonishing. From the outside the Hindutva agenda did not seem to drive Modi's government; development was the leitmotiv. I was involved in a development project in Rajasthan concerned with nutrition, public health, toilets, water, and sanitation, as well as the roles of schools and Anganwadis in improving the lives of tribal families in Banswara. The Hindu nationalism of the early 2000s seemed very far away. It was only when peeling back the layers that moves towards communalism could be discerned: reports on the effects of the cow slaughter ban, love jihad, and in the schools I visited new portraits of national heroes not seen before. When Modi won in 2019 it was again no surprise, but the swift actions on Kashmir and the Citizenship Amendment Act were. The concept of Indian citizenship had joined up with the narrative of Indian national identity, as described in many of the country's textbooks.

Then the pandemic came, and there was time to fit all the pieces of the puzzle together. The reforms, the neoliberal agenda, the changes to national identity, and finally the changes to citizenship and how everyone reacted to it was all one big story. I finally had time and space to comb through over 25 years of data and materials collected and filed over the years. Kusha Anand, my former PhD student and now my colleague joined me in the endeavour. It felt less daunting sharing the burden of the work as well as the realization that India had irrevocably changed. The Nehruvian doctrine and the India it created are dead. There is a 'naya Bharat' we have to contend with. The cover of this volume – showing both the inauguration of the Ram Temple at Ayodhya and student protests against the National Education Policy 2020 exemplifies the contemporary trajectory of this new India. Personally I believe India was stronger in its Nehruvian form; but all things change; even countries. As an academic I have cast a critical eye over how India has developed during the past

30 years. That is part of my job. However, I am not only an academic. This has also been a very personal book, describing the changes I have witnessed and experienced. As an Indian bahu, India remains my country no matter what direction it takes.

Marie Lall
London, 26 January,
Republic Day 2022

Introduction

India will soon be the world's most populated country and its political development will shape the 21st century. Yet Hindu nationalism – at the helm of contemporary Indian politics – is not well understood outside India, and its links to the global neoliberal trajectory have not been much explored. This book argues that it is because of the neoliberal education trajectory chosen after the 1991 economic reforms that India changed from a largely inclusive society to one where nationalist and religious populism results in minorities being denied their basic rights. This volume discusses how education was the vehicle that linked neoliberalism with Hindu nationalism and allowed to it permeate through Indian society.

India's 1991 economic reforms not only engendered economic liberalization and growth, but also brought about neoliberal structural changes that seeded a revived and reconfigured Hindu Nationalist political movement (Ahluwalia, 2019). Less than a decade after the start of the reforms, the first BJP-led government was in place. After a hiatus between 2004 and 2014, Hindu nationalism came back with even more vigour, delivering two thumping electoral victories for Narendra Modi. The Hindu nationalist rhetoric has stuck, even though the first five years of Modi rule did not bring about the kind of development that had been promised (Flaten, 2017). India is one of a number of developing countries – such as Brazil – that is choosing to stick with a populist regime even when their leaders do not deliver.[1] In India, the reasons for this lie within education.

This book examines how the increased neoliberal reality led to economic disaggregation and deregulation as well as decentralization, the rise of regional

---

[1] The COVID-19 epidemic might break some populist regimes and has certainly posed a threat to Modi's government, as exemplified in the state assembly elections held in May 2021 in Assam, Bengal, Tamil Nadu, and Karnataka – where the BJP only won in Assam despite a massive campaign in Bengal. The bad results at the polls can be linked to the large number of COVID-19 infections and deaths during India's second wave; the government is widely perceived as having mismanaged the situation. However, the BJP's win in UP in March 2022 showed that this government failure seems to have been forgotten just a year later.

parties, and larger inequalities between India's north and south. Neoliberal policies required the government to reduce public expenditure, which led to the commodification of services, with an emphasis on measurable outputs. In the first instance, economic reforms supported the growth of aspirational Indian middle classes. Rising wealth across this section of society brought with it concerns about globalization and westernization, resulting in the search for a 'traditional' identity that in turn underwrote the political rise of Hindu nationalism. The BJP's education reform slogan in 2000, 'Indianise, nationalise, spiritualise', directly tapped into the fears and hopes of the middle classes (Lall, 2009). In parallel with this, the rise of wealthier middle classes also resulted in the demand for changes in education, and a parallel private education system developed, serving different strata according to affordability, forever altering the role of state responsibility in public services. Both neoliberalism and Hindu nationalism have over time reframed the concept of Indian citizenship in terms of identity and rights, with devastating consequences for religious and other minorities.

This book aims first to offer a greater understanding of how neoliberalism was at the origin of the rise of Hindu nationalism. Although the link between neoliberalism and the rise of populist regimes has been explored in relation to other countries (see discussion later in this introduction), this has not yet been undertaken in any detail for India. In doing so, this book challenges the current understanding of Indian politics that sees Hindu nationalism mostly as a reaction to incompetent and corrupt domestic Congress-led politics and a tiring with a left-wing system of caste-based reservations, rather than being engendered by a global phenomenon. This book goes beyond the current trend of exploring how neoliberal economic policies engender populist regimes by showcasing the instrumentality of education in propagating India's new identity within a neoliberal system, including ideas around citizenship and inclusion/exclusion. In particular it explores how the Indian government's political choice of neoliberalism and Hindu nationalism has been accepted by the wider population across India. Without major changes in curriculum, textbooks, and teacher training, the Hindu nationalist political project would have encountered much more domestic contestation and resistance. Education has produced Modi-supporting citizens who will not question his failure in delivering his promises of development. [2] This has resulted in discrimination against minorities, something the book engages with in Part III. Hindu nationalism is bringing about the disenfranchisement of hundreds of thousands of Muslims and other minorities, and the vast majority of ordinary Indians do not see anything wrong with this, because of how they are being educated.

---

[2]   Perhaps 'fans' rather than citizens, as detailed later.

Figure 0.1: The Indian government's political choice: the triangular relationship between Hindu nationalism, neoliberalism, and education

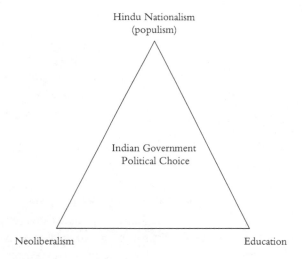

This introduction first introduces neoliberalism and the links between neoliberalism and the rise of populist national regimes, drawing parallels with the Indian experience that will be explored in depth in this volume. It then turns to the role education plays in propagating the new hegemonic discourse of both neoliberal economics and populist religious nationalist political rhetoric. In linking these two policy concepts, education emerges as the third corner in a kind of self-reinforcing triangle, one that is at the heart of contemporary Indian politics and the political choices that have been made by the BJP government, underpinning Hindu nationalist power (Figure 0.1).[3] The introduction goes on to explain the sources and fieldwork that this volume is based on before summarizing each chapter.

A short review of neoliberalism and its effects on education

The new neoliberal economic realities across the developing world have led to increased disaggregation, deregulation, commodification, emphasis on measurable outputs, managerialism, accountability, and a reduction of state responsibility. This in turn has affected societies across the developing

---

[3] The media – in particular social media – has been explored as another way in which populist regimes embed the new hegemonic discourse. However, in India education was used much earlier than the media, and social media as we know it today did not even exist at the time of the first BJP textbook revisions. It is therefore pertinent to examine the role education plays in embedding the 'new normal'.

world, with middle- and aspiring middle-class families choosing private education provision (and that of other services) over government schools and services, altering a key part of the social contract (Lall and Saeed, 2019; Lall, 2021a and b). The new reality across much of the developing world has increased the disparities and lessened social justice. It has been seen that such economic changes favour the rise of religious nationalist movements in the South Asian region (e.g., Pakistan, Myanmar, and India). This section offers the theoretical backdrop for the following chapters, engaging with the political science as well as education debates on globalization, neoliberalism, and the rise of religious nationalism.

The path of social democracy and redistribution marked the post-Second World War (mostly Western) world.[4] At the core was the state's responsibility to provide equal public services – including education – to all its citizens. The collapse of the Bretton Woods system in the early 1970s, the liberalization of exchange rates, the reduction of tariffs and transport costs, and the progressive removal of all controls on financial flows brought about the emergence of the neoliberal order and greatly reduced the capacity of governments to regulate their economies (Cayla, 2021) This resulted in the rise of neoliberalism – what some have called market fundamentalism, the doctrine to diminish the role of the state in the economy in order to let market mechanisms operate spontaneously. This doctrine presupposes those free markets are naturally efficient while political interventions distort the market order, resulting systematically in negative long-term effects (Cayla, 2021, pp.60–1). However, neoliberalism is not about lessening state control, but rather represents a new form of state involvement. At the heart of a neoliberal system is the changing nature of the state from a provider to a regulator (Olssen and Peters, 2005; Wrigley, 2007).

> Whereas classical liberalism represents a negative conception of state power in that the individual was taken as an object to be freed from the interventions of the state, neoliberalism has come to represent a positive conception of the state's role in creating the appropriate market by providing the conditions, laws and institutions necessary for its operation. [...] In neoliberalism the state seeks to create an individual that is an enterprising and competitive entrepreneur. (Olsen and Peters, 2005, p.315)

As the market logic is extended to the public sector, the state becomes a regulator rather than a provider of such services, with the state being

---

[4] The social-democratic framework as the foundation for governance was also the basis for India's development, as well as a number of other post-colonial developing countries.

instrumental in facilitating the market to take on these responsibilities. As such the state uses the market as a new control mechanism. Whilst there is a general withdrawal of the state, it is not from the arena of control, but rather from its position as the entity responsible for safeguarding all citizens, especially the weaker sections of society, a key socio-democratic function of the state. Globalization has ensured that these notions have influenced the development and aid agenda, with aid agencies exporting these notions to the global south (Lall, 2021a) through the Washington Consensus for economic policy, 'namely to privatize, deregulate, open up to external competition, and cut public spending and taxes' (Galbraith, pp.101–2, cited in Cayla, 2021, p.126). This globally adopted logic has led to an increase in inequalities both within countries as well as between countries, with political consequences elaborated on later.

It is argued that the marketization of society has influenced all spheres of life, including education, and this has led to profound changes in the nature of social relations, in particular the narrowing of the notion of student into that of consumer, and a concomitant commodification of the learning experience (Giroux, 2004). The emphasis on competition and increased performance means increased surveillance and evaluation, which has led to the development of national curricula, national testing regimes, and managerialist systems of performance evaluation that have eroded teachers' professional autonomy (Apple, 2004).[5]

Neo-liberal market-oriented reforms have affected most services in developed and developing countries, but education in particular. In many countries primary and secondary education have opened up to the market, allowing new private providers to offer educational services, which compete with the public education provided by the state. This has brought with it a new education discourse that changes the aim of education; it is developing a society that is adapted to the global knowledge economy. Education reinforces neoliberalism (Lall and Nambissan, 2011) through a new education discourse that changes the aim of education, that of developing an educated society, to one that is adapted to the new knowledge economy both at domestic and international levels. Education, Gamarnikow (2009, p.7) writes, becomes the main 'insurance policy' for individuals, families, communities, countries, and regions, which is invoked to protect from the known (technology and skills) as well as unknown risks and insecurities (the vagaries of markets). Education also underlies the new hegemonic discourse of the primacy of the market, not least through the growth of a private parallel education system.

---

[5] Quite a lot has been written about how teachers have been affected by neoliberal education reforms. The reference to Mike Apple (2004) shows that this is nothing new.

Reforms pushing public services to adapt to markets have been particularly supported by the growing middle classes in middle income and poorer countries, as they tend to benefit most from policies of choice and have the ability to buy themselves out of the public system to the detriment of the poorer and weaker sections of society (Hill and Rosskam, 2009). Globally the middle classes have been seen to access the lion's share of opportunities that have come with the new economy, using education as a key cultural resource.

The influx of new educational providers has also led to increased opportunities for students from poorer backgrounds to attend school. Nevertheless, as Roberts (2001, cited in Reay, 2004) argues, this transformation has only created the illusion of a fairer society as it creates a stratification that relegates the working classes to different trajectories from the middle classes (Reay, 2004). The underlying assumption of market-oriented policies is that the free market allows parents to choose the school that aligns with their expectations and needs. The possibility of choosing a school acts as a natural selection process through which unpopular schools are forced to change or to close if they do not adapt to clients' expectations (Ball, 1993). Policymakers regard a marketized education system as an ideal solution because it allows parents to choose and it compels schools to improve regardless of their resources (Ball, 1993). The rhetoric of choice assumes that all parents have equal cultural capital and are therefore equally informed and capable of making such a choice for their children. The middle classes benefit whilst the lower classes have to make do with the leftovers (Leathwood, 2004; Reay et al, 2005). As a consequence of the new policies and the focus on choice, the vision of a collective good has given way to individualism, with every individual and every family having to develop strategies to compete with everyone else. Those who are weaker and poorer are left behind and lose out.

There have been similar effects in the higher education (HE) sector: marketization across the sector has made performance and accountability two of the cornerstones of HE policy. The role of the university is no longer that of a public interest institution, but that of a site of 'knowledge production' created according to the economic imperatives of the 'knowledge economy.' As academics are ranked according to the number of their publications, their universities compete internationally for those students who will bring in the highest fees.

A central question in all this concerns the role of the state, as the neoliberal polity results in groups that experience discrimination and disadvantage in increasingly unequal societies. How neoliberalism has played out in India since the late 1980s and the economic reforms of 1991 is detailed in Chapter 1.

From economic neoliberalism to nationalist populism

Recent literature discusses how neoliberalism and the inequality it engenders can lead to significant changes in a democracy, with elections bringing populist regimes to power. Populism is a style of politics, and not a particular ideology, that 'arises, according to Laclau, when a large number of demands accumulate which are not satisfied, and a political leader or movement is able to construct an equivalence among them, portraying them in terms of the opposition between the people and the bloc in power, each understood as unitary and undifferentiated' (Hallin, 2019, p.16). Neoliberalism's economic realities have resulted in unequal societies that experience increasing popular discontent, reinforced by economic crises such as the 2008 financial crisis that affect ordinary citizens, yet do not touch the elites in the same way. Cayla (2021, p.1) explains 'that the roots of populism lay in the contradiction between the democratic ideal, which implies that the people should decide, and neoliberal governance, which seeks to make markets and competition the arbiters of major social developments' Mouffe (2018), building on Laclau's (2005) definition, argues that right-wing populism emerged when the West abandoned the Keynesian welfare state. Economic liberalism and a free-market ideology have undermined the two central tenets of democracy, equality and popular sovereignty, and as inequalities have increased, elections have not offered meaningful alternatives for citizens to change their economic conditions. The 2008 economic crisis is seen by Giroux (2019) as a turning point, and Gandesha, (2018) agrees that the insecurity caused by neoliberal austerity has been a key element in the rise of Western populist parties. As elites are seen to benefit, the failure of neoliberal policies in bringing 'the good life' to the wider population has resulted in the election of Bolsonaro in Brazil, Trump in the US, and Orbán in Hungary – leaders whose rhetoric seems to offer alternatives. It has led to Brexit led by Boris Johnson in the UK and brought Marine Le Pen to the final round of presidential elections in France in both 2017 and 2022. Populist leaders offer a break from the past and a people versus elite construction of society; the 'people' are defined on the basis of nationality, race, or ethnicity, leaving out groups such as immigrants or religious minorities.[6] Not all populist leaders are elected democratically, but many find their origins and continued support in global and national neoliberal policies and the resulting economic inequalities. Populist leaders often counter neoliberal narratives by promising to challenge international bodies such as the International Monetary Fund and promise

---

[6] Of course, once in power, they must navigate the contradiction that they have in effect become part of 'the elite', yet still are part of 'the people'.

to offer alternatives to the Washington consensus. Whilst some populist regimes stand against neoliberalism (see Modi reverting to self-sufficiency through his Atmanibar Bharat movement in India),[7] it is not quite as simple. Mostly the neoliberal programmes are not rolled back but are appropriated by the populist governments (Katsambekis, 2017; Hussain and Yunus, 2021). Populist regimes often embrace the parts of domestic and/or global neoliberal policies that suit them and the necessities of their domestic contexts, and then blame minorities or immigration for the effects of those same policies on ordinary citizens, deflecting anxieties through the construction of cultural, religious, and ethnic divisions. While there are different types of populist regimes, many contemporary populist regimes are right wing owing to their views on race, minorities, and purity. Gino Germani calls this national populism, whereby the leaders claim to represent not the whole population, but the majority – defined by language, race, or religion (Germani, 1978). Pluralism is anathema to this type of populism, which sees all citizens as one and anyone not part of this collective being defined as impure (Mueller, cited in Dieckhoff et al, 2016). This can result in a so-called ethnic democracy, where citizenship is reserved for the dominant ethnic group and others are marginalized (Smooha, 2002) or used as scapegoats. One of the main features is a permanent struggle with internal threats such as terrorism and immigration (Hallin, 2019, p.23).

There has been a recent spike in research and publications on different populist leaders and regimes, including China's Xi Jinping, Russia's Vladimir Putin, and the US's Donald Trump (Krastev and Holmes, 2019). Much research has also focused on the effects of illiberal populist regimes and the backsliding of democracy (Diamond, 2015; Diamond et al, 2015; Runciman, 2018; Levitsky and Ziblat, 2018),[8] some with a focus on the role played by populist leaders in Eastern Europe such as Hungary's Orbán or Poland's Duda (Krastev and Holmes, 2019), or India's Modi (Jaffrelot, 2021). What they all have in common is an ultimate aim to transform the state to become more autocratic: 'you may change the government, but you cannot change the rules; democracy becomes a theatre' (Jaffrelot, personal communication, 2021). The key to this process is the marginalization of dissent. Both neoliberalism and populism rely on conformism. In returning to the start of this section, it is important to understand that 'populism and neoliberalism are two sides of the same coin. Neoliberalism theorizes a

---

[7]   In relation to national security, poverty, and digital India.

[8]   Democratic backsliding is characterized by increased political polarization, racism (including the politicization of ethnicity and religion, leading to discrimination and anti-immigration), and the amassing of excessive executive power (Mettler and Lieberman, 2020) resulting in the weakening of democratic institutions and the infringements of rights and freedom of expression.

state that is powerless to respond to social discontent and concerned solely with preserving the order of the market; in response, populism generates an authoritarian state obsessed with satisfying the immediate expectations of its electorate' (Cayla, 2021, p.175). However, what is missed by the wider literature that relates to both neoliberalism and populism is the mechanism that embeds the new hegemonic discourse – education.[9]

Modi's Hindu nationalist government has been labelled a populist regime threatening India's democratic fabric. Over the past few years that the BJP has been in power there have been concerns about the state of India's democracy. Freedom House downgraded India from free to partly free,[10] and the VDem 2022 report changed India's status from democracy to electoral autocracy (Alizada et al, 2022).[11] Since the advent of the Hindu nationalist BJP in government in 1998,[12] and more rapidly since its absolute win in 2014 under Modi's leadership, India has changed from a largely inclusive society to one where polarizing nationalist politics have resulted in minorities being denied their basic rights. This has included discrimination against Muslims through the Ghar Whapsi campaign (*Financial Express*, 2019) and the cow slaughter ban.[13] In its second term in office after 2019, the BJP government dropped most of the development rhetoric, focusing instead on communal goals – such as the changing of Kashmir's status in 2019 (Jaffrelot and Verniers, 2020) that resulted in the shutting of Kashmir's internet for a year (Sherman, 2020) to quell protests, the rollout of the national verification of citizens in Assam (Jaffrelot and Verniers, 2020), and the finalizing and inauguration of the politically controversial Ram temple in Ayodhya (Rashid, 2020) that was not even held up by COVID-19. There is increasing evidence that India's

---

[9] Some of the literature engages with the role of the media and populist political messaging; and Hussain and Yunus (2021) have started to explore the role of education in embedding populism (yet fails to engage with the neoliberalism aspect of the problem). None of the literature has as yet engaged with the triangle we propose for the rise of India's Hindu nationalism.

[10] India's status declined from Free to Partly Free owing to a multi-year pattern in which the Hindu nationalist government and its allies have presided over rising violence and discriminatory policies affecting the Muslim population and have pursued a crackdown on expressions of dissent by the media, academics, civil society groups, and protesters (Freedom House, n.d.).

[11] https://v-dem.net/media/publications/dr_2022.pdf.

[12] The BJP was in power at the head of a coalition from 1998 to 2004, and has been in power again since 2014.

[13] Article 48 of India's constitution directs the state to 'take steps … prohibiting the slaughter of cows and calves', and 21 states criminalize cow slaughter in various forms. Cow protection has been promoted as a key issue by the BJP and the Rashtriya Swayamsevak Sangh (RSS). Lynch mobs, often organized over social media, have attacked minorities – including Muslims, Christians, and Dalits – under suspicion of eating beef, slaughtering cows, or transporting cattle for slaughter (Jha, 2002).

judiciary is no longer fair or transparent, instead being used to intimidate political opposition (Ganguly, 2020). Sedition charges are increasingly used to silence dissent (Vaishnav, 2021). The law allowing non-Muslims from neighbouring countries to fast-track their applications to become Indian citizens is a direct rebuke of India's secular and Nehruvian constitution. This engendered protests (Mujahid, 2020), with many Muslims killed during the riots that followed.[14] However, most of the national media and wider population in India did not so much as bat an eyelid in reaction to the policies pushed through by the BJP, largely because of the fundamentalization of education that had been taking place alongside these policy changes.

There are a number of parallels that can be drawn, not least with the experience in Eastern Europe after 1989 when the end of the Cold War led to economic reforms and the imposition of a Western economic system. As Krastev and Holmes (2019) detail in their seminal volume *The Light that Failed*, 'the striving of ex-communist countries to emulate the West after 1989 has been given an assortment of names – Americanization, Europeanization, democratization, liberalization, enlargement, integration, harmonization, globalization, and so forth – but it has always signified modernization by imitation, and integration by assimilation' (p.7). They argue that imitation of the West has led to the rise of populism as a backlash to what was seen in 1989 as 'the end of history' (Fukuyama, 1989) with the only option as a political system being liberal democracy. India's imitation of the Western economy post-1991 was also modernization by imitation, as left-wing economic policies were dropped in favour of the capitalist market economy. This led to poorer sections of society losing some of the social safety net that had been provided by the Congress-led socialist system. As in Eastern Europe, children began to look westwards through the media as well as the increased availability of Western goods. Krastev and Holmes detail how in Eastern Europe,

> faced with their inability to program their children with their own values, parents in the region began, somewhat hysterically, to demand that the state should do it for them. Government rescue squads must be dispatched to liberate the children from their insidious Western kidnappers. [… this being] another important source of the popular appeal of the region's illiberal populists. (Krastev and Holmes, 2019, p.53)

In India the middle classes were equally worried about westernization and advocated a return to their roots, creating support for the BJP (Lall, 2008

---

14 A detailed discussion of these riots is presented in Chapter 6.

and 2009). It can be argued that the BJP's model between 1998 and 2004, which focused mainly on the woes of the middle classes, contributed to their defeat at the polls in 2004 – India's middle classes are a minority of the voters. However, Congress did not change much: the decade between 2004 and 2014 was an uphill struggle that continued to imitate the Western neoliberal economic model. The resulting inequalities and corruption led to large-scale resentment and a backlash. As in Eastern Europe, the development of an anti-liberal counter-elite began to emerge and to attract considerable popular support, especially outside the globally networked metropolitan centres, by monopolizing the symbols of national identity that had been neglected or devalued in the process of globalization (Krastev and Holmes, 2019). Modi's BJP represented the anti-elite alternative in 2014, first through a discourse of development, and subsequently in 2019 through a discourse of Hindutva that looked at Indian national identity as Hindu (Lall, 2008). As in Eastern Europe, populism in India has been fuelled by the rejection of minorities-centred politics: 'While liberals and leftists were talking about the rights of minorities, Orbán was talking about history and the rights of the majority' (Krastev and Holmes, 2019, p.68). Like Orbán, Modi has fomented anxiety about illegal immigration from Bangladesh – the 'fear that unassimilable foreigners will enter the country, dilute national identity and weaken national cohesion' (Krastev and Holmes, 2019, p.37).

There are other parallels as well. Like Trump, 'who turned the republic of citizens into a republic of fans' (Krastev and Holmes, 2019, p.178), Modi speaks to his fans rather than all citizens of India.[15] Like Trump, who 'feels no obligation to represent Americans who do not admire and respect him' (Krastev and Holmes, 2019, p.178), Modi feels no obligation to represent those in India who disagree with his arguments. Like Trump also, Modi sees 'the internal enemy, rather than the external enemy, who poses the gravest existential threat' (Krastev and Holmes, 2019, p.179). None of this would stick without the new hegemony being reinforced through education.

Education as a political tool

One of the primary aims of education systems in modern states is, and has always been, the political socialization of the young. Whereas much rhetoric surrounding education policy, whether emanating from the 'East' or the 'West', nowadays increasingly focuses on the importance of schooling in

---

[15] '[E]nthralled fans, with their critical faculties switched off, are central to Trump's understanding of politics as centred less on policy-making than on a series of raucous campaign style rallies' (Krastev and Holmes, 2019, p.178).

generating 'human capital', the role of education as a political tool remains as important as ever.

Education systems throughout Asia have their origins in processes of state formation that were aimed at countering imperialism or furthering post-colonial nation-building. State elites across Asia have sought to popularize powerful visions of nationhood, to equip these visions with a historical 'back story', and to endow these with sentimental charge. In most states, particularly those that can trace their roots to a pre-colonial past, the national narrative has tended to be explicitly or implicitly ethno-cultural and primordialist in character (Lall and Vickers, 2009).

Education is viewed by many as the most logical entry point for the process of change in society. Governments have routinely used education or the curriculum amongst other vehicles to disseminate their political ideology in order to achieve desired change in societies (Apple, 1993; Lall and Vickers, 2009). This has been done both covertly and overtly. In all societies, but perhaps especially in post-colonial countries, emphasis has been placed by political elites on the role of education – and particularly on schooling – as a tool for shaping and sustaining political systems. This is evident both in the official knowledge that is imparted to students through textbooks and tested in examinations, as well as in subtler ways – what is often termed the hidden curriculum. The curriculum is chosen to fit in with the political ideology of the day, and the elites who construct the dominant ideology are also those who select the corresponding curriculum. Apple's work underlines how curriculum and political ideology are intertwined in the construction and reproduction of hegemony; that is, how they support systems and structures of class domination (Apple, 1993).

There has been much analysis of the role of textbooks and the curriculum in the West. Michael Apple, Christine Sleeter (2002), and Pauline Lipman have in many of their publications questioned the role of the state with regard to education and drawn connections between education and politics. Vickers and Jones (2005) focus in particular on history textbooks and curricula in East Asia, while Lall and Vickers (2009) look more broadly at how education is used by Asian governments for differing aims. School textbooks have become a primary vehicle through which societies transmit these national narratives (Hussain and Safiq, 2016). They portray a society's ideology or ethos and convey values, goals, or myths that the society wishes to transmit to new generations (Bourdieu, 1971). Textbooks also explain historical conflicts and present political parties in a particular light (Naseem and Stober, 2014).

One can argue that education has been used as a political tool throughout the ages and across the whole world to define national identity and justify the political rationale of governments. However, the role of education, in particular history education, in promoting nationalism and underpinning political legitimacy is a contemporary phenomenon that is evident in many populist regimes.

As can be seen from this discussion, education is a key component in embedding the new normal of populist majoritarian politics as well as neoliberal thought. The BJP has been using education to propagate Hindu nationalism as well as ideas around citizenship and inclusion/exclusion (Adeney and Lall, 2005, Lall 2008, 2009, 2013). As the new Hinduized identity becomes increasingly acceptable there has been widespread anti-Muslim rhetoric across social media (Lall and Anand, 2020). Beyond schools, the role of HE has been a central part of the Hindu nationalist project. It started with the BJP appointments of Hindu ideologues in 2000, moving on to how between 2014 and today particular HE institutions (HEIs) such as Jawaharlal Nehru University (JNU), known for its left-wing politics, are gradually discredited and infiltrated (Sharma, 2020b). In parallel, so-called institutes of national importance are funded, often headed by those who have the 'right' political outlook. Diversity, inclusion, and discrimination are propagated by HE through the intellectual paradigms around religion, ethnicity, and gender on knowledge production and minority student engagement. This includes the use of university spaces to exclude minority students and issues pertaining to academic freedom (*The Guardian*, 2020). The 2020 National Education Policy, published during the COVID-19 pandemic, plans to restructure HE and its mandate to bring India back to its cultural and epistemic roots. These themes are explored in detail in the following chapters.

In sum, neoliberalism has had two effects in India, exemplified in education and reinforced through education. First, the economic reforms of the 1990s created a middle class in search of an identity. This supported the rise of Hindu nationalism, which resulted in the rewriting of history – including in school textbooks – and a redefinition of Indian national identity. Second, it engendered the rise of a parallel private education system, changing the nature of state responsibility. Both these elements have reframed the concept of Indian citizenship in terms of identity and rights.

The aim of this book is not to produce a comprehensive and definitive account of the rise of Hindu nationalism on the back of neoliberal reforms, but to highlight and illustrate one specific aspect of the story that has not yet been examined. This book is also not about electoral choices and who votes for what party. Rather, spanning 30 years of education and politics across India, the book shows how education was the link between neoliberal economic policy and a Hindu nationalist dominated polity that are the hallmarks of contemporary India. The volume uses the voices of teachers to explain some of the educational and political changes and show how they have affected society by normalizing both neoliberalism and Hindu nationalism.

Methodology and data

The book is based on 29 years of work and engagement with the whole of India both in terms of politics and education. It is not just based on one set of data or a singular project. The book takes a macro approach, underpinned by data and information from across the country, collected during travel to most of India's states, rather than focusing on a single city or state. Key policy documents from over 30 years form the backdrop of the analysis. The work takes an interdisciplinary approach, linking political science with education, and linking economic reforms with all education sectors, including schools, HE, and teacher training.

Recent data in the form of teachers' voices were collected in two tranches – first, 110 teachers were interviewed in the summer of 2020 across 15 Delhi government schools and a further 115 were interviewed in the summer of 2021 across 115 government and private schools in Bengaluru, Karnataka (south), Guwahati, Assam (north-east), Jaipur, Rajasthan (north-west), Mumbai (west) and Chandigarh, Punjab (north), as well as 20 supplementary interviews in Delhi.[16] To ensure widespread views, teachers from all over India teaching in schools that cater to different socio-economic classes (Anand, 2019) and from different geographical areas were interviewed. Both government and private schools from each study area were initially randomly selected. A list of schools was prepared by discussing the research with respective District Education Officers and through desk research by using information from the list of websites.[17] This strategy was adopted to create a sizable list of schools from different areas. It was thought that this process would provide enough schools to get respondents for the study. As part of the identification of respondents, a few schools in all locations were contacted by telephone. This was unsuccessful because owing to COVID-19 all schools were closed and not responding to phone calls. The strategy had to be changed, and teachers were therefore identified through contacts, networks, and other sources, including non-governmental organizations (NGOs) working in the field of education, especially teacher training.[18] Whilst this worked for Bengaluru and Jaipur, in Guwahati there were difficulties in identifying sufficient respondents through contacts, references,

---

[16] Marie Lall and Kusha Anand were joined by a team of researchers specifically recruited for this project. We worked with the School for Development and Impact (www.school4 dev.org), an independent research organization based in New Delhi. Dr Benazir Patil (chief executive officer) led the team of three researchers who collected data in Rajasthan, Assam, and Karnataka. In total 225 teachers were interviewed.

[17] Target Study (n.d), UDISE (2019), School Search List. (n.d), Schools. org.in. (n.d.), Government of Assam (n.d), Bangalore Education (n.d), School Education (n.d).

[18] The travel restrictions related to COVID-19 made it impossible to personally visit schools.

and the help extended by Pratham (see https://www.pratham.org/). It was therefore decided to expand the study area. References from the teachers who were interviewed from Guwahati and the Head of Department of Social Work, Assam University, helped to identify three government school teachers from Silchar.

Since the research aimed to explore teachers' views on parents being given a choice between government and private schools, the general effects of the National Education Policy (NEP 2020), and more specifically on citizenship, social studies teachers (teaching history, geography, and civics) were selected from secondary or high schools. One teacher per school was interviewed. The distribution of teachers from the study areas is given in the table in Appendix 2.

A few teachers were identified for interview from different schools before one teacher was selected from each school. Teachers were contacted by telephone beforehand and received an information sheet via email or WhatsApp, both to seek their permission and to provide them with an understanding of the research. The teachers were asked about their preferred language of communication – English or Hindi. When they agreed to make time for a discussion, a particular day and time were fixed to suit them (these teachers were also teaching their classes online from home during much of this period). On the agreed date and time, the research team conducted online interviews. Owing to social-distancing procedures during the COVID-19 crisis, data had to be collected online, via Zoom, telephone, or Teams to virtually replicate face-to-face interviews. Telephone conversations and emails were used to build rapport with head teachers or teachers and to negotiate research permissions. Each interview lasted between 45 minutes and an hour. A few of the teachers refused to participate, giving such reasons as online teaching commitments or insufficient time to prepare.

The semi-structured interviews constituted the key evidence for Chapter 4 and Chapter 6, and covered the ideologies and world views of teachers from the private and public sectors. They have been woven together to portray a myriad of views on the main themes of this book. Data analysis combined the features of content analysis and thematic analysis to examine the research data. Both pre-identified and emergent themes were analysed, linked, and reorganized to correspond to the themes explored in this volume.

Content summary

The background provided in Chapter 1 engages with identity issues and with the advent of neoliberalism in India. This chapter explains the origins of India's national identity and how the Nehruvian doctrine (Lall, 2001) defined Indian citizens. It engages with the inclusive nature of the policy, showing how India's key policies and its constitution embraced this vision and translated it into the education system. The chapter also engages with the Nehruvian vision for an educated India and the development of an HE system, and briefly lists the main education policies and reforms between 1947 and the 1990s. The chapter then turns to the economic reforms of 1991 under the leadership of Prime Minister (PM) Narasimha Rao and Finance Minister Dr Manmohan Singh, in light of the increasing neoliberal global economic climate. This resulted in major domestic political changes, including the rise of regional parties (which then became part of ruling coalitions at the centre) as well as the rise of the BJP as a political force. The chapter engages in detail with the national narrative on identity and the middle-class voices that strove to maintain Indian traditions in light of an onslaught of westernization. The middle classes are projected as agents of change pushing for increased neoliberal reforms whilst fearing the consequences, the antidote to these being Hindu nationalism.[19]

After Chapter 1 the book is divided into three parts. In Part I, entitled 'Education and Ideology', two chapters focus on the propagation of Hindu nationalism in schools as well as changes in access to and quality of education under a neoliberal education model.

Chapter 2, entitled 'Hinduism versus secularism and the social realities of discrimination', starts with the first rewriting of history in the new BJP textbooks as part of the BJP's education policy that was rolled out under the slogan of 'Indianise, nationalise, spiritualise'. It describes how the content was used to underpin Hindu pride and disparage India's Muslim heritage, drawing battle lines between those who believe India is a secular country and those who want to redefine India on Hindu lines. The chapter goes on to look at how between 2004 and 2019 school textbooks become a political football, changing depending on which party was in power across state governments (Lall, 2008), and how the new Congress sponsored books did not alter the Hindutva approach offered in many schools. The chapter turns to the effects of Hindu nationalism as the new Hindu identity became increasingly acceptable, and the Ghar Whapsi campaign, the cow slaughter ban, and widespread anti Muslim rhetoric across social media are all discussed. A brief review of specific Delhi education reforms follows: the Happiness Curriculum and the Entrepreneurial Mindset Curriculum (EMC) both have direct links to Hindu traditions. The chapter ends with an analysis of the NEP 2020.

Chapter 3, entitled 'India's neoliberal schools', explores how the discourse and binary of Hindu nationalist and neoliberal agendas have shaped private

---

[19] ML was living in India at the time of the rise of the BJP and has first-hand experience of the BJP campaign, how it was received by Delhi's middle classes and the wider political processes between 1994 and 1999.

and government school education in India, and discusses the ramifications for social stratification. The first section describes how the Sarva Shiksha Abhiyan (SSA) and the Right to Education (RTE) Act 2009, undertaken for the universalization of elementary education, have led to a growth in enrolments and improvements in retention and transition rates for education, as well as a rise in low-cost private provision. It then outlines how NGOs lead intervention programmes to propagate international frameworks for 'cost-effective teachers' in order to achieve universal elementary education in India. The chapter then turns to the rise of private schools – both low cost and those serving the middle and aspiring middle classes, looking in detail as to how they have increased access but also changed the relationship between India's middle-class society and the state, forever altering the Nehruvian social contract and embedding a neoliberal outlook that is part and parcel of the BJP's economic and political discourse. Finally, the last section outlines an account of the origins of Hindutva through the Rashtriya Swayamsevak Sangh (RSS) and kindred organizations that fill the gaps, acting in parallel with changes in education at central and state levels.[20]

Part II is made up of two chapters that engage with the effects of neoliberalism on teachers, teacher agency, and their training; it includes teachers' voices on neoliberalism and Hindu nationalism in six states. It also shows how neoliberalism and Hindu nationalism have played out in HE.

Chapter 4 discusses how education provision differs between states. It examines the reality of schooling in Karnataka (south), Rajasthan (north-west), Punjab (north), Assam (north-east), Mumbai (west) and Delhi (India's capital). Education plays out differently across India's many states, but the core neoliberal and Hindu national elements are still present. Teachers' voices from government and private schools in all six states illustrate how education has been altered by neoliberal practices as well as the Hindu nationalist discourse.

Chapter 5 engages with the role of HE in the Hindu nationalist project. It starts with the BJP appointments of Hindu ideologues in 2000, moving on to how from 2014 particular HEIs such as JNU (known for its left-wing politics) have been gradually discredited and infiltrated (Sharma, 2020b). In parallel, the funding of 'institutes of national importance' and the rise of HEIs in more remote areas – often headed by those who have the 'right' political outlook – is discussed in the light of wider economic development. The chapter then turns to how diversity, inclusion, and discrimination are propagated by HE through intellectual paradigms around religion,

---

[20] The RSS, the Hindu right-wing grassroots organization and the key ideological provider for the BJP, maintains the view that education needs to be de-westernized and views education as a focal instrument in character building as well as elevating cultural consciousness in India (Athreya and Haaften, 2020). It is regarded as the parent organization of the BJP. The RSS is one of the principal organizations in the Sangh Parivar group.

ethnicity, and gender relating to knowledge production and minority student engagement. This includes a discussion on the use of university spaces to either include or exclude minority students and issues pertaining to academics and academic freedom (*The Guardian*, 2020).

The chapter briefly engages with the rise of private HE across India and its role in increasing access – a key mandate of the NEP 2020. The chapter ends with a discussion of HE's changing mandate[21] in a neoliberal Hindu national India that is analysed through the text of the new NEP.

Part III asks 'Whither India?'. Chapter 6, entitled 'The effects of education on citizenship under the BJP Modi government', indicates how Indian society has been transformed both in terms of its political outlook, with Hindu nationalism taking centre stage, as well as in terms of its economic trajectory – which is set by neoliberal policies. The education reforms across schools, universities, and teacher training have been embedded both through new school textbooks, new courses, and new teaching approaches. Hindutva views on Muslims have become mainstream, as depicted in Chapter 1 with the examples of the Ghar Whapsi campaign and the cow slaughter ban. As the BJP retained power, the Modi government dropped most of its development rhetoric to focus instead on communal goals – such as the changing of Kashmir's status in 2019 (Jaffrelot and Verniers, 2020) and the rollout of the national verification of citizens in Assam (Jaffrelot and Verniers, 2020). The law allowing non-Muslims from neighbouring countries to fast-track their applications to become Indian citizens was a direct rebuke of India's secular and Nehruvian constitution. Most of the national media and wider population in India did not see any problems with this. The book shows that the reason for wider apathy and even support of government policies is the reinforcement of these ideas through mainstream education.

The Epilogue brings the volume up to date by engaging with the effects of COVID-19 on both the central government as well as state elections, such as the ones held in 2021 in Assam, Karnataka, Bengal, Punjab, and Tamil Nadu, demonstrating that a form of 'soft Hindutva' has permeated other Indian political parties in their quest to woo the Hindu vote.

---

[21] The plan to restructure the HE system is presented as bringing India back to its cultural and epistemic roots.

1

The Role of Post-Colonial Politics in Re-Theorizing India's National Identity

Introduction

This chapter provides a backdrop to the rest of the book, showing how education became the vehicle that linked neoliberalism with Hindu nationalism and allowed it to permeate Indian society. In order to do this, a comprehensive look at India's policy development is required, both domestic and foreign, to contrast Nehru's original political and economic vision at independence with that of the Hindu nationalist BJP after economic reforms had taken place. A detailed description of both sets of policies and the contexts in which they emerged allows the later chapters of the book to develop the argument that education became and has remained the vehicle that has propagated the ideology of Hindutva and India's contemporary neoliberalist stand. Whilst others have hinted that Hindutva was a direct response to the neoliberal reforms that emerged out of India's economic crisis of the early 1990s (Corbridge and Harriss, 2000), and some have examined the role of India's middle classes in the process (Hansen, 1999; Zavos, 2000), no one has yet discussed how the two ideologies intertwined and were propagated through education, including through its privatization.

The chapter begins by explaining the origins of India's national identity and how the Nehruvian doctrine (Lall, 2001) defined Indian citizens after independence in 1947. It engages with the inclusive nature of this approach, showing how India's key policies and its Constitution embraced this vision and translated it into the education system. Education was used by the Congress Party to further this vision, to contrast with Pakistan's two-nation theory, and to build a united post-colonial nation in light of wider global decolonization and the Cold War. The chapter also engages with the Nehruvian vision for an educated India and the development of an HE system, and briefly engages with the main education policies and reforms that took place between 1947 and the 1990s. The chapter then turns to the economic reforms of 1991 under the leadership of PM Narasimha Rao and Finance Minister Dr Manmohan Singh, which emerged in an increasing neoliberal global economic climate.

The chapter further examines how the increasingly neoliberal reality led to economic disaggregation and deregulation as well as decentralization, the rise of regional parties, and larger inequalities between India's north and south. Neoliberal policies required the government to reduce public expenditure, leading to the commodification of services and an emphasis on measurable outputs. In effect, India's 1991 economic reforms not only engendered economic liberalization and growth, but also brought neoliberal structural changes with them that seeded a revived and altered Hindu nationalist political movement (Hansen, 1999; Ahluwalia, 2019). Less than a decade after the reforms began, the first BJP-led government was in place.

Key to the BJP's success was the growth of an Indian middle class and an aspiring middle class (referred to here as the middle classes). Rising wealth across these sections of society brought fears of globalization and westernization, resulting in the search for a 'traditional' identity. This chapter engages with the national narrative on identity and the desire voiced by the middle classes to maintain Indian traditions in the face of an onslaught of westernization. The middle classes were key agents of change, pushing for increased neoliberal reforms whilst fearing their consequences, the antidote to which seemed to be Hindu nationalism. The BJP's education reform slogan in 2000 'Indianise, nationalise, spiritualise' directly tapped into their fears and hopes.

The rise of Hindu nationalism was in effect a reaction to the globalization of India's economy. Hindutva at first rejected globalization, but as time went on, the BJP was able to separate India's economic trajectory from its religious and cultural narrative, creating a global India that was compatible with religious nationalism. The key to this change was a redefinition of India's national identity, based on Hinduism, which included the global Indian diaspora and excluded non-Hindus living in India. Education became the link between neoliberal economic policy and a Hindu nationalist dominated polity, which are the hallmarks of contemporary India. The chapter ends with a brief engagement with the BJP education policies that propagated both the notion of a global and a neoliberal Hindu India; this is further explored in the subsequent chapters.

The Nehruvian doctrine

At independence in 1947 India inherited the structures of the Raj, which although national in form were imperial in content. As a result, internal structures and policy formulations had to be changed, no longer to be based on the imperial legacy of divide and rule but rather on unite and cooperate. With the new political elite – the Congress Party and the Indian Administrative Service, both of which transcended Indian society – Jawaharlal Nehru set out to construct a new Indian state that was meant to operate as a unified entity and was expected to deliver equality to all.

Building India on idealism

Nehru's vision of equality in the new India encompassed clear policies of poverty alleviation. In the debate on the Resolution of Aims and Objects in the Constituent Assembly, he declared: 'The first task of this Assembly is to free India through a new Constitution, to feed the starving people, and to clothe the naked masses, and to give every Indian the fullest opportunity to develop himself according to his capacity' (Constituent Assembly Debates, 22 January 1947, cited in Corbridge et al, 2005, p.54). But India had to achieve this on its own – without outside aid or interference. One cornerstone of the new state was the ideal of *swadeshi* or self-sufficiency – India was not to be dependent on other countries either economically or politically (Corbridge and Harriss, 2000). Therefore, education policy in the newly independent country focused on developing not only universal primary education, but also a competent HE sector that would produce Indian doctors to populate Indian hospitals and Indian engineers to build Indian roads, bridges, and other infrastructure. Self-reliance not only affected domestic policy but also heavily influenced India's development of foreign policy. Despite being economically and militarily weak at independence, 'India chose self reliance as an economic goal and the public sector as its tool' (Chopra, 1993, p.57). Nehru believed that any kind of conflict swallowed up the resources that could have been used for development; therefore, he wanted non-alignment in order to preserve the integrity and sovereignty of the country, especially in light of the global division that called for allegiance to either one superpower or the other. The Western political and economic system was rejected since it was believed to be based on economic inequality and exploitation; historically it was this system that was accountable for the worst form of colonialism in Asia and Africa. Seeing India as the model for all decolonizing nations, Nehru wanted a 'third world bloc' that would follow certain moral principles based on anti-imperialism and non-dependency, and India had to set a good example. In general, non-alignment could be seen as the international expression of domestic nationalism after independence: it enabled a country to judge each international problem freely, but this did not mean neutrality or giving up the right of self-defence. Key to all of this was Nehru's desire to give India a global role. He believed that if India wanted to lead the newly decolonized and developing countries, it had to be viewed as irreproachable, both domestically as well as internationally. The new Indian state was to be based on democracy, religious tolerance, inclusiveness, and equality. These ideals were also to underpin the new definition of Indian identity.

Who is Indian in newly independent India? Nehru's vision

Beyond building a post-colonial state, newly independent India also had to define its national identity. Constructing national identity is largely a top-down process in which the state plays a central role. According to Oliver Zimmer, '[n]ational identity relates to the process whereby "the nation"' is reconstructed over time [it is therefore] a public project rather than a fixed state of mind' (Zimmer, 2003, pp.173–4). At independence, post-colonial states had the choice to base the definition of their national identity on one of two possible formulas: either on the ethnicity, culture and religion of the dominant group or on shared history (a civic definition).

The challenge for India's new leaders was to construct India's identity in line with their goal of creating a modern democratic and tolerant state, one that would be a model for other decolonizing states (Adeney and Lall, 2005). However, there was no consensus on how to achieve this. In line with his other idealistic views on domestic and foreign policy, Nehru firmly believed that the only factor that could be the basis of a new Indian identity was its shared historical past, including all who were in India at the time of independence (Lall, 2001). India's society differed on the basis of language, religion, and ethnicity and gave little other common ground for national integration. But this integration, consolidating the nationalist movement and creating a single state on a common path, was one of Nehru's top priorities. He therefore opted for a civic, territorially defined national identity, despite many of his colleagues disagreeing over the issue of secularism as they felt that 'community [was] ... an essential part of national identity' (Brown, 2003, p.185). Nehru focused on the tolerance of Ashoka (Gore, 1991),[1] defining Indian society as all-inclusive and accommodating: '[t]hose who professed a religion of non-Indian origin or, coming to India, settled down there, became distinctively Indian in the course of a few generations' (Nehru, 1946, p.41).

---

[1] In the middle of the third century BCE, Ashoka, emperor of one of the largest empires in the world, had the following inscribed at various sites across his kingdom: 'The king ... honours all religious sects ... with gifts and with honours of various kinds. But he does not value gifts or honour as much as the promotion of the essentials of all religious sects. The root of this is guarding one's speech so that neither praising one's own sect nor blaming others' sects should occur on improper occasions; and it should be moderate on every occasion. And others' sects should be honoured on every occasion. Acting thus,

Nehru clearly rejected Jinnah's two-nation theory as well as the British perception of India as irrevocably divided between its religious communities (Metcalf, 1994).[2] India's Partition on religious lines had given some credence to the view that it should be a Hindu state, a position that led supporters to consider privileging Hindus and Sikhs, even abroad (Rodriguez, 2005, p.224), but secularism prevailed. Nehru's socialist beliefs influenced his attitude towards national identity formation, and he hoped that identities, whether based on language, religion, or caste, would fade away with the onset of modernization (Brown, 2003). His vision was enshrined in India's Constitution, through the exclusion of religion, ethnicity and language from the identity debate.

Religion: The religious minorities (Muslims and Christians) were accommodated through a multicultural strategy of polyethnic rights,[3] whereby the state maintained neutrality vis-à-vis all religions (Article 15 (1)) rather than a strict separation of religion from public life. Polyethnic rights included the recognition and protection of the personal laws of Muslim and Christian minorities. However, this accommodation for minority religious groups did not include reserved seats in government or the creation of states along religious lines. There was no separate protection for the dominant Hindu majority.

Ethnicity: Nehru's definition of who was and who was not Indian automatically excluded the Indian Diaspora, which was linked to the motherland through ethnicity, religion, and language. Having left India, they had not shared in India's history, and were consequently excluded (Lall, 2001).

Language: India's linguistic diversity is immense.[4] Unlike religion, at independence there was no majority group that could easily dominate,

---

one both promotes one's own sect and benefits others' sects. Acting otherwise, one both harms one's own sect and wrongs others' sects. For whoever praises their own sect or blames another's sect out of devotion to their own sect with a view to showing it in a good light, instead severely damages their own sect. Coming together is good, so that people should both hear and appreciate each other's teaching' (Gethin, 2019).

[2] The two-nation theory argues for the need of a separate state for Muslims on the subcontinent. Muhammd Ali Jinnah was the founder of Pakistan.

[3] The explanatory clause attached to Article 25 (1b) states that 'the reference to Hindus shall be construed as including a reference to persons professing the Sikh, Jaina or Buddhist religion'.

[4] In terms of linguistic diversity, the Census of India (1961) recorded 1,652 mother tongues with a much larger number of dialects; these have been classified into 300 to 400 major languages belonging to five language families. But there are only 22 official languages (*Constitution of India*, VIIIth schedule, after the 100th Constitutional Amendment, December 2003, cited in MacKenzie, 2009), along with English (the associate official language). Nearly 80 per cent of Indian languages are endangered; most of them tribal (MacKenzie, 2009). As far as tribal communities are concerned, according to the 1980 census, the population of the scheduled castes was 104,754,623, and the figure for

as Hindi speakers comprised only between 30 and 40 per cent of the population. The Constitution provided that states could adopt their own languages for official use (Brass, 1994). Nehru had wanted to avoid the reorganization of states along linguistic lines, as this could create a separate, and possibly competing, linguistic identity. There was at the time a real fear of a 'Balkanization' of India in light of what had happened with Partition, which informed the Congress position on the issue (Brass, 2015). Following the publication of the report by the States Reorganisation Commission in 1953, disturbances erupted in several parts of the country that felt affected by and unhappy with the recommended changes. Despite Nehru's preference, states were eventually reorganized on the basis of language, starting with Andhra Pradesh in 1953 and followed by Maharashtra and Gujarat. At the end of the 1960s, and in particular during the centralization of the Indira Gandhi period, the language issue re-emerged (Brass, 2015). The linguistic principle of reorganization became a highly political issue that all major political parties used in their campaigns and manifestos to gain popular support (Horowitz, 1985; Al-Shammari and Dali, 2018). Punjab, Haryana, and Himachal Pradesh were created in 1966 out of the former province of Punjab; and much of the north-east was reorganized on linguistic lines in the 1970s.[5] In effect, this created new and separate identities, which came to be politically significant after the 1991 economic reforms and in the era of coalition politics. There were consequences for education as well, as all states and union territories now have an official language as the major medium of instruction. Language policies reflect the contradiction between Nehruvian inclusiveness and later governments' centralization and essentialization drives, which have pushed for the use of more Hindi across the country, resulting in the political issues already described. The official policies of the Government of India (GoI), as well as those of all the state governments, have supported the principle of using the mother tongue (MT) as the medium of instruction at least in the initial stages of schooling. In the case of speakers of the major national languages of the country who reside in their 'home' states, there have been no serious problems when

---

scheduled tribes was 51,628,638. About 23.51 per cent of the country's population consisted of scheduled castes and scheduled tribes (India, 1985, p.18; Shah, 1982, cited in MacKenzie, 2009). The census listed 613 different tribal communities (GoI, 1978, cited in MacKenzie, 2009) using 304 tribal MTs (MTs not claimed by non-tribal communities), which were reduced to 101 distinct identifiable languages.

[5]   Rather than leading to 'political Balkanization' and the break-up of the country, the reorganization solidified support for the Indian state and the Indian nation, as attested by the strength of feelings shown across the country on the 'Only National', 'More National', and 'Equally National and Regional' scale (State of Democracy in South Asia (SDSA), 1998, p.256; Adeney, 2017).

implementing this policy (Groff, 2017); but it has been harder to implement it in small towns and rural areas, where teachers may not be available for small numbers of children or migrants. Speakers of minority languages in particular have not been served well, as the Three-Language Formula does not distinguish between regional/state languages and MTs,[6] thus ignoring the situation of minorities whose MT is not the regional language (Groff, 2017). Unrecognized languages, such as tribal languages, are technically allowed to be used as a subordinate medium of instruction in the primary grades (Chaturvedi and Mohale, 1976, 46; Khubchandani, 1981; Sridhar, 1991), but nevertheless the use of minority languages in education has faced implementation problems owing to pedagogic, environmental, and curricular issues. The dominance of certain languages across certain states has – many decades on – resulted in the kind of politics Nehru was trying to avoid.

Nehru's belief that religion, language, and ethnicity had no part to play in the definition of Indian national identity did not remain uncontested. Sridharan and Varshney (2001) explain that historically there have been three competing themes used to define Indian national identity: geography, culture, and religion. The secular nationalists combine geography and culture and the Hindu nationalists geography and religion (Sridharan and Varshney, 2001, pp.225–6). Khilnani explains:

> Nehru's idea of Indianness emerged through improvised responses to constrained circumstances: its strength was not its ideological intensity, but its ability to steer towards an Indianess seen as layered, adjustable, imagined, not as a fixed property. […] It was fundamental to him that Indian nationalism could not fashion itself after European examples. In contrast to the academic analysts who see nationalism as the diffusion of a standard form devised in the industrialised West – whether in the Gaelic version of a community of common citizenship or the Voelkish idea of a shared ethnic or cultural origin – Nehru rejected the idea that Indian nationalism was compelled to make itself in one or other of these images. To that extent Nehru agreed with the two men whose influence he acknowledged as most important to his thinking about this matter, Tagore and Gandhi. But unlike Tagore and Gandhi, for who the state was a dispensable nuisance, Nehru believed that an Indian identity could emerge only within the territorial and institutional frame of a state. (Khilnani, 1999, p.167)

The state created would be committed to protect cultural and religious differences rather than imposing a stereotype of Indianness – Nehru's vision

---

[6] The Three-Language Formula refers to state language, Hindi, and English.

engendered India's secular politics. The Indian Constitution of 1950 laid the foundations of a secular and democratic political order, and provided in its various clauses protection for religious minorities. Though the term 'secular' was only formally made part of the Constitution in 1976, provisions for the protection of minority communities that gave them equal status to the majority Hindu community were incorporated in the Constitution from the start. Post-colonial, independent, and modern India was to be a country inclusive of all religio-cultural groups. The Constitution would be in tune with the sociocultural plurality of the country, protecting the status and voices of minorities. Secularism meant that religion remained in the private rather than the public realm, with diverse social groups and individuals living their lives according to their cultural beliefs and practices. India did not choose a state religion, and it was understood that the political leadership was not to use religion as a political tool, for instance by favouring one religious community over another. Bhargava described India's approach as 'political secularism', which did not call for a total exclusion of religion from politics but demanded that the state be equally distanced from all religious and non-religious ideals (Bhargava, 1998, p.493).[7] In a society guided by political secularism, believers of different faiths and atheists can live together harmoniously (Bhargava, 1998, p.495). However, Nehru's choice of secularism did not remain uncontested. Those in opposition claimed it was a Western concept that did not fit India's needs, as people were generally religious and the communal aspect of religion was a defining feature of their identity (Madan, 1998; Nandy, 1998). As a result, the debate about the role of religion, language, and ethnicity in defining identity has continued.

In the end, secularism was imposed from above and did not, as Akeel Bilgrami concedes, 'emerge out of a creative dialogue between the(se) different communities' (Bilgrami, 1998, p.395). This 'Archimedean existence' gave secularism a 'procedural priority, but 'no abiding substantive authority' (Bilgrami, 1998, p.395), which accounts for secularism's weakness. However, the proponents of secularism argued that in modern India it was the principle that could 'mediate between the diverse notions of the social good' (Alam, 1998, p.5), becoming not only a value choice but an indispensable need (Alam, 1998, p.11). Secularism had its challenges and challengers, but it was not until economic reforms took place that a political party was able to fundamentally alter the Nehruvian doctrine. As will be seen later in this chapter, the rise of the BJP in the

---

[7]   Bhargava distinguishes between ethical secularism and political secularism – with ethical secularism meaning no contact between religion and politics, thereby excluding all religious beliefs from affairs of the state (Bhargava, 1998, pp.493–4).

course of the late 1980s and early 1990s led to a renewed argument about who was Indian, what defined Indian identity, and the role of religion in Indian society.

Nehruvian education policy

The legacies of the Nehruvian approach to citizenship, national identity, and education are considerable, perhaps the most notable being the entrenchment of a pluralist/secularist perspective in the minds of the Indian people – which happened largely through education.[8] Following independence, school curricula were imbued with inclusiveness, placing emphasis on the fact that India's different communities could live peacefully side by side as one nation. Drawing on Nehru's vision, and articulating most of his key themes, the Kothari Commission (1964–1966) was set up to formulate a coherent education policy for India. According to the Commission, education was intended to increase productivity, develop social and national unity, consolidate democracy, modernize the country and develop social, moral, and spiritual values (Sharma, 2002). To achieve this, the main pillar of Indian education policy was to provide free and compulsory education for all children up to the age of 14. The Commission stated: 'One of the important social objectives of education is to equalize opportunities, enabling the backward or underprivileged classes and individuals to use education as a lever for the improvement of their condition' (Kothari Commission, 1964, p. 66, cited in Thamarasseri, 2008). Other features included the development of languages (Hindi, Sanskrit, regional languages, and the Three-Language Formula), equality of educational opportunities (regional, tribal and gender imbalances to be addressed), and the development and prioritization of scientific education and research. India's curriculum has historically prioritized the study of mathematics and science rather than social sciences or arts. This has been actively promoted since the Kothari Commission, which argued that India's developmental needs were better met by engineers and scientists than historians.

Subsequent Indian governments regarded education policy as a crucial part of their development agenda. Emphasis has traditionally been placed on universality, pluralism, and secularism rather than quality and excellence. Education has been a prime focus in India's development plans ever since independence. It is included as part of the Directive Principles of State Policy

---

[8] Education is used as a political tool by governments and elites to impose their conception of society across their citizens – no matter the type of government or its political persuasion (see Lall and Vickers, 2009).

in the Constitution, which states that 'the State shall endeavour to provide within a period of ten years from the commencement of this Constitution, for free and compulsory education for all children until they complete the age of fourteen years' (Article 21A, the Constitution of India).[9] India's education infrastructure has developed some of the best HE institutions in the world, such as the Indian Institutes of Technology (IITs) and Indian Institutes of Management (IIMs),[10] but, at the other end of the scale, severe problems have persisted with basic education provision in rural and tribal areas (Nambissan, 2006).

In 1986 Rajiv Gandhi announced the NEP, which was intended to prepare India for the 21st century. The policy emphasized the need for change: 'Education in India stands at the crossroads today. Neither normal linear expansion nor the existing pace and nature of improvement can meet the needs of the situation' (para 1.9, NEP, cited in Shukla, 1988, p.2). According to the NEP of 1986, the goals set out by the Kothari Commission in the 1960s had largely been achieved: more than 90 per cent of the country's rural population was within a kilometre of schooling facilities and a common education structure had been adopted by most states.[11] The prioritization of science and mathematics had also been effective. However, change was required to increase financial and organizational support for the education system to tackle problems of access, quality, and quantity. A problem with literacy levels also remained, as despite the increased number of schools, these differed widely from state to state. The NEP was intended to raise education standards and increase access to education, while at the same time safeguarding the values of secularism, socialism, and equality that had been promoted since independence. To this end, the NEP stated that the government would seek financial support from the private sector to complement government funds. The central government also declared that it would accept a wider responsibility to enforce 'the national and integrative character of education, to maintain quality and standards' (Shukla, 1988, p.6). The states, however, retained a significant role, particularly in relation to the curriculum. The key legacy of the 1986 policy was the beginning of overt privatization.[12]

---

[9]   Something that subsequent Indian governments did not achieve.

[10] IITs and IIMs are renowned as world-class institutions. The majority of their graduates end up abroad, contributing to the phenomenon known as brain drain.

[11] How far these objectives have been met is up for discussion, as the Kothari Commission aimed at universal primary education, which India had not achieved. A discussion about the success of the Kothari Commission is beyond the remit of this chapter.

[12] Private schools already existed; however, government education was seen as the main education provision. See Kingdon (2017).

The turning point, 1991 – India goes bust

For over four decades India's domestic and international policies reflected the Nehruvian vision, even though there were some changes as Indira Gandhi took the helm of the Congress Party and led the country, including during the two-year emergency. Nehruvian idealism lost some of its shine. However, India broadly remained faithful to Nehru's vision of a secular democratic polity with economic self-sufficiency, based on a moral, non-aligned foreign policy.

The world after the end of the Soviet Union

A shift in Indian domestic policy was overdue because of the global changes of the late 1980s and early 1990s. With the fall of the Berlin Wall and the subsequent demise of the Soviet Union, the only alternative economic model to the capitalist market system had been removed. Fukuyama (1992) called this 'the end of history'. Economically, it disrupted the 'barter' arrangement that India had with the Soviet Union, which allowed for international trade without expending foreign currency (Jha, 2020). The collapse of the Soviet empire had further political and ideological consequences: the traditional Indian position of non-alignment in international affairs became obsolete. Since there were now no clear-cut oppositional economic and political systems, it made little sense to stand apart as a third group. The world had broken up into a multitude of facets, with trading blocs of different sorts emerging as the dominant groupings (Clark, 1997). India's moralistic stand on anti-imperialism and other political issues had become outdated. Now that economic and trade relations were taking precedence over ideological ties, India had to decide how to manage international trade; consequently it had to rethink its international and regional foreign policy and work out how to keep a heavily subsidized domestic economy afloat. While Indira Gandhi had moved India's foreign policy from a global and ideologically oriented approach to a more realistic regional policy, based on India's hegemonic status, not much had changed in terms of the internal economic model. In addition, the South Asian Association for Regional Co-operation was not very successful.[13] Although the region had over 21 per cent of the total world population, its share of world gross domestic product (GDP) was less than 2 per cent. Its share of world exports was a marginal 0.90 per cent and of world imports an equally insignificant 1.01 per cent (Mehta and Otto, 1996, pp.29–34). Other post-colonial countries were growing, with

---

[13]   Comprising India, Pakistan, Bangladesh, Sri Lanka, Nepal, and the Maldives.

spectacular reductions in poverty around Asia, yet India remained poor and economically isolated from the rest of the world.

The new economic situation

Domestically, India's economy had grown very slowly. In a phrase coined by the economist Raj Krishna, the Hindu rate of growth was around 3.5 per cent for the first three decades after independence. (1950s–1980s). Although from 1981 to 1991 there had been an acceleration in the rate of economic growth to well above 5 per cent per annum, this relatively higher growth rate was combined with an acute macro-economic crisis that reflected itself in runaway inflation, a balance of payments (BoP) deficit, and mounting public debt. The inflation rate was running in double digits. Coupled with these danger signals, the basic macro indicators such as the fiscal deficit were high and industrial production was depressed. The continuous high levels of deficits (both fiscal and BoP) compelled the government to resort to heavy borrowing to finance them, and consequently the public debt increased alarmingly. The strain on the BoP was aggravated by the Gulf War crisis, and this resulted in a sharp drain on foreign exchange reserves.[14] Under normal circumstances such an external shock would not have toppled the country's economy, yet India was extremely weak (World Bank, 1991). Inflation was at 12 per cent and rising, there was a large public and current account deficit (10 per cent and 3 per cent of GDP respectively), and heavy foreign and domestic debts. As a result, India's credit rating went down and private foreign lending was cut off (Joshi and Little, 1996, pp. 14–15). The shortage in foreign exchange forced a massive import squeeze, which halted industrial growth and produced negative growth rates from May 1991 onwards (GoI, 1997). Patel sees the crisis as originating in the age-old policies of keeping subsidies high in order to placate the voters, financial excesses in the defence sector and in public salaries and perks, and too great a reliance on short-term borrowing (Patel, 1992).

India's economic policy had primarily been based on industrial self-sufficiency with a dominant public sector. The public sector had become the largest outside the Communist bloc. The reason for this dominant public sector was based on Nehru's conviction was that the disinterested 'hands of the state' would take care of the Indian population better than anyone who had to make any sort of profit. It could be argued that Nehru believed he could establish a command economy embedded in a westernized and liberal democratic system (Hanson, 1968, p.43). The Nehruvian model ignored matters of efficiency and focused purely on allocative choices: capital

---

[14] Lok Sabha Debates, Q. 392, 19.7.1991.

investment was directed towards industries protected from competition. 'The result was a control-infested system that smothered private initiative and encouraged the proliferation of inefficiencies and corruption within both the state-controlled economy and the political system as a whole' (Khilnani, 1999, p.97). This system, based on the public sector and controls, had led to an economy where industries were kept alive despite low productivity and high losses to prevent job losses, poverty, and the resulting political fallout. It cultivated an atmosphere where the corporate houses of the Birlas, Tatas, and Kirloskars were held back by restrictions and regulations because the concept of profit was mistrusted and any kind of expansion or diversification required a considerable number of permits and licences (Tharoor, 1997). Bank nationalization guaranteed the state an easy source of money, with credentials for a loan not being based on efficiency, but on priorities for allocation. Years of Nehru's socialist pattern, with economic nationalism at its base, though noble in intention, contributed to India's biggest economic crisis ever, and it required comprehensive reforms to remedy the damage. In early 1991 the country's economic system was on the verge of collapse.[15] India had only $1 billion foreign exchange reserves, which would cover only two weeks of imports: the country was effectively going bust.[16]

At the same time as the economic crisis started, the Congress Party was also fighting for its political life.[17] Having won a majority of seats in the 1989 elections, but not enough to form a government, a National Front government was formed with Janata Dal's V.P. Singh as PM. The arrangement fell apart when Singh, along with Chief Minister Lalu Prasad Yadav, stopped the BJP leader Advani's Ram Rath Yatra in October 1990. The BJP, with 85 seats, withdrew its support. An alternative arrangement under PM Chandra Shekar (who had broken away from the Janata Dal and formed the Samajwadi Party in 1990) collapsed in 1991, and new elections were called. The campaign was marred by Mandal-Mandir. Mandal referred to the Mandal Commission's suggested 27 per cent

---

[15] It should be noted that this was not the first time the Indian economy had been on the verge of collapse; it had happened, for example, in 1964. Yet this time there was no alternative but to open up the economy to outside investment. During the previous crises, India had reformed parts of its economy, but the situation had never led to serious liberalization.

[16] Corbridge and Harriss (2000) argue that the economic reforms were not a result of the fiscal crisis but rather an 'elite revolt' against state directed economic development. Whilst we disagree with this assessment, this so-called elite revolt was certainly a factor in sustaining the change process, and will be discussed in more detail in the section on the middle classes later in this chapter.

[17] Congress had won the previous elections by a landslide, but was marred by the Bofors scandal, rising terrorism in Punjab, and Tamil politics in Sri Lanka, including the war between the Tamil Tigers and the Sri Lankan government.

reservation in government jobs for Other Backward Classes (OBCs) and Mandir referred to the Ram Janmabhoomi Mandir that Hindu nationalists wanted to build on the site of the Babri Masjid at Ayodhya.[18] The Mandir issue was a key policy in the BJP manifesto, and the party won 120 seats. Both themes – the right to reservation and the position of the Hindu religion are those that were to determine politics in India for the next thirty years.

During the election campaign former PM Rajiv Gandhi was assassinated in a suicide bombing in Tamil Nadu in May 1991. No party was able to get a majority of seats, resulting in Congress forming a minority government with the support of other parties, led by PM Narasimha Rao. The unstable political scene contributed to the economic collapse and laid the foundations for a new system, which would renounce economic nationalism and favour the opening of the Indian economy. India had to integrate itself into the New World Order; its leitmotiv was terribly outdated. In the words of the new Finance Minister and economist Dr Manmohan Singh:

> Self-reliance in today's world of integrated global markets cannot be achieved merely by reducing import dependence and insulating the economy from the world. Following that path will only lead to more import controls and promote inefficiency and corruption. It will perpetuate an environment in which the Indian entrepreneurs will not have the flexibility they need to compete with other developing countries in world markets. The resulting inability to export will actually make us more, rather than less dependent on the outside world. Our vision of a self-reliant economy has to be of an economy which can meet all its import requirements through exports, without undue dependence on artificial external props such as foreign aid. (*Lok Sabha Debates*, Budget speech, 29.2.1992, cited in Lall, 2001 p.156)

Changing India's economic model – neoliberal solutions in a globalizing world

The new government embarked on immediate and extensive reforms – the New Economic Policy and the Economic Reforms Programme. The first priority was to stop the slide and to restore India's credibility both domestically and internationally. To achieve this, immediate measures had to be taken to avoid defaulting on international obligations and to restore the macro-economic balance; these included a $2.2 billion emergency

---

[18]   More on this in Chapter 6.

International Monetary Fund (IMF) loan (August 1991), guaranteed by a large part of India's gold reserves (Tharoor, 1997, pp.159–60).[19] The IMF recommendations recommended key macro-economic objectives, which included a rebuilding of India's international reserves, steady economic growth, and a reduction of inflation. As part of the conditions for the loan and to achieve these benchmarks, a Structural Adjustment Programme had to be adopted (Kennedy et al, 2013). This included devaluing the rupee by 23 per cent,[20] making India's currency convertible on the current account and the exchange rate more reflective of market conditions (World Bank, 1991, cited in Lall, 2001; Basu, 2004; Kennedy et al, 2013). With regard to trade, customs duties, which were among the highest in the world, were drastically reduced, and procedures for importing and exporting were simplified, including for foreign capital investment (Bajpai and Sachs, 1999; Basu, 2004; Kennedy et al, 2013). Beyond trade liberalization, domestic pricing policies, public enterprise reforms, financial sector reforms, tax reforms, and expenditure control were also a part of the programme. The World Bank (1991) India Country Economic Memorandum Vol. 1 explained the structural reforms as follows:

> The new industrial policy announced on the same day as the budget has eliminated investment licensing requirements for most domestic manufacturers, drastically reduced the number of industries reserved to the public sector, eliminated restrictions on investments and mergers by large concerns under the Monopolies and Restrictive Trade Practices Act, and opened up a positive list of industries in which 51% ownership

---

[19] India has had 3 IMF programmes. The IMF programmes of 1966 and 1981 helped tide over periods of high inflation and difficult balance of payments position.

1966 – US $ 187.5 million – 36.5 percent devaluation of the rupee. In 1965 foreign exchange reserves had already been reduced to a low level by increased payments for food inputs occasioned by the shortfall in domestic production and by delays in the repatriation of export proceeds. In March, a stand-by arrangement of US$ 200 million was approved by the Fund.

1981 – US $ 5 billion – Low Conditionality Program.

The Balance of Payments situation changed dramatically in 1979–1980 as agricultural growth suffered and industrial bottlenecks emerged. Inflation soared from 3 percent in 1978–1979 to 22 percent in 1979–1980 and the external terms of trade worsened significantly owing to higher prices for imported petroleum and fertilizers. Government undertook deficit financing on an unprecedented scale. To meet the short-term cyclical imbalance, India drew SDR 266 million under the compensatory financing facility (CFF) from the IMF, but even so, the country's international reserves slid down to 3 ½ months of imports.

[20] This brought the cumulative depreciation of the rupee against the dollar since the beginning of the year to 43 per cent (World Bank, 1991, p.vi).

by foreign companies is freely permitted. These measures go a long way toward deregulating entry and opening up the economy to increase domestic and foreign competition. (p.v)

According to Finance Minister Dr Manmohan Singh in the Lok Sabha Budget debate in February 1992, the medium-term objective was to place the economy back on the path of high and sustained growth (GoI, 1997), which included deregulating the private sector, reforming the public sector, delicensing industries, liberalizing the financial market, deregulating foreign trade, and allowing the entry of foreign capital. External capital was now allowed into 34 major areas from which it had previously been excluded. Foreign investors could acquire majority shareholdings in some Indian companies. The private sector was permitted to enter some areas that had previously remained reserved for the public sector, such as road building and aviation; tariffs were slashed (from 300 per cent in 1991 to 50 per cent by 1995); and the rupee was made convertible on the trading account (Tharoor, 1997). The government risked two devaluations of the rupee so that India could integrate more easily into the world economy. Part and parcel of these reforms was the reduction in bureaucratic processes, which had meant that any investment had taken a long time to be approved (Tharoor, 1997). The 1991 reforms set out to change the country's economic system by removing the hurdles for outside investment and by creating a new investor-friendly economic climate. The Industrial Policy of 24 July 1991 simplified the long-entrenched industrial licensing system, drastically reducing the number of industries reserved for the public sector from 17 to a mere 6.[21] Although a list of 15 industries requiring compulsory licensing was retained, these accounted for just 15 per cent of value added in the manufacturing sector in 1994–1995 (Ministry of Finance, Government of Finance, n.d.). Recognizing the need to modernize India's industrial and export infrastructure, not only to promote and sustain higher growth but also to facilitate larger inflows of foreign direct investment (FDI) into hi-tech export oriented and employment generating manufacturing sectors, the government offered packages of special incentives to foreign investors in selected infrastructure sectors.[22] With these reforms, India saved itself from defaulting on its international debt, and slowly the open economy started to attract capital investments. The areas into which foreign capital

---

[21] These are defence, atomic energy, coal and lignite, minerals, mining, and railway transport.

[22] These included power, telecommunications, petroleum exploration, refining and marketing activities, transportation, ports and shipping, and air taxi operation. 'The government also liberalized its policies around participation by foreign investors in drugs and pharmaceuticals and in the banking services sector' (Gupta, 1999, p.276).

was welcomed broadened over the years to include telecommunications, power, and oil exploration.

The changes were contested by many, leading to much of the reform process having to be brought in by stealth (Jenkins, 1999), and the Rao–Singh government having to assert that this was in no way making India dependent on other countries (Corbridge and Harriss, 2000).[23] Yet things started to change quite dramatically – in particular India's position in the 'global market place' (Corbridge and Harriss, 2000). With the sign that India's economy had opened up, further foreign exchange rolled in, and the foreign exchange reserves rose to $20 billion in the first few years. Already in his 1992/1993 Budget speech, Dr Manmohan Singh could state that the government had achieved its most immediate objective of restoring India's credibility and pulling the economy back from the slide into financial chaos (1992/1993 Budget, Lok Sabha Debates, 29.2.1992).

Corbridge et al (2005) document that beyond the fiscal crisis and dealing with India's BoP issues, the reforms also included a broader programme of administrative and economic reforms to address India's crisis of 'governability'. Kohli suggests that 'widespread administrative failure in India was being produced by an absence of enduring coalitions and a structural incapacity to accommodate political conflict without violence' (Kohli, 1990, p.23, cited in Corbridge et al, 2005, p.158). PM Rao used reforms to address such issues and to keep rural India on board with the reforms he developed a new public administration system and poverty alleviation policies for rural areas (Corbridge et al, 2005). This included new initiatives in education and healthcare, as well as reformed wage employment schemes and the development of a 'village democracy scheme'– the Panchayati Raj, which was instituted through the 73rd Constitutional Amendment (1993).[24] Reminiscent of Gandhian ideals, the Panchayati Raj was meant in part to provide a better allocation of resources, and chimed with the Congress Party's electoral promises to continue to uplift the rural poor. James Manor argues that the three essential conditions for democratic decentralization (which is what the Panchayati Raj was expected to establish) to work well in India are: that the elected bodies should have adequate powers; that

---

[23] India's *swadeshi* (self-reliance) was not actually as pure as the government tried to make everyone believe, as the country had been dependent on both technical assistance and concessional finance from other countries (albeit from both sides of the Cold War divide) throughout the 1950s, 1960s, and 1970s. In the 1980s India received an IMF loan and the government was borrowing heavily, which is what led to the fiscal crisis in the first place. For more see Corbridge and Harriss (2000).

[24] The theory of globalization (Held and Mc Grew, 2007) holds that power moves up to supranational bodies and down to regional bodies. As such, the Panchayati Raj was seen as a form of glocalization.

they are provided with adequate resources; and that they are provided with adequate accountability mechanisms. With some hindsight, Manor writes that most Indian states failed to satisfy these conditions and that they have consequently lost significant opportunities (Manor, 2010; Harriss, 2010). Issues with the successful rollout and running of the Panchayati Raj system have been state governments that were not necessarily committed to the ideology of grassroots democracy,[25] the power of local political actors and their likely disinclination to 'planning from below', the lack of administrative capacity among local governments to carry out planning and developmental projects, and wide regional variations in the process of decentralization as well as the actual devolution of power with a uniform system and procedures (Jenkins, 1999; Manor, 1998; Mitra, 2001; Heller et al, 2007; Rajaraman and Sinha, 2007). For instance, Andhra Pradesh,[26] as well as Tamil Nadu,[27] have been led by regional parties that have bargained strongly for powers for their state-level governments (Kumar, 2009).[28] Simultaneously, both have sidelined further decentralization in their own states. Although Andhra Pradesh was one of the first states to start Panchayati Raj (along with Rajasthan), as it lacked local bodies, it did not do much to empower those at sub-state level. Tamil Nadu had weak local bodies, yet with a strong tradition of bureaucratic rule, managed efficient service delivery (Kumar, 2009).

Economic reforms, decentralization to the states, and the rise of regional parties

Rewriting the rules of economic governance in India's federal democracy had far-reaching consequences on the relations between the union and the states (Kennedy et al, 2013). Although the reforms were initiated by the government at the centre, state-level politicians and political systems had key roles to play in managing their implications and contributing to their sustainability. According to Jenkins, 'they absorbed much of the political

---

[25] See later in the chapter for the role of state governments and regional parties in the reform process.

[26] Telugu Desam Party (TDP) in Andhra Pradesh since 1982.

[27] Dravida Munnetra Kazhagam and the All India Anna Dravida Munnetra Kazhagam in Tamil Nadu.

[28] The championing of the federal cause is less common among national parties than among regional parties, since they have their high command at the centre; but intra-party dynamics even among national parties contain weighty power equations between a central party and its regional chapters. An increasing tendency in Indian politics, alongside economic reforms, is the rise of coalition politics since 1989, which is adding to the strength of national parties' regional leaders.

burden' (Jenkins, 1999, p.126). Although initially seen as a possible obstacle to the smooth roll out of directives from New Delhi, and the fact that multiple layers of government can increase inefficiencies and corruption, in this case the Rao–Singh decentralization accompanying the reforms was designed to share the economic pain. An assessment made just a few years into the reforms by the Economist Intelligence Unit states:

> [O]ne of the most important changes taking place in India is the gradual diffusion of power to the states after the centralised, statist years of the Nehru-Gandhi family. It is happening for good reasons (political pluralism and the workings of the market) and bad ones (weak leadership at the centre and the growth of parochial, sectarian political parties). (Economist Intelligence Unit, *Country Report – India*, 2nd Quarter, 1995 [London,1995], p.14, cited in Jenkins, 1999, p.127)

The dismantling of controls that had been exercised by central government gave state governments greater scope to construct their own policies with regard to economic development initiatives. This translated into greater policy-making space for state governments and greater responsibility for their own finances (Ahluwalia, 2000; Bagchi, 2003). Subnational political elites reacted differently to this new situation, which was perceived sometimes as a constraint and sometimes as an opportunity. The liberalization of controls on the location of investment resulted in more direct competition between subnational territories, with regional governments vying to outdo each other (Kennedy et al, 2013). According to Jenkins (1999), centre–state conflict was partially displaced by interstate competition, and this lack of unity helped to take some of the stings out of anti-reform dissidence among state-level political leaders.

Regional inequalities deepened, and interstate comparisons of economic growth quickly showed increasing divergence in economic performance (Kennedy et al, 2013). In the south Indian states,[29] per capita incomes rose substantially faster than in the larger north Indian states (Singh, 2008).[30] This transformation resulted in the so-called north–south divide.[31] Part of this was

---

[29] In 1990–1991, per capita income in Karnataka was 1.7 and 1.3 times higher than that of Bihar and Uttar Pradesh.

[30] But it should be noted that despite the south's rapid progress, India's national political agenda was still set by the more populous north – the conservative, Hindi-speaking region often called the 'cow belt' (Kazmin, 2018).

[31] Their interregional inequality appears to have further widened during the neoliberal globalization era (Singh, 2008). In 2000, inequalities in per capita GDP was found to be the highest in two of the richest states (Tamil Nadu and Maharashtra) (Kurian, 2000; Ghosh and Chandrasekhar, 2003; Purohit, 2008). Swain et al (2009) reported that regional disparity in Orissa, one of India's poorest states, declined during the post-reform period

also down to the role of the chief ministers, who took on para-diplomatic roles to further the development of their states (Wyatt, 2017). To ensure their political survival, state leaders adjusted their political strategies to account for changes (Wyatt, 2017).[32] Manor has documented how chief ministers in Andhra Pradesh and Madhya Pradesh used the 'advantages of office skilfully' (Manor, 1995, pp.49–50). Andhra Pradesh is a case in point, as its political leadership embraced the reform agenda as a strategy for pursuing its regionalist political agenda, and contracted loans from the World Bank in a bid to restructure the regional economy and engage with the global economy (Kennedy, 2007; Kennedy et al, 2013). Chandrababu Naidu became Chief Minister of the government led by the regional TDP in 1996.[33] A strategic plan for this state entitled *Andhra Pradesh: Vision 2020* was designed in collaboration with the international consulting firm McKinsey (Kennedy et al, 2013). Naidu had a vision of transforming Hyderabad into a global tech hub – a Silicon Valley outpost, powered by low-cost Indian programmers (Kazmin, 2018).

Kennedy (2004) has looked in detail at the two cases of Andhra Pradesh and Tamil Nadu, and has noted a great deal of overlap in the substance of policy, but a wide divergence in the 'discursive framing of [the] response to liberalization' (Kennedy, 2004, p.30). Chief Minister Naidu was keen to back economic reform, whereas the regional parties in Tamil Nadu avoided 'wherever possible taking a public stand in support of market reform', resulting in a situation where 'Andhra Pradesh's government does less than it announces, Tamil Nadu's does more' (Kennedy, 2004, pp.44–6). Seeking to explain this, Kennedy argues that the narrative used to promote reform was 'modulated' as political leaders balanced the interests of different groups. The government of Andhra Pradesh was more concerned to signal its pro-reform intentions to external investors and domestic elites, whereas ruling parties in Tamil Nadu were more concerned not to alienate poorer voters (Kennedy, 2004, pp.52–3). Such rhetorical strategies resemble a two-level game, with chief ministers setting an economic trajectory and trying not to alienate different interests (Wyatt, 2017).

---

owing to development programmes for backward areas. States responded to liberalization on the basis of their relative economic standing (Bajpai and Sachs, 1999). Rich states are likely to adopt reforms since it is presumed that they stand to gain from the shift towards markets and global economic integration, whereas poor states are not inclined to embrace reforms since they perceive themselves as likely to lose from a greater reliance on markets (Kennedy, 2004).

[32] Chief ministers faced fiscal difficulties as the centre changed the rules for allocating resources and responsibilities, encouraging them to seek out FDI to strengthen their state economies (Rudolph and Rudolph, 2001, pp.1543–4). However, they also gained new opportunities for rent seeking and raising party funds (Jenkins, 2004, pp.133–6).

[33] This regional party was formed in the early 1980s in opposition to the Congress. It claims to protect the interests of the Telugu-speaking people and defend their pride.

These transformations across the states resulted in a specific reordering of economic governance; a redefinition of the respective roles of central and state governments. In his seminal work, Jenkins (1999) emphasizes that

> Despite the complications and uncertainties it introduces, the existence of a federal political system has been an extremely important ingredient in helping to make India's economic reform programme politically sustainable – that is, in reducing the pressure on political decision-makers in the central government to abandon reform. In addition to unloading thankless political burdens on to state governments, in the guise of devolving decision-making authority in certain areas. (pp.127–8)

In fact, the reforms required cooperation from state governments to succeed, and hence state-level politics and governance took on greater importance for India's overall development trajectory (Kennedy et al, 2013).

Owing to the devolution of powers and responsibilities to the states, the role of regional political parties also changed, increasing their powers both locally and at the centre. A notable feature of the national and state party systems in India since the late 1980s/early 1990s has been the strengthening of existing and newly formed regional parties (Kailash, 2014; Tillin, 2015; Diwakar, 2017; Wyatt, 2019). The party system in many of the states was traditionally seen as 'anti-centre fractionalized', but not in opposition to the Indian Union (Wyatt, 2009, p.12). The growth and increased importance of regional parties is associated with a greater diversity of economic policies. State governments are either important regional allies of the central government or they are part of the opposition (Kumar, 2009). This can be explained by the federalization of the party system: a growing number of parties, and the commensurate changes in vote shares, with national parties declining, largely though not exclusively, in the face of strengthening state-based parties (Arora, 2003, pp.84–5) that have clear local agendas and priorities that represent regional aspirations (Kailash, 2014, pp.65–6; Wyatt, 2019). This development has exerted pressure on national parties to cooperate with state-based parties to form electoral alliances and coalition governments (Arora, 2003, pp. 85–8, pp. 91–2; Wyatt, 2019). Regional parties that are active in national politics, with a good chance of winning seats and the potential to form governments or lead coalitions at home, will run their state politics in line with what their voters want locally (Palshikar, 2013, pp. 91–2; Ziegfeld, 2016, pp. 24–5; Wyatt, 2019).[34] The situation has

---

[34] The regional governing parties may well be members of a national coalition government, either gaining a place through membership of a pre-election agreement or by offering support to an alliance after an election (Wyatt, 2019).

again differed drastically between the north and south of the country: in the north (e.g., Uttar Pradesh) the debate has been around the Babri Masjid and Ram Mandir issues, whereas in the south voters (and the parties they voted for, in Karnataka and Andhra Pradesh, for example) were more interested in developing their cities into cyberhubs (Kumar, 2009).

Post-reform education

As reforms began in 1992, when education policy was re-examined, the NEP was regarded as a sound way forward for India's education system, although some targets were recast and some reformulations were undertaken in relation to adult and elementary education (Ram and Sharma, 1995). The new emphasis was on the expansion of secondary education, while a focus on education for minorities and women continued. According to Corbridge et al (2005, p.80), India had 'failed lamentably' to meet its performance targets, and the reforms made this all too visible. Sound policy goals (regarding access and literacy) and the actual effect on the ground of these policies were not congruent in many of the Indian states.[35] In the 1990s government education provision needed to be expanded, resulting in quality being traded for quantity, with new institutions being opened with declining allocations spread thinly. Equity was also sacrificed, as the budget allocations for scholarships and welfare programmes waned fast (Tilak, 2018). The revised National Policy on Education (1992) suggested an expansion of Operation Blackboard to provide three reasonably large rooms and three teachers in every primary school, and to extend the scheme to upper primary level (Tilak, 2018). However, in 1993, when the All-India Educational Survey (NCERT, 19971998) was conducted, more than 20,000 primary schools in rural India (17.1 per cent of them) were found to be operating in open spaces, tents, thatched huts, and katcha buildings (NCERT, 1992, 1997–1998; Tilak, 2018, p.122).[36] Most of these schools remained closed during rainy days as well as on severe winter and summer days (Tilak, 2018). With respect to the provision of ancillary facilities, the overall situation was unsatisfactory – for example, more than 60 percent of primary schools and 40 per cent of upper primary schools did not have drinking water facilities (Tilak, 2018, p.123).

---

[35] A notable exception to this has been Kerala, which still boasts the country's highest literacy rates. It is interesting to note that with India's increased globalization and integration into the world economy, public investment in education had increased to around 4 per cent of GDP by 2004, but this was still well below the 6 per cent of GDP level recommended in 1968 by the Kothari Commission.

[36] Katcha buildings are buildings with a limited lifespan made from natural materials.

The new education agenda relied on private provision coming to the rescue of the learning deficit. The required budget cuts that had been agreed as part of the structural adjustment programme did not allow the government to increase public spending on education to a level that would allow radical reformation of the system (Tilak et al, 2018).[37] The expansion of education through private and not for profit sectors would in turn allow for parental choice, congruent with the neoliberal reform policies that the government had embarked upon. Private provision was not new, as the NEP agreed under Rajiv Gandhi had already started to encourage the growth of that sector. However, the post-1991 government shifted its focus from the allocation of public resources to mobilizing non-governmental resources, then to alternative methods of cost recovery, and to the privatization of education. Private institutions began to increase in number at the cost of the growth of public institutions. This was broadly in line with the new economic policies adopted by the government from the beginning of the 1990s, which favour downsizing of the public system and its privatization (Tilak et al, 2018).

Field surveys in the 1990s began to report a surge in parental demand for education, and accompanying this a new phenomenon – small fee-charging private schools (often referred to as 'low cost') for the less privileged (De et al, 2002, pp.131–3). With the dwindling quality of government provision, it appeared that low-income groups not only desired education, but they were willing to pay for it. This new phenomenon was welcomed by education bureaucrats since the government system was struggling with both access and retention issues, and many felt that the new private schools could be allies in achieving the target of universalization of elementary education (De et al, 2002). Enrolment in private unaided schools thus rose most sharply following the economic liberalization that raised incomes in the early 1990s (Venkatanarayanan, 2015). In 1993–4, the private upper primary schools increased in proportion from 11 to 22 per cent (Tilak, 2018, p.527).[38] Between 1999 and 2003, studies (PROBE, 1999; Aggarwal, 2000; Tooley and Dixon, 2002) reported a burgeoning sector of low-cost private schools.

The evidence available indicates that private schools have grown largely in response to the prospect of making quick profits, and/or for reasons related to political power (Tilak, 2018). It is widely acknowledged that private schools turn out to be socially and economically divisive, and the

---

[37] In education financing, the trends in India correspond with global trends – high rates of growth in public expenditure on education in the 1960s, negative rates of growth in the 1970s, steady but slow positive growth in the 1980s, and declining growth in the 1990s, accompanying the adjustment policies (Tilak, 2018).

[38] Recent figures show that between 1993 and 2017 enrolment in private unaided schools grew rapidly by 25.6 percentage points (Central Square Foundation, 2020, p.100).

government school system has not been adequate to counteract these forces; as a result, the whole educational system has been found to be a 'de-equalizer' that accentuates income inequalities (Tilak, 2011; Tilak, 2018). In the new neoliberal thinking India, this was something the middle classes did not necessarily object to. After years of Congress-led reservations in HE and public sector jobs, and with the opening up of the economy, the middle classes found that there was increased competition for good jobs and careers, for which a good education, notably with English as a medium of instruction, was becoming essential. Differentiation on the basis of public and private schools became a central part of the middle-class push for reforms, with many lamenting that as part of the 'general category' they had to throw everything they had into the ring to give their children the best chance to be successful (Menon and Vincent in Lall and Nambissan, 2011).[39] This in turn reflected the anti-reservation policies of the BJP, which increasingly spoke of a meritocratic system, rather than one that helped to elevate backward sections of society. With the increasing availability of choice, the lower middle classes also started to opt for private provision, and as time progressed, even those considered poor would rather skip a meal in order to send their children to a private school. Sarangapani and Mukhopadhyay (cited in Jain et al, 2018) agree that the socio-economic transitions resulted in an aspiring middle class as well as an increasing social distance between government school teachers and families, both of which contributed to the desirability of private institutions and a simultaneous reinforcement of deficit assumptions regarding government schools (Jeffrey et al, 2005; Sancho, 2015).

This development, key to the argument of this book that education became the link between neoliberalism and Hindu nationalism through the choices made by the middle classes, has to be seen in the context of economic reform. It was the changed economy that allowed the aspirations of the middle classes to find new expressions (Jain et al, 2018). With their professional and social interests intertwined with the emerging forms of corporate capital that came to dominate both the formal and informal economy, the new middle classes started to leave the government's and government-aided provision of vernacular education in favour of a burgeoning range of private unaided schools (Lall, 2013; Jain et al, 2018). These schools ranged from those offering international baccalaureate school education programmes at high fees for the elite, to a spectrum of schools with a graded fee structure that catered to the highly segmented new middle classes, and on to low fee unrecognized schools catering to those from the lower stages of the stratified social order who were aspiring to reach the middle classes (Tilak, 2018; Jain et al, 2018).

---

[39] General category refers to those for whom there is no reservation.

The rise of Hindu nationalism and BJP politics

In 1991 India had been forced to open its economy in order to prevent collapse, but once the economy had been saved, the process of liberalization started to stagnate. Policy implementation is always slower than the rhetoric preceding it, especially when the country is as large and diverse as India. But in this case, the willingness to break with the Nehruvian tradition and to jump head over heels into a new neoliberal system in which outside capital would dictate the Indian state of affairs was initially not supported by the majority of the population or the politicians. The middle classes needed to be brought on board.

The results of the liberalization programme – what changes?

'After the initial burst of reforms, the absence of any overall economic design or strategy, and consequent inability to explain the logic of government actions to the citizenry became uncomfortably clear' (Khilnani, 1999, p.99) The government was trying to pacify as many demands as possible, without any clear goal in sight, and this remained the case throughout the 1990s as coalition government after coalition government (first two United Front governments, then the BJP coalition) struggled with the country's economic conditions. At first, it seemed as if a discourse of liberalization had simply replaced a discourse on planning. It remained a debate about good versus bad, without any clear direction, and as a result implementation severely lagged behind the rhetoric. The argument that national economic sovereignty was threatened by liberalization that opened India to the world was the standing argument of both the political left and Hindu nationalists.[40] They argued that the reforms only touched a fraction of the Indian population and that the masses had nothing to gain but everything to lose. Indian industrialists complained of the reforms, as they took away the protectionism they had become used to, and exposed their weakness to competition. The outside investor was still regarded as an economic predator who wanted to take advantage of the Indian economy for his own benefit. He was seen as relying too much on imported machinery, rather than using the indigenous options, and did not reinvest the profits he made but took them all abroad. At the root of the debate were the effects of the reforms on Indian society and the resultant changes for the population. The leading criticisms of liberalization were that it had not brought about growth as quickly as expected, did not

---

[40] In this case, the BJP was referring not only to investment by non-resident Indians (NRIs), which it had appealed for earlier, but also to the fact that opening the Indian economy had let in various multinational companies, which the BJP disliked intensely.

improve the country's credit rating, did not upgrade the technological level of Indian industry, and did little for the masses of poor and unemployed (Tharoor, 1997, p.181). Growth that did not help to solve India's poverty, illiteracy, poor health, and inequality problems would widen the gap between the rich and the poor, urban and rural areas, and different regions.

The effects of the reforms on society

Owing to its size and large population, India was hardly in a position to implement economic reforms smoothly. Although these reforms led to the economic uplifting of around 30 per cent of its population, the economic growth unfortunately did not trickle down to all sections of society. The opening up of the market quickly brought about increased disparities between the wealthy and the poor. According to Kumar, disinvestment in the public sector allowed the private sector to grow, and this quickly led to the casualization of the workforce (Kumar, 2009, p.144). To mitigate the effects of the changes, the Congress-led government put in place pro-poor programmes (Corbridge et al, 2005). One of the key anti-poverty programmes was the Employment Assurance Scheme (EAS) that started in 1993, when it was deployed by the Ministry of Rural Development in New Delhi 'to provide gainful employment during the lean agricultural season in manual work to all able-bodied adults in rural areas who are in need and who are desirous of work, but who cannot find it' (GoI, India 1993, p.1 as cited in Corbridge et al, 2005, p.80). The funds (80 per cent from New Delhi, 20 per cent matching funds from state governments) were to provide up to 100 days of waged employment for a maximum of two adults per household in need.[41] The aim was to make sure that poor rural areas were not left behind whilst India underwent its reform process. Despite anti-poverty and pro-poor policies, rural dwellers who still make up over 80 per cent of the population did not benefit in the same way as those based in urban settings. According to Harriss-White (2004, p.3):

Some eighty-eight per cent of India's population lives and works in settlements with fewer than 200,000 people. This still rural and small town economy is dominated by agricultural- and food-related goods

---

[41] The EAS guidelines stipulated that village open meetings would have to be called to decide on the sorts of schemes that villagers might like to see commissioned (the results to be passed upwards to higher-level panchayat bodies and the Block Development Office), and for the selection of the contractor charged with executing a scheme. They also required that the accounts of EAS schemes should be presented to villagers each year through their open meetings (the *gram sansads* of West Bengal, for example) (Corbridge et al, 2005, pp. 80–2).

and services. In 1997, an average of a little over 10 per cent of total consumption expenditure in this part of the economy was estimated to be devoted to the output of the corporate sector. The other 90 per cent was spent on the output of the informal economy, in which most of the 88 per cent worked. The informal economy either lies outside the scope of state regulation, or is officially subject to state regulation but nevertheless does not operate according to the rules and laws through which the formal intention of regulation is inscribed. In the first sense it is familiar as 'unregistered' and 'unorganised', and defined as consisting of firms with electricity but under 10 workers or without electricity and over 20 workers (conditions which are very rare outside agriculture).

Harriss-White goes on to argue that the policies of the World Bank would not work in India because of the large scale of India's informal and rural economy. She also states that the government's main problem was tax evasion rather than corruption. For her, the reforms that brought in privatization created a shadow state 'for the accumulative projects of local capitalist classes' (Harriss-White, 2004, pp.100–1, cited in Corbridge et al, 2005 p.161). Reforms therefore benefited the middle classes rather than the whole country.

The reforms and opening up of the economy did – as Harriss-White correctly analyses – result in the development of new and wider middle classes (rather than one monolithic middle class), the top layer of which was able to take advantage of the market economy and imported goods. Those just below and the 'aspiring' middle classes increasingly saw access to Western goods as a marker of success. However, in the mid-1990s, the general feeling was that the newly arrived multinationals were benefiting from the Indian markets whilst the population – no matter from which class – had to put up with staggering price rises, and more goods on the shelf that the majority could not afford. This is why popular support for the more nationalist BJP started to increase. Their (initial) call for investment, which would help to develop India's infrastructure, yet leave multinationals such as Coca-Cola and KFC at the door, struck a chord with a majority of the public. We now turn to the relationship between the growing middle classes and Hindu nationalism.

The identity crisis of the middle classes

Hansen (1999) asserts that since the 1970s and 1980s the educated urban middle class had gradually come to question the state's commitment to the policy of secularism, as secularists were seen to defend all kinds of religious discrimination, for example religion-based civil codes, against the genuinely and quintessentially secular system of equality of all citizens before the law regardless of their religion. He gives the Ayodhya campaign as an example that portrayed the Congress government of the day as pseudo-secular.[42] The middle classes felt that the government's pledge to respect all religious communities had failed. Affirmative action demands by the lower castes squeezed the space available for the middle classes, who increasingly resented the reservation system. Whilst the system had worked in its early years because the state wielded enough authority to accommodate diversity, it started to fail later, when rather than creating more equality, there were more and more groups clambering for reservation rights, resulting in a 'creamy layer' (Jaffrelot, 2003) that in turn opened the door to religion-based politics and the 'saffron wave',[43] as it was known, of Hindu nationalism.[44] As discussed later, the economic reforms supported this trend.

Slowly but surely the influx of Western goods started to change the way India looked; with such a large population, the country was an ideal market for imported consumer products. The internet was increasingly becoming more accessible, and soon India's traditionally restrictive TV channels (there was only one government channel, Doordarshan,[45] until the early 1990s, when DD2 was set up) expanded, with private investment bringing in Star TV, CNN, and new domestic chains such as ZEE that aired Western programmes. All this material novelty was well received by the middle classes, who until then had not had much access to either Western goods or media. However, the rapid changes also fuelled something else – an identity crisis, at the heart of which was the question of what it meant to be Indian in light of globalization and the onslaught of westernization. The answer came through politics: reassurances about the insecurities

---

[42] Hansen also remembers the hard-line rhetoric of a Sadhvi Ritambhara (a Hindu nationalist ideologue and the founder-chairperson of Durga Vahini); the emphasis was on Rama as a national (as opposed to a Hindu) hero, and on Babar as a foreign invader (as opposed to an Islamic iconoclast), who had been fought 'by Indian Muslims and Hindus jointly' (Hansen, 1999, p.10).

[43] The rise of the BJP in Indian politics (termed the 'saffron wave') thus intersects with the increasing political participation of lower castes (termed the 'silent revolution') (Jaffrelot, 2003).

[44] Hansen situates Hindu nationalism – in the form of a family of Hindu political and cultural groups, the Sangh Parivar – within public culture. He avoids reducing this movement to politics or religion and argues that it derives from and seeks to shape an Indian public culture at the 'turbulent intersection of various democratic, demographic, consumerist, and globalising forces' (Hansen, 1999, p.10). Hansen argues that Hindu nationalists have gained momentum from middle-class anxieties regarding the social flux accompanying these forces, especially the increasing involvement of 'competing populisms' based on 'plebian movements' (Hansen, 1999, p.10).

[45] Popular for airing *Ramayan* (1987–1988) and *Mahabharat* (1989–1990).

presented by the rapid change were offered by the BJP, whose aim was to redefine India according to its Hindu cultural legacy and to integrate the ideology of 'Hindutva' into future generations.[46] Hindutva is founded on the basis that India is primarily a Hindu nation, and non-Hindus living in the country have a choice either to accept the majority's domination or leave (Flåten, 2017). Hansen's work shows that Hindu nationalists have been successful because 'the movement [acted as] as a receptor of a disgruntled and frustrated Hindu middle-class' (Hansen, 1999, p.10), which sought explanations and easy solutions to its problems. Such grievances and sentiments were reframed, organized, and aggregated by the Hindu nationalist discourse, and staged as a spontaneous upsurge of cultural identity in the political arena.[47]

The rising middle classes not only focused on the acquisition of material wealth. As certain sections of Indian society became richer they were also able to opt out of government provision of health, education, and other public services as a vast array of new private institutions offered these at varying levels of affordability to various groups – both in urban and not much later in rural settings.[48] This posed risks to the unifying system that had been envisioned by Nehru around 50 years earlier that had transcended India's many fault lines of caste, class, religion, and ethnic groups. Choice was the new leitmotiv for the more affluent classes, and increasingly throughout the 1990s public education was left for the poorer sections of society (Kingdon, 2007). As discussed earlier, the market of low fee

---

[46] In the essay 'Hindutva: Who is Hindu?', Veer Savarkar wrote: 'Hindutva is not identical with what is vaguely indicated by the term Hinduism.' The Hindutva forces want to amend the Constitution of India, removing key words, and turn India into a theocratic state based upon 'systemic inequality', 'anti-egalitarianism' and 'elitism' – so the Hindus have supremacy over all other religious minorities (Chaudhury, 2020).

[47] Hansen focuses on the phenomenon within the context of specific 'economy of stances' (1999, p.187) in the political field. He studies how idioms, practices, and stakes that define political practices in their localized forms in neighbourhoods and villages, the contest over religious sites, rituals, shared spaces, and symbols of Indian culture, lead to interventions in the political arena and modify sociocultural identities in a specific manner. However, according to pro-Hindutva scholars (such as Ashis Nandy, Tarun Vijay, and Koenraad Elst), Hansen's *The Saffron Wave* – like Craig Baxter's *The Jana Sangha* and Walter Andersen and Shridhar Damle's *Brotherhood in Saffron* – relies on partisan secondary accounts. According to Nandy and Vijay, Hansen expresses reservations about majoritarian politics and their potential ill-effects for minority and religious groups. Elst (2002) also expresses concern about Hansen's over-reliance on the partisan selection of secondary sources and the usage of quotations from secondary anti-Hindutva sources (such as Bipan Chandra, Raimon Panikkar, Parambrata Chatterjee, Christophe Jaffrelot, Asghar Ali Engineer, Sudhir Kakar, Gyan Pandey, and S. Gopal).

[48] Whilst there has always been private education in India, this was reserved for the tiny elite and had little effect on the wider population.

private schools was soon to expand exponentially to serve the aspiring middle classes.

Whilst the functions of education include the promotion of social justice and the creation of a functional workforce, it is often forgotten that education is also a political tool to promote what Gramsci termed hegemony – 'the power to establish the "common sense" of a society, the fund of self-evident descriptions of social reality that normally go without saying. This includes the power to establish authoritative definitions of social situations and social needs, the power to define the universe of legitimate disagreement and the power to shape the political agenda' (Fraser, 1992, p.53). In every country, one of the prime functions of education is to build a cohesive society – one held together by shared values, purposes, and activities. Most education systems have been designed to more or less impose one culture, usually that of the elite: a dominant race, class, political party, or colonial power. Determining and imposing a dominant culture from above is directly related to elite ambitions to control the wider population (Lall in Lall and Vickers, 2009). In post-independent India, education reflected the visions of the largely Western educated and secular elites of the day with a modicum of commitment to equity. After 1991 the new middle classes set the agenda (Despande, 2003). They supported the liberalization process and a pro-choice agenda for education. Their choice of private schooling meant that as a consequence public education lost value in the eyes of the masses, and even the poorer sections of society aspired to leave the public system (Lall, 2013).

Beteille (2001) has argued that the middle classes have long supported differentiated schooling, which would equip their children with better credentials, thereby giving them an edge in the employment market. Middle-class parents had previously supplemented public schooling with private tuition, and made sure their children accessed HE. One could argue that before the emergence of the plethora of private schools, the main differentiating factor between the classes was the length of schooling and whether or not a child went to university.[49] Nevertheless, public education was still a unifying factor, promoting a secular national identity and intending to provide equal chances for access to HE. When the middle classes chose to opt out, the poorer sections of society had no option but to take whatever the state gave them. This led to a trend of deteriorating public education, meaning that more and more aspired to leave the system, thereby creating a vicious circle (Nambissan, 2006; Nambissan and Ball, in Lall and Nambissan, 2011).

---

[49] This is also why reservations for Scheduled Castes (SC) and Scheduled Tribes (ST) were limited to HE and not seen as relevant at school level.

India's (new) middle classes were important because of their economic choices, and they became increasingly important because of their role in creating hegemonic discourses, which legitimated certain ways of being and behaving, as well as certain attitudes (Zavos, 2000; Skeggs, 2004). In focusing on the competing ideologies of Hindu nationalism and Indian nationalism, Zavos (2000) charts how the middle classes were able to shape the discourse around an open economy and a Hindu identity because they were close to the focal points of power. Much of this was underpinned by notions of assertiveness and pride that have also been noted by scholars of Hindu nationalism (Hansen, 1996, 1999; Vanaik, 1997; Zavos, 2000; Rajagopal, 2001), who connect it to the effects of globalization and the rise of the Indian middle class, which almost exclusively consists of Hindus (Flåten, 2019). Their behaviour affected the public sector, and its provision for poorer sections of society (Vincent and Menon in Lall and Nambissan, 2011), underpinning an increasing neoliberal attitude towards the economy and education, yet in parallel supporting the Hindu nationalist political discourse.

How India went through three elections in five years

After five years of a Congress-led government, with its half-finished reform programme, general elections were held in 1996 that produced a hung parliament, with the BJP as the largest party. The debates were dominated by how far the reforms should go and by Congress corruption scandals. The BJP had campaigned against unfettered market reforms, promising to safeguard Indian businesses and only allow international and multinational corporations into India to supply technology that the country did not have. Its four-point plan advocated probity in public life, self-reliance in the economy, social harmony, and greater security. The BJP also stressed the role of Hindutva for India, promising to ban cow slaughter, introduce a uniform civil code, and remove the special status of Kashmir. The Congress Party campaigned on its foreign policy record, its handling of the numerous natural and ethnic crises that had emerged over the past five years, and better concessions for ethnic minorities and separated state governments. It also stressed the economic gains already made by the government (although these were brought about by Congress-inspired liberalization policies to post-1992). The results of the election show that the public was not convinced.

The BJP was called to form a government, but conceded after 13 days that not enough support from elected party members across parties could be gathered (only 200 out of 545 seats). Regional and smaller parties then united as a third force to keep both the BJP and Congress out of power, and a United Front government came together first under Deve Gowda of the Janata Dal, later replaced by I.K. Gujral. For the first time, Indian politics dealt with serious coalition negotiations. The United Front government was able to survive until Congress withdrew support, resulting in new elections in 1998. These did not result in a clear result, even though the BJP won the largest number of seats and managed to get support from 286 out of 545 MPs. The BJP-led government collapsed on 17 April 1999, leading to fresh elections between September and October that year, just after the end of the Kargil war with Pakistan.

In the 1999 elections, the National Democratic Alliance (NDA, a coalition of regional parties and the Shiv Sena headed by the BJP) rose to power; it lasted for the full five-year term (Adeney and Saez, 2007). Unlike in 1998, the BJP had agreed on a common coalition manifesto *before* the elections – 'For a Proud, Prosperous India: An Agenda' (NDA, 1999) (more often referred to as the 'National Agenda for Governance').[50] The opposition coalition led by Congress comprised far fewer parties, and its alliances were generally weaker than those of the NDA. The fact that Congress was led by Sonia Gandhi, Italian by birth, resulted in a debate on 'videsi' (foreign) versus 'swadesi' (home-grown) politicians, advantaging Atal Bihari Vajpayee. During the previous two years, India had posted strong economic growth on the back of the economic and financial reforms, as well as a low rate of inflation and a higher rate of industrial expansion. However, the BJP had come to power fighting *against* the Indian economic reforms – advocating more limitations on the operations of multinational corporations in India and pushing for greater involvement of the NRIs. Under the slogan 'Microchips yes, potato chips, no', the BJP promised that the already stark economic divisions in Indian society would not be exacerbated by the opening up of the market.[51] On the ground, however, after winning the elections, the economic reforms continued unabated, with the gradual opening of the Indian market to foreign trade and investment, and financial devolution to the Indian states; this despite the fact that Hindu nationalist thought favours a strong central government committed to Hindu unity, viewing federal forms of government – especially around 'ethnic criteria' – as potentially destabilizing (Adeney in Adeney and Saez, 2007; Hansen, 1999).[52] But

---

[50] The joint manifesto of 1999 was toned down, with the BJP's previous commitment to introduce a Uniform Civil Code, their pledge to build a temple at Ayodhya, and their vow to revoke the special status of Kashmir in the Constitution omitted. When in government, partial restraint was seen in relation to minorities (Adeney and Saez, 2007).

[51] The BJP's 1996 manifesto, prior to first taking office, was also careful not to dismiss globalization entirely, instead referring to the need to adopt a 'calibrated' approach to global economic integration. These fine distinctions were, of course, an attempt to have it both ways, something that most parties try their best to achieve (Jenkins in Adeney and Saez, 2007).

[52] Hindu nationalist thought does not see decentralization at the local level – to the panchayats – as incompatible with this (Adeney in Adeney and Saez, 2007).

requiring political alliances with regional parties to create a coalition, the BJP had to compromise on some of its agenda. A key example of this is the continuation of the reforms. As mentioned earlier, the BJP had campaigned against the reforms for ideological reasons. Its links with the RSS,[53] and RSS-linked organizations, which were calling for *swadeshi*, made BJP relations with external actors such as the World Bank and the IMF complex, in particular making it difficult to justify the continuation of the structural reforms, which included multilateral trade negotiations and a reduction in public finances. One can argue that the coalition forces (and the pragmatism required to keep the coalition together) made it possible for the BJP to step back from the economic nationalism they had advocated; but coalition politics also required trade-offs, and there were some acute political dilemmas (Jenkins in Adeney and Saez, 2007).

Deeper second-generation reforms meant that the NDA faced a more complex set of challenges than previous governments (Jenkins in Adeney and Saez, 2007). It would probably have been impossible for the NDA government to advance its reforms had the Indian economy not improved significantly since the crisis. Jenkins reminds us that:

Inadequate progress on certain indicators, such as the consolidated (central plus states) fiscal deficit as a proportion of GDP, has been eclipsed in public discussions by the high annual GDP growth figures (particularly in a world marked by meagre economic growth in most countries during the period under investigation). Likewise, headline-grabbing statements such as the size of India's foreign-exchange reserves (which stand in such great contrast to the 1991 situation), or the fact that during at least one quarter during 2003–04 India balanced its

---

[53] It should be remembered that the BJP's relationship with the RSS was not always straightforward. Manor states: 'Another part of the problem is the tendency of the RSS to be a diffident partner for the BJP. This has happened at different times and in different places for different reasons. In some parts of India – and, to a degree, in India as a whole – between 1980 and 1989, when Indira Gandhi and then Rajiv Gandhi were clearly in the ascendancy, many RSS cadres turned to the INC as the party that was most likely to achieve some of its cherished goals. They did so in part because they found the BJP's political prospects depressing, but also because they were dismayed at the party's dilution of Hindu nationalist ideology, its "efforts to attract Muslims", its strategy of alliance-building with other parties, and its aim to form a coalition government (Jaffrelot, 1996, p.327). In that period, Paul Brass witnessed RSS cadres canvassing for INC candidates in Uttar Pradesh – as a result of a decision by the RSS leader in the state. Andersen and Damle (1987, pp.231–2, 234), Graham (1987, p.15), Katju (2003, p.63) and Jaffrelot (1996, pp.374, 377) offer evidence from other states to reinforce this point. That problem was eased when the BJP's fortunes revived after 1989, but some hesitations in the RSS remain (Manor, quoted in Adeney and Saez, 2007).

current account for the first time in a quarter-century also have taken precedence in economic debates. All of this has taken place in a low-inflation context. (Jenkins, in Adeney and Saez, 2007, p.176)

In the end it seems that pragmatism was a key part of the BJP's coalition politics, putting reforms above ideological constraints and bending towards powerful regional parties as opposed to the RSS. Jenkins explains how the large block of TDP MPs who were part of the NDA (Chief Minister Chandrababu Naidu's party that ruled Andhra Pradesh) made it difficult to exercise fiscal restraint, and that Railways Minister Mamata Banerjee insisted that the central government approve the proposals contained within her self-proclaimed 'Bengal package'. The regionalization of politics with the push from state-based parties was a key element in India's new politics; this allowed the BJP to embrace neoliberalism, making the party increasingly attractive to the growing middle classes who just wanted India's economy to open up. It also allowed for some level of ideological politics to take root, as will be discussed next.

Beyond reforms, the NDA win changed much in Indian politics, as the Hindu nationalists were now at the helm of power. Their politics was a challenge to the Nehruvian secularism that had been the bedrock of Indian politics until then.[54] For decades, a strong political challenge to secularism has been posed by the politics of the Hindu right represented by groups such as the RSS, of which the BJP is the political party, the Vishva Hindu Parishad (VHP), and the Shiv Sena. This Hindu right looks at secularism as a policy of minority appeasement, mainly Muslim appeasement, and of Hindu subjugation. In their view, the Congress Party has favoured the Muslim community by agreeing to Partition and then allowing communities to have separate laws, and is therefore not truly secular. Their argument is that India is a Hindu majority country and therefore Hindus constitute the nation and the citizenry of India and have the first claim over it. The conception of a majoritarian political rule is justified in the name of democracy, meaning that Hindus as a majority have a right to steer the country. Corbridge and Harris (2000, p.xix) discuss the rise of Hindu nationalism as the second 'elite revolt'. According to them, Hindu nationalism would allow India to be fully itself, secure global status, and

---

[54] The Congress party has not been consistently secular despite its Nehruvian origins. Two prominent instances illustrate the point – the Shah Bano case and the opening of the locks of the Babri mosque site for worship to Hindu devotees during 1986–1987. These two instances (among others) brought the state's secular credentials into question since Congress was in power. In both instances, the government pandered to the communal/fundamentalist elements – Muslim and Hindu fundamentalists, respectively.

receive recognition in a globalizing world. The Sangh was not seen as anti-modern, but offered a different road to modernization that was the right way forward in light of the reforms.

There have been many other arguments put forward against secularism in this age-old Indian debate.[55] As mentioned earlier, T.N. Madan (Madan, 1998) and Ashis Nandy (Nandy, 1998) both argued that secularism is essentially Western. Madan has also argued that secularism by its very nature is incapable of countering religious fundamentalism and fanaticism (Madan, 1998, p.298). Both see traditional religion rather than secularism as a source of tolerance and harmony, and also as a source for containing religious fundamentalism. For them, Gandhian ideas and praxis are good instances of a functioning religious plurality. These arguments supported the BJP anti- westernization and anti-globalization approach at the start of their tenure. But anti-secularism did not remain anti-globalization; and, pushed both by pragmatic coalition politics and the middle classes, the BJP further developed India's neoliberal trajectory. Between 2000 and 2004 India witnessed the contradictory developments of opening up through increased participation in the world economy as well as a return to its roots through the rise of a Hindu-inspired nationalistic movement and the redefinition of its national identity.

National identity in an age of globalization

By the mid-1990s it was clear that the debate on the role of religion in India's national identity had not faded away, as Nehru had expected, but instead had been reinvigorated with the advent of globalization. With the rise of the BJP and the onslaught on secularism, India's national identity was also being redefined. Any identity is a social construction that draws on historical, cultural, and social resources, of which there are many available in any given community. Politicians can mobilize some of these resources and suppress others. However state-sponsored discourses need to find resonance in the public sphere, and therefore they draw on the available

---

[55] Others include Chatterjee and Chandhoke. Partha Chatterjee argues that the Indian situation has seen the onslaught of the Hindu right against religious minorities, in particular against 'a specific religious minority' (Chatterjee, 1998, p.348); in such a situation, 'Is the defence of secularism an appropriate ground for meeting the challenge of the Hindu right? Or should it be fought where the attack is made, i.e. should the response be a defence of the duty of the democratic state to ensure policies of religious toleration?' (Chatterjee, 1998, p.348). In her argument against secularism, Chandhoke (1999, p.4) argues that all religious groups will only be treated equally if a polity is committed to the generic principle of equality. This argument showcases that the existence of pluralism and minority rights necessitates the prevalence of democratic equality much more than secularism.

elements in that sphere – often simply amplifying the rumblings on the ground. Post-reform the rumblings were for a return to the roots and defining India as a Hindu motherland, suppressing the commonalities and emphasizing the religious and divisive aspects. The debate on the role of religion in Indian national identity could have been based on the premise of Hindu inclusiveness; but Hindutva has moved far away from its traditional Hindu roots:

> To the extent that the BJP promotes a broad Hindu identity in a society where Hindus have always been split across language and caste lines, it resembles an ethnic party, ethnicity being defined in terms of religious-cultural markers. The BJP's ideological aim is to create a unified, pan-Indian – or even diasporic – Hindu ethnicity. It sees Hindus not primarily as a religious group – many BJP workers and supporters may not even be religious, and the founders of the RSS were definitely not – but as a people/potential nation with a broadly common culture that must be moulded, or unified, into a consciously Hindu nation by the politics of polarisation. (Sridharan and Varshney, 2001, pp.224–5)

The Hindu nation as defined here differentiates itself from Muslim Pakistan (implicitly accepting the two-nation theory), as well as setting itself apart from those Indian citizens whose religion (Islam and Christianity) does not allow them to integrate into this new Hindu identity. It is striking how far the Hindu nationalists have strayed from the original inclusive Hindu values of the past:

> Hindu culture has been described in terms of the juxtaposition of numerous religious and cultural identities that constitute a singular family in which each enjoys the same respect, importance and tolerance. The unity of all religions is based on the fact that they each constitute different paths to God. Contrary to the Western model of universality, which is premised upon a self-other binary in which the other's agency and identity must necessarily be negated, Hindu culture's universality doesn't require the suppression of difference, given that each of the particularistic identities that comprise it are viewed as legitimate and equal parts of a unified whole. In consequence, implantation of self-other distinctions characteristic of Western modernity has been extremely difficult in the Indian context. (Tickner, 2003, p. 304)

Traditionally, as this passage suggests, the Hindu notion of identity has been a tolerant and inclusive one. It recognizes the other as necessary to make an identity complete; it sees difference as inherent in any formation of identity.[56] This is radically different from the conflictual dialectic of self and other, which most Western thinkers employ to explain the origins and persistence of national and other forms of identity.[57] It would seem in fact that contemporary Hindu nationalism uses a Western mode of social theory to define the new Indian national identity, as it externalizes difference. One might reasonably argue, therefore, that the inclusion of religion in today's national identity is actually a westernized invented tradition rather than a genuinely traditional identity.

The question of why the BJP and the Hindu right moved from an inclusive Hindu identity to an exclusive, discriminatory one is directly related to the economic reforms and globalization/westernization that started to change India in the 1990s. Globalization always has winners and losers, it is therefore important to give the losers someone to blame and to deflect their protests and criticisms away from the policies and the government implementing these policies. Creating a separate and 'different' minority (mainly the Muslim but also Christian Indians) was therefore a politically expedient ploy. To the world India was becoming a more open, accessible place; however, it can be argued that internally India was slowly becoming increasingly intolerant as the politics of difference and disunity were promoted under the guise of the search for a more traditional national identity.

This dramatic change in the definition of national identity was not a necessary or foregone conclusion, even with the rise of Hindu nationalism. It is the westernization of this form of nationalism – arguably brought about by the liberalization of the economy – that created the new schisms in society, making the definition of Indian national identity a divisive as opposed to a unifying issue. In the same way that Nehru had used education to propagate the Nehruvian secular and inclusive identity after independence, the BJP also turned to education to entrench the new approach.

Drawing the battle lines: the use of education to promote a new national identity

A large part of identity creation happens through the formal education process at school (Apple, 1993; Apple and Franklin, 2004). Education is seen as one of the central tools in modern society for shaping national

---

[56] If difference is inherent to identity, then it is valued as equal and necessary. If identity is externalized (as in the more primordial brands of Western nationalism), difference becomes devalued, and possibly the target of discrimination and eradication.

[57] Most studies of identity formation rely on an unreflected acceptance of Western modes of identity formation that externalize difference as the universal norm.

identity. Education was a central tool used by Congress to develop a civic and territorial identity and to separate religion from public life, as far as possible, leaving it firmly in the private domain. It was hoped that by educating a few generations of the Indian masses in a secular system, differences such as caste, religion, and language would no longer play a role in society.

As will be seen in detail in Chapter 2, between 1998 and 2004 the BJP used education policy as an instrument for promoting and spreading its Hindu nationalist ideology (Taneja, 2003), tapping directly into middle-class fears of the effects of globalization. With the rise of Hindutva and the renewed debate on the role of religion in national identity, the battle of ideas moved to the classroom. From this point of view, the emphasis on difference as opposed to traditional Hindu inclusiveness is dramatic: In 2001, the National Curriculum Framework (2000) for school education was heavily based on the Hindutva ideological agenda and on the premise of 'Indianise, nationalise, spiritualise'. The discursive implications of this slogan are enormous.

'Indianise': India was not really Indian; it needed to be 'indianized'. 'Nationalise': it was not a proper nation, because it contained too many un-Indian elements, so it needed to be nationalized. All foreign elements therefore had to be purged from the curriculum (Sharma, 2002). These included the British legacy as well as aspects of Indian culture that were seen as having been introduced by the Mogul (and Islamic) invaders. 'Spiritualise': India had no soul, as the foreign, non-Hindu elements (as opposed to the consumerism advanced by economic globalization) had taken it away.

The new policy engendered a massive textbook revision that justified an anti-minority outlook. In these books, Muslims across history were homogenized, described as invariably antagonistic, perpetual aggressors, and violators of the sacred Hindu land, women, cows, and temples.

The BJP appointed scholars to rewrite the history textbooks because the old textbooks were secular (as well as out of date), and did not focus on Hindu achievements (Guichard, 2010). The revised curriculum surrendered accuracy to meet the nationalist goals and utilized history as an instrument for propaganda (Hasan, 2004, pp.165–6). For the Hindutva historian, revisiting history is not simply about differentiating the other, but finding the 'self' – that is, the Hindu nation that has been oppressed for so long. For Hindutva, the self is present in the culture of the country. It does not need to be created but simply recognized and communicated. This is therefore the start of a political project, which seeks to mobilize cultural resources to produce recognition for every Hindu. This process of awakening is associated with new pride: 'Pride is crucial to this awakening, for it is the loss of pride in one's Hinduness as a consequence of Muslim and British invasions, especially colonial indoctrination (resulting in secularism of course) that has obscured the self from the recognition that they possess the land' (Datta, 2003, p.22).

This was therefore the start of a political project that aimed to mobilize cultural resources to produce recognition for every Hindu. The main product of history, as a part of education, was highlighted as the development of the 'national spirit' and 'national consciousness' by instigating pride among the youngest generations regarding India's past or distinctive religio-philosophical ethos, presented as Hindu (Lall, 2008).

In effect, the advent of the BJP meant an end to the separation of religion and education in state schools.[58] Under the BJP's logic of majoritarianism, the Indian nation was reconceptualized as Hindu. But not an inclusive Hindu-ness, but one that draws the lines of differentiation between itself and the other (Muslim, Christian, etc.) The main argument behind this, espoused by the then government, was that previously the Hindu majority had suffered as the role of minorities had been unduly emphasized. The BJP hoped to 'rectify' the situation by giving the Hindu population their rightful place, starting with the school textbooks.

The nationalist agenda meant a radical rearticulation of Indian identity in that it turned whatever Indian identity was not into its very core. In the view of their opponents, the agenda shifted the basis of identity from secularism to religion, from plurality to unity, from equality to hierarchy, from coexistence to oppression. The moves to desecularize and fundamentalize the Indian education system were an attempt to strengthen the BJP's future voter base. They were, however, also part of a new form of elite control vis-à-vis the wider population through a type of 'fundamentalization from below' operation.

The greatest success of the BJP's 2001 education policy was neither the introduction of new textbooks nor the emergence of RSS activists at the helm of national education institutions. It was that the discriminatory discourse was accepted by the public, many of whom had grown up with Nehru's secular ideals that had been aimed at constructing an inclusive Indian national identity (Lall, 2007).

Conclusion

In 2004 the BJP lost the elections. This had nothing to do with the ideological shifts that had taken place, but rather more with the effects of reforms on the poorer sections of India's rural society. The 'India Shining' campaign resonated badly with communities where increasing debt had led to farmer suicides. The BJP had also alienated some core voters because of the party's attitude to foreign capital and wider liberalization. The fact that

---

[58] Although the Indian government has funded schools of all major denominations, the Constitution forbids religious teaching in state funded schools.

GDP was over 8 per cent was not enough. Reflecting on the 2004 elections, Meghnad Desai stated:

> Had the BJP/NDA coalition won, there was little doubt that the BJP would have become the natural party of power, much like the INC used to be in the first 40 years after independence. It would have moved into a hegemonic position in a Gramscian sense and controlled the discourse along its own ideological tramlines. School textbooks would have forever changed children's views of Indian history and minorities would have had to come to terms with a precarious state of existence, henceforth under suspicion of their loyalty. When this did not happen, the question about BJP's future choices becomes urgent as much for the party activists as for students of Indian politics. (Desai in Adeney and Saez, 2007, p.254)

The return to a Congress-led government in 2004, however, did not mean a return to the Nehruvian ideals. Hindutva was no longer promoted as a national policy; nevertheless the question of religion, national identity, and who is Indian had entered a new stage. Congress took the ethnic national identity definition on board and decided to include the Diasporas in its direction on who is Indian. At the 2005 Pravasi Bharatiya Divas, PM Manmohan Singh called for overseas nationality to be extended to all Indians and their descendants who had left India after 1956. The Indian Diaspora is today firmly linked with the motherland. Largely owing to the needs posed by a quickly globalizing society, they were expected to act as political and economic ambassadors for their country of origin. Congress took on the ethnic dimension of national identity, not clarifying how this affected the civic, Nehruvian definition.

As India rises in global power and influence, as Nehru had originally envisaged, it is important to return to the question of the role of religion in national identity and how education propagates it. As argued in this chapter, the home-grown reaction to the increased westernization encouraged by globalization has in effect been a westernization of the approach to and the debate about the role of religion in national identity – all this in the name of returning to the roots and rediscovering a Hindu identity. This ultimate reversal of those very Indian Nehruvian ideals has meant that India today and the India that Hindutva promotes is more Western than anything that the empire could have imposed.[59]

---

[59] This is not particular to India – in other parts of the world as well, rather than fading away, the issues of religion primarily, but also language and ethnicity, have been reaffirmed as cornerstones of who we are in a globalizing age.

Chapter 2 will show how schools and textbooks became the vector to propagate a Hindu national identity, in a wider context of neoliberal economic policies reinforced through the education model. The chapter will move beyond the 1999–2004 administration and engage with the curricula and textbook changes between 2015 and 2020 as well. The chapter then describes the Modi administration's education policy changes that have firmly married Hindu nationalist education with neoliberal policies both inside and outside schools.

PART I

Education and Ideology

2

Hindu Nationalism Versus Secularism and the Social Realities of Discrimination

Introduction

This chapter starts by describing the rewriting of history in new textbooks as part of the BJP-led NDA government's education policy, which was rolled out under the slogan 'Indianise, nationalise, spiritualise'. It describes how the content is used to underpin Hindu pride and disparage India's Muslim heritage, drawing battle lines between those who believe India is a secular country and those who want to redefine India on Hindu lines. The chapter goes on to look at how between 2004 and 2019 school textbooks become a political football, changing according to which party was in power across state governments (Lall, 2008), and how the new Congress-sponsored textbooks did not alter the Hindutva approach offered in many schools. The chapter turns to the effects of Hindu nationalism, including the Ghar Whapsi campaign, love jihad, and the cow slaughter ban, as the new Hinduized identity became increasingly acceptable amidst widespread anti-Muslim rhetoric across social media. The chapter then briefly reviews how specific Delhi education reforms have brought in the Happiness Curriculum and the EMC, both of which have direct links to Hindu traditions. It ends with an analysis of the NEP 2020, which also reflects some of the Hindutva discourses and approaches.

The rise of the BJP to political power in central government as part of the NDA coalition meant an end to the separation of religion and education in government schools.[1] Under the BJP's logic of majoritarianism, the Indian

---

[1] By this time secularism in politics was long dead. The Congress Party has at times also sought to downplay its secularist roots and embrace pro-Hindu sentiments (Jaffrelot, 2019). However, until 2000 the Indian curriculum and textbooks had remained secular.

nation had to be reconceptualized as Hindu. However, as mentioned in Chapter 1, this was not based on an inclusive Hinduness, but one that drew lines of differentiation between itself and a constructed non-Hindu. The main argument behind this, espoused by the government of the day, was that previously the Hindu majority had suffered as the role of minorities had been unduly emphasized. The BJP hoped to 'rectify' the situation by assigning the Hindu population their rightful place, starting with school textbooks. The religio-nationalist agenda meant a radical rearticulation of Indian identity in that it turned what Indian identity was not into its very core. This move, however, did not (yet) touch on issues of citizenship such as rights, responsibilities, and political participation.

In order to change Indian identity, the BJP-led NDA government turned its attention to India's textbooks. School textbooks are a primary vehicle through which societies transmit national narratives (Hussain and Safiq, 2016). They depict a society's ideology or ethos and impart values, goals, and myths that society wishes to transmit to new generations (Bourdieu, 1971). Textbooks also explain historical conflicts and present political parties (Naseem and Stober, 2014) in a particular light. School history serves the dual function of transmitting historical knowledge and creating a shared national identity (Carretero et al, 2013). It constructs the myths of origins and draws geographical, ideological, and affective boundaries to distinguish the nation from 'others'. Textbooks are 'authoritative accounts' of 'real' information, representing specific constructions of 'reality' through their 'content' and 'form' (Apple, 1993, p.15). They also provide an authoritative pedagogic version of received knowledge by positioning people in hierarchical relations of power (Chris, 1994).

Textbooks are fundamental to the educational system in the global south. The notion of a 'textbook culture' fosters the prescription of an official hegemonic curriculum (Kumar, 2005; Apple and Christian-Smith, 2017). Textbooks have been essential for Indian schools ever since an education system was officially introduced in the early nineteenth century, during the colonial era (Kumar, 1988). Their relevance has been sustained, with the government still recommending textbooks to state-run schools. They not only delineate teacher instruction but also dictate student assessment patterns. One of the significant criticisms of this system is that it controls teacher autonomy, whose curricular choices are bound by the text (Kumar, 1986; Apple and Christian-Smith, 2017). Thus, for over two decades there has been a demand for widening resource systems for teachers in India (GoI, 1993, 2020a; NCERT, 2006). However, within a financially constrained educational system, textbooks remain the only accessible material resources in most schools. Hence, they have become the basic equalizer, ensuring that all children have access to some educational opportunities (Morris and Hiebert, 2011). Textbooks thus merit attention as a valuable means of understanding both schools and society. Although they are only one part of the school environment and offer only a partial picture, they are the part that is open to central control as well as to uniformity: they give an accurate impression not so much of what children actually learn but what the state intends them to learn. This is not restricted to India – in other countries too, power operates through educational practices, social interactions, and the normative language of schooling to create social identities, social relations, and dominant modes of thought (Lipman, 2004). The state and social movements interact to form certain conditions in which conflicts arise over what makes up official knowledge (Apple, 2001). As will be seen later in this chapter, what was included or omitted in Indian textbooks began to play a major role in Indian politics not long after the economic reforms took root.

Background to textbooks' revisions in India

The textbooks that were conceived in the 1960s and 1970s were political instruments that helped to construct a united India in the Nehruvian tradition; the elites accepted that for India to be united, it needed to be secular (Guichard, 2013). In 1969, the Report of the Committee on School Textbooks emphasized the crucial role of history textbooks in building 'national unity' (Guichard, 2013, p.72). The authors of these textbooks – many of whom were professors at JNU, and included eminent left-wing secular historian Professor Romila Thapar – belonged to diverse historiographical traditions that were influenced by Marxist historiography; however, they shared a secular understanding of India's history. Thapar's seminal *History of India* (1966) departed from imperialist traditions and included social and cultural history. The JNU historians rejected the British interpretation of Indian history and the 'nationalist and the communalist/ Hindu nationalist' view, in which a 'Hindu golden age' was ended by Arab invasions, which began a 'Muslim period' that was followed by a 'British period' (Guichard, 2013, p.72). Secular historians disagreed with the idea of Hindus and Muslims as two distinct and antagonist groups – rejecting the two-nation theory that had engendered Pakistan. They highlighted the fact that 'most of the Indian past saw a peaceful and harmonious living together', with socializing and an enrichment of relationships between Hindus and Muslims (Guichard, 2013, p.72; also Bhattacharya, 2008; Thapar, 2009). In the late 1990s the National Council of Educational Research and Training (NCERT) textbooks, which had been published in the early 1980s, were criticized as 'Marxist' and replaced between 2002 and 2004 under the Hindu nationalist BJP-led NDA government (Lall, 2008; Guichard, 2010). How this situation evolved is described in the next section.

'Indianise, nationalise, spiritualise': 2000–2004

Despite the NDA being a coalition government, the BJP kept control of the two most senior positions in the Ministry of Human Resource Development (MHRD), which included education policy. Two party hardliners, Murli Manohar Joshi and Uma Bharti, took the positions of Union Minister and Minister of State. Murli Manohar Joshi oversaw the expansion of the network of RSS schools and the appointment of RSS members or sympathizers to top national education bodies such as the NCERT and the University Grants Commission (UGC).

The National Council for Educational Research and Training (NCERT)

In India, education is both a state and a central government subject, meaning that different types of textbooks can coexist across different states, depending on which political party is in power at state level, regardless of the government in Delhi. In central government, the NCERT is a key institution in India's education system. It defines the official guidelines for curricular development and develops 'model' textbooks for different school subjects (Flåten, 2017). The NCERT develops curriculum frameworks, which are used in schools across India that are affiliated to the Central Board of Secondary Education (CBSE) (Naseem and Stober, 2014). It is thus in charge of determining curriculum standards for the whole country. Over the past few decades, the NCERT textbooks have been revised as successive political parties have come to power centrally. The political party in power decides who is appointed as NCERT director and other key posts in charge of creating education policy and the curriculum. Consequently, the nation's educational mission changes when the dominant party changes at national level.

Nation-building has been a key concern of NCERT education policies and textbooks throughout independent India's history. The National Curriculum Frameworks (NCFs), written by the NCERT as guidelines for national education, have always maintained the importance of nation-building, regardless of which political party has been in power (Guichard, 2010). Nation-building, as elsewhere, is done by constructing a mutual national past, mythologies of ancestry, historical recollections, and culture, to instil a national identity (Miller, 1988).

In 2000, the NCERT published the NCF for school education based on the Hindutva ideological agenda under the slogan that has already been mentioned: 'Indianise, nationalise, spiritualise'. This policy resulted in a massive textbook revision with an anti-minory outlook – as described in Chapter 1. This was therefore the start of a political project that aimed to mobilize cultural resources so that the worth of every Hindu would be recognized. The main product of history education was highlighted as the development of a 'national spirit' and 'national consciousness' by instigating pride among the youngest generations regarding India's past and its distinctive religio-philosophical ethos, which was presented as Hindu (Lall, 2008, p.176).

The textbooks between 2000 and 2004

In this section we explore some examples of the narrative that Hindutva-inspired textbooks presented to children, and how by omission or by exaggeration, or simply by the peddling of fictional accounts, an extremist Hindu view of history was given preponderance over all other interpretations.

Kumkum Roy undertook an in-depth analysis of the social science textbook that was introduced by the BJP-led government for Class 6 (Roy, 2002). Amongst a number of issues, she highlights the fact that the four-strata varna (caste) system is presented as having existed in Vedic society.[2] This means that the caste system and the Hindu social structure that comes with it are essentially represented as having been in existence since time immemorial, as no dates are supplied for the Vedic era. What is not mentioned is that the only evidence for this is a single verse from a single hymn that some historians regard as a later addition to the Rig Veda (Roy, 2002). But the issue goes beyond the social science textbook for one particular class. The sort of unsubstantiated assertions that were highlighted by Roy were made in the context of inaccurate over-glorifications across all the new history textbooks.

Each history textbook is related to a distinct period of Indian history. In grades 6 and 7 students are introduced to history through a two part series entitled 'India and the World', which covers Vedic times to the struggle for independence. Each year thereafter focuses on a particular period: grade 8 on historical pasts, grade 9 on Contemporary India, grade 10 on Ancient India, grade 11 on Medieval India, and grade 12 on Modern India. Themes that are addressed in grades 6 and 7 are repeated in more depth in grades 9 to 12. All these books were published between 2002 and 2003 and replaced the previous history textbooks.

The analysis that follows aims to look at two specific themes: that of Hindu cultural superiority vis-à-vis other cultures and that of the demonization and pathologization of Islam.[3] The themes highlighted here, of Hindu

---

[2]   Varna refers to the Indian caste system.

[3]   The basis for the analysis of textbooks below was the NCERT Historians' report in 2004 (commissioned after the Congress victory in the elections of that year) – *Learning History*

cultural superiority and issues with Islam and the Muslim community, are of course related. There are, however, some important differences. Hindu pride, especially with regard to the Vedic period, is emphasized, whilst the descriptions of Islam and Muslims go beyond this, pathologizing the Islamic community in more or less obvious ways. Hindu superiority is expressed not only in relation to Islam but also in relation to other religions, cultures, and civilizations, this aspect mainly being associated with ancient history or myth. The issues with Islam, though, are addressed in all periods of history.

Hindu cultural superiority

Hindu cultural superiority emerges in the textbooks for Classes 6, 7, 10, and 12. In Class 6, the descriptions of the *Upanishads* as 'the works of most profound philosophy in any religion' (Lal et al, 2003, p. 91) and 'the greatest works of philosophy in the history of humankind' (p. 134) indicate the overall tone, as the authors attempt to establish Hinduism as the 'best' of all world religions. Similarly, 'Indian and Chinese civilisations are the only ones which have survived right from the time they came into existence till date. ... All other early civilisations have disappeared and the present people/ civilisations have no connection with the past ones' (Lal et al, 2003, p. 58). Aside from being incorrect, such discourse leaves the reader in no doubt as to which civilization is the greatest and which ones can be looked down upon. Statements such as this encourage pupils to believe that the Hindu civilization was greater than all others, including the later Mughal civilization that was essentially Muslim. In Class 7 ancient India is again portrayed as an ideal society, with the oppression of women having been imported in the Middle Ages as the result of Muslim invasion and oppression: 'with Muslim contact there began the purdah system' (p.99).[4] This is a clear oversimplification, as during Mughal rule Hindu and Muslim customs were combined. On p.88 there is another example of the glorification of Hinduism in the context of a discussion of Southeast Asia. Buddhist and Islamic influences are marginalized, leading students to ignore the historical significance of other religions in the wider region. The Class 10 textbook again over-glorifies certain aspects of the Indian past, especially those connected with the Vedic tradition and Hinduism. The Vedic people are depicted as having extensive scientific knowledge – in certain cases knowing things that were only discovered by others much later (p.100):

Without a Burden, which pointed to factual inaccuracies and omissions in the various textbooks (https://vdocument.in/learning-history-without-burden.html).

[4] Purdah refers to the segregation of women from men in society.

Vedic people knew the methods of making squares equal in area to triangles, circles and calculate the differences of squares. The Zero was known in the Rig Vedic times itself [...] Cubes, cube roots, square roots and under roots were also known and used. In the Vedic period astronomy was well developed.[...] They also knew that the earth moved on its own axis and around the sun. (Class 11: *Ancient India* by Makkhan Lal, p.100)

In Class 12 the focus on Hindu pride is taken beyond the ancient history period: Chapter 7 (pp.136–41) of *Modern India*, the social and cultural awakening in 19th-century India is described, but this focuses exclusively on Hindu revival movements: 'Rammohun [the founder of the Brahmo Samaj revival movement] did not shirk from establishing the superiority of the Hindu religion on the basis of his interpretation of the Vedas and Upanishads' (Class 12: *Modern India* (2003) by Satish Chandra Mittal, p.142). There are no references to Islamic modernism, Parsee reawakening, or other social movements. In the same chapter the role of Christianity is discussed: 'The Brahmo Samaj, thus, awakened the Indian society from within and saved it from the engulfing tide of Christian influence' (p.144).

Sixteen pages in three history textbooks for grades 6, 7, and 11 were removed. These included a paragraph suggesting that there was no archaeological evidence for settlements in and around Ayodhya around 2000 BC.[5] The importance of this cannot be underestimated, as the lack of any evidence of settlements dating from that period exposes the illegitimacy of Hindu fundamentalist calls for the building of a Ram temple on the ruins of the destroyed Babri Masjid.[6] The dispute between Hindus and Muslims with regard to this site has sparked violent intercommunal disputes, including the 2002 carnage in Gujarat. The vast majority of medieval historians agree that there is no substance to the claim that the Babri Masjid had been built by destroying a Ram temple, yet by omitting discussion of the archaeological evidence, the new NCERT textbooks effectively allow a different interpretation to be taught in class.

---

[5] Archaeological evidence should be considered of far more importance than the long family trees given in the Puranas. 'The Puranic tradition could be used to date Rama of Ayodhya around 2000BC but extensive excavations in Ayodhya do not show any settlements around that date' (Sharma, 2002, p.198).

[6] It is alleged by Hindu Nationalists and the BJP that the Babri Masjid was built upon a temple that commemorated the birthplace of Ram, a Hindu god.

The demonization and pathologization of Islam and the Muslim community

This theme emerges principally in the textbooks for grades 7, 9, and 11. The grade 7 textbook reduces the socio-religious diversities in medieval India to two homogeneous categories: the Hindus and the Muslims, which is highly inaccurate as other religious groups such as the Sikhs, Jains, and Buddhists have had an important influence on Indian culture. This is problematic in two ways: first, it endorses the Hindutva trend to forcibly include Sikhs, Jains, and Buddhists within a broad definition of the Hindu family; secondly, it oversimplifies Muslim society, as it is inaccurate to speak of a uniform Muslim entity. Arabs, Turks, and Afghans all came to India at different times and all had distinct political and cultural identities, yet the pupils are presented with a homogeneous image of Islamic invaders. In fact, throughout the book the Muslim population of India is shown in an unfavourable light, with the sections on the Delhi Sultanate and Mughal Empire emphasizing an image of warfare and destruction in which Muslims are termed 'Muslim invaders' and 'Muslim rule' is shown to be particularly brutal. In *Medieval India*, the history textbook for Class 11, the process of conquest by Muslim and Hindu rulers is characterized by discriminatory language: Hindus are generally described as conquering, expanding their kingdom, and marching triumphantly, whilst the Muslim expansionist acts are invasions and incursions, with the rulers referred to as intruders and depicted as foreign. Class 12's *Modern India* describes the Muslims as resorting to the wholesale plunder of temples, depicting the Muslim rulers as brutal and the ruled Hindus as oppressed by them.

The Class 9 book, *Contemporary India* (2002) by Hari Om, has a number of important omissions. For example, there is no reference to the historic Karachi session of the Indian National Congress (1931) or the contribution of Sir Sayyid Ahmed Khan as a reformer and educationist. The role of the Muslim League in the independence movement against the British is depicted in a bad light. Again, there is a tendency to downplay the role that Indian Muslims have played in shaping contemporary Indian society.

In the Class 11 textbook, the information pertaining to the Muslim community in the medieval period is inaccurate. It is said that 'In the Indian context, Sufis meticulously resolved their differences with the ulema and emphasised the need to follow the *Sharia*' (p.127). According to the revising historians,[7] this is incorrect as: 'It views *ulema* and Sufis as two opposing groups. This is not necessarily true as many Sufis were fine scholars (*ulema*). And in several well-documented instances there were clear disagreements between the *ulema* and the Sufis' (NCERT, 2004). Aside from these inaccuracies, the important assimilative aspects of medieval Indian culture

---

[7] After the elections in 2004 a committee of historians was set up to revise the inaccuracies of the textbooks. More on their work is discussed later in the chapter.

are ignored, and no instances of Hindu–Muslim interaction are depicted in a positive light. The development of Islam and Hinduism is shown as hermetically separate, and art forms such as the Sufi–Bhakti interaction are entirely neglected.

These selected examples are just a few amongst many of what was changed in or omitted from certain textbooks. There seems to have been a trend across all these books to focus on the ancient Vedic civilization and on the role that Hinduism has played in India's cultural history. Other religions are ignored or shown as inferior. The focus is on ancient times, glorifying that epoch. Nalini Taneja from Delhi University gives the following analysis:

> In the name of 'Indianised, nationalised and spiritualised' education there is an attempt to polarise and divide people along religious lines by communalising their consciousness. Through a distortion and concoction of facts there is an effort to reconstruct history and tradition along communal and sectarian lines. [...] Uma Bharti, the Union Minister of State in the Ministry of Human Resources did not take long to pronounce that the Kashmir problem finds its roots in the teaching pattern in the Madrasas and that there is a need to closely monitor them. (Taneja, 2003)

In general, the slant of the textbooks was pro-upper-caste north-Indian, anti-minority and anti-leftist.

Aside from what was happening in state schools, the advent of a BJP-led government meant that the RSS was able to expand its influence over the provision of education and health. The regional committees affiliated to Vidya Bharati, the largest voluntary association in the country, expanded quickly.[8] Education has been a major area of work for the RSS, and it has made efforts to promote its views through Shakhas, Sarswati Shishu Mandirs, and Ekal Schools (Puniyani, 2017). The first Saraswati Shishu Mandir was set up in Gorakhpur, Uttar Pradesh, in 1952. The Vidya Bharati coordinate over 13,000 institutions with 3,206,212 students,[9] according to its website (Vidya Bharati, n.d.). Other RSS affiliates – Shishu Mandir Sewa Bharati, Bharat Kalyan Prathisthan, Vanvasi Kalyan Ashram, and Bharatiya Jan Seva Sansthan – also work in riot- and disaster-hit areas, or places where few state agencies provide basic amenities (Mohan, 2016). The expansion of RSS schools has been a major pillar in the Hindutva strategy, essentially circumventing the traditional separation of education and religion and

---

[8] For a more detailed description of the RSS-sponsored Vidya Bharati network see Sharma (2002).

[9] Vidya Bharati institutions function under a variety of names such as Shishu Vatika, Shishu Mandir, Vidya Mandir, and Sarasvati Vidyalaya.

underpinning the new message on Indian identity. This expansion has been funded in various ways, including through charities operating in the West. According to the report published by Awaaz, almost a quarter of Sewa international earthquake funds raised in the United Kingdom to help Gujarat in 2001 were used to build RSS schools (Awaaz, 2004).[10] Apart from opening more schools, the Sangh is also training youth in villages to become counsellors and tutors for children enrolled in government schools (Mohan, 2016).

As shall be seen in Chapter 5, on HE, the RSS has also been successful at putting its followers in top university positions and major research institutes across the country (Puniyani, 2017). The Sangh's strong defensiveness about growing criticism drives a more aggressive education campaign. It checks the growth of convent schools and missionary-run educational institutions, many of which also operate in underdeveloped villages (Mohan, 2016).

Contestations

In the view of opponents to Hindutva, the official education agenda has shifted the basis of identity from secularism to religion, from plurality to unity, from equality to hierarchy, from co-existence to oppression (Mukherjee and Mukherjee, 2001, p.22). Secular and liberal authors have challenged these measures as tools of Hindu nationalist communication (Kumar, 2001; Sharma, 2002; Subarmaniam, 2003; Taneja, 2003; Nanda, 2005; Setalvad, 2005; Lall, 2008). The Communist Party and left-wing historians have introduced various campaigns against history textbooks. In 2001, polarization reached new heights when Arjun Singh, who was later to be appointed Education Minister under the Congress-led coalition government in 2004, criticized the BJP for 'talibanising' the writing of history (Lall, 2009, p.176). The textbook revisions were contested by a petition to the Supreme Court that was brought by three activists, who argued that the NCERT had not followed the correct procedures of consultation with the states and that it was attempting to introduce religious teaching, which is forbidden by the Constitution. However, the petition was rejected by the Supreme Court.[11]

The BJP defended itself by claiming that it had actually helped to free history from the vestiges of colonization. It argued that one-sided interpretations of history were being corrected. In an interview, Murli Manohar Joshi explained that the changes were made following complaints from Jains, Sikhs, Jats, and others, who felt aggrieved by the way in which certain events were depicted in the old textbooks:

---

[10] There is more on RSS schools in Chapter 3.

[11] Judgement by Justice M.B. Shah, D.M Dharmadhikari, and H.K. Sema in Writ Petition (Civil) No. 98 of 2002, Ms Aruna Roy and others vs. Union of India and others.

We examined them and the NCERT made a decision to delete them. […] Certain authors of history have tried to distort history. They have given it a purely leftist colour. They say that India had no history of its own because they are guided by Marx. They teach the history of a nation that was mainly defeated and conquered by foreign powers. It's a travesty of facts and an attempt to kill the morale of a nation. (Sharma, 2002, pp.215–18)

The changes introduced by the nationalists were an attempt to increase pride in being Indian, but concerns were raised that Indian culture was presented as solely Hindu, ignoring India's pluralistic roots. The Human Resource Development Minister responded to the widespread criticism from professional historians by calling the criticism 'intellectual terrorism unleashed by the left … more dangerous than cross border terrorism' (Indian Express, 2001, cited in Lall, 2009).

The secular press described the moves as the 'saffronization' of education, and this became a national issue in 2001 when non-BJP parties within the NDA said that even if the Human Resource Development Ministry insisted on the new curriculum, they would not accept the changes in states they ruled. There were two main criticisms of the new education policy: first, that reforms were dictated by the communal agenda of the Sangh Parivar and were contrary to the principles enshrined in the Constitution; and second, that, according to the Constitution, education was the responsibility of the states, and changes could not be centrally imposed. No curriculum, they argued, could become national policy without mandatory endorsement by the states. The debates and 'the virulence of the arguments' between the opposing parties (BJP and Congress) clearly show that the controversy was not about scientific and educational concerns but rather opposing views of Indian history and Indian national identity (Guichard, 2010, p.13).

Moving the debate to the states: 2004–2014 Congress rule

In the 2004 election campaign, the BJP-led NDA manifesto on education had changed in emphasis, moving towards an even more communal and nationalistic stand. Three points emphasizing the Hindu heritage stand out:

- The focus on Indian culture, heritage, and ethical values in syllabi will be strengthened. Character-building and all-round development of the student's personality will be emphasized. Sports, physical training, and social service will be mainstreamed into the educational system.

- The growing de-emphasis of Bharatiya languages in school and college education will be checked. Teaching in the mother tongue will be encouraged.
- Efforts will be intensified for the propagation of Sanskrit. (BJP, 2004)

However, whilst the NDA did not win, it is important to remember that the educational changes introduced by the BJP did not play a major role in the election. Access to education might have been an issue in some rural areas, but roads, power, water, and jobs were more important.

The Congress-led United Progressive Alliance (UPA) government had to deal with both the inherent problems in the education system and, for its own long-term political survival, needed to reverse the changes introduced by the NDA.[12] Only a few weeks after the elections, on 12 June, the new government ordered a panel of historians to be constituted to advise on the issues of communalization and inadequacies of the history textbooks of the NCERT. The three historians, Professors S. Settar, J.S. Grewal, and Barun De, submitted a report that concluded that 'the textbooks prepared since 2000 are so full of errors and sub-standard that we find it impossible to recommend their continuation' (MHRD, 2004). The panel acknowledged that though there were different interpretations with regard to historical facts, at school level history teaching should reflect the current scholarly consensus. A note was subsequently issued to all schools in which the Executive Committee of the NCERT explained that the report had been accepted, but because the academic session 2004/05 was too advanced, the books would only be withdrawn for the 2005/06 academic year. The note also gave some advice on how to cope with the flawed history books, detailing errors and page numbers, and promising to reprint and make available the old textbooks again (NCERT, 2004). The revisions ran to between 20 and 30 pages. The committee also emphasized that history was not to be used for political purposes: 'The past has a value of its own and distinctive facts of its own, not to be twisted for present purposes, either of the state or regional predilections of that element of the past as it was, distinct from the past as we would like it to be today' (NCERT, 2004).

The restoration of the pre-BJP books was promised quickly, yet this led to a debate that heightened awareness of the flaws in the old textbooks, which were seen as too dry and lacking narrative drive. The NCERT

---

[12] Member parties of the UPA were the Indian National Congress, Dravida Munnetra Kazhagam, Nationalist Congress Party, Rashtriya Janata Dal, Indian Union Muslim League, Jammu and Kashmir National Conference, Jharkand Mukti Morcha, Kerala Congress, Marumalarchi Dravida Munnetra Kazhagam, Revolutionary Socialist Party, and Viduthalai Chiruthaigal Katchi.

framed another document, known as the NCF of 2005. Countering the communal textbooks of 2003 was one of the stated aims for producing the revised NCERT social science textbooks between 2006 and 2007. The goal was to produce 'secular' textbooks, in line with the Constitution, which defines India as being secular (Guichard, 2010). In the NCF, social science was considered as an important method of delivering knowledge to construct a fair and peaceful society – the political message of the day (NCERT, 2005, p.50). Congress's revisions of the NCERT textbooks were not without controversy, as key information was omitted in order to meet the 'de-saffronization' objectives. A key example, which shows how the Partition of India was presented, is described next.

A chapter entitled 'Understanding Partition: Politics, Memories, Experiences' (p.376) (Bhattacharya, 2006, the NCERT history textbook for Class 12), highlighted the importance of mutual respect for one another's culture and beliefs. The textbook focuses on secularism and the value framework ('directive principles') of the Constitution that are prescribed in the National Curriculum Framework (2005, p.53). The chapter, however, raises questions about the insufficient engagement of Indian textbooks with the Partition of 1947. India is incorrectly depicted as a country in which there were no communal difficulties prior to the British (Sandhu, 2009). The British, the Muslim League, and Muhammad Ali Jinnah are criticized for 'sowing the seeds of communalism' (pp.384–5). The dominant message is the sacredness of a unified India (Sandhu, 2009, p.10). This version of Partition is depicted as an event that 'was done to us by the other, an event that could and should have been avoided if it were not for the British and the Muslim League and Jinnah, resonates with the narrative in the earlier textbook and is also a popular line of rhetoric in India' (Anand, 2019, p.148).

The chapter also depicts the role played by the Hindu Mahasabha in British India.[13] In addition, a history of the electoral politics between the Muslim League and the Congress is provided,[14] which refers to the Lucknow Pact,[15] the Pakistan Resolution, and the growth of the RSS.

---

[13] Hindu Mahasabha is a Hindu nationalist political party in India. It was formed to protect the rights of the Hindu community in British India 'in 1915. It was a Hindu party that remained confined to North India. It aimed to unite Hindu society by encouraging the Hindus to transcend the divisions of caste and sect. It sought to define Hindu identity in opposition to Muslim identity' (Bhattacharya, 2006, p.385).

[14] The Muslim League, also known as the All India Muslim League, was founded in 1906 to safeguard the rights of Indian Muslims at the time of the Partition of British India (1947).

[15] The Lucknow Pact was drafted by the Indian National Congress (headed by Bal Gangadhar Tilak) and the All India Muslim League (headed by Muhammad Ali Jinnah). The meeting

The Pakistan demand was formalised gradually. On 23 March 1940, the League moved a resolution demanding a measure of autonomy for the Muslim majority areas of the subcontinent. This ambiguous resolution never mentioned partition or Pakistan. In fact Sikandar Hayat Khan, Punjab Premier and leader of the Unionist Party, who had drafted the resolution, declared in a Punjab assembly speech on 1 March 1941 that he was opposed to a Pakistan that would mean Muslim Raj here and Hindu Raj elsewhere … If Pakistan means unalloyed Muslim Raj in the Punjab, then I will have nothing to do with it." He reiterated his plea for a loose (united), confederation with considerable autonomy for the confederating units. (Bhattacharya, 2006, p.386)

…while the leading Congress leaders in the late 1930s insisted more than ever before on the need for secularism, these ideas were by no means universally shared lower down in the party hierarchy, or even by all Congress ministers. Maulana Azad, an important Congress leader, pointed out that in 1937 that members of the Congress were not allowed to join the League, yet Congressmen were active in the Hindu Mahasabha – at least in the Central Provinces (present-day Madhya Pradesh). Only in December 1938 did the Congress Working Committee declare that Congress members could not be members of the Mahasabha. Incidentally, this was also the period when the Hindu Mahasabha and the Rashtriya Swayamsevak Sangh were gaining strength. The latter spread from its Nagpur base to the United Provinces, the Punjab and other parts of the country in the 1930s. By 1940, the RSS had over 100,000 trained and highly disciplined cadres pledged to an ideology of Hindu nationalism, convinced that India was a land of the Hindus. (Bhattacharya, 2006, p.386)

The origins of the Pakistan demand have also been traced back to the Urdu poet Mohammad Iqbal, the writer of 'Sare Jahan Se Achha Hindustan Hamara'. In his presidential address to the Muslim League in 1930, the poet spoke of a need for a "North-West Indian Muslim state". Iqbal, however, was not visualising the emergence of a new country in that speech but a reorganisation of Muslim-majority areas in north-western India into an autonomous unit within a single, loosely structured Indian federation [sic]. (Bhattacharya, 2006, pp.386–7)

---

at Lucknow marked the reunion of moderate and radical wings of the Congress. The pact dealt with the structure of the government of India in relation to the Hindu and Muslim communities.

These quotes show that the purpose of Bhattacharya's 2006 book is to suppress the real root causes of Partition. Omissions are indeed blatant and problematic. The chapter repeats the same clichés, elusiveness, and (mis-)understanding of the Muslim League (Anand, 2019). While underscoring growing communalization in the 1920s and 1930s, and pointing to mixed electorates as a threat to Muslim identity, the two-nation theory is rejected despite being the declared premise of the Muslim League and Jinnah. Bhattacharya's (2006) work is descriptive and topics on partisan lines (such as beef consumption) are omitted. It is also silent on wider conflicts between Hindus and Muslims (Anand, 2019). The purpose of the textbook was to construct equality and to depict the country as secular (Guichard, 2010). Silence on particular subjects was an explicit decision that had been taken by the government (Anand, 2019).

The new NCERT textbooks contrasted with textbooks used in some states, where the Hindutva narrative was maintained. As mentioned earlier, education is both a state and a central government subject. Research by Vernoff (1992), Banerjee (2007), and Benei (2008) indicates regional content in textbooks used by states such as Maharashtra and West Bengal, thereby showcasing how states have used the autonomy granted to them to craft history textbooks that are more in line with local conditions. However, given that states have the power to decide what is taught in their schools, the BJP books were not removed everywhere. Relations between the central and state governments became strained, and in August 2004 the BBC reported that ministers from five BJP-run states had walked out of a meeting called by the government to devise a new national education policy.[16] Versions of the BJP textbooks continued to be used across states with BJP-led governments, such as Gujarat (Guichard, 2010). This led to the absurd situation whereby textbooks and curricular content changed when state governments were voted out of power. It also meant that children in different states learnt different versions of Indian history, annulling in effect Nehru's project of unifying the Indian nation through a shared sense of history.

Veronique Benei has studied the textbooks used in the state of Maharashtra (Benei, 2008). She develops the notion of 'banal nationalism' (p.2), wherein nationalism is so ingrained in people's lives that it goes unnoticed most of the time. She remarks that 'arguably the neglect of vernacular categories has precluded an understanding of both their attendant social and cultural

---

[16] The ministers (belonging to the states of Madhya Pradesh, Chattisgarh, Rajasthan, Jharkhand, and Goa) objected to a statement by the federal Education Minister, Arjun Singh, that distortions should be removed from school textbooks. This followed claims by the governing Congress-led coalition that the BJP had attempted to introduce a Hindu nationalist agenda through the books. The BJP ministers also said they wouldn't implement a changed syllabus in their states (BBC, 2004, cited in Adeney and Lall, 2005).

semantic repertoires and local negotiations. Their unravelling remains indispensable for a thorough comprehension of the cultural entailments of political processes, forms and models, especially of the nation state' (Benei, 2008, p.64). The regionalization of heroes who underscore nationalism is reflected in her study of Shivaji in the Maharashtra textbooks. Shivaji's encounter with Afzal Khan was one of the favourite subjects of study for both teachers and students in the schools that Benei visited – underscoring the Hindu–Muslim rivalry with a positive Maratha masculinity being projected in opposition to a fantasized Muslim other (Benei, 2008, p.154). More on how individual states such as Gujarat and Rajasthan have included Hindutva themes in their textbooks is detailed in the next section.

As the states had retained much of the power to decide what was taught in their classrooms, the BJP textbooks remained in use across various states in India. As a result, when the BJP returned to power, there was no immediate need for the Union government to revise curricula and textbooks again.

The BJP returns in 2014 – a new Hinduized identity led by state governments

For the 2014 elections, Narendra Modi redefined Hindutva in a new manner that combined development, nationalism, and Hindu identity. Modi declared that 'nationalism is development' and that 'being nationalist is the essential aspect of Hindutva' (Flåten, 2017, p.392). The Modi-led BJP won an absolute majority across India, delivering a fatal blow to Congress and for the first time establishing the BJP as a pan-India party. In the first term of the Modi-led BJP government education did not figure as a central tenet at Union level – but major changes were still made.

The RSS takes charge of education policy

Between 2014 and 2016 the Ministry of Human Resources and Development was occupied by Smriti Irani, a former television actress, who routinely consulted influential members of the RSS, including Dinanath Batra, who was instrumental in having many portions deleted from Congress NCERT textbooks. According to Pradyumna Jairam (2021, p.75), the BJP mentioned that 'there is need for a better coordination between the government and the RSS and it was felt that regular meetings should be held so that representatives of the government are made aware of concerns of organizations affiliated to the RSS'. Irani also accused the JNU of indulging in 'anti-national activity', in light of the event that took place there in February 2016, as discussed in Chapter 6.

Irani was replaced by Prakash Javadekar as Union Minister; he had previously been affiliated with the RSS, and was indeed seen as the RSS choice for the ministry (India Today, 2019). Javadekar's first meeting after being appointed was attended by several organizations affiliated to the RSS, including Vidya Bharati, Akhil Bharartiya Vidyarthi Parishad (ABVP) (its Student Wing), and the Akhil Bharatiya Itihaas Sankalan Yojana (All India History Compilation Scheme), an affiliate that sought to remedy the ills of history writing introduced under British rule, which were continued by historians even after independence.[17] The purpose of the meeting was to once again ensure that the message of the RSS and the broader Hindu Right was reflected – that 'new education policy measures would instil nationalism, pride and ancient Indian values in modern education' (NEP, 2020, p.14).

Dinanath Batra, a former teacher, convenor of the Shiksha Bachao Andolan Samiti, became chairman of the Bharatiya Shiksha Niti Aayog (Indian Education Planning Commission), an RSS council that advises the Narendra Modi government on what they refer to as 'Indianising' the country's education system (Mohan, 2016). The Bharatiya Shiksha Niti Aayog was set up in 2014 under the leadership of Dinnath Batra, to align MHRD policies more closely with RSS beliefs. Along with Batra, the other proposed members of the committee included Rajput, along with RSS member Atul Kothari, both prominently involved in earlier education policy debates on the side of the BJP.[18] RSS groups have been actively lobbying central government's new education policy for changes to value education, local and cultural history, and India's achievements in all fields. They are also pushing for the MT as the medium of instruction in primary schools, as reflected in the NEP 2020 (Mohan, 2016).

Owing to these connections right at the top of the MHRD (renamed the Ministry of Education in 2020), the Sangh Parivar was able to push for significant changes to the school textbooks that had been drafted during the Congress period to return to a pro-Hindutva agenda in the name of cultural nationalism (Sharma, 2016b).[19] Javadekar's focus with regard to the

---

[17] The Akhil Bharatiya Itihaas Sankalan Yojana is believed to have carried out research projects, which established among other things that 'Aryans originated among Adivasis (Tribals) or janjatis, thereby establishing their indigenous roots to India' (more on this in Jairam, 2021).

[18] 'The Rashtriya Swamayamsevak Sangh has set up a consultative body to ensure that the Narendra Modi government moves ahead with the saffronization of the country's education system – a move that seems to mirror the establishment of the extra-constitutional National Advisory Council by the previous United Progressive Alliance regime' (Jha, 2014, para.2).

[19] The Sangh Parivar has always shown interest in the teaching of history, not only because it contributes to defining the national identity, but also because the Parivar believes the version of the past portrayed by secularists does not reflect reality. Its influence on the Modi government is also evident (Jaffrelot and Jairam, 2020).

NCERT textbooks was on omitting historical content to match the party's ideology. This was referred to as a 'curriculum rationalisation exercise' (India Today, 2019). According to Jairam, one example of this included Dalits being completely omitted from discussions on caste.[20] During the COVID-19 pandemic, the NCERT decided to remove the chapter on Partition from the Class 12 history textbook as part of simplifying the syllabus and reducing its content by 30 per cent (Jairam, 2021). However, a section on the French Revolution was retained (Bakshi, 2020).

In 2017 a committee was set up 'quietly' in New Delhi by culture minister Mahesh Sharma to institutionalize through education the RSS philosophy that 'India belongs to Hindus' (Jain and Lasseter, 2018).[21] Manmohan Vaidya, RSS spokesman, stated that 'the true colour of Indian history is saffron and to bring about cultural changes we have to rewrite history' (Jain and Lasseter, 2018, para.2). According to the committee, the rewriting of history was necessary because Indian schools taught a deeply 'Congress-ized version of history', which they said praised Congress leaders to the exclusion of all others. The committee drafted conclusions including 'archaeological findings, DNA to prove that Hindus are descended from the land's first inhabitants, the ancient Hindu scriptures are fact, not myth', and that it intended to work backwards to find evidence to support these conclusions (Jain and Lasseter, 2018). The conclusions were divisive, conflated history and mythology, and sought to establish the supremacy of one religious group over all others (Jain and Lasseter, 2018). Prakash Javadekar mentioned that he would take the conclusions of this committee 'seriously' (Jain and Lasseter, 2018).

In his first term, the Modi-led government mostly left the Hindutva reforms of the education sector to Sangh Parivar-related civil society organizations such as the VHP,[22] and also the RSS.[23] Modi also deliberately

---

[20] Dalits are a group of people belonging to the lowest caste in India and characterized as 'untouchable'. They are excluded from the varna system of Hinduism. Ambedkar campaigned against social discrimination towards the untouchables.

[21] Reuters states that Modi had not requested the committee's creation. The committee may have been prompted by Sharma but its mission was in resonance with Modi's viewpoint. During the 2014 launch of a hospital in Mumbai, Modi referred to the scientific achievements acknowledged by ancient religious texts and of Ganesha (a Hindu deity with an elephant's head) (Jain and Lasseter, 2018).

[22] The family of the Sangh also consisted of the VHP, along with its youth wing that is known as Bajrang Dal. The members of these groups often participated in the Hindu–Muslim riots (Jaffrelot and Therwath, 2007, p.15).

[23] Vinayak Damodar Savarkar was the first person to articulate Hindu nationalism through his goal of a Hindu Rashtra (nation) in 1925 (Jaffrelot and Therwath, 2007). Savarkar described Islam and Christianity as 'foreign elements' existing in India, and he suggested that their religious practices or activities should be restricted to the private sphere (Pandey,

left the Hindu nationalist ideas or ideological reforms to the individual states (18 states are currently governed by the BJP),[24] in the knowledge that these reforms would underpin the Hindutva political communication message. In Madhya Pradesh and Rajasthan, the Vidya Bharti and other RSS affiliates are involved in writing part of the curriculum and training teachers. Haryana schools have outsourced moral education to Dinanath Batra, mentioned earlier in his position as chairman of the Bharatiya Shiksha Niti Aayog, an RSS council that advises the Narendra Modi (Mohan, 2016).

The role of the state governments

A number of BJP-ruled states, including Rajasthan, Gujarat, Haryana, Goa, and Maharashtra, have taken 'creative liberties' to reinforce a Hindutva revivalist agenda and attempt to erase Muslim identity (Syed, 2019). One of the main goals of the new editions of Gujarat and Rajasthan textbooks (superseding the old textbooks drafted under Congress) is to insist that 'the rule of non-Hindutva communities was disastrous' in medieval times (Syed, 2019; also see Traub, 2018; Westerfield, 2019).

Historical events and exclusion of Muslims: distortions and omissions

The BJP-led state government in Rajasthan amended key historical facts in school textbooks that were issued in 2006 (Sharma, 2016a).[25] Traub reports that 'the early Hindu era is depicted in the Rajasthan books as an unrivalled Golden Age' (Traub, 2018, p.7). The revised textbooks in Rajasthan glorify the role of Hindutva ideologue V.D. Savarkar in the Indian independence movement in order to instil patriotism and nationalism in the young generation. Savarkar overtakes even Gandhi in prominence, losing

---

1991, p.3005). Inspired by Savarkar, Keshav formed the RSS, a militant Hindu nationalist organization that was also defined as fascist (Basu, 1993). The chief aim of RSS was 'to penetrate the entire social structure to forge a Hindu nation that would be physically, morally and socially sound'. RSS expanded its aims by establishing different organizations targeting distinct sections of society, such as women, youth, students, secluded/excluded castes, and ethnic groups; they were known as the Sangh Parivar, the family of the Sangh (Jaffrelot, 2005, p.5). The Sangh Parivar has attempted to homogenize the Hindu community in order to create a sense of Hindu national identity (Fearon and Laitin, 2000).

[24] In 2020, at the time of writing, the BJP holds a majority in 12 states: Arunachal Pradesh, Assam, Goa, Gujarat, Haryana, Himachal Pradesh, Karnataka, Madhya Pradesh, Manipur, Tripura, Uttar Pradesh, and Uttarakhand.

[25] In the Congress Party's textbook on India's modern history, members of the Nehru/Gandhi family are glorified.

any explicit Hindutva credentials in the process (Outlook India, 2017). In the Grade 10 political science textbook, Savarkar is depicted as a great revolutionary, patriot, and 'sangathanwaadi' (organization man) (Sharma, 2016b). His problematic views on Indian citizenship will be discussed in Chapter 6.

Pradyumna Jairam's unpublished thesis (2021) on the textbooks in Rajasthan offers a detailed critique of the changes that took place, including how they returned to the narrative of the NDA from 2003 – with the nation tracing a journey 'from a golden ancient age to a period of struggle in the Medieval period [...] with more stress on local (Hindu) protagonists'. The focus was on resistance to foreign invasion and the vernacularization of history around Rajput heroes, especially in grades 9, 10, and 12. Rajasthan's Education Minister Vasudev Devnani played a key role in how history textbooks were written:

> [T]he BJP textbooks also went one step further than any of the other previously mentioned sets of textbooks, in so-far as they indulged in overt altering of historical narratives. This was evidenced in the Battle of Haldighati, which previously was seen as a historical stalemate, but was now re-written to project a victory for Maharana Pratap over Akbar, thus in the view of Devnani 'tell students the truth and fix an aberration'.[26] This particular theme was so crucial for the BJP that it was mentioned in both the Class 10 and Class 12 textbooks, to ensure students remembered the outcome as much as possible. (Jairam, 2021, p.245)

Jairam also traces blatant omission and inaccuracy when discussing two prominent historical figures – Ashoka and Ambedkar. He states:

> The erasure had to do with the need to continue a linear progression of history, demarcated by Hindu and Muslim periods, with any mention of Ashoka's change of religion marking a fissure, where-in Buddhism would be the reason for his change of heart after the Battle

---

[26] This particular event was significant for the BJP, because in both Class 10 and 12 textbooks it was explicitly stated that Rana Pratap defeated Akbar, in a creation of two dichotomous antagonists divided by religion and nationality. The new texts disregard this characterization and mention that the battle 'between the two sides was not a religious war but a clash for superiority between two political forces' https://www.indiatoday. in/india/story/maharana-pratap-not-akbar-won-battle-of-haldighati-rajasthan-history-book-1026240-2017-07-25, and https://indianexpress.com/article/education/savar kar-loses-veer-as-congress-rewrites-school-textbooks-in-rajasthan-5779772/ [Accessed 28 January 2021].

of Kalinga. In the case of Ambedkar, labelling him a 'Hindu social reformer' displayed a marked unwillingness towards acknowledging his radical ideology, something which the previous narrative also was guilty of, when it only focussed on his achievements as a constitutionalist. (Jairam, 2021, p.246)

The revised textbooks in Gujarat that depict the second era of history lead to a complete erasure of Muslim identity and culture. Traub writes that 'One book reduces over five centuries of rule by a diverse array of Muslim emperors to a single "Period of Struggle" and demonizes many of its leading figures' (Traub, 2018; see also Westerfield, 2019, p.7). The 2002 Gujarat carnage is titled the 'Gujarat riots',[27] instead of 'anti-Muslim riots', in the revised NCERT textbooks.[28] Apart from the title and the opening line, the text in the passage on the 2002 Gujarat violence remains the same and continues to highlight critical observations about the role of the then BJP state government (Pandey, 2018).

There are also distortions to be found where events from the medieval period are recounted, an example being the name of Qutub Minar, a prominent Mughal structure in Delhi that was built under Qutab-ud-din Aibak.[29] The battles for power between Shivaji and Afzal Khan, Akbar and Maharana Pratap, Guru Govind Singh and Aurangzeb are given a religious flavour by statements that all the kings who fought against the Muslim rulers were Hindu nationalists (Puniyani, 2017). Whereas Gujarat's textbooks 'take a more moderate line on ancient India' than their Rajasthan counterparts, they 'still tend toward the view that "the most glorious and prosperous age of Indian history" occurred before Muslim rule' (Traub, 2018, cited in Westerfield, 2019, p.7). Major components of Indian history, science, and philosophy are interconnected with more than 700 years of rule of Muslims over the subcontinent. This chapter

---

[27] In February 2002 the western Indian state of Gujarat, governed by the Hindu nationalist Chief Minister Narendra Modi, witnessed one of the country's biggest massacres. Responding to reports that Muslims had set fire to a train carriage, killing 58 Hindu pilgrims inside, mobs rampaged across the state. The riots flared up again and killing, raping, and looting continued. More than 2,000 Muslims were murdered, and tens of thousands rendered homeless in carefully planned and coordinated attacks of unprecedented savagery (Mishra, 2012). This massacre was carried out by organized Hindu right-wing groups who raped and murdered Muslims (Ghassem-Fachandi, 2012).

[28] *Politics in India since Independence*, NCERT textbook in political science for Grade 12. A chapter titled 'Politics in India since Independence' (p.187) includes a passage under the heading 'Anti-Muslim riots in Gujarat'.

[29] The textbook changed the name of Qutub Minar to 'Vishnu Stambha', and states it was built by Emperor Samudragupta.

has been rejected by right-wing Hindu nationalists, ushering in an era that has been referred to as bringing about the 'Murder of History' in the Indian polity (Syed, 2019).

Muslims have seen their influential history during the Mughal era distorted, their accomplishments erased from textbooks. In Rajasthan, the selection of notable Indians in the '*Hamare Gaurav*' (Our Pride) sections of the environmental science textbooks is a giveaway (cited in Westerfield, 2019, p.14). There is not a single Muslim among the 15 notable Indians featured (Chowdhury, 2018). All religious minorities such as Muslims and Christians have been termed as the 'other' or 'foreigners' who invaded the country (Traub, 2018; Westerfield, 2019, p.7). In the political science textbook for Rajasthan, the section on the Uniform Civil Code depicts the different laws for different communities and sections that it claims creates separatism (Bharadwaj, 2017).[30] The chapter also makes a case against positive discrimination and the grant of any special facility to any religious community. These textbooks are continuing to shape the narrative of Muslim and Hindu identity in a way that perpetuates division and hate.

Consequently, history is being distorted and interpolated, and Indian youth are thus being inspired by Hindutva ideologues to believe that the Muslims were and are the real cause of all that is wrong with India (Syed, 2019). BJP textbooks are promoting a Hindutva agenda in which they consider Indian revolutionaries and heroes. The writing of history textbooks to include all those 'great' men who fought against the Muslim 'invaders' is the constitutional commitment to religious diversity and the plural fabric of India that has been invariably invoked. These instances of anti-Muslim discourse in school textbooks are reinforced by the media and political actors (Waiker, 2018). The states are motivated to adopt national forms of education that are centred on character building and the creation of good citizens. They therefore become laboratories for testing reforms, which can then be scaled up to a national level (Chowdhury, 2018; HRW, 2019).

Discrimination on the ground – Ghar Wapsi campaign, love jihad, and the cow vigilantes

The first term of Narendra Modi was marked by a 'de facto ethnicization of Indian democracy:[31] Hindu nationalist vigilante groups have implemented articles of faith of the Sangh Parivar in the streets, including its cow protection

---

[30] Uniform Civil Code is an ongoing point of debate regarding the Indian Constitution's mandate to replace personal laws based on the scriptures and customs of each major religious community in India with a common set of rules governing every citizen.

[31] More on how discrimination on the ground has played out against Muslims is depicted in Chapter 6.

agenda, the fight against "love jihad",[32] and reconversion programmes to Hinduism' (Jaffrelot and Verniers, 2020, p.3; see also Jaffrelot, 2019). Several BJP-ruled states adopted stricter laws and members of the BJP used communal rhetoric to spur a violent vigilante campaign against the consumption of beef and those engaged in the cattle trade. As a result, between May 2015 and December 2018, according to Human Rights Watch (HRW), at least 44 people – including 36 Muslims – were killed (HRW, 2019). The following section presents how these issues were linked nationally to textbooks.

In Hinduism, the cow is considered sacred. Article 48 of India's Constitution directs the state to 'take steps … prohibiting the slaughter of cows and calves', and 21 states criminalize cow slaughter in various forms. Cow protection has been promoted as a key issue by the BJP and the RSS. Lynch mobs, often organized over social media, have attacked minorities – including Muslims, Christians, and Dalits – under suspicion of eating beef, slaughtering cows, or transporting cattle for slaughter (Jha, 2002). Since the BJP came to power in 2014, there has been an increase in these attacks. The mythical cow, and its divinity, is another axiom held by Hindu nationalists, but Jha has proved that this may not be based on fact.[33] Jha writes:

> [T]he sanctity of the cow has … been wrongly traced back to the Vedas, which are supposedly of divine origin and the fountainhead of all knowledge and wisdom. In other words, some sections of Indian society trace the concept of sacred cow to the very period when it was sacrificed and its flesh was eaten. (Jha, 2002, p.18)

However, while Hindutva leaders claim that beef-eating was first introduced to India by Muslims and other foreigners, in reality, 'the cow was not always all that sacred in the Vedic and subsequent Brahmanical and non-Brahmanical traditions … and its flesh, along with other varieties of meat, was quite often a part of haute cuisine in early India' (Jha, 2002, p.20). Since Modi came into power, cow vigilantism has been on the rise, which has resulted in Muslims and Dalits being killed over the protection of cows, sacred in Hinduism. As already mentioned, the cow and its protection have also been converted into a symbol of the communal identity of the Hindus, and fundamentalist forces

---

[32] 'Fears around "love jihad," a supposed form of religious warfare by which Muslim men lure Hindu women away from the faith, have circulated in one form or another in India for more than a century' (Bhatia, 2017).

[33] Jha (2002) uses considerable historical and archaeological evidence to prove that beef was routinely eaten during the Vedic period. After his book was published, Jha received many death threats in 2001, leading to the withdrawal book in India (Dalrymple, 2005).

have led to major rioting and violence towards Muslims throughout India for eating beef and towards those engaged in the cattle trade (Ramachandran, 2017; Anand and Lall, 2022).

Ignoring the evidence to the contrary and refusing to include any mention of the debate in textbooks feeds the flame of communal violence. In 2016, the Rajasthan Class 5 Hindi textbook contained 'a letter in which the cow declares herself a purveyor of strength, wisdom, longevity, health, happiness, prosperity and glory, enjoins children to serve and protect her, and signs off with – Yours, Kamdhenu Gaumata' (Chowdhury, 2018, p.4; see also Westerfield, 2019).[34] The glorification of ancient India has been a recurring theme of the Hindu right-wing discourse in India. Modi made several pseudo-scientific claims between 2014 and 2019, while Pragya Singh Thakur, a member of the ruling BJP, claimed that cow urine can cure cancer (Solomon, 2019). Today there are claims that cow urine can help prevent COVID-19 (Baker, 2020).

As mentioned earlier, those who have suffered most in the ban on cow slaughter and the subsequent vigilante movements have been Muslims. On a larger scale, Muslims as a community are being otherized through the marginalization of Urdu.[35] The mutually constitutive relationship between identity and language is the subject of an exploration of the tensions brought about by the status of Urdu and English in Indian schools (Matthan et al, 2014; Anand and Lall, 2022).

This section has shown that the 2016 and 2018 textbooks differ substantially from their 2002–2004 counterparts. The explicit inclusion of Modi's and other BJP politicians' agendas are not just about synthesizing a common national identity but are also intended to pacify the public on social justice issues (Waiker, 2018). They have three main objectives. First, they create links between the historical and mythical achievement of Hindu figures and gods, highlighting the essential relationship between the nation-state of India today and the ostensibly Hindu politics of the past. Second, this discourse seeks to categorize Hindu as having been eternally dominant in India and imposes a contemporary vision of a Hindu past (Thapar, 2014). Third, monopolizing the economic development discourse with Hindu experiences effectively negates the significance of Muslims, which feeds into the larger context of the Hindutva narrative (Waiker, 2018).

---

[34] It is a divine bovine goddess described in Hinduism as the mother of all cows.

[35] There is a linguistic diversity among Muslims. However, Muslims are reduced to being Urdu speakers, which is political, communal, and exclusionary.

Delhi's Happiness Curriculum, Entrepreneurship Mindset Curriculum – Hindu traditions and role models

In the last five years, the Aam Aadmi Party (AAP) has led the Delhi government. In February 2020 it won another mandate for five more years. Unlike the BJP, the AAP has presented itself as secular. Its main platform has been based on an anti-corruption campaign as well as on improving public services. In light of this, the AAP has focused on increased education funding to improve schools across India's capital. Some other components of its school reforms include the introduction of new teacher training courses, curricular reforms such as the Happiness Curriculum, student learning programmes to improve learning outcomes, and investment in school infrastructure to provide better facilities for the school community (Sharma, 2020a). The AAP claims that certain government schools are now as good as or better than private schools (Goan Connection TV, 2020).

A closer look at two flagship programmes launched in 2018 – the Happiness Curriculum and the EMC – however shows links to Hinduism and a Hindu mindset. Whilst this is not the same as Hindu nationalism or Hindutva, the fact that these programmes are not regarded as breaking away from a secular education tradition is in itself interesting, and shows how far the Hindutva approach has been mainstreamed. Fieldwork undertaken in summer 2020 during the COVID-19 lockdown with 110 teachers helped to explore some of the Hinduism-related themes.

The rationale behind the Happiness Curriculum lies in India being ranked 140th out of 156 countries in the World Happiness Report (n.d.). As a response, the Delhi government launched this initiative in all 1,030 government schools from nursery through to Grade 7 in July 2018. The aim was to focus on the holistic development of all learners, invest in their well-being, and improve the overall quality of education in line with the Sustainable Development Goals (SDG-4) (Kim et al, 2019). A study by Narula et al (2019) aimed to explore in-service teachers' beliefs about happiness and the happiness curriculum revealed that teachers perceived the Happiness Curriculum as positive, a desirable endeavour that would improve lives by bringing joy and happiness to students, and would provide enabling conditions for students to flourish and succeed. The teachers pointed to positive outcomes from the curriculum's class activities. One explained: '*The Happiness Curriculum* fosters a fearless environment, mindfulness, and learning without burden in the classes from nursery to grade VIII. It should be for all classes.'

Happiness classes focus on mindfulness, instilling moral values, and reflection. According to the teachers, 'the mindfulness activity helps in relaxing the child. We also tell stories to children. The stories in the happiness curriculum are based on moral education. They are more concerned with instilling values in children' (FT3SV4 Delhi). Teachers narrate stories from reference books, some of which have their roots in Hindu traditions – such as the stories *Nirmal Paani* and *Bekar Paudha* that refer to guru and disciples. Several also refer to saints or holy men.[36] Only one of the 20 stories about Alexander the Great, *Ek glass pani ki kimat*, refers to a fakir.[37] From this, the students learn about 'reflection and expression' (FT2SV11 Delhi); 'we will not ask about the moral of the story but how it is related to their real lives' (FT1SV9 Delhi). Mornings begin with the happiness classes, so 'we mentally prepare them, so that they can study in their 2nd period onwards. The student should be ready to learn, and without which no activity can be successful' (FT1SV9 Delhi). Teachers explained that this was 'their favourite class. Every child wishes to attend it and enjoy it' (FT3SV12 Delhi). Some of the activities are meditation based, a Hindu/Buddhist tradition and children sit with their hands in a mudra;[38] the meditation and 'the mindfulness activity make them stress-free and attentive in the class. [Through] the story reading, children share their thoughts and experiences related to the story, so they enjoy this period thoroughly' (FT8SV4 Delhi).

Along with the happiness classes, schools provide an opportunity for students to gain real life-based experience through the EMC. These sessions enable the teachers to provide experiential teaching and give them opportunities to motivate students towards vocational education. Through EMC, the students can 'interact with entrepreneurs who studied at government schools such as [...] Arjun Takral, Rajiv Takra, and other famous personalities. These personalities share the issues of funding and how they became famous after facing barriers at home. So students get very motivated and feel that if they won't get a job, still they can start their own business' (FT8SV2 Delhi). It helps students to 'think creatively, out-of-box and make them imaginative' (FT5SV5 Delhi). One of the teachers explained that through EMC, the students

made such beautiful uniforms out of newspapers. ... The students will not be dependent on anyone; they can think for themselves [...] The students can stand on their feet, and if the students want to do something in the future, it should not be that they have to take only science, commerce, there should be so much creativity in the children that they can do anything. (FT5SV5 Delhi)

---

[36] Some of the stories also have an international context – one is on Thomas Edison and another on Stephen Hawking.

[37] The word 'fakir' could refer to either a Muslim or Hindu religious ascetic who lives solely on alms.

[38] A symbolic or ritual gesture or pose in Hinduism, Jainism, and Buddhism.

Teachers explained that EMC also motivates academically less able students: 'for weaker students, it is important to teach them so that they don't have a feeling that they can't do it' (FT6SV4 Delhi). For instance:

> In EMC, there is an activity which states that Sachin Tendulkar is not an educated person but famous through cricket. We have stories on how a person started with a small business. We told them that they could start working under a tailor and earn Rs. 100. [...] They can learn and recruit tailors under them [...] In our school, we allow students to sell diyas within the school on Diwali [...] They are also stitching clothes for their parents. (FT6SV4 Delhi)

The intention behind this curriculum reform is disclosed in Delhi Education Minister Manish Sisodia's own words: 'The bigger idea is that we want to impart the Entrepreneurial mindset' (cited in Sandhu, 2021, p.181). In the literature, this "entrepreneur self" is a critical reconstruction of the identity that is dictated by 'neoliberal governmentality'. Here, the entrepreneurial government 'makes up' the individual as a person – as an 'entrepreneur of the self' (Du Gay, 1996, p.156). Using Foucault, Du Gay elucidates that individuals are made to realize that they are responsible for their success or failure in the 'business of life' (p.156). Therefore, the neoliberal logic not only governs the state, the economy, and civil society, but it also governs behaviour and the subjective identity of the self (Sandhu, 2021).

EMC also focuses on Hindu personalities; according to the teachers who teach it and were interviewed, there are no examples of Muslim entrepreneurs. Both the Happiness Curriculum and EMC have positive learning aims, yet are not inclusive of minorities and show Indian society in a monolithic Hindu way. The fact that this has remained unquestioned is proof of how far this mindset has become mainstream.

Deshbhakti (patriotism) curriculum in Delhi government schools

In September 2021 the AAP government started rolling out its deshbhakti curriculum,[39] to instil patriotism among students and inspire them to feel proud of their nation (Bose, 2021). The curriculum is being rolled out in every class – from nursery to grade 12 – across all government schools in Delhi (Bose, 2021). It mandates one period every day for patriotism studies for students in nursery to grade 8, and two classes per week for students in grades 9 to 12 (Bose, 2021). According to a circular released by

---

[39] The framework of the curriculum was approved by the governing council of the State Council of Educational Research and Training on 6 August 2022.

the Directorate of Education, 'Every deshbhakti period shall start with a five-minute "Deshbhakti Dhyaan",[40] where the teacher and students shall practice mindfulness, reflect on their gratitude for the country, freedom fighters, and any five persons that they consider deshbhakts, and pledge their respect for the country' (Bose, 2021, para.2). Arvind Kejriwal said that the deshbhakti curriculum will not be based on rote learning and there will be no exams. 'It will be activity-based, and students will be told stories about independence and the nation's pride. Children will be made to realise their responsibilities and duties towards the country' (cited in Bose, 2021, para.3). He added, 'They (the students) will be prepared to fulfil their responsibilities and contribute towards the nation's progress. They will also be prepared in a way that if the need arises, they can lay down their lives for the nation and be willing to give their all to the country' (Bose, 2021, para.4). The deshbhakti curriculum framework also aims to develop a deep sense of respect towards constitutional values and seeks to bridge the gap between values and action (Bose, 2021).

To implement the curriculum in classrooms, two separate teachers' handbooks have been designed – one for students of grades 6 to 8 and the other for grades 9 to 12. For both groups of students, the fundamental chapters are the same – love and respect for the country; who is a deshbhakt; what is deshbhakti; my country, my pride; why is my country not developed; and the India of my dreams (Baruah, 2021, para.7). The course does not have textbooks, and the teacher acts as a facilitator for discussions by introducing each topic with a central question so that children can express their ideas and views (Baruah, 2021).

The teachers' handbooks come with a set of 'dos and don'ts' for conducting these classes. They are instructed not to criticize children's answers if they do not agree with them, and not to present their personal thoughts or opinions about correct answers; not to stop children from asking questions or cutting them off, but to listen to them with patience; not to stop discussions on sensitive topics or present their own views; and to let children form their own thoughts through the discussion (Baruah, 2021). For instance, for Grades 6 to 8, there are simple topics such as 'Mera flag, mera saathi [My flag, my friend]' but also some complex ones, such as respect for the country's people within the larger subject of 'Respect for the country' (Baruah, 2021, para.4). An exploration of a

---

[40] 'Each class begins with a five-minute activity called "Deshbhakti Dhyaan" in which teachers encourage students to run the lines "Main apne desh ko pranaam karta hoon/naman karta hoon. Mai apni Bharat Mata ka aadar karta hoon" [I salute my country. I respect my country] through their minds, and then ask the children to take a vow to honour their country and preserve its respect. The children are then to think of five people whom they consider "deshbhakt" and thank them in their minds' (Baruah, 2021, para.7).

critical topic – 'Mera Bharat mahaan phir bhi viksit kyun nahi [My India is good but it is not growing]' – for grades 9 to 12 begins with teachers explaining the concept of developed, developing, and underdeveloped countries, before posing a question: 'In your everyday life, what are the difficulties you face or see people around you facing, which stop India from being a developed country?' This implies that the AAP government is promoting the deshbhakti curriculum in tandem with the notion that India is a knowledge economy and society.

The curriculum reforms by the AAP-led government cannot be seen in a vacuum as they reflect wider societal and political changes across India. The new curricula feed into this by promoting new values that lead to the construction of new identities.

The 2019 elections and the new NEP 2020

After the 2019 elections, in which the BJP won an even greater majority of seats than in 2014, a big reshuffle took place in the cabinet; about half of the new or promoted ministers had strong RSS connections. Of the 303 BJP MPs in the Lok Sabha, 146 or 48 per cent have an affiliation to the RSS. In the Rajya Sabha, of its 82 MPs, the BJP has 34 links to the Sangh (Pandey and Arnimesh, 2020). Such links are increasingly visible in the decision-making of the government. The most important panel in the Modi cabinet, the cabinet committee on security, is dominated by the Sangh (Pandey and Arnimesh, 2020),[41] with the explicit goal of promoting and disseminating a radical Hindu ideology. Part and parcel of this is a redefinition of Indian citizenship. National education reform is also back on the agenda, with the new NEP 2020 being published.

The NEP 2020

The NEP 2020 was released in the summer of 2020. Key features of the new policy are the restructuring of the education pathway into 5+3+3+4 years, the freedom for children to mix and match subjects across the science/arts and social science divide, increased vocational training, and greater use of Indian languages with an emphasis on MT education. Teachers interviewed in Delhi as part of a wider project on classroom practices (Lall et al, 2020) mostly viewed the new policy as positive, although some had reservations on how it would eventually be implemented. The NEP text has clear links to Hindutva thinking, as detailed in the next section.

---

[41] It only has two non-RSS members.

The NEP's saffron edges

The policy's promise to 'revamp all aspects of the education structure' (p.3) in order to align it with the needs of the 21st century (as well as SDG4) has at the heart of it both modernization in light of globalization as well as a return to roots by promising to align the reforms with 'India's traditions and value systems' (p.3). This reflects the BJP's external outlook with regard to the economy and internal view of identity already discussed. Early on the policy states:

> The rich heritage of ancient and eternal Indian knowledge and thought has been a guiding light for this Policy. The pursuit of knowledge (*Gyan*), wisdom (*Pragyaa*), and truth (*Satya*) was always considered in Indian thought and philosophy as the highest human goal. The aim of education in ancient India was not just the acquisition of knowledge as preparation for life in this world, or life beyond schooling, but for the complete realization and liberation of the self. World–class institutions of ancient India such as Takshashila, Nalanda, Vikramshila, Vallabhi, set the highest standards of multidisciplinary teaching and research and hosted scholars and students from across backgrounds and countries. The Indian education system produced great scholars such as Charaka, Susruta, Aryabhata, Varahamihira, Bhaskaracharya, Brahmagupta, Chanakya, Chakrapani Datta, Madhava, Panini, Patanjali, Nagarjuna, Gautama, Pingala, Sankardev, Maitreyi, Gargi and Thiruvalluvar, among numerous others, who made seminal contributions to world knowledge in diverse fields such as mathematics, astronomy, metallurgy, medical science and surgery, civil engineering, architecture, shipbuilding and navigation, yoga, fine arts, chess, and more. Indian culture and philosophy have had a strong influence on the world. These rich legacies to world heritage must not only be nurtured and preserved for posterity but also researched, enhanced, and put to new uses through our education system. (NEP, 2020, p.4)

Ancient India and pride in 'India's rich, diverse, ancient and modern culture' (p.6) are recurring themes throughout the document – reflecting the BJP textbooks from two decades ago. In particular, ancient Indian heritage is made reference to a number of times – including ancient languages. Sanskrit is referred to as an 'important modern language' (despite the fact that no one has spoken it for centuries (§4.17, p.14). The policy claims that Sanskrit 'possesses a classical literature that is greater in volume than that of Latin and Greek put together'. In the same section, the policy promises that

> [E]very student in the country will participate in a fun project/activity on 'The Languages of India', sometime in Grades 6–8, such as, under the *'Ek*

Bharat Shrestha Bharat' initiative. In this project/activity, students will learn about the remarkable unity of most of the major Indian languages, starting with their common phonetic and scientifically-arranged alphabets and scripts, their common grammatical structures, their origins and sources of vocabularies from Sanskrit and other classical languages, as well as their rich inter-influences and differences. (NEP, 2020, p.14)

These languages will include other classical languages such as classical Tamil, Telugu, Kannada, Malayalam, Odia, Pali, Persian, and Prakrit. Urdu is not mentioned anywhere. In fact, the NEP engages with the issue of languages in two sections – chapter 4 and chapter 22 – which are about the promotion of Indian languages, arts, and culture.

Beyond languages, the aim is to inculcate 'Knowledge of India' (§4.27, p.16) that comprises 'knowledge from ancient India and its contributions to modern India and its successes and challenges'. It also includes tribal knowledge and indigenous and traditional ways of learning, as well as being included in 'mathematics, astronomy, philosophy, yoga, architecture, medicine, agriculture, engineering, linguistics, literature, sports, games, as well as in governance, polity, conservation'.

The inclusion of Indian art and culture in the teaching and learning process to strengthen the links between education and culture and to imbibe the Indian ethos (Saraswathy, 2020) is also reflected by the discussion about using indigenous toys as pedagogical tools. BJP members have asserted that toys can be used to promote experiential learning and are useful in the teaching and learning of mathematics, languages, science, and so on, as they have existed since the Indus Valley Civilization (Arora, 2020). Given the NEP's special emphasis on local entrepreneurship, students are introduced to toy-making from the sixth standard, as part of the government's effort to boost the toy-making industry. As part of NEP 2020, local crafts such as toy-making are made part of vocational education in schools (Saraswathy, 2020), to instil a sense of pride in national goals.

In HE, the NEP promises to replicate ancient Indian universities such as Takshashila, Nalanda, Vallabhi, and Vikramshila, 'which had thousands of students from India and the world studying in vibrant multidisciplinary environments' (§10.2, p.34). This is given as a justification to move away from subject-specific HEIs. Multidisciplinary research and teaching is presented as a 'great Indian tradition to create well-rounded and innovative individuals, and which is already transforming other countries educationally and economically' (NEP, 2020). HE is also positioned to develop a more 'holistic' education.

Ancient Indian literary works such as Banabhatta's Kadambari described a good education as knowledge of the 64 Kalaas or arts; and among these 64 'arts' were not only subjects, such as singing and painting, but also 'scientific 'fields, such as chemistry and mathematics, 'vocational ' fields such as carpentry and clothes-making, 'professional 'fields, such as medicine and engineering, as well as 'soft skills' such as communication, discussion, and debate. (NEP, 2020, §11.1, p.36)

The policy document claims that 'the very idea that all branches of creative human endeavour, including mathematics, science, vocational subjects, professional subjects, and soft skills should be considered "arts", has distinctly Indian origins'. HE is also tasked to develop programmes in 'Indology, Indian languages, AYUSH systems of medicine,[42] yoga, arts, music, history, culture, and modern India' (p.39). Students of allopathic medicine will also have a 'basic understanding' of AYUSH (p.50). These themes will be explored in more detail in Chapter 5.

Chapter 2 of the policy document returns to the themes of Indian languages and culture – making the point that Indian culture needs to be preserved and promoted as it is important for the "nation's identity as well as for its economy" (p.53). A reference is made to 'Incredible!ndia', quoting the country's tourism slogan. But beyond the economic argument of tourism, Indian culture and tradition are promoted as an essential part of identity creation: 'It is through the development of a strong sense and knowledge of their own cultural history, arts, languages, and traditions that children can build a positive cultural identity and self-esteem' (p.53). In light of this, HEIs are also expected to provide more programmes in local languages, and under the 'Ek Bharat Shrestha Bharat' scheme 100 tourist destinations across the country will be identified so that educational institutions can send students to study them (p.54). Sanskrit makes another comeback on p.55, being offered in schools and HEIs. The policy promises that 'it will be taught not in isolation, but in interesting and innovative ways, and connected to other contemporary and relevant subjects such as mathematics, astronomy, philosophy, linguistics, dramatics, yoga, etc' (p.55).

The NEP 2020 does not mention the word secular even once (MHRD, 2019), which raises questions about what it might mean for the idea of citizenship and education in contemporary India (GoI, NEP, 2020). These issues will be further explored in Chapter 6.

Conclusion

This chapter has described how textbook content has been used to underpin Hindu pride and disparage India's Muslim heritage, drawing battle lines

---

[42] AYUSH is Ayurveda, Yoga and Naturopathy, Unani, Siddha, and Homeopathy.

between those who believe India is a secular country and those who want to redefine India on Hindu lines. The BJP's education policy has led to broad nationwide policy changes that impact notions of belonging and citizenship, which are further explored in Chapter 6. During both its terms, India's history and defining characteristics of the Indian identity became the target of the BJP's education policy. The textbooks that were produced contextualized and de-contextualized certain events depending on the topic that was being covered, accentuating and consolidating the image of Hindu nationalists as the liberators from British colonial rule. Education was consistently used during both terms as a tool to form the dominant discourse, placing Hindus as the core group of the Indian nation, determining the true inheritors of the state, and mobilizing the core ethnic group (Bäckman, 2020).

The previous BJP-led NDA regime had already started the process of saffronization by changing school textbooks and by introducing courses such as Paurohitya (priestcraft) and Karmakand (rituals). The attempt to popularize their viewpoint on ancient, medieval, and modern history has been intensified during the last few years (from 2014), while BJP has been in the seat of power. The current BJP–RSS government is trying to rewrite the history of the subcontinent through the lens of the 'Pundit Hierarchy'. At the same time the BJP has fostered changes in education, in particular through the NEP 2020, aiming to align India's classrooms with globalization alongside the Hindutva agenda of *manuwad* (Puniyani, 2017).[43] These ideological messages are seen as acceptable across society because schooling is understood as the site of hegemony; where students and teachers practise the perpetuation of 'common-sense ideas' on a par with the leading mainstream political images (Gramsci, 1971). These hegemonic discourses become an integral part of common-sense beliefs. Chapter 3 contributes understanding to how schools, government, private, and RSS, reproduce key ideologies of the society in which they are embedded.

---

[43]   Ancient Hindu legal texts.

India's Neoliberal Schools: The Hindu Nationalist and Neoliberal Agenda in School Education

Introduction

As discussed in Chapter 2, education in India was envisioned as a leveller that would combat prevailing systemic inequities through policies that were aimed at the inclusive development of India's stratified society. The constitutional provisions of equitable education directed the Indian state to provide free and compulsory education for all children until they reached the age of 14 years (Article 45, part IV) (Raina, 2020). Article 46 directed the state to promote with special care the educational and economic interests of the SCs, STs, and other weaker sections of society. After the reforms had taken place there was a gradual but noticeable change in the direction of policy. This new direction became particularly evident after Modi's 2016 election win, when there was not just an intensification of neoliberalization of school education, but the essentialization of 'neoliberal-common sense' (Raina, 2020, p.156). These changes have resulted in a worrying outcome: the structural distortion of school education into multilayered hierarchies of access has been legitimized, while policy solutions have been abandoned to reduce these distortions (Raina, 2020). The policy shifts have supported, reinforced, and further entrenched a binary between the public and the private school education systems, and also deeply embedded a multilayered graded hierarchy within both. Contemporary enrolment in government schools is mainly from disadvantaged social groups such as SCs, STs, Dalits, and minorities (Sadgopal, 2016, p.18), which is 'turning state schools into a colony of the underprivileged' (Raina, 2020, p.68). Post-reform, students who can afford 'quality education' exit government schools, as discussed in Chapter 1. The socio-economically marginalized poor who remain are devoid of voice and therefore fail to have any impact on the 'dysfunctional government school system' (Mukhopadhyay and Sarangapani, 2018, p.12). Each school type is attended by children who belong to a certain socio-economic section of Indian society. The social differences of class are firming up because of this, with education exacerbating social differences and leading to further social divisions in an already stratified society (Raina, 2020).

This chapter discusses first how government schools are affected by issues of access, quality, reforms in teaching approaches, and privatization. It then outlines the interventions led by Public Private Partnerships (PPPs). The chapter goes on to review the neoliberal approach of NGOs in teacher education and training. It also provides evidence of the neoliberal and Hindu nationalist agenda 'on the ground' in government schools. The chapter then turns to the rise of private schools – both low cost and others serving the middle and aspiring middle classes, looking in detail at how this has increased access. The discussion briefly revisits the previous arguments about the rise of private schools around demand for 'quality' education and the neoliberal agenda of school choice. It subsequently discusses the impact of the neoliberal agenda on teacher agency to critically counter textbooks and government rituals that serve the Hindutva agenda. Even though private school teachers recognized the dangers of the new textbooks, the school system left them with no options. The last section of the chapter outlines the role played by the RSS and kindred organizations to fill particular education gaps at central and state levels. It shows how Hindutva has been spread by using RSS-drafted textbooks alongside government textbooks in RSS-sponsored schools, highlighting how the rhetoric of these textbooks revolves around the creation of a 'Hindu Rashtra'.

Government schools

Chapter 1 showed how the post-1991 reforms in India chose a neoliberal trajectory that resulted in the rise of private schools. NGOs also started to play a role in government schools, as there was an increased emphasis on performance that was fuelled by increasing school choice for parents. This neoliberal trajectory allowed the embedding of the Hindu nationalist discourse in schools as the middle classes wanted more globalization (such as English medium schools that will be discussed in Chapter 4), while simultaneously wanting to safeguard the Indian culture and their children against the onslaught of globalization.

Both the District Primary Education Programme (DPEP) and SSA were designed under the neoliberal policy framework imposed by the IMF and the World Bank (Sadgopal, 2008). They converted the existing school system into a new multilayered system that was made up of government and private schools, which led to lower quality and credibility for government schools

(Sadgopal, 2008). This resulted in the middle classes moving their children to private schools, causing only the marginalized to stay at government schools (Lall and Nambissan, 2011; Dharmaraj, 2017). The RTE Act had a positive effect on government school infrastructure and teacher absence rates, but it had a negative impact on measures of literacy and numeracy skills for students owing to low teaching quality, as well as problems with the curricula and pedagogical methods (Mukerji and Walton, 2012; Muralidharan and Sundararaman, 2013; Bhat, 2017). Government school teachers have come under attack because of the low performance of their students. Blame is directed at them owing to perceived low accountability in state-run schools (further supporting the argument in favour of neoliberal reform measures (Ball, 2010).[1] As a result, the government has employed monitoring systems, introducing site visits, inspections by the Education Minister, district education officer and assistant educational officers,[2] peer reviews, biometric attendance, and CCTV cameras in classrooms (Sandhu, 2021). Head teachers and principals have started to behave in a managerial way, accepting the necessity of imposing targets, indicators, and evaluations as a means of making the school system more accountable (Sandhu, 2021).

One of the problems identified by the Annual Status of Education Report (ASER, 2018) is that the traditional teaching style in government schools has been teacher-centred rote learning. Since 2005 India has been endeavouring to make a paradigm shift from teacher-centred to child-centred classrooms, through reform efforts such as the SSA, the NCF (2005), and the RTE. The RTE Act's guidelines state that 'learning [ought to take place] through activities, discovery and exploration in a child friendly and child-centred manner' (GoI, 2009, p.9). SSA spent almost US$400 million between 2001 and 2010 to provide 20 days of annual in-service training for government teachers across India (GoI, 2010). However, the teacher training programmes in India have not had the anticipated impact owing to the quality of the training itself, the training methodology, which ignores practical constraints faced in the classroom, and the lack of systemic alignment around child-centred education. These in-service training sessions are based

---

[1] In terms of the corporate culture of monitoring and surveillance, these low-cost options have been critiqued by Nambissan and Ball (2010) for their wide-ranging repercussions on teaching and learning, with the state pointing a finger at the lack of teachers' quality and professionalism.

[2] As representatives of the Department of Education, district education officers are external supervisors for primary and secondary schools. Their responsibilities include regular inspection of schools, checking building maintenance, ensuring adequate supplies are available, writing annual district reports, assigning posts to secondary teachers, and appointing primary teachers, and helping the Director of the Bureau of Curriculum and Extension with in-service teacher training programmes (Singh et al, 2020).

on the Euro-Western model and do not acquaint teachers with contextual classroom experience, thereby creating a dissonance between preparation and actual practice (Gupta, 2020). Such programmes thus tend to train teachers to work in a system in which education is seen as merely the transmission of 'market-worthy information', and has nothing to do with realizing the 'constitutional ideals of democracy, equality, and social justice' (Singh, 2013, p.48). For Tabulawa (2003, p.9), the initiative among international agencies and developing countries to encourage and integrate a child-centred approach (CCA) is by no means 'value free'. There are political, social, and economic gains that have meaningfully influenced this international 'push' (Windschitl, 2002; Tabulawa, 2003; Smail, 2014). The value-laden nature of child-centred pedagogies inevitably reflects the norms of the Western capitalist systems in which they arose (Windschitl, 2002; Tabulawa, 2003). The application of CCA in India has led to reduced rather than increased teacher autonomy (Smail, 2014), a counter-intuitive but real result of education reforms, further discussed later in the chapter.

The twin policies of neoliberalism that are relevant for India's education sector are managerialism and so-called bean counting.[3] Managerialism can be evidenced through the curb on teacher autonomy and agency in Indian classrooms. For instance, Sriprakash (2012) emphasizes the low status of teachers and the lack of teacher autonomy, which makes CCA difficult to implement. Their autonomy is undermined by increasing managerial regulation of their work – accountability and surveillance being products of neoliberalism (Sriprakash, 2012). Since the quality of education is constructed through 'managerial interests in the efficient measurability of outcomes', teachers struggle with the expectation that they will implement child-centred practices within a competitive managerial system (Sriprakash, 2012, p.51). Under these bureaucratic structures of monitoring and assessment, teachers follow techno-managerial and instrumental norms of teaching and learning that are ultimately focused on performance (Sriprakash, 2012); this fosters a bean-counting culture in classrooms that detracts from teacher autonomy and their ability to implement CCA. The politicization of CCA in turn supports the neoliberal trajectory (Smail, 2014).

A study conducted by Singh et al (2019) has revealed that in-service teacher training programmes are fraught with problems at all levels, whether related to policy, planning, implementation, or follow up. A major problem that was identified is that teacher educators, key resource people, and subject matter experts neglect the knowledge, attitude, and beliefs of teachers themselves,

---

[3]   'Bean counting is the consequence of a view of the world as consisting of things to be manipulated, rather than people to be interacted with and conversed with and responded to' (Denning, 2011, para.6). It can threaten thoughtful and well-informed teaching.

thereby disregarding the purpose of training (Dyer et al, 2004; Kidwai et al, 2013; Batra, 2014). Teachers perceive administrative aspects of their work such as documentation, testing, and reporting as taking precedence over pedagogic ones. In Delhi, teachers are obliged to spend about a third of their time on administrative tasks. This 'paper tyranny' means teachers spend more time on paperwork than they do on planning lessons (Anand and Lall, forthcoming 2022). Teachers say they feel like clerks, and this has become worse since the introduction of CCA. Teachers' non-academic administrative tasks thus take precedence over academic duties (Chandran, 2021). A core principle of CCA – teacher autonomy (Nawani, 2013; Kumar, 2019; Chandran, 2021) – has been conspicuously absent from the teacher discourse, including in the conversations underlying this volume. Officials who are overseeing CCA remain steadfast in the belief that completing documentation is more important than spending time on educational processes or challenges (Anand and Lall, 2022).

The neoliberal reforms have also used accountability and efficiency as a reason to introduce para-teachers, or contractual teachers, to try and improve matters. The decentralization of teacher appointments and contractualization helps to curb teachers' resistance to change (Manjrekar, 2013). The recruitment of para-teachers within the government school system and an attitude of resignation towards pre-service programmes have become essential parts of state provisioning for elementary education (Pandey, 2006, cited in Kingdon and Sipahimalani-Rao, 2010, p.60). The rationale for the appointment of contract teachers ranges from cost-effectiveness (Kingdon, 2007; Kingdon and Sipahimalani-Rao, 2010) to increasing access to education in remote and under-served areas (Govinda and Josephine, 2004; Robinson and Gauri, 2010). Though the role of contract teachers is not restricted to isolated villages, an overwhelmingly large proportion of them are assigned to remote locations, where the population is geographically and often socially marginalized (Sandhu, 2021). Their appointment has also been actively supported by international agencies, primarily the World Bank, as a key reform that is intended to make teachers more accountable (Bruns et al, 2011). Proponents of contract teachers, notable policymakers, argue that their wide-scale appointment has played a critical role in the expansion of access to education, contributing to a reduction in high pupil–teacher ratios and the number of single-teacher schools, at an affordable cost (Kingdon and Sipahimalani-Rao, 2010). However, while contract teachers have contributed to increasing school enrolments, the negative consequences for the quality of the education provided are numerous, and studies point to the equity implications of deploying contract teachers (Kingdon and Muzammil, 2013; Pandey, 2006). Opponents of contract teachers (notably teacher unions and a growing number of academics) argue that a lack of qualifications and/ or professional training among contract teachers who are not supported in school environments may sustain the low quality of teaching in government schools (Kingdon and Muzammil, 2013).

Some scholars (see Muralidharan and Sundararaman, 2013; Atherton and Kingdon, 2010; Duflo et al, 2012) advocate for contract teachers as a means of increasing accountability, but most of them disregard other crucial factors for education quality and learning outcomes, such as pedagogical methods, time spent teaching, class size, adequate teaching materials, and the socio-economic backgrounds of students. A lack of formal training, combined with multigrade teaching and poor material conditions, makes it extremely difficult for contract teachers to offer adequate education, and the result is often rote-learning, a practice they have often experienced in school themselves (Verger et al, 2013) and which is contrary to the national efforts to instil more child-centric learning and teaching across the country. As a result, communities such as SCs, STs, OBCs, Muslims, and families below the poverty line experience marginalization within the education system owing to the intersectionality of their economic and cultural identities.[4] A succession of policies and programmes have been conceived to make education accessible to all sections of society, but owing to patriarchal practices, urban–rural biases, social stratifications such as caste and religion, bureaucratic corruption, and lack of contextual knowledge, these programmes have had little success on the ground (Gowda, 2020). One solution straight out of the neoliberal rule book that has been propagated to reduce inequalities has been an increased involvement of the private sector in public education. The following section outlines the interventions led by PPPs and NGOs, and their involvement in government schools.

PPPs as a solution

The Right of Children to Free and Compulsory Education Act, 2009 called on the private sector to collaborate with the government in delivering a quality education that increases learning outcomes, equity, and social cohesion (RTE Act, 2009). In its Twelfth Five Year Plan (2012–2017), the

---

[4]   Fraser (1998) identifies two forms of social exclusion – economic and sociocultural. Economic exclusion results from 'economic injustices such as marginalization, exploitation, and deprivation' (p.102). Sociocultural exclusion is 'manifested as dominant groups make certain groups invisible within the dominant discourse, seeking to impose dominant values, or consistently devaluing certain categories of people' (p.102). This concept is particularly applicable to the Indian education system, where sociocultural exclusion persists (Ramachandran, 2009; Govinda, 2014). Economic inequities interlock with other forms of sociocultural inequity, notably caste, gender, linguistic origins, ethnicity, religion, and geographical location, with children from SCs, STs, OBCs, and Muslim minorities in particular constituting a large portion of the marginalized population.

GoI called upon private actors to increasingly engage in education provision for children from Economically Weaker Sections (EWSs) and Disadvantaged Groups (DGs) through PPPs.[5] A key strategy proposed by the Planning Commission to increase private participation in education delivery is 'easing the regulatory restrictions' (Planning Commission, 2013, p. 64). However, critics argue that rather than establishing a robust public education system that nurtures and fosters social inclusion, equity, and cohesion, the government has failed to fulfil its obligation to provide the right to education through PPPs (Dahal and Nguyen, 2014; Harma and Rose, 2012; Nambissan, 2014). Instead of investing resources and expertise to improve the public education system, which is over-represented by children from EWSs and DGs, the government has adopted a neoliberal approach that is at best described as segmented. The privatization of education leads to socioeconomic inequities, segmentation, and the stigmatization of EWSs and DGs. Children are often discriminated against in the classroom based on their caste, gender, and minority status (this will be discussed further in the section on private schools) (Nambissan, 2013; Verger et al, 2016; Kamat et al, 2018). In the Tenth Five Year Plan (2002–2007) the government encouraged the private sector to contribute towards improving quality and access to education by expanding their role in education delivery, improving the functioning of government schools through PPPs, increasing enrolment opportunities for marginalized groups in private schools, reducing regulations for private schools without compromising on quality, and harnessing the expertise of the private sector to make students e-literate (Planning Commission, 2002). PPPs in India include the target that all private schools will reserve 25 per cent of their seats for children from EWSs and DGs, reflecting the GoI's acceptance of PPPs as a viable alternative for failing public schools.[6] Private schools that enrol students under the PPP model are usually required to meet certain criteria and standards set by the government covering areas such as infrastructure, curriculum, teacher qualifications, student–teacher ratio, school fees, management structures, and student performance letters (Gowda, 2020).[7]

PPPs are increasingly proposed and promoted as a solution for government schools that are failing owing to deficiencies in educational quality, shortage

---

[5]   EWS and DG are official terminology used by the GoI.

[6]   Children from EWSs and DGs experience academic alienation and subtle forms of discrimination within the classroom. Gowda's research shows that differentiated teaching in the form of screening or labelling children from EWSs and DGs increases the negative peer effect and exclusion by peers within the classroom (Gowda, 2020).

[7]   The data about children from EWSs are sent to private schools. The government instructs these schools to admit children from this category, and then pays the private schools for all admissions.

of resources, and inefficient use of those resources (Mundy and Menashy, 2012; Muralidharan and Sundararaman, 2015; Verger et al, 2016). As developmental scholars and international organizations explore and test various policy alternatives and programmes, PPPs have emerged as a key government strategy in reducing educational and social inequities (Nambissan and Ball, 2010; Verger, 2012; Verger et al, 2018; Ashley et al, 2014; Menashy, 2016; Gowda, 2020).

This is not a problem in India alone. Globally, PPPs are encouraged as a policy alternative in the delivery of education services to meet the twin challenges of increasing access to education and improving learning outcomes. This, coupled with financial constraints and shrinking education budgets around the world, has resulted in the emergence of private or non-state actors either as a viable alternative or as a contributor to public education (Patrinos et al, 2009; Draxler, 2012; Ginsburg, 2012; Menashy, 2016; Verger et al, 2016). One of the most contentious issues that elicit heated debates in the field of international and comparative education is the role of private actors in the provision of educational services using public money. This is because PPPs in India are problematic: the government has proposed solutions to support private-aided schools that charge fees, as the RTE Act states that students should receive education free of charge (Mohanty, 2018). Despite growing research that suggests the contrary, the neoliberal positioning of PPPs as the best mechanism for achieving educational rights, something that is enshrined in international declarations and national constitutions, continues to be perpetuated. The global push toward achieving universal quality education as outlined in Education for All and the Millennium Development Goals has made India a focus of great attention owing to group-based inequities in educational inputs and outcomes (Ramachandran, 2009; Govinda, 2014; Hill, 2015; Gurney, 2017). Despite the sweeping expansion of the public education system over the past 25 years, government schools remain underfunded, underequipped, and understaffed. The international development community led by the World Bank and its various partner organizations has therefore identified PPPs as a positive step towards addressing these shortcomings (Verger and Vanderkaiij, 2012; Govinda, 2014; Nambissan, 2014).

Proponents of PPPs argue that partnerships with private providers improve the quality of education through choice and competition, increase access to schools for children who previously never attended for a variety of reasons, improve equity and social inclusion, and provide a cost-effective model for delivering better quality education at lower rates (Patrinos et al, 2009; Barrera-Osorio et al, 2012; Tooley and Longfield, 2015; Mond and Prakash, 2019). However, critics argue that PPPs are the first step towards the privatization of education and reflect the neoliberal agenda that is promoted by market forces, interested in increasing profits for private actors while simultaneously reducing the role of the state. PPPs lead to further stratification of the education system and weaken it as more students exit (Ball, 2009; Nambissan and Ball, 2010; Kamat, 2011; Menashy, 2016; Verger et al, 2016; Kamat et al, 2018). Despite contradictory empirical evidence on the significance of private participation in education provision, school choice advocates in India have been successful in creating a social and policy environment that favours PPPs in management and delivery (Harma and Rose, 2012; Muralidharan and Sundararaman, 2015; Verger et al, 2016; Verger et al, 2018).

Beyond the 25 per cent compulsory enrolment in private schools, PPPs take on various forms of service delivery in private and government schools. Outsourcing of non-curricular support services includes non-instructional activities, school maintenance, student transportation, school meals, budget and financial management, human resources, and information technology (IT) services. Some examples include the Mid-day Meal Scheme,[8] and the Adopt a School programme.[9] Organizations and foundations supporting Adopt a School include the Bharti Foundation, the Varkey Foundation, the Sir Ratan Tata Trust, Care India, the Azim Premji Foundation, and Pratham (Srivastava et al, 2014; Kamat et al, 2018). In addition, infrastructure PPPs have a variety of arrangements in which the private sector is tasked with initiatives such as Build–Own–Operate–Transfer, Build–Operate–Transfer, and Design–Build–Finance–Operate (Gowda, 2020). While the private sector invests in the infrastructure in all cases, delivery of other educational services such as teaching, education supplies, staff recruitment, and so on are dependent on the terms of the contract (Gowda, 2020).[10] In many cases, the private partners use their networks and expertise to help in establishing and operating science and computer labs in under-equipped public schools. Examples include the Bridge International Academies involved in the improvement, construction, and maintenance of public schools in the south-eastern state of Andhra Pradesh. Edureach, a programme of Educomp (n.d.a, n.d.b), has partnerships with more than 13,000 schools in 23 states, and helps to establish computer labs, computer technology instruction, and the assessment of learning skills using computer-based activities. Organizations engaged in this partnership include Intel, Microsoft, and the Azim Premji and Infosys Foundations (Gowda, 2020).

---

[8]   School meal programmes funded by the Akshaya Patra Foundation.

[9]   A PPP extending pedagogical services related to curriculum development, teacher training, provision of teaching material, and learning enhancement for students through technology.

[10] During the period of the contract, the private partner is reimbursed by the state based on performance outputs. This model also includes leasing public school buildings to private operators. Leasing schools to NGOs, businesses, and others provides government schools with much-needed financial and human resources (Gowda, 2020).

In addition, demand-side financing PPPs include a publicly funded voucher, scholarships, stipends, and tax credits for students to attend private schools (Languille, 2017). State and non-state actors participate in the education partnership by financing vouchers and stipends so students can attend a private school of their choice.[11] Voucher programmes are different from education service delivery partnerships, as a payment follows the student rather than being directly provided to a school (Languille, 2017). One such programme is the Andhra Pradesh School Choice Project – a partnership between the Government of Andhra Pradesh and the Azim Premji Foundation, funded by the World Bank. The voucher covers all expenses related to school fees, textbooks or workbooks, stationery, uniforms, shoes, and transportation costs (Muralidharan and Sundararaman, 2015).

PPPs have become part of India's education landscape, with clear support from the ruling BJP. An instance of this can be determined from PM Modi's national address in 2018, in which he took the opportunity to draw attention to exam scores and education by praising the efforts of a poor tea stall owner from a Delhi slum who ran and largely funded a low-fee, private-aided school for poor children (Mohanty, 2018, p.4). This story served to promote these schools, to criticize government-administered government schools, and to skirt the government's constitutional obligation to provide open access, quality, and free education to all students (Boucher, 2020). Following the RTE Act of 2009 discussed earlier, spending on education across states increased to address the constitutional mandate, but since 2016 there has been a drop in educational spending and funding in every Indian state. This corresponds with the rise in private-aided schools, which central and state governments have increasingly subsidized (Kumar, 2019).

The neoliberal approach of NGOs

Non-government involvement in education not only includes the private sector but also NGOs, which focus on improving access to schooling and building a more 'convivial teaching–learning environment', in particular through teacher training (Batra, 2009, p.12). Given the criticism of school quality and teaching practice, teacher training came to be seen as an important variable in improving school quality (Subramaniam, 2019). The government and corporates began to focus their attention on and channel their resources into those NGOs that offered innovative teaching practices that could be scaled up and implemented across the whole school system

---

[11] LaRocque (2008) defines vouchers as a 'certificate or entitlement that parents can use to pay for the education of their children at a public or private school of their choice' (p.22).

(Dasra Report, 2010). Among the wide range of NGOs working in teacher training, a select segment that is largely supported by prominent corporates has been gaining considerable importance in education policymaking circles (Srivastava, 2016).[12] Reflecting India's neoliberal education policies, NGOs employ a managerialist approach in which the teacher is envisioned as a technician imparting literacy and numeracy skills. Teaching is framed within an input–output model, with particular teaching practices needed to produce the desired results, which can be regarded as in opposition to CCA's core principles of participatory and collaborative teaching (Dasra Report, 2010). These NGOs, which are finding an increasing voice and considerable validation in PPP discussions, are keen to promote the neoliberal principles of competition, choice, and efficiency through their interventions. They operate in certain sections of the government school system as well as advocating low-cost private schools as better alternatives for the poor (Subramaniam, 2019).

Menon's work in Delhi (2014) reflects on one such organization, Teach for India (TFI), in which she finds that teachers as well as professional teacher education have become redundant. The TFI programme is a PPP-based intervention working with under-resourced government schools and in low-cost private schools across the country. Like its American counterpart, the Indian programme has similar ideas about reform, and recruits college graduates and young professionals to serve as teachers as part of a two-year fellowship (Subramanian, 2018). Through this, it seeks to address educational inequities among children from low-income and marginalized communities. TFI is also instrumental in facilitating support for poorly functioning government schools in various cities (Subramanian, 2018). The NGOs that have been set up by TFI alumni and associated members focus on providing techno-managerial support to different parts of the school system, specifically by training principals and teachers and introducing better mechanisms of student assessment. The increasing demand for English medium oriented classrooms among the low socio-economic disadvantaged families has also reinstated tuition in English as an aspect of improving school quality (Milligan and Tikly, 2016). TFI has established a skill-based English curriculum for both professional teachers, as well as teacher education (Subramaniam, 2019). According to Subramanian (2019), TFI has 'increased the administrative responsibilities of government teachers

---

[12] The most prominent among them are the Mahindra Group (K.C. Mahindra and Anand Mahindra), Thermax Industries, the Central Square Foundation (CSF, n.d.), the Michael and Susan Dell Foundation, and the Bill and Melinda Gates Foundation. A few NGOs such as the Akanksha Foundation, Pratham, and Door Step School also received funding from the Mumbai and Pune municipal corporations (Subramanian, 2018).

further and relegated them to being regional language teachers for the TFI-led English medium sections' (p.7). Although there is autonomy delegated to TFI fellows when they engage with students, this has led to 'class-based tensions between fellows and government teachers, exacerbated material inequities and reinforced the symbolic power of English within school sites where government teachers themselves had poor pedagogical support' (Erling et al, 2016, cited in Subramanian, 2019, p.16).

TFI is not the only prominent NGO active in government schools. The Delhi education reforms ongoing since 2015 provide an example. Prior to the AAP-led government in Delhi, government schools were criticized for being poor quality in comparison with private schools. At the time the state government was diluting quality by substituting professional teachers with para-teachers. After getting into power, AAP has focused on teacher capacity-building and mentoring programmes, although still relying heavily on NGOs such as Pratham and CREATnet, among others (Anand and Lall, forthcoming 2022). The involvement of NGOs in schools in Delhi has created a 'new bureaucratic field' that highlights 'flexible organisation and efficiency' in place of the 'traditional bureaucratic proceduralism' typical of state systems (Qureshi, 2015; Subramanian, 2019). These procedures have established corresponding organisations of governance, and fragmented teaching and learning, as well as weakening the position of government school teachers (Anand and Lall, forthcoming 2022).

The rise of NGOs' influence in teacher education appears to be directly linked to the politics of neoliberalism and the complex forms of cultural hegemony that have been used to secure consent for the increasingly uneven distribution of power and wealth across the globe (Bourdieu, 1998; Giroux, 2004; Harvey, 2005, 2006; Finnegan, 2008). The following paragraphs review how this neoliberal trajectory has also allowed the Hindu nationalist discourse to be embedded in schools.

Teachers' realities on the ground

In the neoliberal context, a teacher is identified as a provider of services and the student as a consumer (Manjrekar, 2013). Osgood (2006) remarks that within neoliberalism, the discourse of professionalism is upheld, although the government reduces the meaning of professionalism to mean simply 'an outcome-focused approach to teaching' (Duhn, 2010, p.49), with little if any room at all for teachers to resist this viewpoint. Consequently, and as a result of the involvement of the private and NGO sectors, teacher autonomy in government schools has reduced starkly (Ramachandran et al, 2008, p.5; Sriprakash, 2009; Smail, 2014). Teaching is rooted in 'school and bureaucratic cultures' (Sriprakash, 2009, p.304), which govern teachers' perceptions of autonomy in the classroom and control the conditions in which they teach. Tensions have emerged for many teachers between achieving the 'pedagogic ideal' and 'the culture of schooling', contributing to their uncertainty as to how autonomy should be exercised (Sriprakash, 2009, p.633). A growing body of literature (Batra, 2005, 2009, 2010; Smail, 2014; Gupta, 2020) suggests that CCA has been reduced to a prescriptive methodology. Even if government school teachers are willing to implement it in the classroom, the lack of freedom, accountability, and bureaucracy act as a barrier (Ramchandran et al, 2008; Padwad and Dixit, 2018). As a result of neoliberal policies, teachers show increasing disempowerment and practise with low agency (Mukhopadhyay and Sriprakash, 2011), because the dominant bureaucratic mechanisms leave them muted in any instrumental discourse (Mehta et al, 2010; Mukhopadhyay and Sriprakash, 2011). Batra (2010, p.8) further claims that disempowering the teacher is an attempt to continue a system 'largely immune to interrogation and challenge' and to reinforce 'a neoliberal frame within which teachers' work and worth is being viewed and judged' (Batra, 2010, p.26). This increase in accountability also leads to a culture of performativity, where tensions between professional commitments and beliefs and the imperative to meet performative requirements affect teachers' subjectivities, causing a lack of creativity, professional integrity, and fun in both teaching and learning. NGO and private sector involvement across the school sector seems to have reinforced this new culture. In Delhi, teachers stated that there was a policy that they have to teach every student, check their books, conduct a weekly test, record their attendance, and find out reasons for any absenteeism. There is evidence to suggest that many teachers have reacted to these bureaucratic pressures by increasing performativity in schools, which compromises their professional autonomy (Anand and Lall, forthcoming 2022). Bureaucratically burdened teachers are also less likely to critically engage with changes to the curriculum and how they affect students.

As discussed in Chapter 2, alongside the neoliberal frame, the Modi government has placed party people in jobs and government organizations that mould curricula, and they are beginning to get results. Many teachers who were interviewed for this book expressed support for the Hindutva inspired changes. Some government school mathematics teachers from Delhi shared that they are teaching 'Vedic maths',[13] named after the Rig Veda, the Hindu scripture upon which the discipline is based. Teachers explained that this helps to instil pride among Indians of all faiths in the classroom and helps to unify the country based on Hindu values. Hindu and Sanskrit government school teachers shared that their head teacher was urging them to teach the

---

[13] Vedic math holds that calculus problems can be solved with the help of sutras, or Hindu religious precepts (Bellman, 2002).

Hindi language through Hindu scriptures and Sanskrit via mantras. A Hindi teacher shared that before the pandemic she used to sketch a swastika on the blackboard. She added that this Hindu symbol of prosperity always brought positive energy to the classroom. When asked about how they teach students of diverse backgrounds or faith, government school teachers in Delhi mentioned that Muslim students were 'not loyal to India, they have loyalties to Pakistan' (Anand, forthcoming 2023). A few teachers stated that they were not worried about the deletion of topics such as secularism and democracy from the textbooks; they were more concerned about the lack of Hindu leaders in these books. Field trips to these government schools showed that portraits of Hindu heroes and goddesses hang on the walls. These images have become an important component of the visual curriculum and culture of every school, as they illustrate patriotic martyrdom and pride. In Chandigarh, government school teachers also emphasized the importance of 'Indian values'. A teacher shared that 'a government official comes to my school and teaches our students on the Indian values such as Ramayana, mantras ... They are very important which has recently started' (GS2 Chandigarh). Another teacher echoed similar experiences: 'every morning I switch on recorded audio files of Modiji on yogas and mantras ... we spend one hour daily on this. This is our sanskriti' (GS7 Chandigarh). These quotes illustrate teachers' world views and the increasing support for Hindutva discourses in the classroom. Schools are sites of hegemony wherein students and teachers practise the dissemination of 'common-sense ideas' on a par with important mainstream political messages. Those who disagree are likely to suppress their opinions in public for fear of being labelled as anti-national.[14] This is akin to Gramsci's notion of the new normal; abstract notions become factual, with the teacher's consciousness later becoming a part of their students' 'common sense' (Gramsci, 1971).

Teachers also follow new guidelines because they accept individual responsibility for children's learning and assessment outcomes. This then becomes a form of performative capital to be accumulated, signifying the 'good' teacher who is contributing their commitment to the classroom (Pratt, 2018). Within these models, teacher professionalism becomes more instrumental and 'technicist', and quasi-managerial roles are created (Jeffrey and Troman, 2004; Garland and Garland, 2012; Hoyle and Wallace, 2014). Sachs (2016) asserts that the current focus on regulation is fixated on compliance, and that accountability has the negative effect of restricting the enacted curriculum, as teachers increasingly use their time to teach

---

[14] A few teachers mentioned that there was pressure to 'impress government officials' when they visited, and that they had to follow the instructions of their head teacher no matter what their personal opinion was.

to the test. In terms of internal control, Delhi schools have cameras in the classrooms and hallways, this having become a common surveillance practice. The teachers explained that head teachers justified the use of cameras as a protective measure to avoid violence carried out by students against teachers and peers, but some teachers experienced the use of cameras in classrooms as a form of internal control. Teachers feel that they don't have pedagogical freedom, and are left struggling for control over teaching practices (Anand and Lall, forthcoming 2022).

This section has showed how the neoliberal agenda has diluted teachers' identity and agency. Teachers are expected to conform to prescribed performance criteria, and the narrowing of the curriculum and constraints on their pedagogical choices limit their autonomy in the classroom (Sachs, 2005). This in turn has supported the wider unquestioning acceptance of the Hindutva-inspired curriculum and textbook content, with few if any teachers critical of the changes. The next section outlines how the private sector has increased access, but has also changed the relationship between India's middle-class society and the state, forever altering the Nehruvian social contract and embedding a neoliberal outlook that is part and parcel of the BJP's economic and political discourse.

Private schools

The deterioration in the quality of public schooling in many economically developing countries has resulted in increased private provision (De et al, 2002; Tooley and Dixon, 2005; Glick and Sahn, 2006). Especially striking is that increasing marketization and privatization are not limited to changes in schooling provision for middle or elite classes, but in an increasing number of countries they are leading to the emergence of private schools for lower income groups (Alderman et al, 2001; Bangay, 2005; Tooley and Dixon, 2007). Within the context of private schools, the purpose of this section is twofold. First, it briefly revisits the previously discussed arguments on the rise of private schools and demand for 'quality' education and the neoliberal agenda of school choice (as reviewed in Chapter 1 and the previous section of this chapter). Secondly, it presents the impact of the neoliberal trajectory on teachers in private institutions. Thirdly, it discusses the impact of the neoliberal agenda on teacher agency to critically counter textbooks and government rituals to serve the Hindutva agenda. Even though private school teachers recognized the dangers of the new textbooks, the school system in which they operate left them with no options.

Chapter 1 discussed how private provision came to the rescue of the learning deficit during the post-reform period. Contemporary India is characterized by the fast growth of private schools owing to increases in quality, demand, and school choice, particularly during the last quarter-century (Tooley and Dixon, 2007; Nambissan, 2012; Wolf et al, 2015; Sahoo, 2017; Dixon, et al, 2019; Choudhury, 2019). The promise of school choice, quality, accountability, and cost efficiency has led to large numbers of students from low-income families and the lower middle-class abandoning the government schools in favour of private schools. When public investment in state education decreased (Srivastava, 2013), leading to a decline in quality of education, more and more people opted for private education for their children (Lall, 2012). Today private low-budget and expensive for-profit schools in education provide people of all classes access to educational opportunities for their children. As discussed in Chapter 1, the growth of wealthier middle classes resulted in the need for reforms in education, and thus an alternative private education system was established, serving diverse strata of people according to their affordability, changing the role of state responsibility for access to and quality of education.

Educational development across many developing countries indicates the considerable growth of low-fee private schools, particularly in hitherto under-served contexts (Barrera-Osorio and Raju, 2015; Edwards et al, 2017). These have considerably expanded the network of elementary educational institutions in diverse contexts (Jain and Dholakia, 2010; Mousumi and Kusakabe, 2019). Multiple research studies have been conducted to examine the increase in private sector engagement in education delivery across India, particularly through low-fee private schools. Looking at school choice theory in the context of Asian and African countries, Tooley has critiqued state-sponsored schooling, and has argued that government schools fail to ensure quality either in educational standards or in developing the ideal ecology of knowledge (Tooley, 2001, 2003, 2009). He goes on to argue that working-class children are the worst victims of government schools, and advocates for the privatization of education as the only solution to the crisis in government education. According to Tooley, private schools widened the scope for school choice for the poor parent, which was historically a privilege enjoyed by only upper- and middle-class parents across developed and developing countries.

Besides choice, increasing demand for quality education is found to be a major driver in the demand for private schools (Kingdon, 1996, 2007; Tilak and Sudarshan, 2001; Muralidharan and Kremer, 2009; Chudgar and Quin, 2012; Srivastava, 2014; Muralidharan and Sundararaman, 2015; Narwana, 2019; Sahoo, 2017). It is widely accepted (but not necessarily correct) that students enrolled in private schools learn better than their counterparts in government schools, and this learning gap is often referred to as the private school premium (Chudgar and Quin, 2012; Muralidharan and Sundararaman, 2013; Singh, 2013, 2018; Kumar, 2019). This argument is not new: in the early 1990s Govinda et al (2012) observed that in the central Indian state of Madhya Pradesh achievement levels of primary school students in private schools were considerably higher than those studying in either aided or government schools. More recently Muralidharan and Sundararaman (2015) have found that children who accessed private schools performed better than those who attended government schools. This was true even after controlling for differences in family background and school inputs. Using a randomized-control trial, Dixon et al (2019) found that a voucher-based school choice programme in Delhi had a substantial positive impact on student test scores in English in a slum area. However, Srivastava's research (2013, 2016) shows that other low-fee private schools marked tests 'leniently' and kept 'high promotion rates' even if students were found not to be achieving. Srivastava (2016, p.14) explains that the low-fee private schools did this because 'high pass marks' and 'promotions' were how parents evaluated the 'quality' of a private school. Private schools are largely organized as businesses – despite the requirement of being not for profit organizations. Schools are allowed to have surplus funds, and their buildings and facilities can be owned by businesses (Haq, 2004). The incentive to retain and expand their client base is high since funding is primarily from tuition and school fees.

These schools keep their costs low by hiring unqualified, low-paid teachers on short term contracts (Srivastava, 2013) and by operating with substandard infrastructure (Chattopadhay and Roy, 2017). Srivastava (2013) found in her research that hiring untrained teachers was contrary to official regulations, but private school owners claimed that it didn't affect the teaching because they could be easily dismissed, unlike in the government sector. Besides teachers, these schools also had fixed daily timetables, longer school hours, minimal closures, and few holidays, in order to compare favourably with government schools. They also enforced regular teacher attendance (Srivastava, 2016, para.2). Although parents are attracted to these schools because they offer English medium education (unlike government schools, which more often teach in the state vernacular), the level of English proficiency among teachers is often poor (Chattopadhay and Roy, 2017). Srivastava's research (2013) also shows the quality of English language instruction was low because of teachers' lack of fluency. Private school owners admitted that they could not hire more qualified English teachers because it would mean paying higher salaries (Srivastava, 2013).

Private schools in India, both elite and low-fee schools, have been the subject of extensive criticism. High-fee private schools face criticism for operating as elite 'avenues of sponsored mobility' to exclusive HE institutions and well-paid employment, reproducing social hierarchies and exacerbating social segregation (Kumar, 2001, p.52). In contrast, low-fee private schools promote themselves as champions of the poor and promise social mobility to low-income families. But these claims are questionable, as in many cases both the input factors and the outcomes for students are below par (Chattopadhay and Roy, 2017). Lafleur and Srivastava's research (2020) in Delhi shows that children from EWSs and DGs admitted experiencing labelling and stigmatization in private schools they were enrolled in. A number of studies have explored different aspects of education policy processes, quality outcomes, social inclusion, advocacy networks, and the motivations of private providers, and have uncovered problems with private school claims, such as the role of transnational advocacy networks in influencing education policies and programmes, which counters the claims that low fee private schools act as forms of social enterprise (Nambissan and Ball, 2010; Srivastava, 2016; Kamat et al, 2018).

Private education has resulted in a new breed of schools that cater to different communities, classes, and castes, perpetuating rather than negotiating differences (Sarangapani, 2009). This section has indicated that the private sector has been reinforcing economic and social inequalities and weakening the support of public schooling by the more privileged (Nambissan, 2012). Teachers' voices quoted below indicate the realities on the ground thanks to the impact of the neoliberal trajectory in private schools, and the impact of this agenda on their agency to critically counter textbooks and government rituals that serve the Hindutva agenda.

In terms of neoliberalism, private school teachers described their schools as 'business institutions' and themselves as accountable for the relationship with parents, student achievement, and the overall experiences of stakeholders in the private schools. One teacher described her situation as follows:

> 'They [head teachers] expect the teacher to make them responsible for everything ... because private schools run like business institutions, and they keep their teachers responsible for every failure, every mistake ... so parents want to hold someone responsible for the failure of their kids ... Being business institutions or schools, there are of course teaching facilities always...' (PS1 Chandigarh)

One teacher drew a contrast between private- and government school teachers around accountability and performance: 'most of the government school teachers are taking salaries, but they are not working according to the salaries, as compared to private school teachers and facilities we provide to the students. ... And right now, also from home, we are taking classes also' (PS8 Delhi).[15] She elaborated on the rules and regulations (such as 'filling performance sheets' and 'keeping records of students and their parents') set by her head teacher, continuing:

---

[15] Interviews were conducted during the COVID-19 pandemic when much teaching and learning was home-based.

'In the morning we are having the classes ... we are having proper assembly we are having, proper discipline, the proper national anthem will be there. And then we will start with our classes. And one more thing is their parents are also happy with this private institute because of our performance and reliability.' (PS8 Delhi)

These teacher voices imply the presence of managerialism, in particular the oversight by head teachers, which is characterized by bureaucratic culture and intensive accountability.

As far as the impact of the government textbooks on private schools is concerned, a history teacher shared her thoughts:

'My principal who used to teach history herself, she is annoyed with the history curriculum now [because of insufficient coverage of Hindu leaders], I agree with her, we should teach student our own history, we shouldn't teach them about foreigners ruling over us. There are certain topics on the victories of Hindu leaders that can be added... The entire pattern of the political science needs to be more elaborate. We have a few people from the government office [Modi] recently visited us...' (PS6 Delhi)

When probed on visit by government officials, teachers said, 'They used to come as guest teachers; before the pandemic, they used to take lessons on victory of the BJP and why Modiji is a great leader...' (PS6 Delhi). Another teacher painted a picture of her classroom:

'A government member came to my class before the lockdown. He taught us about Hindi scriptures and the importance of Sanskrit language. Me and my students really enjoyed. We learned a lot. I am so happy that the Sanskrit language is getting popular. I saw many students joining my classes. I think the government is helping us.' (PS9 Delhi)

Teachers mentioned that when they went for their job evaluation meetings, their head teachers asked them to include the examples of Narendra Modi and Amit Shah. This shows that certain head teachers and teachers are supporting the Hindutva agenda in the classroom. Even government officials as guest teachers are spreading the Hindutva agenda by regularly visiting schools and participating in classroom discussions.

However, there were also teachers who criticized the 'narrow', 'sectarian', and 'unscientific' nature of their textbooks, and made efforts to reduce the damage to students by promoting critical thinking. A teacher explained that before the pandemic he started sharing items of news and knowledge and modified prayers to go beyond the overtly religious Saraswati Vandana such as mantras. On critical thinking, a primary school teacher said: 'I ask students to ask questions and challenge their textbook […] I tell students to respect all animals not just the gaumata [cow]. I also tell them to respect all religions – one is not above others' (PS10 Delhi). When asked why he had not discussed such concerns with the head teacher, this teacher replied: 'I tried to convey my feeling in the meeting about how the Modi government is interfering in my classroom discourses by sending officials to observe while teaching. But other [senior] teachers started saying that I am overreacting and playing politics' (PS7 Delhi). Another teacher echoed similar concerns:

'[T]here are problems with the textbooks, I remain quiet to avoid conflicts with the head teacher and parents. Parents could complain if I say anything against the stereotypes of Hindu culture [such as the cow]. In the past [2017], I said to my students that sati [a former practice in India whereby a widow threw herself on to her husband's funeral pyre] is wrong and this practise broke the law, someone's parents complained to the principal, I can't say anything because they [parents and their children are my clients.' (PS3 Delhi)

Similarly to the new textbooks, which reflect a majoritarian world view, there are serious implications for teachers who protest against anti-Muslim prejudice. A few found that Muslim students stopped attending their schools after February 2020 when the Delhi riots occurred.[16] They explained that in February 2020 certain students started instilling hatred and stereotypes in their classrooms. A teacher said: 'a student whispered to the other and said see they [a few Muslim students] are responsible for riots in Delhi' (PS1 Delhi). Another teacher shared: 'After riots, you know students used to come but I think they don't use to like us insisting on Hindu rituals or mantras in the Sanskrit classroom … I can't do anything … I have to do it as it's my job' (PS2 Delhi). In debriefing sessions after the interviews, a few teachers told of their fear of 'being watched by the Modi government', and shared an incident reported in 2021 of a teacher who was summoned by her principal after a video featuring her comments such as 'the BJP is ruining the country' was used during an online class. This video went viral, and the parents immediately complained to the principal that the teacher was 'brainwashing the children with her political views'. Teachers further shared that a few BJP officials were also targeting a teacher for 'political frustrations' and damaging the 'Hindu culture' by 'laughing on [sic] Hindus for voting for the BJP' and 'praying to the Cow'. Students had made short clips of her online classes and showed these to their parents. Teachers thus expressed their fear of 'losing their job'

---

[16] More on this in Chapter 6.

and 'being summoned by their principal and the government', and therefore they chose to bow to the directives of head teachers and the state.

Besides the fear of losing their job, teachers also explained the pressure created by the examinations that underscore the new narrative. Some teachers mentioned that their job is based on performance, as in any corporate office, in this case that of their students. These examinations are completely based on the prescribed school textbooks, which makes covering the syllabus the priority, and on many occasions they avoid contesting the textbooks owing to time constraints. 'If I correct the information, their answers won't match the answers demanded in the board exams. The questions are directly from the textbooks. I don't want my students to score less, so I don't challenge the textbooks' (PS2 Delhi). The teacher elaborated:

'[R]esults of the board examinations – best or worst are clearly reflected in our [teachers] annual progress reports. If the number of students failing or scoring a class is high, I might be served with a notice as parents will complaint or sometimes, they come to school and ask why I am going against the textbook. So I don't contest a lot, just focus on my performance.' (PS2 Delhi)

It is clear that teachers in private schools focus on teaching the syllabus without critical input.

The next section presents the third alternative for school education, and explains the links between the marketization of education and the saffron agenda in India's RSS schools.

RSS-run schools

As most government schools have deteriorated because of inadequate budgets and teachers' absenteeism, and there has been an increasing push towards private education, the RSS has started opening schools in areas where state governments have neglected to provide functioning, viable, and affordable schools, therefore creating an educational vacuum (Andersen and Damle, 2018). These schools challenge secular and scientific history and use state power to control education and suppress alternative points of view. Some parents will choose these schools over government and low-cost private provision because they believe this is the best quality education in their area (Andersen and Damle, 2018). The RSS schools are also attractive to a wider circle of parents because they perform the requisite educational function of producing good exam results, which appeals to aspiring middle-class parents and children in a certificate- and degree-oriented economy in which state schools are suffering from gross neglect and underfunding (Andersen and Damle, 2018). In keeping with Gramsci's idea that the content of education must be seen to be disinterested to become hegemonic (Forgacs, 1988, pp. 313–18), while some such parents may not desire an overtly Hindu education, in the RSS schools the discipline and *sanskars* become a bonus because they are tagged to exam success (Sundar, 2005).[17] This section starts with a brief account of the growth of the RSS schools by placing these within the neoliberal trajectory of school choice and parental preferences. It then shows how Hindutva has been spread using the RSS-drafted textbooks alongside government textbooks. It highlights how the rhetoric around the creation of a 'Hindu Rashtra' (nation) is expanded, translated, and implemented through these schools.

Chapter 1 outlined the establishment of the first Saraswati Shishu Mandir in 1952 in Gorakhpur in Uttar Pradesh (Sundar, 2005). The school was named after the Hindu goddess of learning and knowledge (Saraswati), its name translating as the Saraswati Children's Temple. It was set up at a time when the RSS was struggling to recover from the ban imposed on it by the Congress government after the assassination of Mahatma Gandhi, while at the same time trying to manage disagreements within its own organization (Nair, 2009; Andersen and Damle, 2018). While the educational role of the *shakha* is viewed by the RSS as an effective way of training a future nationalist leadership,[18] its message was, in its view, often drowned out by anti-Hindu messages coming from the universities, the press, the Congress government, and much of the so-called intellectual class (Andersen and Damle, 2018). With a commitment to restore (or 'Indianize', to use its term) Hindu values in the schools of India, the RSS first made a foray into formal education by supporting a private school at Kurukshetra in Haryana before independence in 1946, with the RSS chief Golwalkar taking part in the ground-breaking ceremony (Andersen and Damle, 2018). During the colonial period, the RSS leaders did not seriously consider setting up a separate school system, in large part because of the existence of alternative national schools that were run by individuals and groups with a nationalist outlook acceptable to the RSS. Prominent among such groups was the Arya Samaj (a Hindu reform organization), whose schools incorporated its message of the unity of Hinduism that was found in early Vedic literature (Andersen and Damle, 2018).

In independent India, a planned process of education emerged as an effective and non-controversial way in which the ideology of a Hindu Rashtra could be propagated, while at the same time developing alternative models of education through a network of schools (Sundar, 2005). The RSS realized that education in independent India might revolve around the concepts of democracy, secularism, and socialism, as propagated by Congress, and hence would not be rooted in a national ethos – a fear that they believe has been proven right

---

[17] *Sanskars* translates as values.
[18] The *shakha* is the branch where the work of the RSS takes place.

(Nair, 2009). Gradually the single school in Gorakhpur was extended out of its rented building, and then new schools multiplied, spreading across almost the entire length and breadth of the country and becoming the largest organized RSS-affiliated movement. The primary schools were all called Shishu Mandir (Children's Temple), while the high schools came to be known as Vidya Mandir (Knowledge Temple). They were also known by other names, such as Geeta Vidyalaya and Bharatiya Vidya Niketan, all of which reflected the links with Hindu culture and cultural nationalism (see Chapter 1) (Nair, 2009). The educational mission was founded with the objective of training children to see themselves as protectors of a Hindu nation:

> The child is the centre of all our aspirations. He is the protector of our country, Dharma (religion) and culture. The development of our culture and civilisation is an impact in the development of a child's personality. A child today holds the key for tomorrow. To relate the child with his land and his ancestors is the direct, clear, and unambiguous mandate for education. We have achieved the all-round development of the child through education and sanskar i.e., inculcation of time-honoured values and traditions (*sic*). (Vidya Bharati, cited in Sundar, 2005, p.206)

Following a rapid expansion in the number of schools in the 1960s and 1970s, the RSS in 1978 established a separate affiliate, the Vidya Bharati, to manage its burgeoning network of 700 schools (Andersen and Damle, 2018, p.64). By 1998, it was running 14,000 schools in all areas of the federation, except for some of the north-eastern states and Lakshadweep. By then, the BJP was in power in the north Indian states, possibly contributing to their steady growth (Nair, 2009).[19] As part of its expansion, Vidya Bharati has managed to penetrate some of the remote areas of India, particularly the eastern and north-eastern regions, which were dominated by Christian missionaries, in the mid-1980s through specially designed interventions such as the Haflong and Uprangsu (both in Assam), projects that targeted the local population (Nair, 2009).

Vidya Bharati's 2016 statistical report shows the quick growth in the number of affiliated schools since 1978, noting that it was overseeing more than 13,000 schools with 32,00,000 students and 1,46,000 teachers, making

---

[19] These schools have even been established in states such as Kerala and Tamil Nadu, where neither the RSS nor the BJP has much influence. About 5,000 of the schools, especially in the BJP-dominated states, are recognized by and affiliated to the Central or respective State Board of Secondary Education, so that the children have access to mainstream education (Nair, 2009, p.52).

it the largest non-government school system in India. Besides Vidya Bharati schools, another RSS-affiliated educational group, the Ekal Vidyalaya,[20] established in 1986, has about 15,00,000 students in 54,000 one-teacher, one-school facilities located in remote rural and tribal areas (Andersen and Damle, 2018, p.65). This large number of schools also ensures a large market for textbooks; RSS-affiliated groups have commissioned textbooks on history and ethics for the Shishu Mandirs and other RSS-affiliated schools. Some of these groups, such as Shiksha Sanskriti Utthan Nyas, lobby the MHRD to ensure that textbooks recommended to the states include some with a value orientation they consider appropriate (Andersen and Damle, 2018). The RSS and its educational affiliates review their own performance four times a year, with new initiatives being proposed to make their schools more relevant to India's changing needs. A case in point was the discussion in the 1980s to set up study centres for students in slum areas to counter the poor quality of instruction, especially in mathematics, science, and English (Andersen and Damle, 2018).

The rise of these schools also reflects the relationship between the BJP and Vidya Bharati. They both have a common area of interest – that of promoting a national identity based on a common national culture that is defined by Hindu values. This symbiotic relationship has led the BJP to support the growth of the network of schools, albeit discreetly, with allocations of land and other resources (Sundar, 2005). Vidya Bharati denies any interference from the RSS, claiming that the organization is RSS inspired but not RSS managed (Nair, 2009). Emphasizing its managerial autonomy and indirect relationships with the RSS, the senior functionaries of the Vidya Bharati have suggested that the Sangh should not be seen as a '*parivar*' or family, but as a philosophy of life, and that, although Vidya Bharati's fundamental opinions are linked to the RSS, they are neither managed nor funded by it

---

[20] The Ekal Foundation of India, Ekal Foundation (United States), and Ekal International are the three main nodes in the far-reaching chain of volunteers, teachers, NGOs, donors, and various Ekal chapters. Ekal or 'one-teacher' schools are non-formal pre-schools and supplemental schools that focus on local culture and involve community members as teachers. These schools design their own curriculum based on *samskaras* (or *sanskaras*) or moral Hindu teaching, along with a blend of local customs. While Ekal is known for its work in education, the scope of its activities also includes skill development in rural areas, health-related initiatives, and promotion of entrepreneurship. According to the official website of the Ekal Vidyalaya Foundation, there are currently '96,559 teachers, 7,717 voluntary workers, 35 field organization (throughout 26 Indian states), and 8 support agencies. It operates in over 96,559 schools' (Ekal Vidyalaya, 2019, cited in Tukdeo, 2019, p.111). Ekal's role in development and education has been questioned on similar grounds: its ties to the RSS, the emphasis on Hinduization in curricula, and its growing networks in the Adivasi region, where the RSS has been strategically active in the last few decades in steering the political project of Hindu nationalism (Tukdeo, 2019, p.111).

(Nair, 2009). In these schools, teachers are given an intensive orientation and training in the traditions and a specific Vidya Bharati curriculum, in addition to skills training on their subject and school management, all focusing on the values and principles of the Sangh Parivar (Nair, 2009). There is an ideological but somewhat fractious relationship between the RSS, a social service organization that promotes a unique brand of cultural nationalism, and its political off-shoot, the BJP (Sundar, 2005). What binds the BJP and Vidya Bharati is their relationship with the RSS (Nair, 2009).

The Vidya Bharati schools are funded through fees and private donations from rich families (Sundar, 2005). While most of the children in these schools are from Hindu families, mostly from lower middle-class households (Basu, 2004; Froerer, 2007; Nair, 2009; www.vidyabharati.org),[21] Vidya Bharati claims that a small but significant number of non-Hindus also send their children to these schools (Nair, 2009). In 2020, it was reported that there had been an increase in the number of students of Muslim background in the schools run by Vidya Bharati – an increase of 30 per cent between 2017 and 2020 in Uttar Pradesh (Dixit, 2020, para.1). Chintamani Singh (the secretary of Vidya Bharati in East Uttar Pradesh) said, 'The urge for good and quality education has been the prime reason for the rise in number of Muslim students in our schools' (Dixit, 2020, para.4). The principals also reported that 'Muslim families' enrol their students in these schools because of 'quality education' (Dixit, 2020, para.5). Vidya Bharati claims that the quality of education in its schools is better than in many government-run schools. Out of 25,000 children from the Vidya Bharati network who take the board exams, between 60 and 65 per cent pass with merit (Nair, 2009, p.53). Despite this, the number of children from well-off families has drastically declined over the years because Hindi has continued to be the medium of instruction (Nair, 2009), and the middle classes want their children to be taught in English.

As the RSS and Sangh Parivar have expanded, debates have emerged over the focus of their educational efforts. Among these is how to address the different needs of rural and urban students across the class divide (Andersen and Damle, 2018). On the urban side there is a growing middle-class population advocating merit and a specialized education in an increasing technical world. On the rural side there is a need for a skills-based education that can address the demand for jobs among the huge number of students from farming families who cannot make a living as farmers because of the tiny size of most plots of land. The demand for education in vernacular

---

[21] Consisting of service-wallahs' children (children whose parents are government employees, industrial plant-workers, and small business owners) and children of lower working-class parents (auto rickshaw drivers, unskilled office workers, and others) (Froerer, 2007).

languages is also stronger in the rural areas, though the Akhil Bharatiya Pratinidhi Sabha in 2008 issued two language-related resolutions, one arguing that the 'medium of education must be Bharatiya Languages' and the other that the 'excessive importance given to English in all spheres of governmental activity must be ended' (Andersen and Damle, 2018).[22] In 2015, the RSS started planning model schools for India's 9,000 blocks of area that emphasize improving vocational training to provide the skills needed in India's growing economy. This goal fits the job creation objective of Modi's government (Andersen and Damle, 2018). With this aim in mind, Modi addressed leaders of the Vidya Bharati school system (in 2016) and the Ekal Vidyalaya (in 2015, 2016, and 2017), asking them to come up with ways to provide job-oriented skills that would make Indians more competitive in Indian and foreign job markets (Andersen and Damle, 2018).

As of 2019, many Saraswati Shishu Mandir schools started switching to the English language as their medium of instruction. RSS 'office-bearers' said that 'English textbooks for all subjects taught in grades 1 to 5 have been introduced in many schools and there were plans to do the same for grades 6 to 8 from 2020' (cited in John and Raju, 2019, para.1). These schools had kept their distance from English medium education since their inception. RSS officials claimed that the change was being piloted only in those institutions where the management committees, students, and parents had demanded it (John and Raju, 2019). In 2019, it was also reported that in Meerut 'Prant',[23] many Saraswati Shishu Mandir schools were being upgraded to become 'model schools', focusing on holistic learning through music lessons, sports, yoga, technology, and the option of English medium education (John and Raju, 2019, para.2). According to the 'office-bearers', about 1,223 Saraswati Shishu Mandirs are running in 49 districts of eastern Uttar Pradesh,[24] many of these schools already having begun to embrace English medium education. Besides Hindi and Sanskrit, all other subjects including mathematics are now taught through English textbooks (John and Raju, 2019, para.2). These schools,[25] teaching children in both Hindi and English, were affiliated with both the Uttar Pradesh Board and the CBSE.

[22] Akhil Bharatiya Pratinidhi Sabha is the top policy-making body of the RSS.
[23] This is a historical district in India.
[24] They are in Awadh, Kashi, Gorakhpur, and Ayodhya 'Prant'.
[25] 'We run separate sections for Hindi and English medium students on the same premises. Those who study in English medium get their certificates through the CBSE, while the others get them from the state education board. Almost 50% of sections in the school are English medium, as the demand for English education is growing with every passing year,' said Sharma (John and Raju, 2019, para.15). Baleram Brijbhusan Saraswati Shishu Mandir is one such 'model school' located in Meerut. Principal K.K. Sharma proudly claimed that his school was on par with the 'best public [government] schools' – and not only in education but in extracurricular activities, including sports (John and Raju, 2019). Jindal (the district

The Hindu orientation of these RSS-affiliated schools includes Hindu rituals and festivals, the practice of yoga, the teaching of Sanskrit, classes on Indian civilization from a Hindu perspective, and a plethora of Hindu symbols (Andersen and Damle, 2018). A day in any of the RSS-run schools starts with Vande Mataram (the national song of India) and Saraswati Vandana (a Hindu mantra) in order to inculcate cultural values, history, patriotism, and moral values in students (Kumar, 2019).

While these schools are required to follow a mandated state curriculum, they have an element of discretion in their choice of textbooks and extracurricular activities (Andersen and Damle, 2018). The curriculum and pedagogy of Vidya Bharati is a 'socialization process' – an extension of the RSS strategy (Sundar, 2005). A school follows the syllabus and textbooks prescribed by the respective state or central examination board to which it is affiliated. However, many of the textbooks being used by the Vidya Bharati schools were designed to promote 'bigotry and religious fanaticism' in the guise of culture (Sundar, 2005, p.4), as will be seen.

This section traces the visuals of the Bharat Mata that are incorporated in Saraswati Shishu Mandir Prakashan, Mathura in primary class textbooks that aim to build a Hindu Rashtra (Chaudhary, 2017).[26] The visual representations in this series of textbooks are purely Hindu-centric and do not identify other religions that are part of India's cultural heritage. The textbooks demonstrate the Hindu character of the nation through 'its restricted manners and visuals' (Chaudhary, 2017, p.1155). As reflected in Chapter 2 on the cow slaughter ban, even the chapter on 'The Cow' in the Saraswati Shishu Mandir Prakashan textbook, 'Saraswati English Reader 3', instructs the reader to save 'Gaumata' as it is their moral duty (Class III: Saraswati Shishu Mandir, 2006, p.18). The content shows the holy image of cow equated with the mother. The Hindu nationalists personify the geographical territory of India by calling the country Bharat Mata as well as calling the cow Gaumata. According to Mohan Bhagwat, *sarsanghchalak* of the RSS,[27] 'rearing of cow is not only our moral duty but it also enhances the values that are lacking in women' (Suraiya, 2013, p.42). In a function aimed at organizing India's first cow sanctuary, he stated that: 'Cow is our mother. Service to cow is service to mankind, which in turn helps to build morals' (cited in Suraiya, 2013, p.44). The status of the cow as a sacred animal is one of the symbolic components of the Hindutva ideology (Chaudhary, 2017). The generosity of the cow is not limited to the animal alone, with the textbook assuring

---

coordinator) said, 'English is a global communication language, so we can't deprive our students from its benefits as they chart their careers' (John and Raju, 2019, p.15).

[26] Bharat Mata maps are also distributed to government schools for public display (see epilogue).

[27] The head of the RSS.

its readers that cow urine can cure fatal diseases. There is also a claim that 'not only do human beings love cow, but Gods also love her very much [*sic*]' (cited in Chaudhary, 2017, p.1156). In picture 1 on page 18 of the English textbook, a woman is shown applying a 'tikka' to a cow with a 'pooja ki thali' [worship plate] in hand. It portrays the cow as god. In picture 2 on page 39 of the personality development textbook, a girl is shown feeding a cow as a moral duty.

Furthermore, the textbook outlines the different uses of cow's products,[28] urine and cow-dung cakes, and its sacredness (Chaudhary, 2017). Textbooks of Saraswati Shishu Prakashan also continuously remind children about their duties towards the cow (Saraswati Shishu Mandir Prakashan, 2016, *Vandana*; *Vyaktigat*).

Apart from other recommended textbooks for the children of Saraswati Shishu Mandir Schools for the primary class, a compulsory textbook named Vandana is supplied to all students studying at the Shishu Mandirs (Chaudhary, 2017). This was incorporated into the education system of RSS schools in order to revive the cultural heritage of India and to build a social character in the children that would uplift the nation. This textbook derived its content from the assumed glorious past of the *Akhand Bharat* (undivided India) (Chaudhary, 2017). Its main agenda is to build an Indian character by engaging children with Indian historic characters, gods and goddesses, Bharat Mata, Vedas, and Upanishads (Chaudhary, 2017).

The specific focus of the RSS schools is to teach ideas about Hindu superiority to protect the Hindu nation against threatening cultural and religious minorities. Symbolic visualization of elements of Hindutva in the textbooks describes the glorious Hindu past, where most or all the fighters belong to the Hindu religion. The Hindu-centric illustration of the book's cover reveals the militant nature of warriors and the diplomacy of Chanakya (Chaudhary, 2017). The historical Hindu characters who fought against foreign invasions were also placed on the cover of Saraswati Shishu Mandir textbooks (cited in Chaudhary, 2017, p.1161). Savarkar further justified the otherness of all other religions: 'Their holyland [*sic*] is far off in Arabis [*sic*] and Palestine. Their mythology and Godmen, ideas and heroes are not the children of this soil. Consequently, their names and their outlook smack of foreign origin. Their love is divided' (cited in Jaffrelot, 1999, p.31).

The most important issue underpinning this discussion is the relationship between educational attainment and opportunities that are provided by the school and valued by students, and a pedagogical agenda that has the propagation of Hindu superiority at its core. With this emphasis, which

---

[28] The exercise questions at the end of the chapter also strengthen the notion of the 'sacredness of the cow'.

includes the physical defence of the Hindu nation, such an educational regime offers little in the way of communal understanding or constructive intercommunity dialogue. What continues to distinguish the Shishu Mandir from other schools is thus the way it harnesses pedagogy to the clear political end of inculcating Hindutva ideals (Sundar, 2005, p.1611). It is through such a regime, ideologues and scholars alike believe, that the production of an 'imagined community' (Anderson, 2015, p.3) of young Hindus who are prepared to use potentially violent means to establish and defend the Hindu Rashtra is likely to occur (Andersen and Damle, 2018). Curricular and extracurricular activities and cultural knowledge exams all serve to remove non-Hindus from the discursive space of the nation. The RSS-run schools are legitimized as an alternative form of schooling for parents owing to their aim of inculcating discipline and Hindu culture in students, in addition to quality and good results (Sundar, 2005). What is crucial here is how education and neoliberalism have become vehicles to consolidate the base for the Hindu right, and these RSS schools essentially provide a cover for both the Hindutva and neoliberal agendas (Chatterji, 2020).

Conclusion

This chapter has discussed how a neoliberal trajectory has allowed the embedding of the Hindu nationalist discourse across different types of schools, and how both neoliberalism and Hindu nationalism are deeply intertwined. It shows the implicit involvement of teachers in the rise of neoliberalism and Hindu nationalism in education. Teachers conform to prescribed performance criteria and the curriculum in classrooms, and therefore choose to bow to the interests of head teachers and the state. Some might argue that teachers are victims of the neoliberal process, but they can also be regarded as (unintentional) perpetrators of the neoliberal agenda through passive acceptance: 'a tacit invoking of the invisible hand by the profession' allowing teachers to do what is 'best for themselves (i.e. conform to government policy)' (Leaton, 2006, p.313). Teachers in India have become habituated into perceiving neoliberal policy as 'natural' or the norm. It may also be that teachers are more consciously supportive of neoliberalism if one accepts the view that an 'expression of concern for the quality of work is in fact mere rationalization masking [financial] self-interest' (Freidson, 2004, p.201). The chapter has also presented teachers' views and their support and critique for Hindutva discourses in the classroom. Overall it is clear that in India, as elsewhere, teachers practise the dissemination of common-sense ideas alongside important mainstream political messages.

Chapter 4 builds on this by presenting teachers' views on the NEP 2020 (GoI, 2021a) and the language of instruction in Delhi, Mumbai, Chandigarh, Bengaluru, Jaipur, and Guwahati.

PART II

The Effects of Neoliberalism on Teachers and Higher Education

4

Teachers' Voices: Neoliberal and Hindu Nationalist Agendas in School Education in Delhi, Mumbai, Chandigarh, Bengaluru, Jaipur, and Guwahati

Introduction

This chapter builds on the arguments presented in Chapter 3 to focus on teachers' voices in order to show the impact of neoliberal and Hindu nationalist agendas on school education at six research sites. This chapter first provides a contextual background to school education in Delhi, Mumbai, Chandigarh, Bengaluru, Jaipur, and Guwahati (Assam), and the state-led educational initiatives envisioned by their respective state governments. The research sites from across India (north, west, south, and north-east) showcase how education plays out differently across the country by briefly highlighting how neoliberal politics shape discourse around the accountability of state governments. The next section highlights teachers' voices to show the impact of the neoliberal agenda at the six research sites. It further presents their views of parental school choice based on the quality of education and English as the medium of instruction, reflecting the arguments about this aspect of the neoliberal agenda that are discussed in Chapter 3. The third section discusses the neoliberal agenda of the NEP 2020 and its impact on teacher agency and their pedagogical practices in schools. It also engages with the NEP 2020 recommendations on the use of MT (home language or regional language) as the medium of instruction, and how this reflects the government's Hindu nationalist agenda.

Background to school education in Delhi, Mumbai, Chandigarh, Bengaluru, Jaipur, and Guwahati

This section offers some descriptive background on school education at the six research sites from all over India follows (see map below), including the proportion of government and private schools, the medium of instruction and their performance, as well as some details about state-led educational initiatives.[1]

INDIA MAP

1	Andhra Pradesh	16	Maharashtra
2	Arunachal Pradesh	17	Manipur
3	Assam	18	Meghalaya
4	Bihar	19	Mizoram
5	Chhattisgarh	20	Nagaland
6	Goa	21	Odisha
7	Gujarat	22	Punjab
8	Haryana	23	Rajasthan
9	Himachal Pradesh	24	Sikkim
10	Jammu and Kashmir	25	Tamil Nadu
11	Jharkhand	26	Telangana
12	Karnataka	27	Tripura
13	Kerala	28	Uttar Pradesh
14	Ladakh	29	Uttarakhand
15	Madhya Pradesh	30	West Bengal

Source: Adapted from 'India Map', Shutterstock/mars-design.

Note: Jammu and Kashmir are no longer states but three Union Territories (UTs).

---

[1]	This chapter only focuses on the private and government school teachers' views from Guwahati, as data was collected from only three government school teachers in Silchar, and their views

In Delhi, the number of private schools increased by 0.1 per cent in 2019–2020. In the same year, enrolment declined in both private (by 5.5 per cent) and government schools (by 4.3 per cent). However, during 2020–2021, enrolment in government schools increased from 16.28 lakh to 17.6 lakh (Express News Service, 2021, para.3). Government schools comprised 2,797 Hindi and 1,692 English medium schools, while private schools accounted for 2,558 English and only 157 Hindi medium schools (UDISE, 2019, p.109, n.d.). The School Education Quality Index (SEQI) (Niti Aayog, 2019, p.109) report stated that,[2] in terms of quality and performance of government schools, Delhi had 100 per cent adjusted Net Enrolment Ratio (NER) at elementary level (the highest amongst all Union Territories),[3] while at secondary level it was 83.10 per cent in 2015–2016, which increased to 85.90 per cent in 2016–2017. Delhi ranked sixth in the learning outcomes indicator, with average scores in Class 3 for language (58 per cent) and mathematics (54 per cent). For grades 5 and 8, Delhi ranked fourth and third among other Union Territories. These good results can be explained by the AAP-led education reforms between 2015 and 2018 (Sandhu, 2021, Anand and Lall, forthcoming 2022). For decades government schools had been criticized for their poor-quality education and for lagging behind private schools in terms of academic performance (Sandhu, 2021). AAP, in power for seven years, made efforts to 'fix' public education through a four-pronged approach that involved modernizing infrastructure, capacity-building for teachers and principals, making school administrations accountable, and improving learning outcomes (Raina, 2020).

In Chandigarh (the capital of Haryana and Punjab),[4] a Union Territory ruled directly by the BJP government, the number of private schools increased from 21.1 per cent to 32.3 per cent and enrolment increased by 5.5 per cent in 2019–2020. During the same period, the number of government schools

---

were no different from their Guwahati colleagues. See the Appendix for a table with the main information. However, segregated education data for Guwahati was not available.

[2]   The report evaluated the performance of all the states based on 33 parameters. While Maharashtra's overall performance score increased from 58.6 per cent in 2015–2016 to 62.5 per cent in 2016–2017, other states such as Gujarat, Haryana, and Himachal Pradesh, which had earlier scored lower, moved up on the indicators (Bhatkhande, 2019). Punjab was ranked ninth, with an increase of just 8.4 per cent in the overall performance score from the previous assessment year. Punjab's rank was the same in the previous report too. States such as Haryana, Assam, Uttar Pradesh, and Odisha have improved their scores by 18.5, 16.8, 13.7, and 12.4 per cent respectively (Prakash, n.d., para.1).

[3]   SEQI (2019) defines Adjusted NER as the total number of pupils in a particular stage of school education enrolled either in the corresponding stage or the next stage, expressed as a percentage of the corresponding population.

[4]   Punjab, however, has been ruled by Congress since 2017. Legislative elections were held in February 2022 and Punjab is now ruled by AAP.

decreased from 69.9 per cent to 52.8 per cent, while enrolment decreased from 58.3 per cent to 57.6 per cent. Overall in Punjab, there was an increase in enrolment in government schools during 2020–2021 from 23.3 lakh to 24.2 lakh (ASER, 2021, p.21). Both types of schools offered Hindi, English, and Punjabi languages as the medium of instruction. Government schools offered 133 Hindi, 107 English, and 19 Punjabi medium schools, while private schools accounted for 16 Hindi, 96 English, and 6 Punjabi medium schools (UDISE, 2019). Chandigarh achieved an overall performance score of over 50.0 per cent. Though Chandigarh has been ranked first among Union Territories in the SEQI ranking, in 2015–2016 the NER at elementary level was 85 per cent, which decreased to 82.7 per cent in 2016–2017. At secondary level, Chandigarh had a 100 per cent transition rate from primary to upper primary level. Regarding learning outcomes, it also had the highest average language and mathematics score of 75 per cent and 71 per cent respectively; Class 3 students scored 69 per cent (language) and 64 per cent (mathematics), and Class 8 students scored 61 per cent (language) and 46 per cent (mathematics) (SEQI, 2019, p.21). The Department of School Education in Chandigarh started a number of projects such as the Kilkaari Project to support government school teachers.[5] Government school teachers also underwent comprehensive capacity-building and professional development initiatives organized by the Central Board of Secondary Education (CBSE).

In 2019 in Mumbai, the capital of Maharashtra and India's financial hub governed by the Hindu right wing Shiv Sena in coalition with the BJP, the number of private schools increased from 1,576 to 1,620. In 2019–2020, enrolment in private schools decreased from 857,592 to 851,426. Both the number of government schools and enrolment level decreased from 905 to 894 and from 813,935 to 797,698 respectively. However, during 2020–2021, there has been an increase from 64.3 per cent to 70.3 per cent in enrolment in government schools (Iftikhar, 2021, para.4). Both types of schools offered Hindi, English, and Marathi languages as the medium of instruction. Government schools had 134 Hindi, 414 English, and 389 Marathi medium schools, while private schools accounted for only 2 Hindi medium and 16 Marathi medium but 785 English medium schools (UDISE, 2019). Besides these languages, government schools also catered to Gujarati and Urdu speaking communities – a total of 57 and 88 schools respectively. Overall, Maharashtra has seen a sharp fall by three ranks in the SEQI report of 2019 from third to sixth out of 20 states, with the state performing poorly especially in areas such as infrastructural facilities and outcomes and equity (SEQI, 2019, para.54). In 2015–2016 the NER at elementary level was 91.4 per cent, which increased to 91.8 per cent in

---

[5]   This project was launched to improve the quality of learning. Its main idea is to make classrooms learning spaces that bolster curiosity and imagination.

2016–2017. Mumbai's learning outcomes are low – only 50 per cent (of primary students) could read a paragraph, 50 per cent could not write at all, and 30 per cent did not recognize numbers as per the Annual Status of Education Report (ASER) (cited in Dasra, 2019, p.10). One prominent education intervention, Naandi, conducts mathematics and English remedial classes in Mumbai schools for low performers, who are then reintegrated into their regular classes (Dasra, 2019).

In 2019, in Bengaluru, the capital of Karnataka, ruled by the BJP, the number of both private and government schools increased from 2,570 to 3,317 and 2,542 to 3,283 respectively. That same year also saw an increase in the number of enrolments in both private and government schools. Both types offered Hindi, English, and Kannada languages as the medium of instruction. Government schools had 728 Hindi, 85 English, and 2021 Kannada medium schools, while private schools accounted for 255 Hindi, 213 English, and 901 Kannada medium schools (UDISE, 2019, n.d.). During 2020–2021, enrolment in government schools went up from 68.6 per cent to 77.7 per cent (ASER, 2021, p.24). Niti Aayog placed Karnataka in third position for its overall performance in the delivery of quality school education in the SEQI. Karnataka was also found to be better than other states in its performance in terms of learning outcomes, access, equity, and infrastructure (Kumar, 2019, para.1). In 2015–2016, the NER at elementary level was 94.1 per cent, which increased to 95.7 per cent in 2016–2017. At secondary level, Karnataka had a 96.8 per cent transition rate from primary to upper primary level. Karnataka topped the learning outcomes of language and mathematics for Class 3, Class 5, and Class 8 students. The Karnataka government has been trying to enhance the access for and enrolment of students and also to prevent dropouts by introducing different programmes such as Samudayadatta Shale,[6] and Nali Kali English (Avinash, 2017).[7] To improve the learning outcomes of students and teaching quality, a number of innovative practices were put in place that included a tracking system for student attendance, a state achievement survey, and a 'making schools safe' initiative.

In Jaipur, the capital of Rajasthan ruled by the Congress party, the number of private schools increased from 3,088 to 5,145, and the number of enrolments in these schools also increased in 2019–2020. In the same year the number and enrolment for government schools also increased but remained lower than in private schools. Similar to other states, enrolment in government schools jumped from 56.7 per cent to 68.4 per cent (ASER, 2021, p.24). Both types of schools offered Hindi, English, and Sanskrit as the

---

[6] This was introduced in November 2020 to improve dropouts and student learning levels by improving infrastructure and training teachers.

[7] This programme was launched to improve English education.

medium of instruction.[8] Government schools had 2,373 Hindi, 476 English, and 402 Sanskrit medium schools, while private schools accounted for 3,949 Hindi, 3,443 English, and 594 Sanskrit medium schools (UDISE, 2019). The previous BJP government of Rajasthan made Sanskrit a compulsory third language for students from Class 4 to Class 10 and also designed the curriculum in order to make the learning of the Sanskrit language more job oriented. Minority groups in Rajasthan at the time saw this development as a plan to eliminate minority languages from the curriculum. Linguistic minority schools in Jaipur, with over 1,500 students in total, were merged with Hindi medium schools. At the time of writing, under the rule of the Congress government, students have the choice of Sanskrit, Punjabi, Gujarati, Urdu, Sindhi, or Bengali as their third language (Jain, 2020). In terms of quality and performance of government schools, the SEQI (2019, p.54) report stated that Rajasthan's NER was between 86.5 to 86.8 per cent at elementary level, while at secondary level it was 94.9 per cent in 2015–2016, which decreased to 93.7 per cent in 2016–2017. Rajasthan ranked second in the SEQI 2019 owing to the highest average scores for class 8 in language and mathematics, with 67 per cent and 57 per cent respectively (SEQI, 2019, p.89). Improvements in Rajasthan's education status were the result of continuous efforts by both central and state governments, including specific schemes and public participation (PRS, 2020). In Rajasthan, schemes such as the Shiksha Karmi Project,[9] as well as the Lok Jumbish Project,[10] were put in place to improve education levels across the state. The state also introduced 'Adarsh', or model schools, with the intention of improving the overall enrolment rate and infrastructure (Rao, et al, 2017).

In Assam,[11] ruled by the BJP, the number of government schools increased by 0.4 per cent in 2019–2020. In the same year, enrolment for government schools decreased by 2.9 per cent. However, in 2019–2020 enrolment in private schools increased by 0.6 per cent. Both types of schools offer Hindi, English, and Assamese as the medium of instruction. Government schools had 1,427 Hindi, 4,519 English, and 40,124 Assamese medium schools, while private schools accounted for 520 Hindi, 2,512 English, and 3,718 Assamese

---

[8]   The fact that Sanskrit is advertised as the medium of instruction in some schools is extraordinary, but underlies Rajasthan's deep Hindutva agenda (UDISE Plus, n.d.)

[9]   This project was initiated to universalize primary education. It was implemented in 1987, with the objectives to overcome teacher absenteeism in schools located in remote and difficult areas and to increase the enrolment of students. The project also aims to reduce the number of dropouts, especially girls (Ramachandran and Harish, 2000).

[10]   It aims to provide primary education for all children (Mondal, n.d.). It emphasized to incorporate children belonging to poor sections of society, tribal and so-called 'lower castes' people, to participate in basic education (Lok Jumbish Parishad Jaipur, 1992).

[11]   Segregated data for Guwahati was not available (UDISE Plus, n.d.).

medium schools (UDISE, 2019). In terms of the quality and performance of government schools, the SEQI (2019, p.91) report stated that in Assam the NER increased from 96.2 per cent to 99.0 per cent at elementary level, while at secondary level it was 87.4 per cent in 2015–2016, which increased to 94.5 per cent in 2016–2017. Enrolment in government schools increased from 64.3 per cent to 70.3 per cent in 2021 (Umarji, 2021, para.2). The Government of Assam (2019) also promoted significant schemes such as AAROHAN for primary and secondary education to enhance the student's enrolment and engagement in schools. AAROHAN was announced in the 2017–2018 budget announcement and aimed to establish 100 new schools in tea garden areas in Guwahati by upgrading lower primary and upper primary schools to high schools, a move that was initiated to improve the quality of secondary education (Government of Assam, 2019).

Of all the research sites, Assam has the worst retention rate among secondary school students, whereas Chandigarh and Punjab recorded over 90 per cent at secondary level. Assam and Rajasthan have the lowest retention rate at primary level in government schools in comparison with the other research sites (Krishna, 2021, para.2). Nationally, schools are not well prepared for, and teachers are not sufficiently experienced in, the use of digital technology, as hardly one-third of schools have functional computers and only one-fifth have internet access. In this respect, government schools are at a greater disadvantage than government-aided private schools and private unaided schools. By the time of the outbreak of COVID-19, government schools across the research sites had only limited exposure to a hands-on experience with digital technology (Tilak, 2021, p.498). With huge regional and household disparities in access to the internet and technology, the required transition was not possible for all students and educators, irrespective of who was in power at state government level. The rapid shift to e-learning prompted by the pandemic has thus brought to the surface once again long-standing issues of inequality and a digital divide in India that was not addressed by economic, education, and digitalization policies introduced by the central and state governments before the pandemic (Modi and Postaria, 2020). The implementation of neoliberal policies or schemes introduced by central and state governments (as discussed in previous chapters) has not addressed the educational inequalities that have emerged as a crisis in the caste and class struggle across India.

This section has showed that there has been an increase in the number of private schools across Delhi, Chandigarh, Mumbai, Bengaluru, and Jaipur, and a drop in the number of government schools in Mumbai and Assam. The report by ASER (2021) shows that there was a fair amount of variation in enrolment at state level during 2020–2021. The national increase in government school enrolment is driven by large northern states such as Uttar Pradesh, Rajasthan, Punjab, and Haryana and southern states such as Maharashtra, Tamil Nadu, Kerala, and Andhra Pradesh. In contrast, in many north-eastern states government school enrolment has fallen during this period, and the proportion of children not enrolled in school has increased. The major change in enrolment that is evident in ASER (2021) is a big jump in government school enrolment accompanied by a fall in private school enrolment. The increase in government school enrolment is across the board – all age groups and grades, and for both boys and girls. The next section presents teachers' reflections on parental choice of schools, the quality of education, and English as the medium of instruction.

Neoliberalism and private schools: teachers' views on parental choice

School choice is a thorny subject in India. As discussed in Chapter 1, the neoliberal movement equates choice with liberty and freedom. Friedman's seminal *Capitalism and Freedom* (1962) outlines the reasons why parental school choice is required in a free capitalist society. In these different contexts with different types of school choice mechanisms, two key aspects of human rights appear to clash – the liberty of a parent to choose their child's education on the one hand, and the right of a student to access free, quality education without discrimination or systemic barriers on the other. In recent years, private schooling has witnessed substantial growth around the world (Tooley and Dixon, 2006; Härmä, 2008, 2013; Tooley, 2009; Akaguri, 2014; Day Ashley et al, 2014). Private schools that run entirely on student fees have been mushrooming in the context of low- and middle-income countries where government schools are considered comparatively inefficient (Härmä, 2008, p.133). As discussed in Chapters 1 and 3, the exploration of parental school choice has dominated Indian educational discourse since the early 2000s. Previous chapters highlight the noticeable increase in private schools across India – a direct result of the government's neoliberal policies.

This section presents teachers' views on the key factors set out in neoliberal reforms: freedom of choice, affordability, autonomy, and quality. These issues are political across India. The promise of free and high-quality education for all is a key pledge in election campaigns across the six research states.

In the interviews, teachers discussed parental school preferences and how parents choose where to send their children. Both private and government school teachers at the six research sites stated how the main consideration for parents was the cost of schooling. In terms of financial affordability, a private school teacher from Guwahati said:

'Parents that choose to enrol their children in government school is mainly because of their financial situation. If a family is financially strong then they generally go for private school. On the other way, if a family is financially not so strong then they opt for government school, where there is less fee for school education. ... financial condition of parents is also a factor that influencing parents' preference for school.' (PS4 Guwahati)

Similar perspectives on affordability and the financial condition of parents were voiced by teachers in Bengaluru, Chandigarh, Mumbai, and Delhi. A government school teacher from Jaipur explained:

'The main reason parents choose a government school, or a private school is affordability and financial condition. [...] Some parents are aware that quality of teachers in Government schools is better, and they are skilled. They have been appointed as teachers after a certain process. [however] Mostly ladies [students' mothers] think that if someone else's child is going to private school so should mine. Hence, they enrol their child to private school. Some private schools have special schemes like if parents enrol two children in their school, they give free education to third child.' (GS5 Jaipur)

These kinds of interventions make it easier for parents to move their children to private schools. They are brought about by the impact of the neoliberal politics of Congress, BJP, and Shiv Sena. These political parties are now emphasizing bringing the private sector forward to improve the quality of education in government schools.

As has been discussed in Chapter 3, those who can pay school fees in areas with both government and private schools are abandoning government provision to send their children to private schools. This practice has been widespread amongst the middle and upper classes for a long time, but it has become increasingly common amongst the poorer sections of society (Lall, 2012, Härmä, 2021) as they are perceived as elite, even if they are low cost (Srivastava, 2008). Nevertheless, family income remains a crucial issue in determining the spending pattern for education, particularly for low-income families. Findings from Mehrotra and Panchamukhi (2006) on eight states show that the financial burden is much higher on households that send children to private unaided schools rather than government schools.[12] Similarly, research on Uttar Pradesh (Srivastava, 2008) and Andhra Pradesh (Woodhead et al, 2013) show that access to private schools is limited owing to financial constraints (Akaguri, 2014). Despite the appearance of abundance of choice for families it remains limited by the ability to pay school fees

---

[12] Rajasthan, Madhya Pradesh, Uttar Pradesh, Bihar, West Bengal, Assam, Andhra Pradesh, and Tamil Nadu.

and associated costs.[13] Because those who can pay end up attending private schools, some families are 'left behind' in under-resourced government schools and receive less attention. In effect, school choice exercised by some parents negatively impinges on the right to free, quality education for the poorest and most marginalized students by further stratifying educational provision (Härmä, 2021).

Beyond cost, school choice is based on the elusive factor of quality. Some parents equate quality with good infrastructure, while others consider examination results or discipline as marks of excellence. Manners and safety also shape parental perceptions of quality and influence their school choices (Lahoti and Mukhopadhyay, 2019; Ayyangar et al, 2020). Participating teachers focused on how school choice is dependent on school facilities such as well-established infrastructure, smaller class sizes, low teacher–student ratios, and improved teaching and learning materials. They shared how parents consider the physical factors of the school such as security, the quality of the resources and equipment, cleanliness, and hygiene. A government school teacher from Jaipur said: 'Some parents think that in government school students have to clean the classes etc., so the parents get a bit sceptical to send their children to government schools. Private schools have better facilities like library etc.' (GS5 Jaipur). Teachers consider their local government schools to be lacking the necessary infrastructure and resources to provide an adequate education for their children – this despite examples of government schools that are better equipped than private schools (Mehrotra and Panchamukhi, 2006). A private school teacher from Guwahati provided a detailed reason for this:

'[P]rivate schools are better equipped with modern facilities, infrastructures than government schools. Few government schools like Navodaya,[14] etc. also have good facilities but those are very few in numbers. That's one of the reasons parents prefer private schools over government schools. Parents also want quantity as well as quality in education and environment in schools.' (PS4 Guwahati)

Teachers from the six research sites also stated that a school's technological capabilities, instructional equipment in the classrooms, and the availability of advanced laboratories appear to influence parental choice. The AAP (in Delhi) spends a huge amount on education, yet still lags behind in terms of

---

[13] The costs of starting at a private school (registration fees as well as new books and uniforms, which come on top of the recurrent costs of tuition fees, examination fees, and other charges) sometimes also curtail school choice and school switching (Härmä, 2021).

[14] Jawahar Navodaya Vidyalayas are central schools for talented students who are predominantly from rural areas.

technological development in its government schools, as evidenced during the pandemic (Anand and Lall, forthcoming 2022). Similarly, there has been an improvement in education conditions in Rajasthan, but there is a need for infrastructural reforms at national level. In Guwahati and Bengaluru, the BJP strengthened its election campaign on the ground, promising improvement in technological resources via the private sector ahead of state elections, which were held in March 2022. In the six research sites, the pandemic has called into question the efficacy of remote or online learning and technological solutions to a crisis of access and inequality. Smartphones became the predominant source of teaching and learning when schools shut down and moved to a remote model of teaching and learning, giving rise to concerns about the most marginalized being left behind. The availability of smartphones has increased from 36.5 per cent in 2018 to 67.6 per cent in 2021. More children in private schools have a smartphone at home (79 per cent) as opposed to children at government schools (63.7 per cent) (ASER, 2021).

In the discussions, some teachers also gave examples of where parental choice had developed in a less planned manner. The closure of government schools (as discussed in Chapter 3), meant that parents were worried about access to education for their students. A private school teacher from Delhi said: 'last year, you know, the riots [Delhi in February 2020] happened, and they closed the government school. A lot of students joined our [private] school' (PS3 Delhi). Similarly, private school teachers from Chandigarh and Mumbai said that 'government schools closed permanently so they came to our [private] school' (PS2 Delhi) and 'there is a very bad government school no one wants to go there, now it is closed' (PS5 Mumbai). The main reason for the sharp decline in government schools is the practice of merging schools with low enrolments in the name of consolidating resources. NITI Aayog's SATH-E project alone led to the merger of about 40,000 schools in Madhya Pradesh, Jharkhand, and Odisha in 2018 (Sharma, 2020b, p.23). Shutting down government schools in disadvantaged areas has also led to limited access for girls; a serious setback for gender justice, which had been a major achievement in several states (Sharma, 2020b). This is a particular issue in the BJP-controlled states. The number of enrolments in government schools in Delhi has increased, whereas it has decreased in the BJP-controlled states. Education officials from Congress and BJP-controlled states have started referring to Delhi's education model for guidance. Despite this, the NEP 2020 legitimizes the practice of school mergers by recommending the rationalization of small schools that are considered 'economically sub-optimal and operationally complex to run' (NEP, 2020, p.28). In the states where the public sector is contracting, private provision will continue to expand. This has repercussions for government teaching jobs. A few government school teachers from Delhi, Chandigarh, Bengaluru, and Mumbai mentioned the resulting issues related to their contracts. A government school teacher from Bengaluru shared that:

'[T]hese days, as for the new policy, government schools are going for only contractual employees, but somehow, it's not successful. Whereas if the extraction of work is concerned, in private schools the management is very effective and efficient. But because of the policy, government sector has failed. Affordability is one thing, and managing the staff, controlling authority in fact, is a failure.' (GS6 Bengaluru)

In the six research sites, teachers reported salary cuts during the pandemic owing to a significant drop in revenue for the state. The COVID-19 pandemic has deeply impacted the 9.43 million teachers in India who are working across private and public sector schools as well as in unaided and education department-run institutions (Bose, 2021). The NEP 2020 has laid fresh impetus on the importance of teachers in the education system. However, they continue to remain some of the lowest-paid public servants in the country. UNESCO's State of the Education Report for India 2020 found that 42 per cent of the teachers across private and government sectors were working without a contract and earning an average salary of under Rs 10,000 a month. Only 8 per cent of teachers have contracts spanning between one and two years. The problem is worse in private schools, where as many as 69 per cent are working without contracts, leaving them without any benefits and vulnerable to unemployment without notice, salary cuts, inhuman working conditions, or deferred pay (Bose, 2021).

Another key reason for the choice of private schools seems to be accountability. A teacher from Guwahati said:

'The main reason I would say is accountability. In the private schools the schools are accountable to the parents. They have to explain if the children are not doing well & they will be called if there are any lapses. In the government schools there is no accountability. The teachers whether they are imparting education, that the education is getting across to the children or not the government school is not very particular about it [...] They will have responsibility & nobody will take accountability...' (PS5 Guwahati)

Private school teachers expressed greater autonomy in decision-making, and their headteachers face stronger incentives to deliver high student performance. A teacher from Jaipur shared:

'People think that in private schools teaching is good, they are disciplined, teachers take care of students, give them homework, teachers are keeping eye on if a child is coming regularly or not. If the child is absent, they ask reason to parents. So, there is perception that children do better in private schools.' (PS9 Jaipur)

Private school teachers seemed to suggest that providing greater autonomy to employees while keeping school headteachers accountable can be effective in student achievement. Private school performance data is made publicly available through websites and the creation of league tables. These processes are central to the creation of markets in schooling, where data is deemed necessary to enable parental choice of schools and, in turn, to raise standards. Parents want the best for their children and will therefore turn to information on school performance nationally, not knowing that research evidence shows that, irrespective of quality related parameters, there is no significant difference in the education attained in either a public or a private school (Chudgar and Quin, 2012; Karopady, 2014; Wadhwa, 2014; Srivastava, 2016; Härmä, 2021). It is therefore no surprise that both private and government school teachers said that parents perceive teaching quality as being better in private schools.

Parents are also seeking an alternative to the traditional pedagogies of government schools. When asked about using child-centred pedagogies (see Chapter 3), government teachers mentioned the issues of 'time', 'teacher–pupil ratio', 'teacher shortage', and 'government policies of no corporal punishment'. A government school teacher from Guwahati explained:

'People [parents] think that students learn better in private schools because they feel that private schools have standards, school uniform, they are strict, they teach better & children learn more there. Government teachers are not allowed to punish or shout at the students. They have taught by play way method if students don't listen or study or follow the rules teachers are not allowed to shout at them.'[15] (GS2 Guwahati)

Another government school teacher held similar views:

'In private school there is separate teacher for each subject while in government schools there is always shortage of teachers. Subject wise teacher is not available in most government schools. Few teachers are there & they have so many responsibilities in government schools, so they can't teach properly.' (GS3 Guwahati)

---

[15] Play way method is a local way of referring to child- or learner-centric approaches to teaching and learning.

The issues were made worse by the COVID-19 pandemic, with government teachers struggling:

'Now during lockdown, we have to prepare videos & send them to children, we are sending but there is a question mark on how many students are able to access these videos. In private schools, teacher uploads video or pdf & asks students if they have downloaded the video & also if they have understood the video or pdf. This is called individual attention which we are not able to do in government schools...' (GS3 Guwahati)

In the BJP, Congress, and AAP-controlled states, lack of connectivity and technological amenities remain a significant issue. For instance, in Delhi – despite the successful reforms – it is well known that government schools have fewer resources, and since they cater to the poorer sections of society, their pupils also struggle more (Jain et al, 2021).

Private school teachers shared that they are more accountable than government school teachers – regardless of the circumstances. A private school teacher from Bengaluru said:

'there is perception that the students perform better in private schools as compared to government schools. ... If we look at the scenario that we all are hooked since the last two years from the pandemic situation, government schools are not able to cope up with the situation, whereas private schools have done it. I will give you my example, in a school where I teach, when the lockdown was announced – within one week, we were able to take from offline to online ... our school was ready & within the first week we were on online mode. On the other hand, government schools couldn't do it...' (PS9 Bengaluru)

When asked how government teachers are coping with the students without digital devices, the private school teacher elaborated:

'Every student over there do not have smart phone, as they are from economically weaker sections, as well as the teachers have inhibitions. They had nearly for two to three months there was no schooling, there was no classes at all. So, that was one big challenge. That way I feel private schools perform much better. The infrastructure they have, the facility they have, the exposure that they give to the student and they keep their students at far as challenge of the 21st century. They prepare the students much better as compared to a government school.' (PS9 Bengaluru)

Further discussions with the teachers elucidated that in government schools teachers lack direct accountability to the families they serve, since staff are hired and paid through civil service structures. School leadership is often weak both in terms of management skills and the authority needed to run a school. These weaknesses lead to well-documented teacher absenteeism, poor-quality instruction, and overcrowded and under-resourced classrooms – all of which have provided the incentive for many families to seek an alternative.

Teachers' voices highlight where parental choices have developed as a result of purposeful policy and where it has developed by default. School choice and related accountability mechanisms are not sufficient to bring about quality improvement, and increasing choice appears to be highly associated with increasing segregation (in the BJP-controlled states) and stratification of school systems (AAP is recreating the hierarchies in and through education based on learning abilities in classrooms). The lived realities on these school campuses are, however, quite different: education remains a site of struggle for students from economically weaker sections and backward castes as they are the most affected by the neoliberal schemes. Although Delhi's AAP government is famous for the improvement of government schools, the segregation created in classrooms is problematic, as most students who are placed in the lower sets entitled Nishtha (determination/those we believe in),[16] and Neo-Nishtha (students who have failed Class 9 twice) belong to the SCs, STs, and the Muslim community (Anand and Lall, forthcoming 2022). This labelling reinforces casteism by creating a separate space between students from the upper class and lower class.

The strong emphasis on choice has helped to turn citizens into consumers, who shop for the 'best deal' for their child, rather than supporting a school that belongs to the whole community. In Delhi, initiatives such as the Happiness Curriculum and Entrepreneurship Curriculum showcase ideal citizens who are 'mindful, aware, awakened, empathetic, and firmly rooted in their identity', and will become future business leaders who develop society through their private ventures (Kochar, 2020, para.2). These initiatives can produce exclusion and inequality in classrooms. They also reflect a state agenda of progress and development that excludes certain sections from this system altogether (Kochar, 2020). Similar initiatives have also been observed in the BJP-controlled states (see Epilogue).

While the more motivated and able may reap benefits from school choice, these benefits may be understood in only a narrow sense, as they ignore the externalities of having to live in an increasingly unequal society (Starnawski

---

[16] The Delhi government's Chunauti 2018 scheme has attempted to address 'the issue of learning deficit from classes six onwards'. The grouping of students (grades 6 to 8) into homogeneous groups of Pratibha, Nishtha, and Neo-Nishtha, in different sections, was acknowledged as regular practice by most of the teachers of the government schools in Delhi (Anand and Lall, forthcoming 2022).

and Gawlicz, 2021). This type of consumer behaviour reflects the effects of globalization across Indian society. Globalization is also a push factor when it comes to the medium of instruction – in particular the English language – as an important reason for choosing private schools. English Medium Instruction (EMI) is seen as an important historical and political dimension of school education in India (Sarangapani and Winch, 2010). The development of EMI is frequently linked to the process of neoliberal globalization, in which the expansion of EMI is recognized as the demand for English for global communication and increased job opportunities across a global market (Park and Wee, 2013; Seargeant and Erling, 2013; Phillipson, 2017; Sah and Li, 2018; Sah, 2021). The teaching of English and its use as a medium of instruction is rooted in India's colonial history, during which the introduction of English education was aimed at acculturating Indian people in European attitudes and for imparting the skills required for working in the colonial administration (Kumar, 2009, p.10). As the language of the new national elites, it continued to maintain its status and desirability in post-colonial India (Sarangapani and Winch, 2010).

There are a number of reasons for the preference for English instead of vernacular languages as the medium of instruction in post-independence India. Faust and Nagar (2001) perceive English education, along with the changes in attitude, lifestyles, mannerisms, and aspirations that it brings, as a form of cultural capital that brings higher economic and cultural status. The opening up of the Indian economy in the 1990s (as discussed in Chapters 1 and 3) coincided with an explosion in the demand for English in schools, because as the global language it is perceived to open opportunities both domestically and internationally (NCERT, 2006). Underlining the monopoly over English education by the upper caste and class, Rao (2008) argued that English medium education has been the 'exclusive privilege of caste and class situation and life's chances' (p.66). Who chooses, or who was chosen for, the English medium schools are largely dependent on what Bourdieu (1973, p.74) terms the 'cultural capital of children': a student with an English medium education is destined to be highly mobile and expected to join the elite ranks of society. Deardin (2014) observed that income levels have a clear influence on the nature of school enrolment among households: government (vernacular medium) school enrolment declines in higher income segments, while the demand for English medium schools increases for the same income group. Today Hindi medium schools are usually less expensive and under government control, whereas English medium schools usually charge higher fees and are affiliated with one of the private administrative boards.

As discussed in Chapter 3, parents prefer private schools, in particular those that use English as a medium of instruction. This is a typical school choice across different social classes (Srivastava, 2008; LaDousa, 2014). English carries the mark of elitism, and some government school teachers associated choosing an English medium school with its socio–historically informed symbolic value (LaDousa, 2014). In a study on low-fee private schools in Delhi, Ohara (2012) noted that parents emphasized the importance of English education and considered English language schools to be superior to education that is provided in Hindi. Given the parental preference for English medium education, there has been a noticeable development in state policies that introduce English as a subject and medium of instruction in government schools: in the last fifteen years, English has been introduced as a subject in government schools by about 27 states (out of 30) at primary level (Jena, 2016).[17] The use of English in certain schools further supports the stratification of society.[18]

Government school teachers stated that parents think students in English medium schools are 'superior' and 'elite'. A government school teacher from Delhi shared that 'Parents think English is a superior language that's why they want to send their children to private schools, we also teach in English. This is everywhere in the government schools now' (GS4 Delhi). Another government school teacher echoed similar thoughts: 'English is for status symbol now. Parents think by sending kids to private schools. They will become elite...' (GS6 Delhi). Besides Delhi, private school teachers from Chandigarh and Mumbai viewed the English language as important for parents to ensure the successful careers of their children in the future: 'English language is some parents' dream. I meet a lot of parents who say that they are worried of their children ability to speak. They think without English they can't get any job' (PG4 Chandigarh). Another teacher explained: 'Parents always go to the English teacher. Parents are not interested in other subjects. They ask me if I speak in English or Marathi with them. Parents ask me to just speak English for their better career. I have to' (PG7 Mumbai). It is clear that parents value English for its perceived use in putting their children at an advantage in the labour market (Bénéï, 2005; Ganguly-Scrase and Scrase, 2008).

Private school teachers from Delhi, Guwahati, Jaipur, and Bengaluru understand that parents planned their children to be physically mobile within India and outside, and that proficiency in English will equip them to navigate their career path with ease. On the face of it, this global aspiration contradicts the idea of an inward-looking Hindutva inspired India, also supported by the same middle classes. The BJP's stand on the Hindi language issue has

---

[17] Jammu, Kashmir, and Nagaland have made English the main medium of education in all schools. The other states, such as Kerala, Punjab, Tamil Nadu, Andhra Pradesh, Maharashtra, and Delhi, also saw an increase in the number of English medium schools, up to more than 90 per cent (Jena, 2016).

[18] As will be seen later in this chapter, the NEP actually pushes for increased instruction in the vernacular MT or local language.

been clear for decades. The RSS has pitched 'Hindi, Hindu, Hindustan', and that has been core to its Hindutva agenda (Misra, 2019a). Amit Shah's call to make Hindi one language to 'bind the whole country' is a step to push the 'one nation, one religion, one election, one culture, one leader, one party, one language' ideology of the RSS–BJP. Misra argues that 'the RSS–BJP is trying to push for uniformity in place of unity. Unity comes from voluntary association and identification of a cause or concept and not by forcibly pushing a language down the millions of non-Hindi speaking citizens' (also observed in the Congress-ruled state of Rajasthan) (Misra, 2019a, para.11).[19] This is further discussed in the next section.

Teachers' views on the NEP 2020 and the BJP's language policy – the merging of neoliberal and Hindu nationalist agendas

As discussed in Chapter 1, the NEP 2020 proposed revamping the curriculum and pedagogy and recommended a paradigm shift from content-based to experience-based learning. A key part of the proposed changes is dependent on teachers. Given over one million teacher vacancies in India's schools and a large proportion of poorly qualified teachers, the NEP 2020 was expected to implement the Supreme Court's Justice Verma Commission's recommendations, including enhancing public investment in teacher education, strengthening institutional capacity in states, and redesigning the curriculum to incorporate diversity and inclusion (Batra, 2020). However, the NEP 2020 only pays lip service to teachers and their status, motivation, and service conditions, which required serious attention. While the policy acknowledges that no reform will work unless teacher are brought 'centre-stage' (NEP 2020, pp.4–5), the policy document does not provide recommendations to transform the way in which teachers are positioned and treated in the education system (Ramachandran, 2020).

The NEP 2020 continues to further consolidate central control over education but provides some leeway for states (Raveendhren, 2020). This policy could create tension between states that are governed by secular parties (such as Delhi, Kerala, and West Bengal), and the central government. As stated in the previous section, the BJP's agenda of imposing the Hindi language and a saffronized education agenda could be devastating to Muslims in BJP-governed states where Hindutva ideology will not only radicalize the Hindu population but also alienate Muslims and other religious minorities (Khan and Lutful, 2021). This section highlights teachers' attitudes towards

---

[19] This could be down to the impact of the BJP's agenda to impose the Hindi and Sanskrit languages, as Rajasthan was ruled by the BJP before Congress gained power in 2019.

the NEP 2020, the changes they are expected to incorporate in their classroom practices, and the BJP's language policy.

Teachers across the six research sites were asked about the NEP's proposals and how this affected their teaching. A government school teacher from Guwahati said: 'NEP 2020 gives much importance on practical rather than theoretical. Therefore, we will have to change our teaching by making it more practical oriented rather than theoretical explanations only' (GS1 Guwahati). She elaborated: 'Tests of students should be based on 80 per cent theoretical and 20 per cent practical at least. It may extend up to 30–40 per cent in practical to gain knowledge. Teachers should adopt play way method in teaching. We need to use more teaching learning materials during teaching. Teachers need to take students to field or lab for more practical experience' (GS1 Guwahati). She also discussed private schools, saying that they 'don't have to change much, because they already have the infrastructure and facilities to teach children in a play way method. Government schools have to change things, because they are still using the traditional method of teaching...' (GS1 Guwahati).

Similarly, a government school teacher from Jaipur felt that parental support and cooperation are integral in order to teach in a 'playful manner'. She said:

'Some changes that are mentioned in the national education policy 2020 are to teach in a playful way, behave in a friendly manner with students. I think that parents should also co-operate with teachers and government for better results of students. Previously teachers were free to teach in their own ways now we have restrictions or guidelines on how to teach.' (GS1 Jaipur)

This reflects the fact that government school teachers have limited agency and autonomy to teach in their own way and are expected to follow guidelines (see Chapter 3). A few private and government school teachers from Delhi, Chandigarh, and Mumbai labelled the NEP 2020 as an 'old policy' and the 'same as other [previous policies]'. The government school teachers from all research sites also expressed their need to be trained so as to be able to align themselves with the new education system. This included having opportunities to enrich their skills 'digitally' and 'practically' with respect to the best possible ways of integrating the play way approach to teaching.

In terms of assessment, the NEP 2020 strongly advocates formative, over-the-year assessment patterns, as opposed to year-end summative exams (NEP, 2020, p.17). However, on assessment and evaluation, a few teachers from each research site expressed fear of a decreased focus on examinations. A government school teacher from Bengaluru said: 'NEP is not giving more importance to examination up to a particular level. It is important to test students' knowledge. [otherwise] Students will not study' (GS1 Bengaluru).

Another government school teacher from Delhi said: 'Exams are important for students. I am not happy that the policy is not focusing on exams and testing. This is important for our students' (GS8 Delhi). Similarly, a government school teacher from Mumbai said: 'I was shocked that we don't have exams. Students will be happy but their parents won't' (GS7 Mumbai). Teachers' quotes show support for the legacy of an accountability system introduced by political parties based on exams, which in turn makes it easier to quantify performance. On one side, the NEP 2020 recommends the use of a descriptive progress report card of students for assessment; the policy also talks of the mushrooming coaching culture, and the introduction of flexible and easier board exams to counter assessment so that students do not have to put in additional effort while attending classes (NEP, 2020, p.18). However, none of the ideas discussed in the NEP 2020 can be operationalized without transforming the way teachers are positioned in the educational system. Teacher autonomy in the schools and classrooms has been eroded over the years as they are expected to teach to a preset schedule, regardless of whether their students are learning or not (Ramachandran, 2020). They are expected to furnish a wide range of input-related data without having the freedom to structure their classroom in a way that enables every child to learn (Ramachandran, 2020). Such requirements are incompatible with formative assessment. In 2022, it is unclear how the legacy of the neoliberal trajectory of schooling, including 'bean counting' and accountability will allow teachers to apply the NEP's more nuanced teaching and assessment policies. This is also the case for the central debate on language and medium of instruction that the NEP has reopened.

The NEP 2020 language policy and teachers' views

There is widespread consensus among educationists, linguists, early childhood education experts, and cognitive psychologists that instruction in the MT of the child is the most suitable medium for cognition and comprehension in the early years (Ball, 2010, 2011, 2014; Kosonen, 2017; Kirkpatrick and Liddicoat, 2019; Khaitan, 2020; Daniyal, 2020). According to the Global Education Monitoring Report (2016), children taught in a language other than their own can have their learning negatively impacted. The imposition of a single dominant language as the language of instruction in schools leads to wider issues of social and cultural inequality (UNESCO, 2016). MT-based bilingual or multilingual education significantly enhances the learning outcomes of students from minority language communities (Bühmann and Trudel, 2008; Ball, 2010).

There is formal recognition of the importance of MT instruction in the Indian Constitution and the national and state education policies formulated thereafter. Article 350A of the Constitution states that the 'shall endeavour to provide adequate facilities for instruction in the MT at the primary stage of education to children belonging to minority groups' (Ministry of Education, n.d., p.9, cited in Khaitan, 2020). The Three-Language Formula of 1957 proposed the use of a MT/regional language, Hindi, and/or English at different levels of education. The Three-Language Formula endorsed in the National Education Policies of 1968 and 1986 emphasized that the medium of instruction at elementary level should be in the MT of the child, directing states to ensure its implementation in state-run schools (Mohanty, 2008). The National Education Policy (NEP) 2020 of India broadens the definition of medium of instruction to include local and regional language at least till Class 5 and preferably till Class 8 (cited in Khaitan, 2020), emphasizing the importance of Indian languages. Part of this relates to the fact that Hindu nationalist policymakers still view English as an imperial language: doing away with it is one of the ways to de-westernize and de-colonize the Indian education system. While some have welcomed this move, others point out that the reduced importance of English in schools will pose an obstacle in reducing inequity arising from language instruction as it is seen as a way of climbing the social ladder (Khaitan, 2020).

As seen from these quotes, the demand for English education continues to dominate, despite attempts over decades, including the Three-Language Formula, to promote and incorporate vernacular languages in Indian education. There has been a drastic increase in the number of English medium schools both in urban and rural areas (Lightfoot et al, 2021). However, the poor quality of English teaching in rural areas continues to further the divide between the rich and poor. Census 2011 data reveals that only 0.02 per cent of Indians identify English as their MT/home language (Jolad and Agarwal, 2020).[20] UDISE 2017–2018 statistics show that 17,000 out of 154,000 schools (11.2 per cent) use English as the main medium of instruction (UDISE, Ministry of Education, GoI, 2017–2018 cited in Lightfoot et al, 2021).

The NEP 2020 stressed that attaining foundational literacy and numeracy for all children is an urgent national mission. One of the reasons for the crisis in foundational learning is the disconnect between the language of the child at home and the language used in schools for instruction (Lightfoot et al, 2021). Although the importance of instruction in the MT/home language has been recognized in the Constitution and reiterated in national policies, the medium of instruction in schools continues to be languages of political and economic pull such as English, Hindi, and other dominant languages of the respective states.

---

[20] The Census of 2021 has been postponed owing to COVID-19.

The NEP 2020 has questioned the increased focus on English; nevertheless the policy highlights that 'English must be available and taught in a high-quality manner at all government and non-government schools' in order to eliminate the divide between the higher and lower socio-economic groups (MHRD, 2019, p.82). In the NEP (2020), references to the importance of English were downplayed, although English is listed as an additional subject to be taught alongside state languages. There thus appears to be a reluctant acceptance at national level of the need for English, but a strong desire for a revival of (other) Indian languages in education and across society. This is at odds with current practices at the state level, where decision-making around education is largely made. Andhra Pradesh, Telangana, Karnataka, Punjab, and West Bengal (see section 1 of this chapter) have all recently committed to increasing EMI in their government schools (Aman, 2018; *Hindustan Times*, 2018; D'Souza, 2019; Rao, 2019; *The Telegraph*, 2019). The NEP 2020 appears to be advocating a move towards the teaching of English as a subject (instead of schooling where English is the medium of instruction across the curriculum). It states: 'all languages will be taught with high quality to all students; a language does not need to be the medium of instruction for it to be taught and learned well' (NEP, 2020, p.13). Since the release of the final NEP, there has been considerable reluctance of private schools and states to switch to MT instruction, especially where English has been used as a medium of instruction (Khaitan, 2020). In tandem with the official policy on language change, the NEP 2020 has also announced the formation of curricular content and textbooks in local languages.

The rationale for this language policy is to celebrate the 'Indianness' and rich cultural, regional, and linguistic diversity of India (Khaitan, 2020). RSS officials claim that the last education policy completely ignored the Indian knowledge system, which they say is thousands of years old. The idea of the NEP 2020 therefore is to create a more holistic teaching system based on Indian values that is flexible and suitable for the growth of students and future employment. According to the RSS, the policy aims to neutralize some fundamental elements that were imposed by Western culture and leftist ideology (Srivastava, 2020). As mentioned in Chapter 2, the NEP 2020 also places a considerable emphasis on mainstreaming Sanskrit, the ancient language known for its rich body of classical literature, and aims to offer it at all levels (Athreya and Haaften, 2020). The Modi administration had earlier demonstrated its sympathy for Sanskrit by spending 22 times more on promoting the language and establishing centres of excellence than it has spent promoting the five other classical languages, Tamil, Odiya, Malayalam, Telugu, and Kannada (Athreya and Haaften, 2020). Historically, Sanskrit has been accessible only to the upper castes of the Indian society, notably the Brahmins, and hence was never a language of the masses. Today Sanskrit is clearly part of the saffronizing Hindutva agenda. By prioritizing Sanskrit, the NEP risks alienating Muslims and Christians, India's oppressed castes, and people from the north-east who trace their history back to different origins, as the evolution of the language has been increasingly dictated by the Brahmins (Athreya and Haaften, 2020). The emphasis on a revival of Indian languages such as Sanskrit, Pali, and Prakrut is another achievement for the RSS.[21] One major argument in favour of Indians learning Sanskrit has been that it allows them to access ancient texts written in Sanskrit, such as the Rig Veda (Athreya and Haaften, 2020).[22]

Given that the MT or regional language received primacy in the NEP, this has been introduced in several BJP-controlled states, albeit on a pilot basis. Karnataka became the first state to implement the language policy in August 2021, and Madhya Pradesh and Himachal Pradesh launched a series of NEP initiatives that gave a push to the language policy (Sahoo, 2021). However a number of opposition-controlled states have been raising strong objections to the language policy and the manner in which this is being rolled out (Sahoo, 2021).

When teachers in Bengaluru were asked about the use of the MT and its impact on numeracy and literacy, a government school teacher said:

'[I]f they [students] learn vernacular, they learn the content very clearly that is advantage. Without any kind of difficulties concepts understanding will be better, that is the advantage the learner can learn very clearly without any difficulties if they learn in regional language [...] If the medium of instruction is mother tongue or regional language it will enhance the literacy rate.' (GS2 Bengaluru)

The teacher also mentioned the key issue of teacher shortages in regional languages: 'There is already shortage of competent teachers this teaching oriented and competency teacher getting in competent manner will be somewhat stumbling block...' (GS2 Bengaluru). A private school teacher had similar views: 'mother tongue or regional language ... when you are using it out at times it is very helpful. Nowadays Hindi is our common

---

[21] According to Atul Kothari, the national secretary of Shiksha Sanskriti Utthan Nyas and an RSS *pracharak* (worker), 'No education system can succeed without moral values. The new policy will be built on moral values which are inherent to India. Students will not only be taught the fundamental rights but also fundamental duties through the education system which borrows from the ancient texts and cultural practices' (Srivastava, 2020, para.3).

[22] A collection of observations made by Chanakya (an ancient Indian teacher/philosopher) from the various shastras.

language we can speak in Hindi. But the regional language is really a must' (PS11 Bengaluru). Most teachers in Bengaluru found that learning in the regional language strengthens literacy and numeracy. Interestingly, in Guwahati, when asked about the impact of the MT on numeracy and literacy skills, a government school teacher agreed to the use of the MT because:

'[I]n English medium schools, they keep mother tongue as a subject, but they do not give much attention to mother tongue. So, many students who are studying in English medium schools, are not good at mother tongue. They cannot read newspaper in mother tongue. They can converse in mother tongue but cannot read a book written in vernacular language. They even cannot write in mother tongue (Bengali).'[23] (GS3 Guwahati)

When probed on the NEP 2020, the teacher said, 'According to NEP 2020, education should be in local/regional language till 5th standard. I think this step has been taken to preserve local/regional languages because of extreme westernization of education recently' (GS3 Guwahati). The teacher held the view that westernized education through the English language was responsible for deteriorating the impact of 'vernacular languages', 'values', and the 'culture' of India.

Similarly in the Congress-ruled state of Rajasthan,[24] Jaipur, teachers endorsed the use of the MT in education. A government teacher explained in detail:

'If at the age of 3, a child comes to school & teacher teaches 'A for apple', 'B for ball', it will be a new thing for that child. It's absolutely new language for the child. The child may not develop interest in attending the school. In that case, use of mother tongue will definitely help the child in developing interest of learning. English is an international language. There is no doubt in its importance.' (GS2 Jaipur)

---

23 Issues regarding the MT in Assam and relations between the Bengali and the Assamese speaking communities are discussed in Chapter 6.

24 Linguistic minority students in Rajasthan have been deprived of education in their MT, with the books in Urdu, Sindhi, and Punjabi not being supplied to over 20,000 government schools and the teachers not being appointed in the academic session of 2021–2022. In a clarification on the staffing pattern, the Directorate of Elementary Education ordered the withdrawal of teachers of more than one 'third language' from the schools. This has effectively resulted in the teaching of Sanskrit as the only third language, to the exclusion of all others (Iqbal, 2020).

When asked about parents' preferences, she commented:

'In places like Rajasthan very few families use English language as medium of conversation at home … Use of mother tongue or local language will definitely help children to understand not only instructions but also for giving examples of the surroundings and also basic concepts of everything they see.' (GS2 Jaipur)

A government school teacher from Chandigarh commented that 'learning via Punjabi can develop comfort among students and promote better learning outcomes in the classroom' (GS3 Chandigarh). Another government school teacher stated that 'Punjabi can help students understand concepts of history better than English. But my students sometime failed at writing in better English' (GS4 Chandigarh). A few government school teachers from Delhi expressed appreciation of the idea of teaching in MT at a primary class and then switching to English in secondary grades. One stated: 'My students are taught in Hindi till grade 5; they learnt social science and science in Hindi. We also use the translation method for teaching English in our class' (GS7 Delhi). Another Delhi teacher shared: 'I don't mind teaching in the mother tongue actually we use Hindi in the classroom. This way students understand better' (GS5 Delhi). Government school teachers from Mumbai and Delhi also endorsed the use of the regional language, or the MT, for pedagogical purposes, whereas private school teachers expressed concern about the heavy usage of a regional or mother language in the classroom. When asked about the use of MT or regional language in a classroom with students of migrant parents or minority communities, teachers across the six states shared concerns about resources and expertise when using an MT or regional language in a multilingual classroom. Teachers also shared that similar resistance is shown by some parents, who argue that their children already know their MT and they go to school to learn new skills, such as speaking and writing the dominant languages and English, which they see as essential for employment opportunities. A private school teacher in Chandigarh said: 'Students are okay to understand the chapters in English, but classroom interaction might cause problems in too much usage of the regional language. Parents will complain and we will be in trouble' (PS2 Chandigarh). A private school teacher from Mumbai expressed similar views: 'It is okay to explain some concepts in Hindi or Marathi but then parents won't send their kids to us as they prefer English medium schools. Parents won't like this as they prefer their students to grow by learning in the English language that's why they sent them to our school' (PS4 Mumbai).

A few government and private school teachers in Mumbai and Punjab also expressed confusion about the use of the MT. A private school teacher from Mumbai said: 'Parents speak Bengali, and their daughter comes to my classroom in which there are students of different backgrounds and speak different languages, so what is the mother tongue to teach in the classroom? I don't understand' (PS5 Mumbai). Similarly, a government school teacher in Mumbai said: 'I think Marathi is the local language here, but I don't know Marathi fluently, how will I teach my subject?' In Chandigarh, a private school teacher expressed her lack of fluency in the Punjabi language: 'I have students who are local but also from Uttar Pradesh. I recently moved to Chandigarh. I can't speak fluent Punjabi. I fear losing my job' (PS9 Chandigarh). A government school teacher also voiced confusion: 'I have a lot of students from different backgrounds. I can't teach history in Hindi or any other regional language as I am not trained as such' (GS7 Chandigarh). This section shows mixed reactions to the use of an MT or regional language in teaching. This seems to be particularly challenging in states or classrooms where teachers or students come from diverse backgrounds. Teachers are also constantly grappling with the issue of which languages should be the medium of instruction, particularly with reference to speakers of minority languages, some of which lack standardized written forms. The major issue highlighted here by teachers is that the emphasis on the MT does not cover the entire classroom population, which leaves them worried that this could result in a group of linguistic minorities being left behind in their schools.

Conclusion

This chapter has presented teachers' views on key education issues, including parental school choice. Part and parcel of this is the parental demand for EMI. The commercialization and privatization of English language teaching has made English education an open and competitive 'linguistic marketplace', which is shaping language policies at local, state, and national level. English is increasingly receiving a greater space in instruction policies, preparing citizens so they fit into this neoliberal world. Buying into this, the Indian government has justified the adoption of EMI in schools owing to parental demand as English provides the necessary efficiency and capability to remain competitive in the global market (Ferguson, 2013; Sah, 2020). Needless to say, the increase of English has wide parental support, since the promotion of English in language policy is largely tied to a perceived belief of English as an agent for upward socio-economic mobility, empowerment, and quality education in a globalized world (Vaish, 2008; Heller and Duchene, 2012; Arcand and Grin, 2013; Erling, 2014; Sah and Li, 2018). At the same time, and in almost direct contradiction, the NEP 2020 promotes a return to vernacular language instruction, including placing greater emphasis on Hindi and Sanskrit. The imposition of Hindi and Sanskrit through changing education policy as per the ruling party has pushed the RSS agenda of homogenizing the country by aiming to 'colonize' a large section of non-Hindi people and wipe away their culture, language, customs, and identity, rendering them second-grade citizens in their homeland (Ibrahim, 2019). Though the emphasis is on the use of MT or regional language to promote community and keep its roots strong, teachers' responses on this are mixed. They shared conflicting narratives, revealing that they embraced their states' linguistic policies yet did not seem themselves as agents of change. Teachers' voices from the research sites show no big differences between responses from central (BJP) and state governments (no matter whether BJP, Congress or AAP) to both the neoliberal and Hindu nationalist agenda. Rather, their views were influenced by the impact of the pandemic on educational initiatives, as well as those policies that are set to earn state governments votes at the next election.

5

Higher Education, Neoliberalism, and Hindu Nationalism

Introduction

This chapter engages with the role of Higher Education (HE) in the Hindu nationalist project and how a neoliberal trajectory was able to embed the Hindutva discourse across Indian HEIs. As Indian HE expanded rapidly after economic reforms, there was a parallel growth in the number of private institutions as well as new regulatory policies that encouraged competition between government-funded institutions. The NEP of 2020 is taking this forward by moving towards a quasi-market model; this includes proposing increased technology for wider access and delivery, reflecting the wider neoliberal agenda across India. Although the NEP promises more autonomy for institutions and individual academics, the planned regulations and monitoring parameters actually make real autonomy in research and teaching impossible (Chattopadhyay, 2020). For the last 30 years, the focus of Indian HE has been on expansion and increasing access, rather than critical inquiry. As has been seen in previous chapters, and as also reflected in the wider literature on the links between neoliberalism and populism, the neoliberal trajectory increasingly attempts to stifle free speech and criticism of the government, which includes criticism of the marketization of HE and the government's Hindutva agenda.

HE has traditionally been a space where critical views of policy could be debated safely. Instead of delivering autonomy and creativity, neoliberalism in HE 'has delivered a semi-privatised authoritarianism more oppressive than the system it replaced' (Monbiot, 2019, para.2). Government HEIs have been forced to conform to new rules, including the Performance Based Appraisal System that includes numbers of publications and teaching hours amongst other metrics to 'measure' faculty performance and compare/rank institutions in a central government-controlled standardization process. This is not just driven by a desire to compare institutions domestically, but also by a drive to get Indian HEIs into international university rankings. Chattopadhyay (2016) describes how this type of control is part of New Public Management, a key feature of neoliberalism and also part of endogenous privatization (Ball and Youdell, 2008). Rather than increasing autonomy and freedom, these regulations force HEIs to be subjected to monitoring and assessment in the name of efficiency, where managerialism becomes an end in itself.[1] As expected, public services being subjected to market discipline have resulted in a fragmented system due to imposed competition – a major critique of India's HE system in the NEP. As elsewhere, the marketization of public services such as HE is in conflict with democracy. Attempts at resistance by staff and students have been met by ever more extreme methods, such as lawsuits, crackdowns, and arrests, to try and dissuade both faculty and students from exercising their right to free speech and taking part in political activities. This reduction in academic freedom, with academics unable to critically discuss issues around identity, citizenship and religion, has also allowed the Hindu nationalist philosophy to expand across the sector. As critical voices in academia are silenced and academics are told to focus on teaching larger cohorts of students more efficiently and effectively, society has been deprived of a space where different viewpoints can be debated. In addition, pro-Hindutva vice chancellors ensure that what is taught at their HEIs increasingly conforms to the Hindutva ideals propagated by the government. Unlike in schools there are no textbooks in HE that can be changed to rewrite history; nevertheless India's HE curriculum has been equally affected by the saffronization agenda.

The chapter begins with a brief review of India's HE sector and the funding issues that have led to increased marketization and neoliberal policies since 1991. Funding has also been made available to increase the numbers of 'institutes of national importance' and the rise of HEIs in more remote areas in light of wider economic development (Sharma, 2020b). The chapter then turns to the BJP appointments of Hindu ideologues in 2000, moving on to how between 2014 and today particular HEIs such as JNU (known for its left-wing politics) are gradually being infiltrated and discredited (Sharma, 2020b). It also examines how diversity, inclusion, and discrimination are propagated by HE through the intellectual paradigms around religion, caste, and gender that affect knowledge production and minority student engagement. This includes a discussion on the use of university spaces to either include or exclude minority students and the issue pertaining to academics and academic freedom (*The Guardian*, 2020).

---

[1]   This reflects what is happening in schools, as discussed in Chapter 3.

The chapter then briefly engages with the rise of private HE across India and its limited role in increasing access. This discussion of HEs' changing mandate in a neoliberal, Hindu-national India is analysed through the text of the new NEP of 2020.[2] The chapter ends with a review of how the NEP presents technology as the panacea for India's access and quality issues, and how this reinforces the neoliberal quasi-market.

India's HE sector

India's HE history starts with British colonialism and the establishment of institutions such as the Presidency College in Calcutta and CMS College in Kottayam in the early 19th century. In the middle of the 19th century, more emphasis was placed on HE with the establishment of the universities of Calcutta, Madras, and Bombay. In 1944, the Sargent Report on the status of education recommended that central government should take over more of the financial responsibility of universities and professional education. It also suggested a central Indian University Grants Committee, which would function as a regulatory body for all universities. The report states clearly that the committee should not interfere in the autonomy of the provincial universities. Based on this, the University Education Commission under the chairmanship of Professor S. Radhakrishnan set up the UGC,[3] through an executive order passed in 1945. Similar suggestions were made regarding technical universities, following which the All India Council for Technical Education (AICTE) was set up in 1946 to 'stimulate, coordinate, control the provisions of the technical education facilities' (Sargent Committee Reports, p.93, cited in Panigrahi, n.d., p.33).

India has witnessed a dramatic growth in HE since 1947 when the country had 20 universities and 500 colleges, and 210,000 students. By 1950–1951, India had 25 universities and 700 colleges with an enrolment of 100,000 students (Agarwal, 2009). The latest UGC Annual Report (2019, pp. 3–4) states that since independence the numbers have increased 52.35 times in the case of the degree awarding universities (1,047), 83.87 times in the case of colleges (41,935), and students' enrolment (37.40 million) has gone up by over 178.1 times. The expansion of the sector accelerated as of 2000. Enrolment increased from 8.8 million in 2001–2002 to 37.4 million in 2018–2019. According to Varghese (in Chattopadhyay et al, 2022), the

---

[2] The plan to restructure the HE system is presented as taking India back to its cultural and epistemic roots.

[3] The UGC is a statutory body set up by the GoI under the Ministry of Education, in accordance with the UGC Act 1956, and is charged with coordination, determination and maintenance of HE standards.

first decade of the 21st century experienced an annual addition of nearly 2.0 million students, making it the largest expansion ever experienced by the sector in any decade. The annual additions in enrolment, although lower, still continue to be at around 1.2 million students between 2011–2012 and 2018–2019 (Marginson et al, cited in Chattopadhyay et al, 2022). As of 31 March 2019, the number of universities listed by the UGC under Section 2(f) of the UGC Act 1956 has gone up to 911 – 51 central, 397 state public, 334 state private, 126 deemed universities, three institutions established under state legislation and 12,070 colleges listed under Section 2(f); out of these colleges, 9,755 are under Section 12B of the UGC Act (UGC, 2019). These institutions further reflect India's student density, as enrolment in HE is nearly 37.4 million every year – a gross enrolment ratio (GER) of 26.3 in 2018–2019, with 1.4 million teachers (MHRD, 2019, cited in Varghese in Chattopadhyay et al, 2022). Further growth is planned, as the new NEP 2020 (NEP, 2020) expects to double enrolment in India's tertiary sector by 2035. Different universities have varying entrance criteria: for example, universities established by central government admit students through entrance examinations administered at national level. They are required to reserve close to 50 per cent of their seats for students of SCs, STs, and OBC backgrounds. Universities established by state governments follow their own admission process and provide preferential admission to students from their respective states (Misra, 2019a).

The MHRD, Department of Higher Education, which the NEP now designates as the Ministry of Education,[4] is responsible for the overall development of the necessary infrastructure of the HE sector, both in terms of policy and planning.[5] However, as has been explained previously, under the Constitution, responsibility for education is shared between central and state governments. Central government sets policy and plans frameworks. The state governments are responsible for running the education system on the ground. This has exacerbated problems across the HE sector, since states have different resources for education, including HE. Those states with better economic performance offer more HEIs and HEIs of higher quality. This is illustrated by the large number of engineering colleges and the concentration of high technology industry in South India.

Institutes of National Importance

Institutes of National Importance (INIs) were established by central government as an independent category of HE institutions in a single

---

[4] The NEP 2020 changed the designation of the ministry.
[5] See the MHRD website: https://www.mhrd.gov.in/higher_education.

disciplinary area, grouped according to their disciplines. For example, all the INIs in the area of technology are called IITs, and they have campuses in various locations. Students are admitted through a common India-wide admissions test. The INIs are independent institutions and enjoy autonomy from central and state governments with regard to designing their curriculum, research and collaborations with industry.[6] The MHRD only stipulates the number of staff, who are paid by the central government (Agarwal, 2007; Ministry of Law and Justice, 2019, cited in Misra, 2019a). Each INI has a board of governors that oversees research and academic matters.

The first INI was established in the 1950s in technology, science, and management. Since then INIs have established a strong domestic and international reputation, and attract the best faculty and students from across India (Altbach, 2009, cited in Misra, 2019a). They enjoy higher prestige than private universities in India. However, the quality of their research outputs has been questioned (Hiremath and Komalesha, 2018, cited in Misra, 2019a). Their elite status is in part made possible by the hierarchical nature of the sector and the large number of non-elite HEIs that cater to the ministry's objective of massively increasing the number of students (Misra, 2019a).

Between 1995 and 2015 central government established a number of new INIs and upgraded some of the existing HEIs to INIs to cater for the growing need for access to high-quality HE across India. Most of these were established in semi-urban or rural areas – their location a deliberate political choice (Misra, 2019a) According to Misra (2019a), an independent committee of experts, convened by the MHRD, prepares a detailed project report for each new INI according to which MHRD funding is allocated, including per capita, and for buildings, programmes, and faculty. This is followed by the appointment of a board of governors and a director, who take responsibility for developing and running the institution. INIs have remained a funding priority for the government, which faces a shortage of resources given its desire to increase the size of the sector, as discussed later.

Funding issues in HE

The UGC is the key funding body for government HE. As well as providing grants for universities and colleges, it is also responsible for academic standards, framing policies, and advising central and state governments about expanding and improving HE.

---

[6]   This is unlike other universities that are regulated by the MHRD.

As India's population grew, access to HE became a major issue. The 1986 reforms reiterated the independent status of HEIs but led to a gradual decline in government expenditure. The proportion of the education budget allocated to HE gradually decreased from 24 per cent in the 1970s to around 9 per cent in early 2000 (Carpentier et al, 2011). The government faced a serious resource crunch and decided to reduce HE subsidies. Two committees were set up to mobilize additional resources for universities and technical education institutions, which were encouraged to raise fees and to turn to the private sector for additional funding (Carpentier et al, 2011). The measures suggested in the reports of both committees used typical neoliberal language, talking about improving efficiency in order to reduce waste and to save resources, mobilizing the latter from sources other than the government. Privatization, as discussed later in this chapter, took place mainly in the realm of professional and technical education in response to the growing demand for these courses (Carpentier et al, 2011). The lack of proper regulation of the expansion that took place has led to its own set of problems.

Negotiating the need to share the burden of funding HE between the public and private sectors has remained a key issue for India's policymakers. The resulting balance between public and private sectors has become almost synonymous with a balance between excellence and access. Quality control issues resulted in the creation of the National Assessment and Accreditation Council of India in 1994, with the objective of assessing and grading HEIs.

The economic reforms of 1991 increased the fall in budget allocation for education, and HE was affected. During the period between 1989–1990 and 1994–1995, HE's share of planned expenditure decreased from 12.6 per cent to 6 per cent (Tilak, 2008). As argued by Tilak (2008), during that period there was a gradual change in the way HE was conceived. 'The White Paper on Subsidies (GoI, 1995) questioned subsidization of HE in general classifying it as a non-merit good while primary education was identified as a merit good as it generates externalities' (Carpentier et al, 2011, p.137).[7] Cost recovery measures were accompanied by policies that allowed for the direct privatization of HE (Tilak, 2002). After the reforms of 1991, based on World Bank suggestions,[8] HE was seen more as a private than a public

---

[7] HE has generally been classified as a public good or at least a quasi-public good to advocate greater support from the government (Tilak, 2004, 2008).

[8] The reform measures suggested (World Bank, 1994) for developing countries include (i) encouraging greater differentiation of institutions of HE, including the development of private institutions; (ii) cost-recovery mechanisms, including cost-sharing with students; (iii) redefining the role of the government by evolving a policy framework to make the sector more market-friendly and public institutions more autonomous; and (iv) prioritizing investments towards quality improvement (Varghese, n.d.).

good as the government began structural reforms even in the social sector. The debate on this subject has gone hand in hand with a discussion about autonomy. The government has adopted a policy of granting autonomy to high-performing HEIs, allowing them the financial freedom to explore cost recovery measures. However, there has been pushback from faculty at some government HEIs who are worried that the quality of well-funded public universities may suffer without government funding and fear that the growth in autonomous institutions will invariably lead to an increase in fees, affecting access (Shamika et al, 2019).

In 2017 the Higher Education Financing Agency (HEFA) was set up as a non-profit joint venture company by the Ministry of Education and Canara Bank in order to mobilizing extra-budgetary resources such as corporate social responsibility funds from public sector undertakings or corporates (who are required to keep aside 5 per cent of their declared profits to spend on social causes). According to Chattopadhyay and Panigrahi (in Chattopadhyay et al, 2022), HEFA was launched with an authorized capital of INR 20 billion (2,000 crores) and it can leverage the equity to raise up to INR 200 billion (20,000 crores) for funding projects for infrastructure and development of world-class labs in IITs, IIMs and National Institute of Technology and such other institutions. HEFA can extend ten-year loans to finance infrastructure that allows institutions to expand and/or upgrade. The repayment of these loan puts extra pressure on HEIs to make money, which affects the academic courses they can offer, and by extension their autonomy with regard to both teaching and research.[9] As expected in a neoliberal environment, Chattopadhyay and Panigrahi (in Chattopadhyay et al, 2022) believe that 'Not all central universities are on the same level playing field. The best ones will be able to take the plunge and surge ahead in this highly competitive situation and the rest will find it difficult to compete and sustain' (p.62).

As in all sectors of education reviewed in this book, HE has been affected not only by the post-1991 reforms neoliberal approach, but also by a rising tide of Hindutva. In the case of HE, Hindutva did not emanate directly from neoliberalism as clearly as in the case of school education, but, as will be seen in the rest of this chapter, the loss of academic autonomy and the increased control of the sector by Hindutva ideologues has played directly into the Hindu nationalist agenda, with academics and HEIs mostly powerless to stop the process.

---

[9] The principal portion of the loan has to be repaid through the generation of internal accruals (earned through fee receipts, research earnings, etc.). The government shoulders the responsibility of interest costs. This requires the HEIs to escrow a specific amount from their internal accruals to HEFA for a period of ten years (Chattopadhyay and Panigrahi, in Chattopadhyay et al, 2022, p.62).

The BJP's Hindu nationalist agenda in HE
Hinduism takes its place in universities 1998–2004

In 1998, the NDA government inherited a post-reform HE sector in which funding was spread very thin. Beyond the hard choices related to financing HE after 1991, the BJP part of the NDA government also had a saffronization agenda. Although the BJP manifesto for the 1998 elections was very clear that it supported the independence of HEIs, once in power the BJP-led NDA government actually increased control and centralization.

> For anyone under the illusion that the Ministry of Human Resources Development would limit its myopic designs for higher education to rewriting a few textbooks, the last few weeks should come as a wakeup call. Every major institution of higher education, from the Indian Institutes of Management to the Indian Institutes of Technology, from universities to professional bodies such as the council of architects, from private institutions to foreign players are now subject to a single-point agenda that defines higher education policy: control and centralisation. (Mehta, 2003, cited in Lall, 2007, p.165)

Control and centralization served a particular purpose – the appointment of sympathetic staff, and the removal from senior positions of those with critical views of the new government. Vice chancellors of various universities were appointed with the sole criterion of sympathizing with the new policies, and democratic norms were flouted as institutional governing bodies were filled with BJP sympathizers. Once the leadership had been changed, this policy was extended to teaching staff (Taneja, 2003). Similar problems were observed across India – in Himachal Pradesh, for example, all three state universities appointed RSS cadre to senior positions. Qualifications were no longer the main criterion. The Indian Institute of Mass Communication appointed a new chairman on the executive council who was known to have RSS affiliations, and the advisor to the director of the All India Council for Technical Education also had RSS links. In Shimla, the Indian Institute of Advanced Studies received a pro-RSS chairman. Resulting problems included the Student Union president at the Aligarh Muslim University being dismissed illegally by the vice chancellor.[10]

Beyond HEIs, the UGC had its authority and autonomy undermined with regard to academic salaries, promotions, and working conditions. Historians appointed to the Indian Council of Historical Research (ICHR) were known to have supported the VHP campaign on Ayodhya. The Indian

---

[10] See Nalini Taneja (n.d.) for more details on personnel changes.

Council of Social Science Research was filled with RSS supporters. In the National Museum, galleries were renamed, and the choice of items displayed reflected the Sangh Parivar's view of Indian history. Personnel at the National Institute of Planning and the NCERT were also changed. Three Marxist historians (Romila Thapar, Bipan Chandra, and Satish Chandra) whose texts had been removed from the national textbooks were dropped from the NCERT board (Mehta, 2021). They were all Delhi-based historians, who were either teaching at the University of Delhi or JNU, and were the co-founders of the Centre for Historical Studies at JNU (Special Correspondent [The Hindu], 2014). 'According to historian Sumit Sarkar, the NCERT cleansing was a part of a general obscurantist drive, which had to be seen in conjunction with the BJP-led government's strident campaign to introduce courses in Vedic mathematics and astrology' (Mehta, 2021, para. 2). The NCF started to push research into what was seen as traditionally Hindu or Vedic 'science'. State universities and colleges received substantial grants from the government to offer particular post-graduate degrees, including PhDs in astrology; research into meditation, faith healing, cow-urine, and priest-craft was promoted with substantial injections of public money (Nanda, 2005).

More significantly, there was a rapid change in discourse amongst certain academics on the ground. One of the senior professors interviewed at IIT in Delhi said:

> For 50 years – since independence there has been a policy to enhance the history of minorities disproportionately. All this government is doing is putting the history of the Hindus into the right perspective. [...] If you go to JNU you can still find those who toe the old socialist line that the old interpretation of history is right and the new take on it is wrong. (cited in Lall, 2007, p.166)[11]

It would have been inconceivable to have heard such a statement even a few years earlier anywhere in the academic community. The greatest success of the BJP education policy was not the introduction of new textbooks with revised history and science curricula, or even the emergence of RSS activists at the helm of national education institutions – it was how the logic of their discriminatory discourse permeated the intelligentsia. The greatest danger from this was the erosion of the concept of the Nehruvian inclusive, statist identity, which allowed the different communities to live with each other (Lall, 2007).

---

[11] Anonymous interview conducted at IIT Delhi on 11 January 2004.

At JNU, there were further changes. Professors and students commented that *pujas* (Hindu prayers) had started in the student halls of residence, and as a reaction Muslim students had started doing *namaz* (Muslim prayers) in the refectories. Consequently, the university gave a neutral space outside the halls but on campus for all religious activities to take place.[12] One of the professors tried to sound reassuring: 'India is such a large country that changes like this cannot happen overnight. There are plenty of people who oppose these changes' (Lall, 2007, p.166). Despite opposition, the speed at which discourse amongst the urban middle class changed was breathtaking (Lall, 2007).

What was also notable was the lack of any significant change in the decade between 2004 and 2014, when Congress returned to power. While there was a clear de-saffronization agenda with regard to NCERT textbooks (as covered in Chapter 2), not much was done to undo some of the damage to HE. The only notable HE policy between 2004 and 2014 was the National Education Mission, or Rashtriya Uchchatar Shiksha Abhiyan, in 2013 that provided strategic funding to higher and technical institutions in states. Under this central scheme, states were required to develop comprehensive HE plans with an interconnected strategy that addressed issues of expansion, equity, and excellence. Central funding under the scheme was linked to academic, administrative, and financial reforms of state HE, supporting the continuation of the neoliberal agenda. This funding incentivized well-performing institutions. The scheme was designed in such a manner that grants were dependent on outcomes and based on state HE plans that benchmarked state and institution performance (Shamika et al, 2019, p.43).

Post-2014 HE – the RSS Hindutva agenda

It was noted earlier that once the BJP was back in power after the 2014 elections, the party did not make significant and direct policy changes with regard to the school curriculum and textbooks, leaving much of this to state governments and influential RSS cadres. A similar policy was followed in HE. HE is important to the RSS as it provides an opportunity to rewrite established historical narratives and to sponsor its members. To do this, the prevailing academic consensus and structures of power have been attacked (Bhatty and Sundar, 2020).

Since 2014, the RSS has (again) influenced the appointments of vice chancellors and heads of research institutions, and has also recruited pro-RSS faculty across public universities (Venugopal, 2018; Kanungo, 2019).

---

[12] It should be emphasized that even until the late 1990s it would not have been possible to imagine that religion would play any kind of public role in JNU's student and university life.

One example is the ICHR, which appointed Y. Sudershen Rao whose perspective on the direction that social science and history education was taking mirrored that of the RSS:

> I honestly feel that Indian social science research in general and history research in particular is dominated by Western perspectives, in the name of liberal or left perspectives. Most of us see India through western prism. Every nation has the right to write its own history from its own perspective, with certain national objectives. I call this process as 'Indianisation'. At best you can call it a patriotic approach. (cited in Jaffrelot, 2015, para.1)

Growing job insecurity (albeit a global problem) has made academics less resistant to ideological agendas that are being pushed by the establishment.[13] In addition, RSS appointees have by and large lacked the requisite qualifications. Thus, Bhatty and Sundar (2020) believe that while they may use the social and cultural capital generated by their positions to achieve greater respectability for their views, they will be unable to sustain this.

One of the most noticeable aspects of the BJP government since 2014 has been the fundamental war waged against public universities in general, and the social sciences in particular, though the sciences have also been attacked by diverting funding to unscientific beliefs and the proliferation of pseudoscience (Padma, 2019; Anand and Niaz, 2022). Delegitimizing scholars – especially English-speaking cosmopolitan scholars who are critical of BJP policies – is something that the Modi regime shares with other anti-intellectual regimes (Conolly, 2017; Stanley, 2018). As in the late 1990s, the RSS/BJP vision for universities involves funding centres of Sanskrit, yoga, astrology, and other subjects that are related to India's ancient past (Bhatty and Sundar, 2020). Much of this 'revivalism' is appealing to an Indian spirit that is still suffering from Macaulay's infamous dismissal of all Indian indigenous learning, but the BJP's project does not go beyond Ancient India to study the reservoir of knowledge that is embodied in the practices of indigenous/tribal communities or its rich Muslim and Dravidian scholarship (Bhatty and Sundar, 2020); rather it serves to underpin the Hindu nationalist fear of globalization and westernization. Institutional resources are being provided to BJP projects; for instance, an inter-ministerial funding programme on developing products from indigenous cows,[14] SUTRA-PIC India (GoI, n.d.), was announced in 2020, while AIIMS Rishikesh has been asked to

---

[13] See Ericksen (2012) on the Nazi takeover of universities.

[14] Hindus consider the cow to be a sacred symbol of life. In the Vedas (Hindu scriptures), the cow is referred to as the mother of all the gods as in the school textbooks in Chapter 3.

undertake clinical trials on the efficacy of the Gayatri Mantra (a Hindu prayer) in treating COVID-19 (Koshy, 2021). Refresher courses, which all faculty who want promotions must take, are used as occasions for RSS propaganda (Anand and Niaz, 2022). The wider acceptance of Hindutva in HE rhetoric is reflected in the IIT Kharagpur calendar for 2022 that promotes the Hindu nationalist agenda and pseudo-scientific attitude by challenging the 'Aryan invasion theory' of ancient Indian history through pieces of evidence embedded in the Vedas in order to counter colonial and Western teachings (Mihindukulasuriya, 2021). The aim of the calendar is also to encourage research in domains such as Indian history, advanced archaeological exploration, Indian language systems, Indian systems of geometry and mathematics, cosmology, positional astronomy, and Indian constructs of ecological and working ethics (Mihindukulasuriya, 2021).

In general the BJP's cultural attack on public universities has connected well with a neoliberal economic downsizing of education. Yet there is one major contradiction between the RSS's cultural vision and that of the government: the desire for Indian HEIs to figure in global university rankings. An Institute of Eminence Scheme started in 2018 aimed to increase the number of Indian universities in the Top 500, with the help of additional resources and autonomy in framing courses and hiring faculty. But if HEIs operate in the forcefield of an RSS-controlled understanding of history and science, they are unlikely to attract foreign students or the foreign investment that will make India's HE sector globally competitive (Chakrabartty, 2019; Bhatty and Sundar, 2020).

The Indian elite has not engaged much with the saffronization of HE, increasingly withdrawing from the public university system and preferring to send their children to private institutions or colleges abroad, even for undergraduate degrees, something that was rare just a generation ago (Bhatty and Sundar, 2020). This contradiction – whereby the middle classes support saffronization across India's public sphere (Nanda 2011), but still prefer Western or Western-inspired HEIs to educate their children – has yet to be resolved. For the rest of the population, the problem goes much deeper than the Hindutva agenda, as discussed later.

Reductions in scholarships and fee hikes

The neoliberal agenda of the Modi government has been observed in the further decline of funds to HE (Jayal, 2019), fee hikes for students, increased precaritization for faculty and changing regulatory structures that encourage HEIs to depend on loans rather than state funding (Bhatty and Sundar, 2020). The government has also been prioritizing 'skill development', designed to create 'enterprising self-motivated individuals for the private sector' (Gooptu, 2009, p.1); this despite government employment remaining the single largest goal for youth nationwide (Centre for the Study of Developing Societies [CSDS], 2017).

Fee hikes have triggered nationwide protests and strikes across the country, resulting in on-campus confrontations. In October 2019 – in the middle of an academic semester, the JNU administration announced that it had amended the hostel manual and increased charges for students. It also changed the rules related to hostel allotment, alongside introducing student dress codes and timings to enter and leave the hostel premises. This decision, as well as the manner of its implementation, created a strong sense of outrage among students (Pandey, 2020).[15] At Jamia Milia Islamia (JMI), in 2016 and 2017, fee hikes were also proposed. Both times the fee hike was rolled back owing to student protests. The reasons cited for the increase refers to the MHRD's expectation that universities should mobilize resources internally. In 2019, hostel fees were hiked by Rs 1300, in addition to the nominal increase made every semester. However, the students were successful in getting these increases rolled back (Panigrahi, n.d.).

In Maharashtra, students of the Mahatma Gandhi Antarashtriya Hindi Viswa Vidyalaya protested against fee increases in 2015. Most of these students belonged to the SC/ST/OBC categories, and hence additional costs would mean that many would have to drop out (Panigrahi, n.d.). The Tata Institute of Social Sciences (TISS) is another example of an institute that has been asked to raise its own funds. TISS started in Mumbai and now has campuses in Guwahati (2012) and Hyderabad (2013) as well as new affiliated centres in Patna and Tuljapur. The 180 ad hoc faculty are funded by private agencies such as the Tata Trust. Since 2013, TISS has been asked to fund itself, and to raise 30 per cent of its own expenses. This forced the institute to hike its fees by at least 46 per cent and in some cases by up to 100 per cent. In 2014, fees went up to Rs 61000 for OBC students per year and the SC/ST students are paying Rs 60,000. The repercussions are already there to see – the OBC student community is seeing an increased dropout rate (Panigrahi, n.d.).

In October 2019, students at the Indian Institute of Technology (Mumbai) protested against a proposed fee hike for MTech courses. In December 2019, six students from the Satyajit Ray Film and Television Institute began an indefinite hunger strike in Kolkata. Students at another premier film institute, the Film and Television Institute of India in Pune, also went on an indefinite hunger strike to protest against the 10 per cent fee hike in December 2019,

---

[15] The JNU administration explained that fees had not been raised in nineteen years. The University Registrar has said that JNU has a deficit of over 45 crores ($6.3 million); the university has been spending a massive amount on water, electricity and service charges (Pandey, 2020).

and the students at the Indian Institute of Mass Communication in New Delhi have been demanding a decrease in the existing course fee since December 2019 (Pandey, 2020). Even open universities that cater mostly to the unprivileged sections have seen a fee hike. A total of 163 courses at the Indira Gandhi National Open University (IGNOU) are to see a fee hike of 10–20 per cent. This again has been due to the reduction in the fund for the central universities and colleges (Panigrahi, n.d, p.40).

The resulting students' protests have been resisted by the administration, but some HEIs have had a particularly tough time, with student protests going well beyond the issues of fees and with increasing brutal government reaction.

Student protests and academic freedom

Student protests have been widespread across India; beyond fee hikes they have taken place regarding a range of issues such as unqualified faculty, longer library hours, the right to eat non-vegetarian food in canteens, liberal hostel timings for women, the right to hold meetings on issues such as Kashmir or the Citizenship (Amendment) Act (CAA) and reactions to the suicide of the Dalit student Rohit Venula (Bhatty and Sundar, 2020). How some of these issues have affected India's society at large will be elaborated in Chapter 6, but the role played by the universities and their students is discussed here.

Wider political issues such as the anti-CAA protests in 2019–2020 even reached usually apolitical spaces such as the IITs and IIMs. These protests became particularly polarizing: on 13 December 2019, JMI students, locals, and teachers began a march towards Parliament demonstrating against the CAA, triggering protests across the country. Clashes broke out between the protesters and the police when they were stopped. As many as 50 students were detained as police used tear gas and lathis (batons) to disperse the protesters (Ahmad, 2019). Another protest march was stopped on 15 December 2019, and several students were allegedly attacked by the police. The same evening, police stormed into Jamia Millia Islamia's (JMI) central library and attacked students, leaving many severely injured. The videos of policemen beating students who were studying in the library triggered local uproar and international condemnation. Thousands of students gathered outside the police headquarters to protest against the attack and demand the release of the detained students. Students then gathered at the university to protest against the CAA and police brutality. Local residents also joined them for the next three months, until the protest was called off due to the COVID-19 pandemic in March 2020 (Iftikhar, 2021).

In a case from Hyderabad Central University, a Dalit student committed suicide, bringing to light the extent of caste discrimination and arbitrary decision-making within universities, and sparking nationwide calls for legislation to address campus discrimination (Sundar and Fazili, 2020).

Following an altercation between the Ambedkar Studies Association (ASA) and the ABVP, the union education ministry intervened on behalf of the ABVP students, putting pressure on the university to take action against the ASA. The university did this in an unprecedented and extreme way: the ASA students were not just removed from their hostels and their fellowships withheld; they were institutionally ostracized. The students responded by sleeping under a tent in the open, symbolically recreating a Velivada, or Dalit ghetto, on campus, highlighting the aspect of caste discrimination (Farooq, 2016).

Across the nation, student protests have been delegitimized and put down brutally. University students have been physically attacked by ABVP vigilantes and policemen on campus (Bhatty and Sundar, 2020). The ways to stifle criticism and protests now also include judicial means and policing (including police on campus, such as at Delhi University) (Chattarji, 2019).[16] Sedition and anti-terror legislation are now regularly used to intimidate academics. Harsh Mander, an academic charged with incitement to violence because of a speech he made at an anti-government protest in 2019 stated: 'The government feels now that its only opposition is some voices in academia and civil society, and they are the only barriers to recasting India into a Hindu supremacist nation' (Perrigo, March 2021, para.5).

Public universities have tried to impose service rules that would prohibit faculty from writing for the press and participating in demonstrations (Vajpeyi, 2017). This means academic voices are stifled, and the Indian press has had a key role in stoking the fire. India's leading media outlets have camped out in the vicinity of the country's leading universities, from Aligarh Muslim University to Jamia Millia Islamia or JNU in Delhi (Anand and Niaz, forthcoming 2022). Students have been making the headlines with their raised fists and bruised bodies, inspiring many others to join protests in solidarity with their demands (Sanu, 2020). But some Indians have asked why these young people, who had gone to study at taxpayers' expense, were protesting when they should have been studying in the library. According to Sanu (2020), students are protesting because they understand that they must struggle in defence of their rights to education and free debate, and to protest against injustice. The student leaders feel that they act for the wider community. Emotions are particularly high when students are their family's first generation to attend HE (Sanu, 2020). Many of the protests are also against the aggressive Hindutva political agenda, as students realize how the

---

[16] 'The permanent presence of police on campuses such as DU backed up by surveillance cameras and the moral policing of foods consumed, dress, religiosity, plays performed, lectures delivered, films screened and so on is the new normal, not only for DU but many public universities' (Chattarji, 2019, p.84).

neoliberal economics promoted by the ruling BJP that has seen education budgets slashed is linked to it (Sanu, 2020).

The onslaught on certain HE institutions – JNU as an example

JNU was set up in 1969 with a mission to promote principles of national integration, social justice, secularism, a democratic way of life, international standing, and a scientific approach to the problems of society. (Sharma et al, 2022). JNU was expected to chart a new course of national integration, providing HE access to people from every area of the country no matter what background they came from (Batabyal, 2014, cited in Sharma et al, 2022). Academics were seen as key in creating and maintaining a space for critical thinking and democratic debate. In their chapter on political actors in HE, Sharma et al (2022) state that even in the face of the neoliberal reforms of the 1990s, JNU was able to withstand the effects and interference of such policies owing to the role played both by the students and the teachers' unions.

Over the last decade, however, JNU has come under increasing attack, accused of being 'infested with left-wing extremism on campus' (Mishra, 2020, para.2). Professors Bipan, Chandra, and Thapar, the previously mentioned academics whose scholarship had been removed from Indian history textbooks, were JNU professors who symbolized India's left-wing: anti-colonial, secular, egalitarian, and modernist. Thapar has been accused of being a Marxist; of 'having a very negative opinion of Hindu religious beliefs, and consistent with Marxist ideology, she has tended to promote the antiquated colonial-missionary racist paradigm of ancient India'.[17] Left-wing accusations, however, are no longer enough; JNU has also been accused of harbouring 'agents of Pakistan on the JNU campus to intensify their vicious campaign for a full-scale secession of Kashmir from India' (Tripathi, 2016, para.1).

JNU was always known as a place with a culture of dissent, especially after the 1977–1979 emergency – and this position was generally respected by wider society. However, after the 2014 BJP win, the government set out to break this dissent. A famous incident in 2016 brought JNU to the top of the news across India: it was accused of harbouring 'anti-national activities calling for the breakup of India' (PTI, 2020c, para.1). Amit Shah, the Home Minister, believed that 'those chanting anti-national slogans in JNU should be thrown in jail (PTI, 2020c, para.3). An incident on 9 February 2016 saw

---

[17] See Vishal Agarwal's (2002) assessment of Thapar's work. More about his work, which discredits the JNU historians and propagates a Hindu nationalist version of Indian history, can be found on his home page – Agarwal (n.d.).

the President of the JNU Students Union, Kanhaiya Kumar, arrested on charges of sedition along with three other students, accused of raising 'anti-national slogans'.[18] Since then, the term 'anti national' has been employed by the BJP against those it accuses of working against the interests of the nation. JNU students saw their actions as their democratic right to protest against the political rhetoric of nationalism. The JNU Teachers' Association (JNUTA) started a 'Save JNU' campaign, which was quickly picked up by other universities across the country and opened up the debate on the academic freedom of expression and autonomy. The JNUTA organized teach-ins at the freedom square to defend the tradition of intellectual debate and discussion on campus, focusing particularly on the meaning of nationalism (Azad et al, 2016, cited in Sharma et al, in Chattopadhyay et al, 2022, p.225).

But the anti-national label has stuck, with the media and pro-BJP social media accusing students and academics of using government funded university subsidies to finance a left-wing political movement. 'Television coverage in particular was ideologically aligned with the dominant discourses

---

[18] 'The Indian Penal Code of 1860, Section-124-A-Sedition, reads: 'Whoever, by words, either spoken or written, or by signs, or by visible representation, or otherwise, brings or attempts to bring into hatred or contempt, or excites or attempts to excite disaffection towards the Government established by law in India, shall be punished with imprisonment for life, to which fine may be added, or with imprisonment which may extend to three years, to which fine may be added, or with fine.' This section was enacted in 1870, not long after the anti-colonial rebellion of 1857 and consequently the establishment of direct British rule in 1858. It stayed in force after independence in 1947 with minor amendments (replacing or deleting phrases such as 'British India' and 'Her Majesty' and 'Crown Representative'). It can obviously be misused to restrict the freedom of speech enjoined in the Constitution of India (1950), especially any expression of dissent and protest. It has been used to such effect with increasing frequency of late (pp.1–2). The sedition law was used to arrest Kanhaiya Kumar, Student Union President and PhD student at the JNU, on 12 February 2016, having allegedly participated in an 'anti-national' discussion event on campus on 9 February. 'It is a charge used frequently in the country, with government data showing that IPC section 124A (sedition) was invoked 47 times in 2014, making up 27 per cent of all charges under the category "offences against the state"' (Tiwary, 2016, para.1). Recent cases have involved sedition charges being brought against: journalist Manoj Shinde in August 2006 for using 'abusive words' about Narendra Modi, then Chief Minister of Gujarat; *Times of India* editor Bharat Desai in June 2008 for publishing articles questioning the appointment of the Ahmedabad Police Commissioner (under the jurisdiction of the state government under Modi); author Arundhati Roy in October 2010 for saying that Kashmir had not been an integral part of India; cartoonist Aseem Trivedi in September 2012 for insulting national emblems in a series of anti-corruption cartoons; 11 protesters in Kudankulum in March 2012 for objecting to the construction of a nuclear power plant; and 67 Kashmiri students in a university in Meerut in March 2014 for cheering the Pakistan team while watching a cricket match on television (Gupta, 2019).

of the nation and nationalism, and projected protestors as anti-nationals' (Chattarji, 2019, p.80). The media contributed to the nationalist versus anti-national narrative, with those protesting against government policies labelled as anti-national. By doing so, the media has played a significant role in reducing academic free speech. According to Chattarji (2019), the reaction of the media points to a symbiotic relationship between the media and the state at a time when 'a privatised media is seeking to create an ideological consensus about the privatization of public goods, which includes public universities' (p.85).

As mentioned earlier, JNU erupted in protests again in early January 2020 at a proposed fee hike, demanding the resignation of the vice chancellor. This time the continued agitation was broken up by thugs on 5 January, when they entered the university campus and went on a rampage, injuring over 28 people, despite the police presence at the gates. According to Sharma et al (in Chattopadhyay et al, 2022), the refusal of police to step in and protect students and staff has fuelled speculation that the university administration and the police were complicit in the attack.

The ramifications for academic freedom

The marriage between neoliberalism and Hindu nationalism has come at the cost of academic freedom – defined as allowing academics and students to work without external interference. Academic freedom is a philosophical cornerstone of the academy (Austin and Jones, 2015), as the pursuit of free enquiry defines the core mission of any university (Bruneau, 2015; Lüde, 2015). The discussions on academic freedom pertain both to what the academic says in the classroom where the individual speaks and writes from a particular knowledge base (Tierney and Sabharwal, 2016) and to what an academic might say outside the classroom, where he or she claims no disciplinary expertise. Both areas have become points of contention in India. According to Sharma et al (in Chattopadhyay et al, 2022 p.225) academic agency has been progressively shrinking owing to neoliberal policies as well as the government's attempts to silence critique and alternative views, and Apoorvanand (2018) explains how universities destroy the very essence of HE when they silence critics.

A notable case was the resignation of Professor Pratab Banu Metha from Ashoka University in March 2020. The founders of the university had apparently made it clear that his public critique of the government had threatened its planned expansion (Perrigo, March 2021). His article (reproduced in the Appendix), which was published in one of India's leading newspapers, criticized the BJP's majoritarian and authoritarian approach. Beyond what happened at Ashoka University, academics and students have been facing an immediate, sharp, and existential threat, as also shown by

India's precipitous decline on the global academic freedom index (The Wire Staff, 2020a).

Part of the attack on academic freedom has gone hand in hand with the militarization of campuses, promoted to project nationalism. There are proposals for tanks (D'Souza, 2017), for towering flags and police bands playing frequently; and army generals are now considered experts on historical topics (The Wire Staff, 2020b). The Indian government seems to be involved in counterinsurgency at universities. The book on the Delhi riots by Monika Arora and others (discussed further in Chapter 6), which the Delhi Police appears to have adopted as its 'intellectual' guide in filing criminal charges against students and faculty, makes the parallels clear (Arora et al, 2020). It describes Delhi's leading universities as hubs of a gigantic foreign-funded criminal conspiracy run by a network of urban-Naxal jihadis,[19] using the constitution as a decoy, to engineer violence (Rai, 2020; Sundar, 2021).

One example of this is the prosecution of a Muslim JNU PhD student Sharjeel Imam. Among various charges against Imam was that he read the wrong kind of books, such as *Forms of Collective Violence: Riots, Pogroms and Genocide in Modern India* by Paul Brass, for his MPhil thesis on pre-partition attacks on Muslims in Bihar (Sundar, 2021). The charge sheet states that the book 'catalogues the various forms of collective violence that has occurred in India during the past six decades, which include riots, pogroms, and genocide … It says that the various forms of violence must be understood not as spontaneous outbreaks of passion, but as an act of organised groups' (*The Federal*, 2020, para.3). The Delhi police said, 'By reading only such literature and not researching alternative sources, the accused (Imam) became highly radicalised and religiously bigoted' (Sundar 2021, para.9).[20]

Teaching has been affected in multiple ways, including censorships of texts. For example, Rohinton Mistry's Booker Prize-shortlisted novel *Such a Long Journey* was eliminated from a syllabus when a student objected to certain passages. The novel tells the story of a bank clerk who belongs to Mumbai's Parsee community (Tierney and Sabharwal, 2016). A few pages in the novel portray Indian politics and a specific political party negatively. Upon the complaint, Mumbai University removed the book from its reading lists. Similarly, a professor at Banaras Hindu University was fired when he tried to screen in his Development Studies class the currently banned *India's*

---

[19] Naxalites are a group of left radical communists, while Jihadis are a group of people engaged in a holy war on behalf of Islam as a religious duty.

[20] Imam is accused in seven cases, including a case stemming from a Special Cell investigation into the north-east Delhi riots.

Daughter, a movie about a rape that occurred in New Delhi. Mathur (2018), teaching at IIM Ahmedabad, describes how in December 2015 the BJP government sought an inquiry against him with specific charges of taking an 'anti-national' perspective in his teaching.

The challenge of what should be taught in the classroom extends to the sorts of seminars, clubs, and activities that occur outside the classroom. Academic seminars have been repeatedly cancelled or refused permission on the grounds that the topics are rebellious or the speakers are anti-national. This also happens occasionally when a speaker is deemed to be too supportive of the Hindu right. The JNU Centre for Sanskrit Studies invited a well-known yoga guru who is looked on as supportive of the conservative government. A group of Muslim students opposed the invitation, terming it a 'silent right-wing onslaught'. The speaker felt obliged to cancel his keynote speech (Tierney and Sabharwal, 2016).

But the onslaught is mainly against those critical of the government or Hindutva. Faculty members have been beaten up or arrested for Facebook posts critical of the government (Sundar, 2018; Jayal, 2019). Surveillance is rising, with CCTV cameras and biometric attendance being set up across campuses. In 2020, the police were tasked with keeping a watch on campuses and infiltrating student WhatsApp groups (Bhatty and Sundar, 2020; Rao, 2020; Sundar, 2021). Consequently, the most obvious implication for students and academics alike is censorship and a move against academic freedom and personal safety (Sundar, 2021). The neoliberal/Hindu nationalist trajectory has also had repercussions on who attends university, as discussed in the next section.

Social diversity, inclusion, and discrimination in HE

Social diversity – in its visible form – is quantifiable and measurable. It is reflected in terms of the relative share of enrolled students from different social and minority groups. Empirical evidence shows that the share of students from socially excluded groups has increased, making campuses across India more diverse (Sabharwal and Malish, 2017). It can be argued that this change in student composition is, in large part, thanks to the strict implementation of reservation policies and the quota system. These trends, however, cannot be generalized. Elite institutions – following selective admission policies based on competitive examinations – often still enrol disproportionally large numbers of students from privileged groups, especially higher castes. Their campuses remain less diverse (Sabharwal and Malish, 2017). Rao (2013) uses Erving Goffman's concept of stigma to discuss the experience of SC and ST students in IITs. While Rao did not actually conduct observations of classrooms, his research showed that institutional processes stigmatize certain students, leading them to withdraw. The share of higher-caste students in institutions following competitive test-based admissions is more than 60 per cent, while the share of students belonging to lower castes is as low as 9 per cent, showing that despite reservations, higher caste students still have an inherent advantage. Since most of the elite institutions specialize in so-called STEM subjects (science, technology, engineering and mathematics), the selective admissions policies also have a significant effect on the choice of study programmes and on employment and earnings after graduation (Sabharwal and Malish, 2017). Dalit students in particular face obstacles in accessing HE, and when they enter institutions, they experience humiliation, segregation, and discrimination (Sukumar, 2008). Studies pertaining to caste-based discrimination in HE indicate that the institutional environment plays a significant role in facilitating an inclusive or hostile environment for vulnerable student groups on the campuses. Over the last decade, a number of cases of Dalit student suicides have come into the public domain (Karthikeyan, 2011; Janyala, 2016), resulting in public protests.

The situation is no easier for Muslim students. Muslims are India's largest religious minority, yet data such as those from the census and the National Sample Survey Organisation (NSSO, 66th Round, 2009–2010) indicate that Muslims occupy India's economic, social, and political margins (Sahu et al, 2017). The Sarchar report of 2006 established that Muslims are poorer and less often employed in the formal sector, which is generally better remunerated than informal-sector employment (NSSO, 66th Round, 2009–2010; Sachar et al, 2006; Mohammad-Arif, 2012). In addition, the Gross Enrolment Ratio (GER) is lowest for Muslims, at 16.54 per cent, compared with a corresponding figure of 42 per cent for other minorities such as Christians, Sikhs, and Jains, and 32 per cent for Hindus. For Muslim girls, gender-based barriers to HE are compounded by their minority status, and Muslim women's access to HE and their educational attainments are generally lower than those of Hindu caste women (Sahu et al, 2017).

Despite India's secular constitution, there are concerns that Muslim students are suffering from persecution and discrimination in HEs, and that conditions have deteriorated in recent years (HRW, 2020). Most of the attacks on campus integrity have come through ABVP students or police action on mostly Muslim students protesting against discriminatory laws. In terms of institutional harassment of Muslim students who dissent, universities are routinely resorting to suspension, expulsion, and withholding of scholarships (Anand and Niaz, forthcoming 2022). For instance, hundreds of fellow students and right-wing Hindu activists gathered outside a university residence in the northern state of Rajasthan accusing four Muslim students of cooking beef. Police arrested these students, although the accusation was just a rumour (AFP, 2016).

During the COVID-19 pandemic that started in March 2021, the Indian administration charged student leaders and activists under the Unlawful

Activities (Prevention) Act, which merely requires suspicion to justify a person's arrest (Marik, 2020). Prominent among the detentions have been two Muslim students, Safoora Zargar and Umar Khalid. Zargar, an MPhil student from Jamia, was imprisoned between 10 April and 24 June 2021 under charges of planned conspiracy. It was alleged that she had participated in the anti-CAA protests in the Indian capital with the aim of triggering the subsequent riots that devastated Delhi in February 2020 (Marik, 2020). Khalid, a former Democratic Students' Union leader at JNU, was charged with facilitating the Delhi riots by making 'provocative speeches' during the anti-CAA protests (Marik, 2020).

As seen here, students from disadvantaged groups find it hard to compete with students from privileged backgrounds, especially with regard to admissions to the top HEIs. Many disadvantaged students are the first generation in their families to attend tertiary education; they come from government schools where the medium of instruction is a regional language and have had limited access to pre-college support opportunities to acquire the necessary academic level to succeed in college (Sabharwal and Malish, 2017).

The attitudes of academics are not always conducive to overcoming the difficulties that are faced by students from disadvantaged groups. Many faculty members tend to believe that the increase in the share of students from disadvantaged groups is a reason for the deterioration in academic quality. Academic diversity affects what happens inside the classroom and has effects on academic outcomes. Lower teacher–student academic engagement negatively impacts the academic integration of students from disadvantaged groups and results in new tensions on campus (Sabharwal and Malish, 2017). This of course varies from institution to institution. Socially inclusive campuses such as JNU, which routinely admit students from disadvantaged backgrounds, tend to have a more inclusive climate. In other HEIs, social group identity and academic differences can become a source of prejudice and discrimination. Prejudice and stereotypes along caste and religious lines are common, and result in overt and covert types of discrimination both inside and outside the classroom (Sabharwal and Malish, 2017). Although there are institutional mechanisms to promote diversity and protect students from discrimination, many of these arrangements do not function effectively (Sabharwal and Malish, 2017).

What emerges is a higher caste-dominated HE sector, which is increasingly supportive of the Hindu nationalist agenda. Caste and other minority realities on the ground have been overlooked in the HE policy domain. Student diversity and campus environment have emerged as significant concerns specifically at premier and professional institutions, despite constitutional reservations and safeguards. Despite these issues the Modi government is trying to end the reservation for SCs, STs, and OBCs.

The BJP government has told the Supreme Court that giving reservations to people from these communities is not its constitutional responsibility (Press Trust of India, 2020). Social tensions around caste identities and recent incidents of open clashes between student groups and administrators point to a range of problems and a deteriorating campus climate.

The rise of the private alternative

With the worsening situation at public universities, India's middle classes have been looking to the growing private HEI sector as an alternative. The 1990s saw a process of HE expansion led by the growth of private HEIs. Non-government HE was not new; private colleges had existed until the 1980s, but these were often publicly financed (Agarwal 2009, cited in Chattopadhyay et al, 2022). The cost recovery methods of the 1980s resulted in a mushrooming of colleges that charged capitation fees and offered courses in engineering, medicine, and management, mostly in South India. The privatization drive after the economic reforms (and after capitation fee colleges were banned by the Supreme Court in 2003) was different, as it was led by India's southern states (Bhatnagar, 2003). The lack of a private university bill at the centre meant that universities could only be set up by state governments under state legislation. Between 2002 and 2019 around 305 private universities were established in India (Varghese, in Chattopadhyay et al, 2022). Many of these are teaching institutions affiliated with a parent university that provides the degree (Kulandaiswamy, 2006, p.48).[21] The lack of a national legislative framework means that the growth of private HEIs has resulted in a large number of institutions with poor infrastructure, less-qualified faculty members, and poor quality HE – all for a fee (Varghese, in Chattopadhyay et al, 2022).

Another type of non-government HEI is the so-called deemed to be university, also in existence since the 1990s. The UGC brought out regulations on the establishment of and maintenance of Standards in Private Universities in 2003 and deemed universities, from then on authorized to offer courses and award degrees, started to proliferate. The private sector has seen the 'deemed to be' mechanism as a way to free themselves from the academic controls of public universities. To this day, all private universities are funded and managed by private organizations or individuals while adhering to regulations specified by the MHRD. But deemed universities

---

[21] The affiliating university system is a model inherited from the British, similar to the one followed by Oxford and Cambridge universities. This model allows the establishment of a network of institutions around a small number of universities.

have more freedom than affiliated colleges when they gain the powers of a university.

A contentious issue has been on how private HEIs fund themselves and what they do with any surplus. Privately owned HEIs are usually registered as charitable trusts, which means that any money made has to be reinvested into the trust. There is little transparency in what has emerged as a parallel economy, largely financed by households taking out private loans.[22] Without such data, it is difficult to regulate the sector (Shamika et al, 2019, p.46). The Brookings report of 2019 accuses these institutions of resorting to unscrupulous means to turn a profit, including that management sell their quota of seats on the black market to the highest bidder or, as established by the Tandon Committee,[23] accept more students than the officially approved intake (Shamika et al, 2019, p.47). A legal way of making profit that has emerged recently is to outsource teaching and management of the HEI to an outside company through a service agreement. The company hires the staff but is not constrained by the non-profit laws that govern trusts and charities (Shamika et al, 2019, p.47).

As the government wanted to see widening participation in the HE sector, the liberalized economy allowed private players to expand the number of HEIs in a way that did not require the treasury to foot the bill. In the decade from 1990 to 2001–2002, enrolment doubled from 4.4 million to 8.8 million, equivalent to the increase in the previous 40 years (Mathew, 2016). This expansion of the private sector picked up pace in the 2000s. The country had only seven private universities in 2005, and this increased to 262 in 2017–2018. Today the private sector accounts for 78 per cent of the HEIs including the aided sector, and more than 62 per cent of the total student enrolment in HE (Varghese and Sarkar, 2022 in Chattopadhyay et al, 2022). There are, however, wide regional variations, and inequalities in the distribution of HE facilities and enrolment have widened. In 2018–2019 the number of colleges per 100 thousand population varied from 7 in Bihar and 8 in Jharkhand to 53 in Karnataka and 50 in Telangana (Varghese in Chattopadhyay et al, 2022). According to Varghese and Sarkar (in Chattopadhyay et al, 2022) India seems to rely on public universities for research and development and on private institutions to cater for the increasing number of undergraduate degrees.

---

[22] Education loans, which funded just 8 per cent of all enrolled students in 2013–2014, exceeded the total government expenditure on HE. It would be safe to assume that student fees are the single biggest source of funding in the HE sector. In fact, private HEIs, which do not receive government funding, are funded almost entirely by student fees. The average tuition fee for a regular four-year B.Tech course at a private institution is almost twice that for a public institution (Shamika et al, 2019, p.48).

[23] The committee also found that the fee charged in many deemed universities is much higher than government- or court-approved limits.

The risks of the marketization of the HE sector, already discussed by Carpentier et al in 2011 when looking at the effects of globalization on social justice in India, include serious implications for access for the underprivileged groups of society as well as quality across the board. As mentioned earlier, the expansion of this sector is funded by household loans, which can only be accessed by middle-class families. The NEP, discussed in the next section, is set to expand this sector even further, in order to increase HE student numbers to the 50 per cent mark by 2035. As a result, it encourages the creation of private universities that can independently determine their fees and proposes to constitute a private corporate board of governors for each institution, encouraging private investment in HE from both India and abroad. This of course shifts the responsibility of paying for HE from the state to students and their families, a typical neoliberal approach. The difficulties in allowing the private HE sector to lead India's HE expansion, thereby emulating Japan and South Korea, are discussed in the conclusion of this chapter.

Looking forward – the NEP 2020 and HE

For HE, there is an inherent tension in the NEP between the creation of a quasi-market and promised autonomy for universities. The earlier sections in this chapter have shown how India's HE charted a neoliberal course that included target-setting and the Performance Based Appraisal System (PBAS), which Chattopadhyay (2016) describes as New Public Management. The neoliberal elements of fostering competition within and between institutions are a key element of the NEP. Chattopadhyay (2020, p.20) explains how the autonomy offered by the NEP has to be 'understood within the overall state–university governance system as proposed' and that 'in practice, this will restrict the scope for the autonomy of both teachers and institutions', creating dissonance within the policy itself. This tension or dissonance reflects the HE systems of other countries, which also find neoliberal accounting systems to be in conflict with academic freedoms. In India, the PBAS does not take into account differences across disciplines and across academics (Das and Chattopadhyay, 2014), and this has resulted in pressured faculty resorting to unethical behaviour, including the fabrication of publications (Sharma 2018, cited in Chattopadhyay 2020) to meet required targets. Yet rather than taking stock of the effects of the earlier neoliberal policies, the NEP deepens these.

The NEP's intention is to transform India's HE system into a regulated quasi-market to achieve local resource efficiencies and give increasing choice to students (Chattopadhyay, 2020). The expectation is that the poor governance of publicly funded HEIs (Chandra, 2017) will improve through a tight regulatory framework,[24] as HEIs are judged based on their Institutional Development Plans, which will make education and research outcomes public (NEP, 2020, 12.3, 13.6). The HEIs will also compete for funds held by the National Research Foundation (GoI, 2019, pp.269–70) and the Higher Education Grants Council (HEGC). The resulting highly competitive situation, made worse by funding constraints, will in the end restrict academic autonomy, as faculty will have to follow the priorities set by their institution (Chattopadhyay, 2020). The NEP promises to shut down institutions that do not meet their own International Development Programmes (IDPs) (NEP, 2020, p.184) However, as Chattopadhyay (2020) points out, this 'state engineered market' comes with two important qualifications: the NEP budget increase to 6 per cent (from 4.6 per cent) of GDP is expected to pay for these changes, including building the educational infrastructure and the operational costs such as teaching staff salaries. This will of course be a challenge to the Indian economy, already suffering from a post-pandemic contraction (Sharma, 2020a; Singh, 2020), which is why private participation (especially philanthropy) is encouraged (Chattopadhyay, 2020). The government is also opening up channels for the infusion of more funds from abroad through ECBs and FDI (Chattopadhyay, 2020). Whilst this might help in post-pandemic India, it is unlikely to be sufficient to reach the stated goals.

The NEP (2020) envisions a complete structural reform for Indian HE. Institutions will be turned into large multi-disciplinary HEIs through mergers and programme expansions, changing India's traditional area/subject-specific approach. How this will affect the INIs is yet unclear. The 20-year blueprint states that the Higher Education Commission of India will be the single overarching umbrella body for the promotion of the HE sector, including teacher education and excluding medical and legal education. In addition, there will be independent bodies for standard-setting, funding, accreditation, and regulation (Highlights of New Education Policy, 2020). This new structure aims to streamline the sector and allow large knowledge hubs to emerge to deal with known problems in India's HE system, such as fragmentation, rigid separation of disciplines, and the lack of quality HE outside the main urban hubs.

The NEP 2020 also aims to almost double HE capacity by 2035 (NEP, 2020). India has always had a challenge with a low GER in HE

---

[24] The Higher Education Commission of India (NEP, 2020, p.18.3) will be the overarching institution to coordinate the functioning of a set of four institutions that oversee four important dimensions of policy intervention for the HEIs, blurring the divide between public and private, general and professional, and centre and states. (Chattopadhyay, 2020, p.13)

(Hossain and Mondal, 2019). Disparities in socio-economic levels, parental education levels, rural–urban disparities, regional disparities, and students with disabilities are a few of the main reasons that make access to HE in India non-equitable, affecting the GER (Sabharwal and Malish, 2017). However, despite this, the NEP is silent about reservations – only scholarships are mentioned. The COVID-19 pandemic has further exposed the vulnerabilities and shortcomings of the current Indian education systems, indicating that increasing and widening access will be challenging. To counter this, technology is presented in the NEP as a panacea, both for expansion and access. HEIs will be encouraged to set up start-up incubation centres; the new National Research Foundation will promote research and technology; and the establishment of an autonomous body, the National Educational Technology Forum (NETF), is expected to operate as a platform to enhance the use of technology in learning, assessment, planning, and administration. The NETF aims to be developed as a dedicated unit to create digital infrastructure, digital content, and capacity building. The NEP outlined that through the NETF, new technologies such as artificial intelligence, blockchain, machine learning, smart boards, computing devices, adoptive computer testing for student development, and other forms of educational software and hardware will be integrated into all levels of education. Through the NETF, the NEP envisages technological advancements that will improve the classroom teaching process, enhance teachers' professional development, improve educational access for disadvantaged groups, and streamline educational planning, administration, and management (Economic Times Government, 2020).

This of course requires the expansion of digital infrastructure across the country (Kerawalla, 2020; Panda, 2020b). To enable the NETF to facilitate various stakeholders, the Internet and Mobile Association of India has recommended a partnership between the ed-tech industry and NETF, which will help streamline research and enable NETF to adopt industry-led best practices (Mitra and Singh, 2020). Technology is seen as an integral part of the way forward in the next phase of India's HE system. This is not exactly new as discussions on the use of IT in India's education system and in HE has been around for a while. The GoI set up the National Task Force on Information Technology (NTFIT) in 1998 to create a knowledge-based information society with the turn of the new century (Rekhi, 1998). The NTFIT Report stated that 'IT is not just a technology, nor is it merely a new enabling tool for economics and education. Rather it will lay the basis for a whole new global civilization in which Indian values and wisdom will play a defining role' (Takwale, 2003, p.6). Though Takwale (2003) acknowledged the crucial role e-education was going to play in developing new processes and ways of communication in the Indian education system,[25] in order to integrate the digital mode of learning, issues of inclusion of marginalized learners would need to be addressed.[26] He was optimistic at the turn of the century that within a decade India would overcome the problems of 'network access and inclusion of the disadvantaged' (Takwale, 2003, p.11); however, these challenges persist, and with the COVID-19 pandemic the digital divide has been widely exposed (Pandey, 2020).

Unpublished research by Banerjee and Lall shows that the digital issue affected both academics and their students. Academics learned how to manage the technology but had not been trained to adapt the teaching to online platforms. Institutions also differed in how much hardware, software, and training support they gave. Students who returned to rural areas during the pandemic, as well as those from poorer sections of society, suffered most, as teaching staff admitted they simplified what was being taught or skipped topics that were too difficult to explain online, expecting to help students catch up once face to face instruction was able to resume.

The NEP 2020 acknowledges India's digital divide, and thus mass media channels such as television, radio, and community radio are to be extensively used for telecasting and broadcasts. The policy further clarifies that educational programmes will be made available 24/7 in different languages to cater to the varying needs of the students, with a particular focus on content to be available in all major Indian languages (NEP, 2020, p.59). However, merely emphasizing the importance and reliance on digital education without having an understanding of the issues faced by university staff and students on the ground and second without any plans to address known access, usage or skill gaps will not achieve the NEP's vision of a 'self-reliant' India (Mangaldas, 2020). It is evident that in the first place there is a need for digital literacy development that educators can adapt to the changing situation worldwide (Rashid and Yadav, 2020).

According to Simon Marginson (in Chattopadhyay et al, 2022), the expansion of HE across developing economies is linked to urban growth, as HE is dependent on physical infrastructure that is more difficult to sustain in rural areas. In India, the majority of the population still lives outside the cities and their immediate needs include water, sanitation, healthcare and sustainable food supplies, rather than HE infrastructure. Marginson cites urban growth at 0.3–0.5 per cent per year: 'At this rate India will not reach an urbanization

---

[25] Prof. Ram Takwale, ex-vice chancellor of three universities in India, delivered a lecture at Shivaji University, Kolhapur, Maharashtra, India, in December 2003 as part of the UGC's Golden Jubilee Lecture Series. Retrieved from http://www.mkclkf.org/about-us/ram-takwale-profile [Accessed 11 December 2020].

[26] Owing to rural inhabitation, poverty or illiteracy, and access to IT (digital divide).

ratio of 50 per cent until well after 2050. Given that, the national GTER [gross tertiary enrolment ratio] is unlikely to reach 50 per cent before that time. In short, it is unlikely that India will achieve the official target of 50 per cent by 2035' (p.7). Whilst in the NEP online education is seen to overcome the urban–rural divide, the pandemic has shown how difficult it actually is to include rural and more disadvantaged communities in online HE. The issues go beyond access to the internet, laptops, and smartphones and to a basic lack of electricity. It is clear that students from rural areas will have specific needs with regard to language and social capital, requiring specially tailored approaches by specifically trained academics via individually tailored courses.[27]

The NEP's saffron edges

Whilst the NEP's intention is primarily focused on expansion, it also has an important aspect of 'indigenization', reflective of the wider Hindutva agenda see across the rest of the education system. This goes beyond the promise to develop more degree courses in Indian languages – a policy that has its critics despite the stated intention to widen participation (Islam, 2020; NEP, 2020, pp 41–2).[28]

The text of the NEP is reflective of the Hindu pride that is to be instilled into the system. Reminding the domestic and international readers of India's ancient glory, the text aims to link the reforms of HE with institutions that operated in the pre-Islamic period such as Takshashila, Nalanda, Vallabhi, and Vikramshila (NEP, 2020, p.34).[29] Linking the modern 'liberal arts' with the Indian tradition, referencing the 64 Kalaas (or arts), the text goes on to state:

> [A]mong these 64 'arts' were not only subjects, such as singing and painting, but also 'scientific 'fields, such as chemistry and mathematics, 'vocational ' fields such as carpentry and clothes-making, 'professional 'fields, such as medicine and engineering, as well as 'soft skills' such

---

[27] According to World Bank data, in India in 2018, 65.5 per cent of the population had no internet access (World Bank 2021). The ratio was much higher in rural areas. Even among currently enrolled students, according to the NSSO (75th round data for 2017–2018), 32 per cent of students in urban areas had no internet access, and this rose to 58 per cent in rural areas. In comparison, 58 per cent of ST and SC students were also without any internet access. Whereas 55 per cent of urban students did not possess a device adequate for online HE, that number was 83 per cent in rural areas (Sarkar, 2020; Chattopadhyay et al, 2022).

[28] While the vernacularization of HE is a democratic goal, it is practically difficult for teachers to teach in the vernacular language at university level in the absence of quality textbooks in these languages (Islam, 2020).

[29] The full text of this is to be found in Chapter 2.

as communication, discussion, and debate. The very idea that all branches of creative human endeavour, including mathematics, science, vocational subjects, professional subjects, and soft skills should be considered 'arts', has distinctly Indian origins. (NEP, 2020, p.36)

The NEP also promises to go back to the traditional roots in other ways – by instilling traditional values steeped in the Hindu tradition:

Value-based education will include the development of humanistic, ethical, Constitutional, and universal human values of truth (*satya*), righteous conduct (*dharma*), peace (*shanti*), love (*prem*), nonviolence (*ahimsa*). (NEP 2020, p.37)

This is not just meant for domestic students: the NEP hopes to transmit these Indian values and wider Indian culture through an explicit policy of internationalization, focusing on the delivery of traditional Indian courses:

The various initiatives mentioned above will also help in having larger numbers of international students studying in India, and provide greater mobility to students in India who may wish to visit, study at, transfer credits to, or carry out research at institutions abroad, and vice versa. Courses and programmes in subjects, such as Indology, Indian languages, AYUSH systems of medicine, yoga, arts, music, history, culture, and modern India… (NEP, 2020, p.39)

The overall aim is to return India to its rightful place as the world's teacher or guru:

India will be promoted as a global study destination providing premium education at affordable costs thereby helping to restore its role as a Vishwa Guru. (NEP, 2020, p.39)

Academic research is also mentioned, reminding the reader that India has a tradition of knowledge contribution that needs to be strengthened and expanded:

India has a long historical tradition of research and knowledge creation, in disciplines ranging from science and mathematics to art and literature to phonetics and languages to medicine and agriculture. This needs to be further strengthened to make India lead research and innovation in the 21st century, as a strong and enlightened knowledge society and one of the three largest economies in the world. (NEP, 2020, pp.45–6)

These policies are not entirely new, as the government has already tried to inculcate Indian values and pride in the nation through programmes such as Vidya Veerta Abhiyan (Learning and Valour) (DHS News, 2017), and Delhi University's 'Code of Professional Ethics' that requires academics to 'aid students to develop an understanding of our national heritage and national goals'. It does, however, underline the issues raised earlier about how the nation is defined, and how these definitions differ between policy writers and academics and their students.

Conclusion

Two key issues with wider ramifications for India crystallize from the BJP HE politics and the academic reaction to these. The first is the debate on defining the nation: universities are seen as Western, with university protesters intent on destroying the traditional Indian nation. 'At the heart of the debate are contestations over the idea of India, which, of course, did not begin with the JNU episode' (Chattarji, 2019, p.82). The definition of the Indian nation pits the homogeneous Hindu Rashtra against other definitions – including that of Dalits, who see Hindu hegemony as caste bondage and who ask for alternative nationhood without caste hierarchies (Chattarji, 2019). Students and policymakers on both sides of the Indian nation definition divide are asking what it means to be Indian, and what it means to be Hindu. Linked to this is of course a space in which to ask these questions without being labelled 'anti national'. This leads to the second issue, which is a debate about the role of universities: this divides those who see HEIs as a space for critical thinking and democratic debate from those who see universities through the neoliberal lens of human capital theory; that is, an instrumental vision where students acquire information that allows them to work within a knowledge economy. This issue is fraught because government funding is the basis for India's public HE, making it difficult for any institution to be completely autonomous. The two issues are deeply intertwined and one facilitates the other. The neoliberal takeover of the academy is linked to the questions about nationhood that are described in these two quotes:

> What we have here then is a seamless convergence of exclusionary nationalist and neoliberal authoritarianism, and it is difficult to tell whether the fascists are piggy-backing on a neoliberal agenda or whether neoliberals are piggy-backing on a fascist agenda. (Chattarji, 2019, p.10)[31]

---

[31] Various academics examine the intertwining of nationalist and neoliberal policies in India, for example Corbridge and Harriss (2000); Oza (2006); Mahajan and Jodhka eds. (2010); Ruparelia et al (2011); Samaddar and Sen (2012); Gooptu ed. (2013).

Drives to transform pedagogy and scholarship in the direction of authoritarian nationalism have generally been sold by using neoliberal tactics of citing metrics, target-setting and cost-accounting rationales. [...] This thrust has grown more ambitious with the advent of authoritarian nationalism as the ruling ideology: critical thinking and academic integrity are countered by skills training and employers' needs (in the national interest); management and policy that is untrammeled by academic principles is de rigueur (as a demonstration of national fiber); maximizing the cost-benefits of education by recourse to the private sector and private education service providers is considered essential (to increase national competitiveness); intensive surveillance and policing of universities is necessary (as a national duty). (Gupta, 2019, p.11)

It is clear that HE in general and university campuses in particular are understood by the government as an important arena in which to win the ideological battle. The reduction of government funding, scholarship, and fellowships, on the one hand, and intervention in student politics, denial of caste discrimination, and the surveillance of university campuses, on the other, reflects how the government defends neoliberal and Hindutva values. There is at the time of writing an ongoing battle – not just in academic and theoretical terms, but as discussed here – and more so in Chapter 6 – in physical violence and lathi charges, resulting in injured students and academic staff.

PART III

Whither India?

6

The Effects of the Indian Political Choice Model on Citizenship under the BJP Government

Introduction

The changes described in Chapters 1 to 6 indicate how Indian society has been transformed both in terms of its political outlook, with Hindu nationalism taking centre stage, as well as in its economic trajectory – led by neoliberal policies. Education reforms across schools, universities, and teacher training have been embedded through new school textbooks, new courses, and new teaching approaches. As has been discussed in previous chapters, education is the key vehicle to disseminate political ideas and messages. As a result of the propagation of Hindutva, there has been a huge debate inside and outside classrooms and across the policy arena over who is a 'legitimate' citizen of India. Ordinary popular views of Muslims have changed, as illustrated in Chapter 1 by the support for the Ghar Whapsi campaign and the cow slaughter ban. There also seems to have been a resultant normalization of Islamophobia, with a negative characterization of Muslims in the mainstream public domain (Waikar, 2018).

This changing public attitude has allowed the Modi-led BJP government in its second term in office to drop most of the development rhetoric, focusing instead on communal goals – such as the changing of Kashmir's status in 2019, a roll out of the national verification of citizens in Assam, the finalizing and inauguration of the Ram temple in Ayodhya, and the CAA 2019 – the law allowing non-Muslims from neighbouring countries to become Indian citizens in an accelerated way. These changes in turn have been widely accepted, resulting in increasing attacks against Muslims and other minorities (Chaudhary, 2019; Azad et al, 2020; Aswani, 2021; Pandey, 2021). This book shows that the reason for the changes in public attitudes is the reinforcement of these ideas through mainstream education. A key result of the Hindu nationalism–neoliberalism–education triangle introduced in this volume's introduction is the effect that Indian political choices have had on Indian citizens and citizenship. Citizenship is the arena in which much of the results of India's Gramscian new normal can be observed; citizenship is where many of the Indian political debates are being played out.

This chapter engages with the question of Indian citizenship and how it has been altered in light of the government's neoliberal Hindutva trajectory over the last two decades. It looks at the rising Islamophobia across society before engaging with four recent cases of changes in Indian citizenship that show how the neoliberal Hindutva approach has become mainstream: Kashmir's changed status, the National Register of Citizens (NRC) in Assam, the CAA (and how the Delhi protests were dealt with), and the farmers' protest movement.

What is citizenship and why is it so important in domestic politics?

At its most basic, the definition of citizenship focuses on the relationship between the individual and the state. While the state has the monopoly on dictating who is included in or excluded from any political community, elites help to decide who can access rights (Kivisto and Faist, 2007). Any definition of citizenship has to encompass three different aspects:

> Citizenship as *status*, which denotes formal state membership and the rules of access to it; citizenship as *rights*, which is about the formal capacities and immunities connected with such a status; and in addition citizenship as *identity*, which refers to the behavioural aspects of individuals acting and conceiving of themselves as members of a collectivity, classically the nation or the normative conceptions of such behaviour imputed by the state. (Joppke, 2007, p.38, italics added)

It was through colonization that the Indian middle classes adopted what was in effect a Western way of organizing the public sphere. The concept of the Indian nation state and Indian citizenship is one that developed slowly over the nineteenth century, a cultural flow brought in by the colonial masters from Britain (Mitra, 2013). Moving out of colonialism meant moving from being subjects to becoming citizens, and a new and relevant concept of Indian citizenship had to be created. As seen in Chapter 1, it was the Nehruvian doctrine of shared history that was at the base of both Indian national identity and Indian citizenship (Lall, 2001). The Indian Constitution and the 1955 Citizenship Act are the legal frameworks that have defined Indian citizenship since independence. Although debates on who should be in or out abounded, Nehru wanted to construct a new unified Indian state that was based on shared history, religious tolerance, and democracy. This secular conception was not uncontested. There was also a Hindutva conception of citizenship, the supporters of which wanted to privilege Hindus and Sikhs, even across the Indian Diaspora (Rodriguez, 2005). At the time of independence, Indian citizens were persons 'who at the time of the commencement of the Constitution had their domicile in India and (a) were born in the territory of India, or (b) either of whose parents were born in the territory of India, or (c) who have been ordinarily resident in the territory of India for no less than five years immediately preceding the commencement of the Constitution' (Rodriguez, 2005, p.212). This secular and inclusive concept was broadly accepted until quite recently.

The Indian government also had another set of goals related to economic development and nation building; these goals were centred around the P.C. Mahalanobis model, Soviet-inspired five-year plans, and a wish to redefine India through its dams and steel factories (Mukherjee, 1960; Kumar, 2022). This model of nationalism underpinned the aspirational model of citizenship, where a good citizen was seen to be contributing to the productive economy of the nation and, therefore, contributing to nation building. Economic citizenship was seen as an integral extension of Nehruvian civic nationalism, which was not merely symbolic but rooted in concrete productive energy to be harnessed by the newly independent nation. This understanding of citizenship linked to nation building was altered by the 1991 reforms discussed in Chapter 1, as liberalization offered the idea of 'consumer citizenship', thereby shifting the base from the producer to the consumer (Kumar, 2022).

The other key transformation of the 1991 reforms related to the rise of other (religious and regional) identities led by new elites that challenged the traditional concepts of an all-encompassing national identity. At that time, national identity and legal citizenship parted ways. This was most pertinently reflected in the curriculum and textbooks changes discussed in Chapter 2. Whilst the concept of Indian national identity was radically changed, the citizenship laws remained untouched. Under the latest Modi-led government, however, the concept of citizenship has been changed, following the trajectory of the exclusionary national identity that was first established in the early 2000s.

Until 2019, most of the academic and political debate with regard to Indian citizenship was located around participatory citizenship and the status of minorities. Oommen has argued that in the elite conception of citizenship there are different visions of India: the Hindu nationalists focus on religion whilst the Cultural Pluralists, who crystallized in the anti-colonial movements, focus on secularism. In both cases, citizenship is differently defined (Oommen, 2005, pp.76–7). Bhargava links the reasoning of what Indian secularism is for to the argument that all Indians, no matter their religion, must have the right to equal (passive) citizenship in that they are to be equally protected and have 'a minimum of material wellbeing and a sphere of one's own in which others ought not to interfere' (Bhargava, 2002, p.9). Active citizenship, according to him, is when all citizens are equal participants in the public domain, and secularism aims to protect this right with regard to minorities (Bhargava, 2002, p.10). As such, citizenship, rights, and duties have very much been part of the wider social justice debate. Yet the concept of social justice, and in particular India's view of equal opportunities for all, has changed since the opening up of the economy in the early 1990s and the inception of a neoliberal state (Lall and Nambissan, 2011). This is reflected in what has been happening in schools over the last two and a half decades. The wider literature shows that in the modern nation state the classroom has become an important arena in which the relationship between the state and the individual is cemented – in terms of learning about the rights and duties of citizens as well as the different conceptions of national identity. So what happens to the concept of citizenship when the neoliberal state withdraws from education provision and the middle classes flee the system?[1]

In India today the common basis of citizenship for the middle classes is built around choice and the market – the old values of social justice are no longer policy priorities (Nanda, 2004; Capelos and Basu, 2022). The state, as seen in earlier chapters, plays a central role, both facilitating the process of marketization and addressing educational disadvantage through specific policies and programmes, in the context of the aspirations of and demands from poorer social groups. Consequently, there are seemingly contradictory trends whereby the new hegemony is that of the partial withdrawal of the state from public services and letting the middle classes choose their provision, yet with increased state involvement at other levels, creating the sense of a 'layered' state that has no clearly demarcated boundaries. This process is linked to the rise of increasingly affluent middle classes who have benefited from India's economic reforms and are able to buy those services that were originally supplied by the state in an open market. Consequently, the concept of rights and responsibilities is eroded as the state responsibility for providing public services changes. The increased importance and involvement of private and non-state actors in the public domain is altering the relationship between the individual and the state. The discourse of choice and the dominance of the markets by the middle classes results in newly excluded groups (see Lall and Nambissan, 2011). This alters the role and purpose of education.

---

[1] Kumar discusses how the resultant pauperization of quality education was not merely instrumental in taking education away from a significant mass of the people dependent on the government schools but also redrew the ideals of equal citizenship by creating different categories of citizens – labourer citizens and consumer citizens – both feeding into the larger idea of 'economic' citizenship (Kumar, 2022).

Today the Indian state is facing a two-tier society that has emerged from the neoliberal reform processes of the last 30 years. As the middle classes, who originally had the highest stakes in the rights guaranteed through citizenship, withdraw from the equation, the state's relationship is only with the second tier of largely poorer urban and rural Indians. Citizenship in terms of rights and responsibilities is changing as society becomes increasingly fragmented and the middle classes make their own destiny away from the masses, who have no other option but to accept whatever the state is still willing to give them. Although status, rights, responsibilities, and duties underpin citizenship, an important part of the discussion still focuses on the other tenet of citizenship – identity.

National identity and citizenship

The relationship between national identity and citizenship is a complex one and differs from country to country. Originally the nation state was the foundation for cultural and ethnic homogeneity (Habermas, 1992, p.2), and became the basis for democratic citizenship in Europe during the 18th and 19th centuries. Yet the relationship between citizenship and national identity has evolved. Citizenship, based on Rousseau's notion of self-determination (Habermas, 1992, p.4), became linked to civil rights, and today much of the Western literature links the concept of citizenship more to democracy and political choice than it does to a common identity. The situation is quite different in India.

Although various groups within one post-colonial state might have differing identities, they still relate to an overarching or umbrella concept of citizenship. Kymlicka and Norman have discussed the concepts of citizenship in diverse societies, and have found that, depending on the system, minorities are sometimes awarded special rights but sometimes have to 'play by the rules of the majority' (Kymlicka and Wayne, 2000, p.1). This, however, is insufficient to address the issues faced by post-colonial societies that are made up of various ethnic and linguistic groups and in which the state has the challenge of not only defining an overarching national identity but also fostering a concept of citizenship that is shared across diverse groups. India adopted a form of multicultural citizenship, with group differentiated rights within the inclusive and egalitarian nature of citizenship that was propagated by the constitution. Group identities and differences were recognized in order to protect minorities from the majority (Rodriguez, 2005). A different treatment was extended to disadvantaged groups. Consequently, SCs and STs were given reservations in HE and public employment.

With regard to religion, Nehru promoted a multicultural strategy – that of polyethnic rights (Adeney and Lall, 2005) – that was based on the state's neutrality to (equidistance from) all religions, reflecting India's definition of secularism. This meant that personal laws for Christian and Muslim minorities were protected. This was controversial as the religious personal laws of the Hindu majority are not protected. With regard to language, a multicultural strategy was adopted, which allowed individual states to use their languages for official business. As discussed in Chapter 1, however, Nehru was opposed to the reorganization of states on a linguistic basis for fear of any state wanting to secede.

In effect, the unifying and inclusive conception of citizenship also had multicultural aspects that allowed for the differentiation of rights and multiple identities that were based on religion and language. Yet despite legally giving space to these multiple identities, the concepts of citizenship and national identity were originally very much linked with each other: neither was based on ethnicity, religion, or language. As discussed earlier, Nehru chose a civic conception over an ethnic one with regard to both. Indian citizenship defined the Indian's legal relationship to the state, and was reflected in the state's desire to forge an inclusive national identity, allowing for different private linguistic and religious identities to be subsumed (Lall 2001). This Nehruvian vision was propagated through education, and remained largely uncontested at the national level until the late 1990s or early 2000s.

At this juncture, when the BJP first came to power, the concepts of citizenship and national identity parted ways. India's citizenship laws did not change, yet the understanding of who was Indian and who was not, and on what basis, started to be debated. Abroad, Indians of the Diaspora who had previously been excluded were reintegrated into a new Indian national identity that was clearly based on ethnic and religious lines (Therwath, 2011). It was now possible to have a foreign passport and still espouse an Indian national identity. Domestically, this debate took place in the realm of education, where the Nehruvian understanding of inclusiveness was challenged and new textbooks propagated religion as a way of distinguishing self from other. Under the BJP's logic of majoritarianism, the Indian nation was reconceptualized as Hindu, ignoring the country's pluralistic roots. Interestingly, though, the changes made to education focused primarily on history and the wider social sciences rather than citizenship education or civics.

Citizenship as a concept does not exist in a vacuum. It has to be transmitted to the citizens of any state. Whilst issues pertaining to national identity are diffused across the curriculum, the concept of any country's citizenship is usually transmitted through a form of citizenship education.

Citizenship education

In India citizenship education has been taught under the title of civics, and later political science. It is meant to familiarize students with political and social institutions, the constitution, and training citizens to develop attitudes and knowledge that support the better functioning of the state (Gupta, 2014; Jain, 2004). The Secondary Education Commission of 1953 focused on the 'quality of character' and inculcating the 'right ideals, habits, and attitude' in citizens (GoI, 1953, p.23, cited in Gupta, 2014, p.56). In 1976, NCERT developed the civics curriculum with the focus on rights and responsibilities of an Indian citizen. The NEP of 1986 introduced a political vision that promoted gender equality, secularism, democracy, and egalitarianism as part of civics. The Yash Pal Commission of 1992 reported that civics as a subject was given very little importance and needed reforming, especially with regard to the pedagogy used; unfortunately, not much was done about this suggestion, and civics has remained a subject that is not regarded as particularly important (Banaji, 2005). The NDA-led textbook revisions discussed in Chapter 2 brought the Hindutva agenda to schools, and the government announced that a new citizenship education would replace civics after 2001 – yet in the end this did not materialize. Changes to social science textbooks more generally did enough to change Indian national identity, yet at this point the overall concept of Indian citizenship was left intact.

The NCF of 2005 that was implemented by the Congress-led government did review civics textbooks and the curriculum, despite the fact that the BJP-led NDA government had not touched them. Pre-2005 civics textbooks were reviewed by a National Focus Group for Teaching Social Sciences (Gupta, 2014), which concluded that the complex and legal language they used made it difficult for students to understand the subject (Jain, 2005). Another problem was that the textbooks did not discuss the realities of the Indian state, including institutional failure and conflicts, and thereby created a distorted image that idealized government institutions and processes. According to Jain (2005) the NCERT textbooks focused on the citizen's responsibility for electing the government, without engaging with issues of caste, religious, and other inequalities. After the review, civics was changed to social and political life (for secondary schools, encompassing students from grade 6 to grade 8), democratic politics (for upper secondary school, grades 9 and 10), and political science (for higher secondary, grades 11 and 12). Gupta (2014) shows that the new textbooks take a more holistic view of the democratic development of the country since independence, explaining some of the conflicts faced by society. Gender and caste, including the problems faced by Dalits, were introduced for the first time, thus engaging with societal power struggles and social justice. The NCERT (2007) claims that pedagogical practices have also been revised through the National Council of Educational Research & Training (2005), although discussions with 110 teachers, which were conducted in 2021,[2] show that most teachers still use rote learning and few engage the students through activities.

Teachers who were interviewed about citizenship education had mixed views on how the concept of citizenship was being imparted to students. Those who spoke about civics or political science explained how they taught the technical aspects of citizenship such as the mechanics of political parties and voting, but maintained that the focus was on diversity, gender, and caste:

> Yes, there are chapters on democracy, diversity, gender and caste. It does not talk about citizenship, but about gender it talks how gender bias existed and how the government is trying to improve the situation. […] I think one chapter from 10th standard civics book has been removed i.e. 'Democracy and Diversity' due to NEP. (PS4 Bengaluru)

A few bemoaned the fact that a key chapter on democracy and diversity had recently been removed, but most teachers did not know much about citizenship either in terms of the concept or in terms of what they were expected to teach. The discussion on rights focused mostly on SC and ST reservations, and why these should be abolished.

> 'Constitutional rights are well guarded by the constitution, but they are not being followed. Reservation for backward classes was OK in the past, but in educational sector there should be no reservation now, because sometimes general class students with good marks are deprived of the seats. Intelligence of students should be given preference…' (PS1 Guwahati)

> 'Due to reservation many people suffer, there should not be any reservation. All should be same.' (PS6 Guwahati)

> 'It [reservations] was implemented for the betterment of the people who had not equal opportunities. But at this point after so many years of independence it is not so wise to continue these provisions. I think reservations in education system & job should be abolished.' (PS7 Guwahati)

> 'Most important thing I think about that is the reservation, which should be removed now.' (PS9 Guwahati)

> 'We don't have chapter on citizenship. We have chapters on gender, caste, religion.' (PS1 Guwahati)

---

[2]   The same teachers who are cited in Chapter 4.

Interestingly – as can be seen here – more teachers from private schools and more teachers from Assam held this view than from other states. But many teachers insisted that there was no such thing as citizenship education, and that they taught democracy, nationalism, and discrimination – raising the question as to how teachers define both citizenship and citizenship education.

'Citizenship chapter is not there in the class. We explain the term democracy & how people are discriminated.' (PS3 Guwahati)

'Since we do not have a specific chapter on citizenship. We have a little bit about Indian democracy & democratic systems of the world.' (PS5 Guwahati)

'We don't have "citizenship" as a separate topic or lesson. When points about nationality and nationalism are to be taught, we used to teach the topic.' (PS5 Bengaluru)

'I didn't see much on citizenship. We did have a chapter on Democracy. I am not teaching about Democracy, but I try with basics … In terms of constitutional rights, we respect and ask students to obey and perform their fundamental duties.' (PS2 Delhi)

'In my school, we have certain rules and regulations for students such as to respect others irrespective of their caste, colour and creed. Though we don't have a specific chapter on Citizenship, but we use different activities to make our students as loyal citizens … Reservation is not needed if we have respect for other minorities.' (PS3 Mumbai)

It is not surprising that teachers find teaching citizenship confusing, not least since 2000 when the textbook changes resulted in the civics or political science texts standing in contrast to what pupils learn in history. However, the confusion has deeper roots, as the basis of Indian citizenship is poorly defined. Research by Shani (2011) shows that there are four different citizenship orientations across India's education policy texts: liberalism, republicanism, 'ethno-nationalism', and non-statism. Using this framework, Nichols (2020) looks at how the four orientations are reflected across what is taught in schools. Starting with the Constitution, he discusses how liberalism is enshrined through a series of individual rights and freedoms – including the protection of life and personal liberty, freedom of conscious and free expression, and the freedom to manage one's own religious affairs (Republic of India, Constitution, Part III). Liberalism is also reflected in India's neoliberal economic approach since the 1991 reforms, when the state withdrew from certain functions, allowing citizens to choose services such as health and education. This is reflected in the curriculum. According to the NCERT, schools should promote '*[a]utonomy of action* – freedom to choose, ability and freedom to decide, and ability and freedom to act' (NCERT, 2006, p.23, emphasis in original). The liberalist approach is further strengthened by the human capital perspective – that educated individuals will be able to take part in India's development – although the 2005 curriculum framework does caution that:

> We need to be vigilant about the pressures to commodify schools and the application of market-related concepts to schools and school quality. The increasingly competitive environment into which schools are being drawn and the aspirations of parents place a tremendous burden of stress and anxiety on all children, including the very young, to the detriment of their personal growth and development, and thus hampering the inculcation of the joy of learning. (NCERT, 2005, pp. 9–10)

Nichols (2020) argues that India also has a pre- and post-colonial republican tradition. The village panchayats of today still allow for public engagement in decision making, reflecting the structures of ancient India. British colonialism enshrined the parliamentary system, reinforcing the republican aspect, albeit at a national level. Republican citizenship is reflected in the NCERT's request that schools allow students to imbibe 'caring concerns within the democratic polity of the country' (NCERT, 2005, p.5), and that there is accountability to the wider political community. The third aspect – 'ethno-nationalist' identity approaches to citizenship – only emerged with the BJP, and has recently gained a dominant platform across schools, textbooks, and the media. Lastly the Gandhian concept of village democracy is a form of non-statism, as Gandhi rejected centralized power (Shani, 2011). This too is taught in schools, when children learn about Gandhi and the freedom movement. However, this non-statist vision of society is not presented as a realistic vision for today's India.

Other authors (Dhuru and Thapliyal, 2021) who have looked at how citizenship is taught in schools have commented that the orientation has tended to be influenced by the upper-caste, male, liberal, ruling elites, not taking into account India's societal realities of caste, class, and gender. The critique offered by Kadiwal and Jain (2020) is that women have been rendered largely invisible. Comments also focus on the lack of engagement with social differences that are based on caste and class. Different orientations and a lack of training seem to result in a largely uncritical rendering of textbook content. Given the rise in Hindu nationalism, citizenship education seems to have failed its original mandate of creating a sense of community and social cohesion across India's religious groups. The rise of Islamophobia and general suspicion between Hindu and Muslim communities is testament to this.

The rise of Islamophobia

Islamophobia was on the rise in India well before the Modi government came to power in 2014; the Shah Bano case in 1985 (Mody, 1987) is a case in point, with a Congress government overseeing a polarization of views across the Muslim and Hindu communities. Institutional and systemic discrimination against Muslims was highlighted by the Sachar Report of 2006, which concluded that the changes in educational policies with regard to access and literacy had favoured SC and ST communities, yet left Muslims behind (Sachar et al, 2006). The same report admitted that the Muslim community was not homogeneous, and that there were significant variations across states and amongst Muslims; however, it was concluded that 'Muslims rank somewhat above SCs/STs but below Hindu-OBCs, Other Minorities and Hindu-General (mostly upper castes) in almost all indicators considered. [...] In addition to the "development deficit", the perception among Muslims that they are discriminated against and excluded is widespread, which exacerbates the problem' (Sachar et al, 2006 p.237).

Over the decades India has seen a large number of communal riots. Many of these have taken place on the watch of a Congress government (Rao, 2014), such as the Aligarh riots (2006), the Dhule riots (2008), the Deganga riots (2010), the Bharatpur riots (2011), the Assam riots (2012), and the Muzaffarnagar riots (2013). Home Ministry data recorded 3,949 incidents of communal violence between 1968 and 1980 (Brass, 2005). However despite claiming that under the BJP government there have been no riots of this kind, the incidence of communal violence actually increased by 17 per cent in 2015 (Sharma, 2016) and 28 per cent in 2017 (Mallapur, 2018), with smaller incidents costing as many lives as the larger, less frequent earlier riots (Deshmukh, 2021). Many of the larger riots also had links to the Hindutva movement, despite Congress being in power at the centre. The destruction of the 16th-century Babri mosque at Ayodhya in 1992 to build the Ram Mandir was led by a number of Hindu nationalist organizations who were questioning the status of Muslims in Indian society. The destruction of this mosque had long lasting consequences for India's political trajectory (Roy, 1992). Although these events were seen by many at the time as an aberration, 2020 saw the inauguration of the Ram Mandir on the site of the former mosque, almost 30 years later, with the RSS and BJP having used the Babri Masjid demolition and Ram Janmabhoomi to create a sense of belonging among Hindus.[3] In those 30 years, the status of Muslims has

---

[3]   'The BJP used Ram as a symbol to rally round all the castes under its banner. It used all sorts of devices for this; it drew up a plan to construct Ram mandir where the Babri mosque stands today; then it gave a call for donation of bricks from all five lakh villages of India; then it drew up plans to take out these donated bricks in the form of processions

changed significantly, with a normalization of Islamophobia (Deshmukh, 2021). How India has become more Islamophobic is illustrated by three interrelated examples: the use of the NRC in Assam, the change of status for Jammu and Kashmir, and the amendment to India's Citizenship Act that resulted in the Delhi riots.

Before looking at the policies and actions of the Modi BJP government at the centre, it is worth returning to 2002, when Modi was chief minister of Gujarat. It was under his watch that an estimated 1,000 Muslims were killed in what has become known as the 2002 Gujarat pogrom, seen by many as state sponsored.[4] The Gujarat pogrom and the increase in anti-Muslim violence since 2015 raises the question as to what Modi's views and statements about Islam and Muslims have been. According to Waikar (2018), who analysed a large number of Modi's political speeches, two themes emerge: the erasure of Indian Muslim histories in Modi's economic development agenda, and the characterization of Hinduism as having a taming effect on Islam in India.

Waikar's (2018) analysis shows that Indian Muslims are seen as unlikely to engage with terrorist organizations such as Al-Qaeda. In fact, references to terrorism are reserved for Pakistan (the country, not its people), and terrorism is de-linked from religion in general and Islam in particular, while Muslim Indians are referred to as patriotic.[5] Many of Modi's statements are hard to disagree with at face value and cannot be accused of blatant Islamophobia; nevertheless, the speeches still paint a picture in which Hinduism is superior to Islam. A recurring theme is India's humanitarian ethos, conceived in ancient times and reflected in modern reformists such as Mahatma Gandhi, Bhimrao Ramji Ambedkar, and Pandit Deen Dayal. Modi claims that compassion, kindness, brotherhood, and harmony are natural Indian and Hindu values,[6] standing against violence.[7] Modi extends

---

from villages, towns and cities and it also planned, with the help of the Vishwa Hindu Parishad, to mobilise lakhs of "karsevaks" on an auspicious day fixed by Dharm Sammelan in Hardwar' (Engineer, 1991, pp. 1649–52).

[4] The chief minister was seen as responsible, resulting in the US Department of State banning Narendra Modi from travelling to the US.

[5] 'While he does tacitly frame India as a Hindu nation located in a complex geopolitical environment, he does not remotely insinuate Pakistan as being a state that uses terrorism to attack Hinduism through India. Pakistan is repeatedly condemned, but not because it is Muslim-majority. At the same time, Modi continues to praise other Muslim-majority countries – UAE, Afghanistan, and Malaysia to name a few – as he would any other non-Muslim majority country. In the context of foreign policy, there is little evidence to suggest he is using Islamophobic language' (Waikar, 2018, p.174).

[6] Buddhism and Jainism are not seen as separate religions by Hindutva proponents; the Constitution also groups these religions under the Hindu ambit (see Jaffrelot, 2009).

[7] 'He claims that Indians today have inherited a "cultural legacy" defined by "Buddha," "Gandhi," and the Hindu God Krishna – one of the central figures who champions righteousness (*dharma*) in the Hindu epic, Mahabharata, the Hindu scripture, Bhagavad

this to Sufism, as Sufism is the version of Islam that has common values with India and Hinduism:

In other words, there are no Islamic values of peace, love, and humanity outside of Hinduism. The very idea, the *very possibility* of plurality and co-existence in Islamic thought can only exist when it is mediated and filtered through Hinduism. Deemed to be "the face of Islam in India," Sufism becomes the Hinduization of Islam. Not syncretic, but fundamentally Hindu in its orientation. In this context, the Islamophobia in Modi's statement, that Indian Muslims are patriotic people who would never be drawn to terror groups like Al-Qaeda, becomes clear. He is in effect stating that Indian Muslims have inherited a legacy of a Hinduized Islam, and are thus predisposed toward being loving and peaceful – just like other Indians. Indian Muslims are peaceful because they are believers of a Hinduized Islam. Given that Hindutva otherwise frames Islam and Muslims as violent, the implication of Modi's narrative is that it is Hinduism that has made the Indian brand of Islam nonviolent and humanitarian. A peaceful Islam would have been impossible without its contact with Hinduism. In other words, Indian Muslims have not joined terrorist outfits because their violent Islamic inclinations have been tamed by Hinduism. (Waikar, 2018, p.173)

In other speeches, Modi dismisses the 'atrocities committed by the Indian army against Kashmiri Muslim civilians' (Waikar, 2018, p.174). Modi's views on Islam have influenced how Hindus view their Muslim compatriots. Public attitudes towards relationships and marriages between Hindus and Muslims can be seen in the anti-conversion laws and vigilante actions towards interfaith couples. India's constitution protects the freedom of practising any religion, but certain states such as Chhattisgarh, Gujarat and Madhya Pradesh have passed anti-conversion laws (IANS, 2006). Gujarat's Freedom of Religion Act Article 5(1) requires permission from a district magistrate to change one's religion. Conversion is also an issue related to marriage, as Muslim women are not allowed to marry outside Islam, and Hindu women marrying a Muslim have to convert. But interfaith marriages and relationships are publicly opposed by Hindutva groups such as the VHP and the Bajrang Dal, which have launched campaigns to 'rescue' Hindu brides from Muslim grooms. As mentioned in Chapter 1, an inter-religious relationship is termed 'love Jihad', with Muslim men being accused of seducing Hindu

---

Gita, and a number of other stories in Hinduism' (Modi 2017d, cited in Waikar, 2018, p.172).

women in order to increase the number of Muslims and weaken the Hindu community (Press Trust of India, 2017, 2018; Mathrubumi, 2018; Gupta, 2019; Ganeshan, 2020). Yet Hindutva's 'morality code' has gone even further: after winning the elections in Uttar Pradesh in 2017, the BJP-led government set up 'Anti-Romeo squads' that disperse couples and stop Valentine's Day celebrations. The stated aim is to protect women, leading to campaigns such as 'beti bachao, bahu lao' (save your daughter, bring in the daughter-in-law) (Deshmukh, 2021).

Islamophobia at government level can be seen in the recent change of status of India's only majority Muslim state, Jammu and Kashmir, when Article 370 was revoked – as discussed in the next section.

Jammu and Kashmir, and the abrogation of Article 370

The state of Jammu and Kashmir is made up of three parts – Jammu, Kashmir, and Ladakh.[8] Jammu is host mostly to Hindus with some Muslim and Sikh minorities; the Kashmir valley is mostly constituted of Muslims; Ladakh's two districts are divided between Buddhists (Leh) and Shia Muslims (Kargil) (EFSAS, 2017).[9] In 1947 Kashmir's Hindu ruler had hoped for independence for his state, not wanting to join either India or Pakistan. However, in 1948, as Muslim tribesmen supported by Pakistan invaded, he turned to India for help and signed the accession document.[10] Kashmir was (and remains) divided between India and Pakistan, and has been a cause for three Indo-Pakistani wars, starting in 1948 when then Indian PM Jawaharlal Nehru first took the issue to the United Nations Security Council (United Nations, 1948). The state has experienced three subsequent wars with Pakistan (1965, 1971, and 1999) and the Kashmir valley has suffered from local uprisings since the late 1980s, with some Pakistani-supported militants fighting the Indian state (Ganguly, 1997; Wirsing, 1998; Widmalm, 2016). The violence decreased between 2002 and 2007, but resumed in 2016 after separatist leader Burhan Wani was killed (Widmalm, 2020). Much of that last uprising was met with brute force, with Indian armed forces using pellet guns that injured many protestors, many of whom lost their sight. Widmalm nevertheless claims

---

[8]   The major ethnic groups are the Kashmiris, Gujjars, Bakarwals, Paharis, Dogras, and Ladakhis.

[9]   Jammu province constitutes 65.23 per cent Hindus, 30.69 per cent Muslims, 3.57 per cent Sikh; 97.16 per cent of the total population of Kashmir province constitutes Muslims, with 1.84 per cent Hindus; Leh has 68 per cent Buddhist; and Kargil 91 per cent Muslim (EFSAS, 2017, p.2)

[10] Instrument of Accession of Jammu and Kashmir State (1947) (Jammu and Kashmir–India), signed on 26 October 1947 by Maharaja Hari Singh of Jammu and Kashmir and on 27 October 1947 by Lord Mountbatten of Burma, Governor General of India.

that the levels of violence were not as bad as those seen in the 1990s or early 2000s. Post-2016 protests have been led by the younger generation in the valley. Singh (2020) holds that this generation is different from earlier ones in that it is far more technology-driven, social media-savvy, and very conscious of its Kashmiri identity. She explains that this generation is angry with the Indian state for the repression instigated by the police and army as well as with hard-line local leaders. The militarization of the valley coupled with the dehumanizing violence experienced by protesters, including the application of the Prevention of Terrorism Act, 2002 (POTA), has reinforced the separate Kashmiri Muslim identity, rather than making Kashmiris feel a part of India (Singh, 2020).[11]

Article 370 was a special amendment made under the Constitution of India to give special rights to the state of Jammu and Kashmir and its residents upon their assimilation in the Indian Union, granting it a level of autonomy that is not enjoyed by other Indian states. This included provisions on who was a resident and who could own or buy property, and the state was allowed its own flag, Constitution, and penal code. On 5 August 2019, the GoI revoked Article 370 – and with it the special constitutional status of Jammu and Kashmir. It also abrogated Article 35A, which had allowed Jammu and Kashmir to define its 'permanent residents' and their rights and privileges. The former state was divided into the Union Territories of Ladakh (without a legislature) and Jammu-Kashmir (with a legislature). This unexpected move included moving 45,000 troops into Kashmir (Chatterji, 2020). A near total telecommunication lockdown was imposed for over a year to stop any protests in their tracks and to stop anyone communicating with others outside the state; 4G internet services were only restored in February 2021. Section 144

---

[11] POTA was passed with the objective of strengthening anti-terror operations in India. With institutionalized communalism increasing every year, it is not surprising that POTA is used as a communalist instrument (Deshmukh, 2021). Within two years of passing the bill, Gujarat witnessed 280 arrests under POTA of which only one was not a Muslim. The ensuing charges resulted in the detention of 189 individuals, most of whom were denied bail. Substitutes were detained in case the person the police were searching for could not be found. Most of the accused did not have a criminal history and were small-time employed individuals engaged as plumbers, electricians, and drivers. According to testimonies, all the accused were aged under 30, and their medical and government identity proofs were taken away by the Crime Branch. The police engaged in death threats to scare families and stated they would file ensuing murders as 'encounters'. Testimonies documented by Preeti Verma also allege torture, including electrocution to the groin, posing with weapons, documenting fake evidence, and moving wooden apparatus across the body. Owing to the torture, several detainees lost consciousness, and those who survived were forced to imitate making bombs. Zakia Jowher's testimony attests the fact that many officers in the Crime Branch are either brainwashed or perpetrate a certain ideology while dealing with Muslims (Verma, 2004).

of the Indian Penal Code was enforced to prevent violent unrest.[12] Political leaders including Farooq Abdullah, Omar Abdullah, and Mehbooba Mufti were arbitrarily detained (Ganguly, 2020). There was hardly any international reaction and domestic protests were muted (Sodhi, 2021 p.3).[13] In part this was because domestic protests were focusing on the CAA, as discussed in a later section of this chapter, but also because of border clashes between India and China in Ladakh and the COVID-19 pandemic taking hold in India and globally. The fact that Kashmir was cut off for so long also means that there were few reports detailing the problems faced by residents during that time.[14]

The political move took many by surprise, but with the benefit of hindsight this should not have been the case. The BJP 2014 election manifesto promised the abrogation of Kashmir's article 370 to make Jammu and Kashmir an 'integral part of the union' (BJP, 2004).[15] The BJP's domestic narrative has been that the Article was a temporary provision and that it ended up impeding development, resulting in a haven for Pakistani sponsored terrorists. Since the abrogation of special status, the government has been portraying itself as the flagbearer of development for Jammu and Kashmir (Sodhi, 2021, p.17), and the move has had widespread support.[16] However, on the ground there has been a severe clampdown on civil liberties. Although the leaders were released in 2020, the media blackout continues and journalists are silenced.[17] According to Amnesty International:

> At least 18 journalists in Kashmir were physically attacked by police or summoned to police stations. Dissent was further suppressed when a new media policy was introduced by the Jammu and Kashmir government to create 'a sustained narrative on the functioning of the government in media' by checking 'anti-national activities'. On 20 October, the Jammu and Kashmir government closed the office of the *Kashmir Times*, without prior notice, after its editor, Anuradha Bhasin, had challenged the communications blockade in the Supreme

---

[12] Section 144 of The Code of Criminal Procedure 1973 is a colonial era law that prohibits the assembly of people.

[13] Sodhi (2021) argues that international powers were only concerned with the humanitarian situation; and that the Jammu and Kashmir issue was seen as a domestic situation, so the international community (apart from Pakistan and China) did not want to upset the Indian government.

[14] There is, for example, a lot more information available on the Delhi riots of December 2019, despite these occurring later.

[15] BJP election manifesto: http://library.bjp.org/jspui/bitstream/123456789/252/1/bjp_lection_manifesto_english_2014.pdf.

[16] See, for example, Dua (2021) and *Times of India* (2021).

[17] One of the authors travelled from Srinagar to Kargil in July 2022, and on every road there was heavy armed police and army presence. In the cities and towns one armed man was posted every 25 metres.

Court. The NIA also raided the offices and residences of civil society activists including Khurram Parvez and three of his associates, and Parveena Ahanger, who had reported extensively on human rights abuses in Kashmir. The NIA alleged that the activists had raised funds for 'carrying out secessionist and separatist activities' in Jammu and Kashmir. (Amnesty International 2020, n.d., para.10).

The changes in the laws have also meant that new domicile certificates for people from outside the state are being issued, changing the demographic composition of the state. The Office of the United Nations High Commissioner for Human Rights (OHCHR) stated that 'The number of successful applicants for domicile certificates that appear to be from outside Jammu and Kashmir raises concerns that demographic change on a linguistic, religious and ethnic basis is already underway' (Amnesty International 2020, n.d.). Muslims might very well become a minority in their only majority state.

Kashmir is not the only state where it has become difficult to be a Muslim. The case of Assam, discussed in the next section, shows that discrimination against Muslims and Islamophobia pervades both current state and national politics.

Assam and the NRC
Background of the problem
Assam is a linguistically and ethnically diverse state: 61.47 per cent are Hindu and 34.2 per cent are Muslim; 7.15 per cent are SCs and 12.4 per cent are STs (Government of India, 2011).[18] Contemporary Assamese politics is focused on the issue of indigenous Assamese identity based on language and the threat posed by illegal Bengali migration, especially from Bangladesh. According to the extensive and detailed study by Saikia et al (2016) on Assam's problem of illegal migration, the consequences for the locals have included visible changes in their area because of the presence of non-Assamese immigrants, including village composition and the use of forest and grazing land, with locals leaving Assam as well as changes in local culture occurring, including those connected to language and religion. Saikia explains that 'the basic problem with religious change is the sense of phobia that if expansion continues at this rate, it will make Assam dominated

---

[18] Major linguistic groups are Assamese (48.38 per cent) and Bengalis (28.91 per cent) (Census of India [Language], 2011). STs include the Barmans in Cachar, Bodo, Deori, Rabha, Miri, Tiwa, Garo, Sonowal-Kachari, Mikir, and Dimasa. Six communities have been demanding ST status (tea tribes or 'Adivasi', Koch-Rajbangsi, Ahoms, Morans, Mataks, and Sootias) (Saikia et al, 2020, p.71).

by Bengalis emigrated from Bangladesh' (Saikia et al, 2016, p.151). The resulting political implications include security issues as well as conflicts between Assamese and other natives and immigrants. One Assamese teacher explained how this affected the classroom: 'We used to teach [citizenship] using dramas and plays about the illegal intrusion happening in our country and how it affects us. I used to teach citizenship classes six–seven years ago to Class 10 students' (GS5 Guwahati).

The causes for illegal migration are numerous, but much blame has been put on the poor policing of the borders as well as the unwillingness of the central government to deal with an ever-growing problem. Saikia et al (2016) state that in their study, except for a tiny minority, the respondents had negative perceptions of immigrants:

> The study reveals the stark realities of an ageing native population as against a young and expanding immigrant population, hinting at an ongoing process of replacement. That an overwhelming majority of 89 per cent of natives are Hindu and 97 per cent of immigrants are Muslim indicates an absolute communal divide and consequential conflict. Immigrants in Assam are less well-off and less educated, thereby complicating the situation. In immigrant villages, 95 per cent of the households interviewed possess land, though the holdings are smaller. (Saikia et al, 2016, p.157)

The problem of immigration began with British colonialism. Dasgupta (2001–2002, cited in Saikia et al, 2016, p.3) points to 1826 as the year when skilled labour migration from West Bengal and later Bihar and Orissa started to further the economic progress of the sparsely populated and underdeveloped region in the north-east. Much of this increased to the tea plantations that were developed across Assam from 1840.[19] Indigenous Assamese were not interested in working in the tea gardens. The population movement that took place formed the second largest stream of migrants in India (the first formed by migration from Bihar into West Bengal). The railways constructed towards the end of the 19th century opened the Brahmaputra valley further. Farmer migration was the second type of migration, taking place due to Assam's extensive fallow land. Muslim peasants from East Bengal began to arrive as of 1881 (Bose, 1989, cited in Saikia et al, 2016, p.5).[20] By the

---

[19] For example, in 1921, 571,000 persons from Bihar and Orissa were enumerated in Assam.

[20] The mass migration of Bengalis to the Assam valley was first reported in the 1911 Census (Davis, 1951). The number of persons born in West Bengal but living in Assam were 159,000 and 348,000 in 1911 and 1921 respectively, excluding those on tea estates (Census of India, 1921, p.5).

1930s issues of loss of forest land, loss of language, and religion (linked to the Muslim League's demand for an independent state) started to fuel fears within the Assamese community that they could become a minority in their own state. The partition of India complicated things further; prior to 1947 no migration could be termed 'illegal' as India was one country. The creation of a border between Assam and East Pakistan began the problem (Hazarika, 2006, cited in Saikia et al, 2016, p.7). The issue of migrants and illegal migration as faced today cannot be separated from colonial history, with the feeling emerging that Assamese were being swamped by Bengali illegal migrants (irrespective of whether they were Hindu or Muslim). Nevertheless, as shall be seen later, the various governments of independent India also carry political responsibility for what has turned into one of India's most polarizing internal dilemmas.

The 1964 anti-Hindu riots in East Pakistan sent Hindus fleeing across the border. This prompted the Prevention of Infiltration from Pakistan Act, and a special Border Police Force was raised to control border crossings (Saikia et al, 2016, p.7). The war between India and Pakistan in 1971, leading to the creation of Bangladesh, resulted in another wave of Hindus fleeing; they were not sent back due to religious persecution.[21] In March 1972 Indian PM Indira Gandhi and the new PM of independent Bangladesh, Sheikh Mujibur Rahman, signed an agreement that legitimized all irregular East Pakistani migrants who had come to Assam before 25 March 1971 (Ministry of External Affairs, 1972; see also Gogoi, 2016). How the local Assamese population felt about this issue was not taken into account. Just eight years later the pot boiled over. In the March 1979 by-elections, there were allegations that illegal migrants from Bangladesh were on the voter lists, resulting in anti-foreigner agitations launched by the All Assam Students' Union (AASU): they demanded 'detection, disenfranchisement, and deportation' of foreigners (Government of Assam, 2012). Militant Assamese nationalists moved to a full-scale secessionist armed insurrection led by the United Liberation Front of Asom (United Liberation Front of Assam, n.d.). In 1983 thousands of Bengali Muslims and hundreds of tribal Assamese were killed in communal violence.[22] The worst was the 'Nellie

---

[21] This can be seen as part of the background to the contested CAA discussed further later, showing that the Congress Party also distinguished between Hindus and Muslims when it came to refugees.

[22] 'Anti-immigrant violence, especially against Bengali Muslims, has continued in the state. In October 1993, around 50 people were killed. In July 1994, assaults on Bengali Muslims in Barpeta district resulted in 100 deaths, mostly Muslim. Clashes between Bodos and Bengali Muslims in 2008 in Udalguri and Darrang districts led to 70 deaths and over 100,000 people displaced (Government of Assam, 2012). In 2012, clashes between Bodos and Bengali Muslims in Kokrajhar, Chirang and Dhubri districts, killed over 80 people, mostly Muslim, and displaced nearly 300,000 people (Firstpost, 2012). In 2014, clashes

massacre', which occurred on 18 February 1983, when at least 1,800 people, mostly Bengali Muslims, were killed (Choudhary, 2019). According to Saikia, the Nellie violence was a result of a complex interplay of many factors: tribal land alienation, breakdown of law and order in the state, and the anti-foreigners narrative of the agitation leaders (Saikia, 2020, p.75). An HRW report explains how the central government responded by passing the Illegal Migrants (Determination by Tribunals) Act (IMDT) in 1983 to detect irregular immigrants who had arrived since March 1971 and expel them (Mediavigil, 2019, cited in HRW Report, 2020).[23]

The 1985 Assam Accords, signed between the Asom Gana Parishad (AGP) party that had won the state elections, the AASU, and the central government under Rajiv Gandhi finally ended the violence. The accord called for the expulsion of all immigrants who had entered Assam illegally after 24 March 1971 and a ten-year disenfranchisement of irregular immigrants who had entered the state between 1966 and 1971. It granted citizenship to those who had come to Assam before 1 January 1966. The 1955 Citizenship Act was amended in 1985 in line with the Assam Accord.[24] This, however, did not settle the issue. In the first instance, the updating of the NRC that had been promised as part of the accord was delayed owing to the ongoing insurgency. The Election Commission of India reviewed the electoral rolls in 1997 and marked a D for 'doubtful voter' next to any persons who could not prove their citizenship status. The D voters were disenfranchised and their cases were sent to the foreign tribunals.[25] These tribunals had been set up in 1964, and over the years there have been serious allegations about

---

between Bodos and Muslims in Baksa and Kokrajhar districts killed at least 30 Muslims (*The Guardian*, 2014).

[23] The burden of proof issue was blamed for insufficient migrants being deported and the law was challenged by the former head of the AASU in the Supreme Court; it was struck down in 2005 in Sarbananda Sonowal v. Union of India; the court establishing that the burden to prove citizenship lies upon the individual accused of being a foreigner. Unlike the Foreigners Act, however, the IMDT law placed the burden of proof on the complainant or the police (White Paper on Foreigners' Issue, Government of Assam, Home and Political Department, 22 October 2012, cited in HRW 2020). According to one official estimate, between 1985 and 2005, 112,791 cases were referred to the IMDT tribunals. It decided 24,021 cases, declaring 12,846 persons as foreigners, out of whom only 1,547 people were pushed back or deported.

[24] The original 1955 Citizenship act adopted the *jus solis* (or birth right citizenship for those born in India). Current legislation is that anyone born before 1987 is a citizen; anyone born between July 1987 and 3 December 2004 would need one parent to be a citizen by birth, for anyone born after that date neither parent should be an illegal migrant. This was contested in Assam, and the law is unclear to date (Azad et al, 2020, p.196).

[25] A total of 231,657 D references were made to the authorities in the 1998 White Paper on Foreigners' Issue, Government of Assam, Home and Political Department, 22 October 2012.

them being arbitrary, discriminatory, inconsistent, and error-ridden (Amnesty International India, 2019). Foreigners Tribunals also tried those referred to them by the Assam Border Police Organization.[26]

The role of the RSS in saffronizing Assam

As has been seen here, the issue in Assam was one of Assamese cultural identity as opposed to Hindu identity. For many decades Assam was ruled by Congress, although Assamese parties have often been part of coalitions. The Congress party was represented primarily by upper-caste Assamese, who pushed through Assamese as the official state language in the 1960s as language riots erupted not only in Assam but also in other Indian states. This discriminated not only against the Bengali speaking population (irrespective of religion) but also against tribal populations, who did not speak Assamese. Saikia maintains that 'the Assamese language movement in the 1960s and 1970s is responsible for two major developments: first, it fragmented the existing constituencies of Congress' catch-all formula resulting in the rise of ethnic parties and second, it created a conducive environment for mass-based anti-foreigners' movement to take shape in the early 1980s' (Saikia, 2020, p.72).

In 2016 and again in 2021, the BJP won power at the state level. In order to understand Assam's contemporary woes, it is key to understand how what has been termed 'nativist' politics based on language and culture (Saikia, 2020) was converted into a Hindutva agenda focused on religion. In the first instance, the BJP's campaign did what the party has also done in other states – appropriate the local history and put a Hindutva spin on it. In this instance the BJP used the late 17th-century battle of Saraighat, at which the Ahoms successfully resisted the entry of Mughals into Assam, to reinforce the discourse of the fear of the outsider – specifically the onslaught of illegal Bangladeshis (Saikia, 2020, p.70). The BJP had already done well in the state in 2014 during the parliamentary elections. For this kind of political success both at national and state elections, more than just a tweaking of the BJP's image had been required. Longkumer's book (2020) on the Sangh Parivar in the north-east shows the work undertaken by the Hindu right amongst tribal populations that had traditionally resisted the 'idea of India' (Khilnani, 1997), and how this fed into support for the BJP. For example, the RSS

---

[26] The burden of proof in both cases is on the person whose citizenship is contested, and not the state. In May 2019, the Ministry of Home Affairs expanded the 1964 Foreigners (Tribunal) Order to allow individuals who have been excluded from the NRC to approach the tribunals. In August 2019, there were 100 Foreigners Tribunals in Assam. The government announced an additional 221 tribunals to handle the appeals of those excluded from the NRC. See Pisharoty (2021).

affiliate VHP-run Pan-India Ekal Vidyalaya Foundation has been offering education and infrastructure in tribal areas since 1986, supporting some of the most marginalized communities in a 'counter proselytization' effort.[27]

Based on the anti-foreigner movement espoused by the AGP, the RSS was able to 'activate religious fissures that were overshadowed by language politics in Assam post-independence' (Saikia, 2020, p.73) The RSS was particularly interested in the north-east because of Christian missionary activity in tribal areas that it sought to counter (Longkumer, 2020).[28] 'The RSS played a key role in transforming the core of Assamese politics 'from being anti-*bahiragat* (outsiders) to being an anti-*videshi* (foreigners) movement' (Sethi, 2017, p.71 in Saikia, 2020, p.74). For the RSS there is a distinction between foreigners, seen as infiltrators, in this case Bangladeshi Muslims, and foreign Hindus, seen as asylum seekers.[29] The RSS worked patiently to adapt the Hindutva ideology to Assamese politics. This included using Assam's 'glorious past' of the Pragjyotishpur and Kamrupa kingdoms (Bhattacharjee, 2016, cited in Saikia, 2020, p.76) and showing how Assam was part of Bharat Mata.

Ironically it was the Bengali Hindus who responded positively to saffron politics, despite being seen as outsiders by the Assamese; the BJP has found its core support in that community. However, Saikia argues that the ideological groundwork done by the RSS and their affiliate civil society organizations allowed the BJP to also expand its voter base among Assamese Hindus in 2014 and later in 2016. (Saikia, 2020, p.77) As religious identity increased in importance, the BJP was able to politicize the issue of illegal migration of Muslims (rather than Bengalis). The promise of deportation secured the vote in 2014. It is nevertheless important to understand that the Assamese and other indigenous groups in Assam continue to see both Bengali Hindus and Muslims as outsiders. How this has affected recent Assamese politics, the NRC, and the CAA is discussed next.

Updating the National Register of Citizens

The issue of updating the NRC re-emerged when a case filed by the Assam Public Works with the Supreme Court in 2009 claimed that 4.1 million immigrants were on the Assam electoral rolls (Indian Kanoon, n.d.). In December 2014, the AASU became involved in the court case, asking the government to update the NRC. The BJP used it to increase religious polarization.

---

[27] The foundation runs single teacher schools.

[28] The Sangh established its first *shakha* in Guwahati as early as 1946.

[29] Hindus are 'sharanarthis' (i.e. asylum seekers) and Muslims are 'anupraveshkaaris' (i.e. infiltrators) (Archives of RSS, n.d., cited in Saikia, 2020, p.75).

The process of updating the NRC started in 2015, monitored by the Supreme Court. According to the India Exclusion Report (Azad et al, 2016), the Supreme Court exempted persons 'who are originally inhabitants of the state of Assam from any further proof or inquiry for automatic inclusion in the NRC'.[30] Two sets of documents were used for the citizenship verification process: legacy data (1951 NRC and electoral rolls up to 24 March 1971 to prove that the applicant's ancestors lived in Assam before 1971) or linkage documents (e.g. birth certificates) to establish the relationship of the applicant to those who had submitted legacy documents (Government of Assam, n.d.). HRW (2019) correctly points out that the kind of documents required (land deeds, birth certificates, etc.) requires a certain level of privilege and financial stability, uncommon with the poorer sections of society across India's north-east. The process has also affected how teachers in Assam define a citizen: 'A person by birth can be a citizen of a country, if he has legal and ancestral documents to prove that he is a citizen of a country. In Assam, if a person has all the NRC documents then only he/she is a citizen of our country' (GS10 Guwahati). Another teacher explained: 'One who is born in India, whose parents are Indian is an Indian citizen. There are guidelines and rules for acquiring Indian citizenship in our constitution' (GS4 Guwahati).

The documents of 33 million people were checked. The NRC was initially described as a mechanism to stop discrimination against Bengalis, many of whom were seen by Assamese as illegal immigrants. However, the process ended up being an arbitrary and opaque exclusion process, fraught with errors (Chakravarty, 2018). The public narrative shifted from 'no genuine citizen would be left out' to 'no ineligible person should be included' (Chakravarty, 2018, cited in Azad et al, 2020 p.201). At first, almost 4 million names were excluded (HRW, 2019). On 31 August 2019, when the final list was published, over 1.9 million residents were excluded, including some indigenous people who could not provide the relevant documents (Express Web Desk [Indian Express], 2019). They had 120 days to file an appeal at a Foreigners Tribunal. Names cleared by these tribunals are supposed to be included on the NRC. However, the India exclusion report (Azad et al, 2020) found cases where they were not.

For those who are unsuccessful, it is unclear where they will go. Bangladesh is unlikely to accept any deported Bengalis, Muslim or otherwise (BBC News India, 2019; First Post, 2019). According to HRW, there are six detention centres in prisons across Assam with 988 people as of November 2019. More

---

[30] However original inhabitants were not defined – and as is seen below, was in any case not applied evenly, as indigenous tribal citizens found themselves excluded alongside Bengali Muslims and Hindus (Azad et al, 2020).

are being built (Choudhury, 2019), and the conditions are horrendous.[31] The whole exercise cost 1,220 crore rupees ($152,795.12) (Saikia, 2020, pp.80–1) and the results have satisfied no one. The ASSU would have wanted more people excluded, while the BJP found that there were not enough Muslims and that many Bengali Hindus had been left out of the NRC (Saha, 2019).

In response to how Hindus were affected by the exercise, the government developed the CAA, so that Hindus who are not citizens of India can receive citizenship in an accelerated way (6 years as opposed to 11).[32] The new law, discussed in more detail later in this chapter, applies to all Hindus, Buddhists, Jains, and Christians from three neighbouring countries – described as vulnerable minorities fleeing persecution.[33]

The BJP faced a backlash for this across Assam; as explained earlier, Assamese politics sees all Bengalis as outsiders, and whilst some signed up to the religious identity issue propagated by the BJP, the CAA meant that more rather than fewer immigrants would be on their way to Assam. Protests erupted across the state. A study on how social media was used to arrange and coordinate such protests showed that Facebook groups against the NRC and CAA increased, especially after the Citizenship Amendment Bill was passed on 12 December 2019 and reached a peak in January 2020 (Roy et al, 2021). The NRC process ended up showing the fissure between Assamese politics and what the BJP was trying to achieve. A new regional party emerged, the Assam Jatiya Parishad (AJP; meaning Assam Ethnic Organization), combining the state's two largest student unions and formed as a result of the anti-CAA protests, reviving the argument that in Assam citizenship is about language and culture more than religion (Saha, 2020). Teachers in Assam have pointed out that protests against the government's policies could put anyone at risk: 'There are constitutional rights but whether those are implemented and followed properly is a question mark. If you talk against the government, they will arrest you. If you will say or write anything against nation you will start getting warning and you may even get arrested' (GS3 Guwahati).

---

[31] A fact-finding report released in June 2018 by the National Human Rights Commission found that people are detained in these centres with no prospect of release and without adequate legal representation. The centres are administered like prisons, the detainees treated as convicted prisoners. The report found that the detention centres also separated children from their parents (Mander, 2018).

[32] This clearly discriminates against Muslims in general, but in particular against Muslim communities that are also persecuted such as the Ahmadis and Rohingyas (Kuchay, 2019).

[33] The CAA excludes the Sri Lankan Tamil community. 'The reason for leaving the Sri Lankan Tamil community absent from the Act is because their persecution was on "ethnic fault lines" and not on religious lines and the war has been over for a decade' (Connah, 2021, p.204).

The BJP has continued to propagate its anti-Muslim/Bangladeshi rhetoric, with BJP president and Home Affairs minister Amit Shah referring to illegal immigrants as termites (Press Trust of India [India Today], 2019). The standoff between the AJP and the BJP resulted in a very polarized state election in 2021 (Verniers et al, 2021), won by the BJP, but clearly indicating the deep communal divide on the basis of religion, as well as on the basis of ethnicity and language. Rather than resolving the issues, the BJP's saffronization has made matters worse.

The CAA, mentioned as a 'solution' to the status of Bengali Hindus, had wider ramifications for the concept of Indian citizenship, and they will be explored next.

The Citizenship Amendment Act, 2019

India's 1955 Citizenship Act is based on the Nehruvian doctrine,[34] allowing for citizenship by birth, descent, registration, and naturalization. 'Illegal migrants' could be imprisoned or deported under the Foreigners Act, 1946 and the Passport (Entry into India) Act, 1920. The BJP seems to have been more concerned than Congress with who could or not become a citizen of India, as it was during their tenures in 2003 and more recently in 2019 that amendments to the Act were promulgated.

In 2003 the BJP-led NDA government amended the 1955 Citizenship Act to define 'illegal migrant' as any 'foreigner who entered India without a passport or travel documents or who entered with valid documents but overstayed beyond the permitted time' (Nair 2019, p.353). Anyone termed 'illegal migrant' could not apply for Indian citizenship by registration or naturalization and faced deportation or incarceration. Section 14A of the law, also inserted in 2003, called for the establishment of a National Register of Indian Citizens (HRW, 2020, p.16), presumably to establish who was legal and who was not. Further changes made in 2003 include any person born after 30 December 2004 also became ineligible for citizenship by birth if either parent was an illegal migrant (Ministry of Law and Justice, 2019, sec.3).

In December 2019, the Indian Parliament passed another amendment to the 1955 Citizenship Act that set out a path to citizenship for certain religious minorities fleeing persecution from neighbouring countries – not including Muslims (Ministry of Law and Justice, n.d.). The most recent amendment states that 'any person belonging to Hindu, Sikh, Buddhist, Jain, Parsi or Christian community from Afghanistan, Bangladesh or Pakistan ... shall not be treated as an illegal migrant for the purposes of this Act' (Ministry of Law and Justice, 2019). Individuals of these faiths from these

---

[34] Religion, ethnicity, or language play no part in it.

three countries can now apply for Indian citizenship provided they have been in India for at least six years and entered India before 31 December 2014. They are in effect exempt from the 'illegal migrant' definition of 2003. The Act is not applicable to the tribal areas of Assam, Meghalaya, Mizoram, Tripura and Manipur, and the area covered under 'The Inner Line notified under the Bengal Eastern Frontier Regulation, 1873, so that it does not violate the Assam Accord or endanger the indigenous cultural identity of the Northeast as a whole' (Nair, 2019, p.364). (However as has been seen earlier, the Assamese still see the CAA as a violation of the Assam Accords).

The government has framed this amendment as a 'humanitarian' exemption (Venkatesh et al, 2020, p.1) In fact, Home Minister Amit Shah explained that 'there is a fundamental difference between a refugee and an infiltrator. This bill is for refugees' (HRW, 2020, p.16). He went on to argue that 'we won't sit quiet (sic) till each oppressed refugee from Pakistan gets Indian citizenship' (Press Trust of India, 2020). While using the principle of international refugees to justify the CAA, it is important to remember that India has not ratified the 1951 Convention on the Status of Refugees nor its 1967 Protocol.[35]

For the first time since Indian independence religion was linked to citizenship criteria. The CAA drew protests and objections domestically and internationally. Three main issues were raised. The first of these is that the amendment is unconstitutional: by excluding Muslims it violates the Right to Equality under Article 14 of the Constitution that states the 'state shall not deny to any person the right to equality before law or the equal protection of laws within the territory of India'.[36] The second objection is that the CAA is anti-secular, violating the spirit of India's secular constitution.[37] The third issue relates to the countries that are included: Afghanistan is not a neighbouring country, and Sri Lanka and Myanmar, both neighbours, are excluded (Bhattacharjee, 2019, p.26).

---

[35] 'In fact, India has a declaration on Article 13 of the International Covenant on Civil and Political Rights that accords aliens the right of due process of the law during expulsion proceedings, stating that India will apply its own laws concerning foreigners. India has traditionally followed an ad hoc policy towards granting status to populations fleeing from its neighbouring countries, including Sri Lankan Tamils and Tibetan Buddhists' (Venkatesh et al, 2020, p.8).

[36] The case of Muslim sects such as Shias and Ahmediyas, who face routine persecution in Pakistan, and the recent persecution of Rohingya Muslims by the neighbouring state of Myanmar are highlighted in this regard (Bhattacharjee, 2019, p.26).

[37] The Supreme Court's verdict in the S.R. Bommai vs. Union of India case 1994, where the Court declared secularism to be a basic feature of the Indian Constitution, has been cited to make this point (Bhattacharjee, 2019, p.26).

As the bill was being prepared, opposition MPs stated that the proposed CAA went against the Constitution (Parliament of India, Lok Sabha, 2016). One of the most vocal was Shashi Tharoor (Congress), who stated: '[T]his is merely a cynical political exercise to further single out and disenfranchise an entire community in India and in doing so, a betrayal of all that was good and noble about our civilization' (Press Trust of India [Outlook India], 2019, para.6). Since the amendment has come into force, over 140 petitions have been filed in the Supreme Court challenging the constitutionality of the law and claiming that the CAA violates articles 14, 15, 21, and 25 of the Indian Constitution.[38] In March 2020, the United Nations High Commissioner for Human Rights also waded into the debate, filing an intervention application through three retired public officials, urging the Supreme Court to take into account 'international human rights law, norms, and standards in the proceedings related to the Citizenship Amendment Act' (Deb Mukharji, IFS (Retd). & Ors. v. Union of India, 2019; Mohan, 2020). Needless to say, this was seen as undue international interference in India's domestic affairs.

As will have been understood from Chapter 2, India's national identity has shifted from a secular conception to one that is in line with Hindutva. Invoking religion as part of legal citizenship was the logical next step for a party that aims to reformulate India as a Hindu nation and that seeks the marginalization of Muslims. The CAA excludes Muslims by not including Muslim groups such as Shia, Ahmadis, and Rohingyas that are persecuted in neighbouring countries.[39] The courts, however, have argued that the CAA has no bearing on the freedom of religion of Indian Muslims. Whilst this may be true, the issue of the CAA cannot be separated from the NRC, as discussed in the section on Assam. The NRC exercise in Assam was set up

---

[38] Article 15 prohibits discrimination on specific grounds, including religion; article 21 guarantees right to life and personal liberty; and article 25 protects right to freedom of religion.

[39] 'The Legislative Department, however, made two broad arguments in defence of the constitutional validity of the CAA. First, it said the law was justified on the basis of a legal doctrine called reasonable classification. According to this doctrine, if there is a special law that is applicable only to certain sections/groups, the court is entitled to 'enquire whether the *classification is founded on a reasonable basis [...] or is arbitrary*' (emphasis added). The reasonableness of classification, in this sense, can only be questioned if a law violates the rights of other persons/communities, which are outside the scope of its legal ambit. The classification of migrants into persecuted minorities and others, by this logic, is called reasonable because it does not affect the rights of Muslim citizens in India. Second, the Legislative Department said the CAA was also justified on the basis of freedom of religion (Art. 25). It argued that this law aims to protect the religious rights of persecuted minorities seeking Indian citizenship. At the same time, it does not have any impact on the right to worship and the religion of other Indian citizens, including Muslims (Ahmed, 2019, pp.22–3).

specifically to identify 'illegal migrants' from Bangladesh. The nationwide extension of the exercise, as first envisioned by the 2003 amendment of the 1955 Citizenship Act, has a profound bearing on Muslims and poor minorities across India. By making citizenship dependent on the possession of the correct documentation, subject to verification, what appears in the first instance to be an administrative act results in the disenfranchisement of anyone who cannot meet these criteria. Once labelled as a foreigner, deportation or detention are real threats, and for Muslims, the CAA path back to citizenship becomes impossible (Siddique, 2020). Venkatesh et al (2020) argue that the NRC and the CAA are at the heart of constructing the 'ideal Hindu Citizen' (p.4), who is adequately documented.[40] The obsession with documentation, verification, and control is nothing new. Desai (2020) points out that despite India's illiteracy rate, families can only access certain everyday 'rights' they hold as citizens by owning a number of official cards and documents, such as ration cards (to purchase subsidized food and other items), Below Poverty Line cards for welfare access, National Rural Employment Guarantee cards to access the government job scheme, voting cards, and so on. These documents are seen by many as confirming their citizenship. In 2009 the Aadhaar card – India's universal identification card, which collects a large amount of biometric data – was supposed to replace much of the other documentation, yet certain poor families have found it difficult to get an Aadhaar card (Kheera, 2019). Birth certificates, ancestry records, land registration documents, and educational certificates are rarely owned by poor, uneducated, and tribal people. Yet these are the 'legacy documents' that are required to determine citizenship and inclusion on the NRC. This verification process transforms the fundamental right to citizenship into a duty for each citizen to produce acceptable evidence to prove his or her status. Both the government and the local bureaucracy now have the power to classify people into citizens and illegal migrants on a case-by-case basis (Ahmed, 2019, p.18).

The protests against the CAA spread across the country, organized by Muslim women, Dalit leaders, students, and hundreds of thousands of people across the caste, class, gender, and religious spectrum (Venkatesh et al, 2020 p.3). The protests have little to do with who is persecuted or not in neighbouring countries, and who might apply for citizenship. Rather, protests are fuelled by Muslims who see this as the first step in a wider disenfranchisement of Muslims in India. Much of the protests have taken place in Delhi – as will be described in the next section, but there have been sizable protests in Uttar Pradesh, Assam, and Karnataka as well, with

---

[40] Venkatesh et al (2020) also argue that these practices resemble colonial practices that are 'adopted to discriminatory political ends' (p.2).

protesters arrested and killed.[41] State governments have imposed section 144 of the Criminal Procedure Code. In Uttar Pradesh police have been accused of using excessive force, sometimes unnecessary lethal force, against protesters in several districts that include Aligarh, Meerut, Kanpur, Bijnor, Sambhal, and Muzaffarnagar (HRW, 2020, p.45). Protesting groups have used national symbols such as the national flag, copies of the Constitution, and images of Gandhi and Ambedkar to show that their protests are not *against* but *for* the Indian state. Despite this legislation affecting Muslims, the protests have been interfaith, and religious texts from the Bhagavad Gita, the Quran, the Guru Granth Sahib, and the Bible have been recited to show the unity across religious faiths, and the unity of the protesters.

Delhi protests, 2019

The protests in Delhi turned violent on 23 February 2020, lasting for five days and resulting in at least 53 people killed and more than 250 injured – most of them Muslim (DMC, 2020, p.17). These numbers are likely to be just the tip of the iceberg. Bodies and body parts were still being recovered in drains as fact finding missions drew to a close, and a number of families have still not been able to locate their loved ones (Youth for Human Rights Documentation, 2020). The violence across localities of north-east Delhi included the looting and arson of homes, shops, businesses, vehicles, and other properties (DMC, 2020), leading to the destruction of 122 houses, 322 shops, 301 vehicles, and 3 schools.[42] Mosques of the area were attacked by the mob, who even placed a saffron flag on top of one of them (Youth for Human Rights Documentation, 2020). Reflecting the violence in Gujarat almost two decades earlier, the police was again accused of not intervening to protect those being attacked, and in some cases even helping when Hindu mobs attacked Muslims, their houses, and their businesses. The government saw things differently – Home Minister Amit Shah, who oversees the Delhi police, praised them for 'effectively containing the riot within 36 hours' (Amnesty, n.d., p.32).

As contesting reports on what happened in Delhi emerged, there has been a debate on whether this was a riot with both communities at fault or an anti-Muslim pogrom. Wahab (2020) has called it 'the war of the narratives'.[43]

---

[41] 'At least 30 people have been killed during protests, all in three BJP-governed states: 23 in Uttar Pradesh, 5 in Assam, and 2 in Karnataka. According to HRW, the vast majority of those killed and injured have been Muslims (Chakravartty, 2019; Jafri, 2020).

[42] North-east Delhi includes Shiv Vihar, Khajuri Khas, Chand Bagh, Gokulpuri, Maujpur, Karawal Nagar, Jafrabad, Mustafabad, Ashok Nagar, Bhagirah Vihar, Bhajanpura, and Kardam Puri.

[43] The 'Report of the DMC fact-finding Committee on North-East Delhi Riots of February 2020'; the Youth for Human Rights Documentation (YHRD) 'An Account of Fear

The Delhi Minority Commission (DMC, 2020) that investigated the events concluded, however, that the violence was 'seemingly planned and directed to teach a lesson to a certain community which dared to protest against a discriminatory law'. The DMC chairperson spoke of a 'pogrom' (DMC, 2020, p.13) and the DMC described the sequence of events as follows. There were anti-CAA protests in several parts of Delhi.[44] The protests against the CAA in Shaheen Bagh had started in mid-December, with Muslim women organizing a round-the-clock peaceful sit-in to show solidarity with the Jamia Milla university students who had been protesting against the CAA and had been beaten by the police. According to the DMC, Shaheen Bagh came to represent a social movement not only against the CAA, but also against 'unemployment, poverty, caste and religious discrimination, and a host of issues at the heart of struggles for social justice and equality in India' (DMC, 2020, pp.24–5). The protests were met with threats by BJP politicians, not only in Delhi. For example, on 3 January Somasekhara Reddy, a Member of the Legislative Assembly of the BJP, warned of serious repercussions in blatantly divisive and dangerous terms at a pro-CAA rally in Bellari:

It's just a caution for those who are protesting against the CAA (Citizenship Amendment Act). We are 80 per cent and you (Muslims) are 18 per cent. Imagine what will happen if we take charge… Beware of the majority when you live in this country. This is our country. If you want to live here, you will have to, like the Australian Prime Minister said, follow the country's traditions… So, I warn you that CAA and NRC are made by Modi and Amit Shah. If you will go against

---

& Impunity: Preliminary Fact-Finding Report on Communally- Targeted Violence in North-East Delhi, February 2020', and HRW's detailed report titled '"Shoot the Traitors": Discrimination Against Muslims under India's New Citizenship Policy' regard what happened in Delhi in February 2020 as targeted anti-Muslim violence. The report published by the Group of Intellectuals and Academicians (GIA) of Advocate Monika Arora (Supreme Court of India) titled 'Delhi Riots 2020: Report from Ground Zero – The Shaheen Bagh Model in North East Delhi: From Dharna to Danga' and the report by Nupur J. Sharma and Kalpojyoti Kashyap of OpIndia titled 'Delhi Anti-Hindu Riots of 2020: The Macabre Dance of Violence Since December 2019', view the violence as 'Anti- Hindu riots'. According to OpIndia, 'the fact of the matter is, it all began when Ladeeda Sakhaloon, Barkha Dutt's Jamia "shero", gave a call for Jihad on the 11th of December 2019. The entire cycle of violence in Delhi began soon afterwards. And since then, it has never been peaceful. It is also pertinent to remember that the Shaheen Bagh protest was masterminded by Sharjeel Imam, a radical Islamist who wished to cut off North East India from the rest of the country' (Sharma and Kashyap 2020, p.15, cited in Wahab, 2020).

44 Locations included Shaheen Bagh, Jafrabad, Chand Bagh, Khajuri Khas, Old Mustafabad, Seelampur, Turkman Gate, Kardam Puri, Sundar Nagari, and Lal Bagh, and Inderlok, Nizammudin, Hauz Rani, and Sadar Bazar.

these acts, it won't be good… If you wish, you can go to Pakistan. We don't have any issues. Intentionally, we would not send you… If you will act as enemies, we should also react like enemies. (India TV News Desk, 2020)

The Chief Minister of Uttar Pradesh, Yogi Adityanath, made provocative and threatening speeches against the protestors. But tensions were particularly high across Delhi, where legislative assembly elections were held on 8 February 2020. During the election campaign, BJP candidates started making divisive remarks against the protesting women at Shaheen Bagh, with BJP leader Kapil Mishra calling Shaheen Bagh a 'mini-Pakistan', On 20 January 2020, Anurag Thakur, a junior minister in the national BJP government, uttered the slogan 'shoot the traitors' (HRW, 2020). BJP MP Parvesh Sahib Singh Verma announced that those protesting in Shaheen Bagh 'will enter your homes, they will pick up your sisters and daughters and rape and kill them' (cited in HRW, 2020, p.34) The Chief Minister of Delhi Arvind Kejriwal was called a 'terrorist' (Press Trust of India, 2020). Consequently, on 29 January 2020, the Election Commission of India ordered the removal of Union Minister of State Anurag Thakur and BJP MP Parvesh Verma from the BJP's list of star campaigners for the Delhi Assembly elections.[45] This did not stop the provocations. On 23 February 2020, as the Delhi protesters occupied an area around a north-east metro station, Kapil Misra led a large demonstration, with participants chanting 'shoot the traitors', and then tweeted that if the roads were not cleared within three days his supporters would not listen to the police.[46] His supporters then gathered in the area, which led to clashes between Hindus and Muslims. Then Hindu mobs arrived with swords, sticks, metal pipes, and bottles filled with petrol, and began chanting nationalist slogans including 'Jai Shri Ram', 'Har Har Modi', 'Modiji, kaat do in Mullon ko' (Modi, cut these Muslims into pieces), 'Aaj tumhe azadi denge' (Today, we will give you freedom). The violence followed a systematic pattern. Different mobs, numbering anywhere between 100 and 1,000 people, stopped men to show ID cards or to check them for circumcision. Testimonies gathered from victims during the fact-finding

---

[45] Since they had made 'statements/speeches contents of which were in violation of the letter and spirit of the various provisions of the Model Code of Conduct for Political Parties and Candidates' (Election Commission of India, 2020).

[46] 'As the violence escalated in the days following Kapil Mishra's speech, the High Court of Delhi on 26 February 2020, while hearing a petition seeking the registration of a First Information Report against BJP leaders Kapil Mishra, Anurag Thakur and Parvesh Verma for their speeches that led to incitement of violence among other prayers, asked the Delhi Police to take a "conscious decision" to register an FIR in 24 hours. […] To date, no FIR has been registered against the BJP leaders' (DMC, 2020, p.32).

mission indicate that the violence was planned and that mobs were armed (Youth for Human Rights Documentation, 2020). Muslim youth threw stones in response, trying to defend their community and families. This was, however, no match for the well-armed Hindu mobs (Youth for Human Rights Documentation, 2020).

The violence escalated to include beatings, looting, gas cylinder bombs, murders, arson: mosques,[47] vehicles, shops, and homes were burnt.[48] Attacks on women included verbal, physical, and psychological assaults (DMC, 2020). According to the testimonies gathered by the DMC, male police officers attacked women at protest sites, and later did not provide any help or support when the mob attacked the protesters in the same area. Several women suffered injuries (DMC, 2020). Police watched and did not respond to cries for help. In some cases, police took part in the beatings; testimonies confirmed that some police officers stopped their colleagues from helping protesters. The police were also accused of not taking action when FIRs were filed, or even refusing to register FIRs when requested to do so. A few accounts state how the police and paramilitary officials even escorted the mobs away once the attack was over (DMC, 2020).

As a result of the violence Muslim residents fled to other Muslim majority areas or relief camps rather than stay to rebuild their homes.[49] The DMC report describes how residents who had identified their attackers or who had complained to the police were particularly scared. This is justified, as the police ignored complaints against instigators such as Kapil Misra and instead focused on arresting anti-CAA protesters under the Unlawful Activities (Prevention) Act (Amnesty International, 2020). The police arrested dozens of Muslim activists and named well-known academics and politicians as part of the conspiracy (Amnesty International Report, 2020).[50] At the same time the planners, instigators, leaders, and perpetrators of that violence have been shielded (DMC, 2020). The Delhi Police have supported

---

[47] A total of 15 religious places – 13 mosques, one dargah, and one graveyard in Ashok Nagar, Gokul Puri, Bhajanpura, Shiv Vihar, Mustafabad, Jyoti Colony, Khajuri Khas, and Ghonda – had been vandalized (DMC, 2000). Hindu temples visited by the fact-finding committee members in the same localities had been left untouched.

[48] Properties owned by Muslims were destroyed while those owned by Hindus, even though adjacent, remained untouched. Reports state that when properties were owned by Hindus, only the content owned by the Muslim tenants was damaged (DMC, 2000).

[49] Many Muslims who took shelter in relief camps were displaced twice when they were, hastily and without any plan, evacuated from the camps in the wake of the COVID-19 lockdown (DMC, 2020).

[50] The Amnesty report points out that the Delhi Police is committing human rights violations including "violence with the rioters; torturing in custody; using excessive force on protesters; dismantling protest sites used by peaceful protesters and being mute bystanders as rioters wreaked havoc" (Amnesty International Report, 2020, p.4).

the conspiracy theory that violence was planned and executed by Muslim and leftist elements, even though two-thirds of those killed were Muslims. The theory of a collaboration between leftist (urban-Naxal) and jihadists to destroy India is also promoted by a group called GIA, who submitted a fact-finding report on the Delhi riots to the Home Ministry in March 2020.[51] The Muslim Women's Forum conducted an analysis comparing the police charge sheets to the GIA book, showing that the GIA theories were replicated in the charge sheets being filed by the Delhi Police in the Delhi riots cases. They conclude that the criminalization of the anti CAA protests was a way of delegitimizing the protests and the protesters, painting them as 'actors in a synchronized conspiracy to destabilise the country' (Karwan-e-Mohabbat et al, 2020, pp.3–4). This narrative means that government supporters will see the protesters as anti-national, further entrenching the BJP views on Muslims and the Hindutva conception of citizenship (Banaji, 2018; Kabir 2020). It is interesting to note that out of the seven seats that the BJP won in the Delhi election in February 2020, five seats were in north-east

---

[51] The group then announced that a book *Delhi Riots 2020: The Untold Story*, based on this report would be launched on 22 August 2020. The guests of honour at the launch event included Kapil Mishra. On the day of the book launch, Bloomsbury India, the publisher, pulled out. The authors subsequently claimed that their freedom of expression was being curtailed (Karwan-e-Mohabbat, Anhad and Muslim Women's Forum, 2020). According to this book, there was a giant criminal conspiracy to create extreme violence and destroy the Indian state. The conspiracy was likely foreign funded, probably by international Islamist organizations, possibly ISIS. The entire movement against the CAA–NRC–NPR in India was the front. The lakhs of protestors, including youth, students, and women of all ages, were part of the conspiracy; sometimes described as gullible and brainwashed, and other times as co-conspirators who were exceptionally violent. The conspirators were 'Urban-Naxals' or Jihadi, and most times both at once. The book does not explain why Naxals were funded by Islamists, despite their known differences. It is fair to say that in this book, all people who express liberal views and take public positions against the ruling BJP are Urban-Naxal. All Muslims – men, women and children – are Jihadi. The tale takes a broad sweep, invoking images of ISIS, Syria, and Egypt, and quotes from purported Maoist pamphlets about guerrilla warfare (Karwan-e-Mohabbat et al, 2020, p.4). According to this book, conspirators – interchangeably Urban, Naxal, and Jihadi – planted highly skilled sharp-shooters, possibly trained in Syria or Egypt, on high-rise buildings in north-east Delhi to kill. Therefore, the authors demand that *all* high-rise buildings in all of north-east Delhi must be subjected to a forensic audit. Many Islamic rioters, the book suggests, had combat training and used 'bunkers'. The conspirators also trained women to hide swords under their burqas. However, it does not indicate a possible location for this burqa/sword training. Delhi Police had no choice but to crush this Islamist–Naxal conspiracy, which was also taking root in the most reputed universities. Therefore, this book also calls on 'vice chancellors of DU, JMI, JNU and all other universities to take an audit of the use of their campuses to engineer wider disturbances in the city in the eight weeks leading up to the riots'. This, then, is the big picture of the Delhi riots portrayed in this book (Karwan-e-Mohabbat et al, 2020, p.5).

Delhi, the epicentre of the communal violence (Youth for Human Rights Documentation, 2020), a lesson certainly not lost on the BJP.

The protests against the CAA (and the NRC, and Kashmir's change of status) were protests against Hindutva's conception of citizenship, but they are not the only ones that have rocked India recently. The best recent example of protests against India's neoliberal turn and what it has meant for Indian citizenship is explored in the next section.

Farmers' protests

Three reform bills – the Farmers' Produce Trade and Commerce (Promotion and Facilitation) Act, the Farmers (Empowerment and Protection) Agreement on Price Assurance and Farm Services Act, and the Essential Commodities (Amendment) Act – were initiated by the Indian Parliament in September 2020. In line with its neoliberal approach, the government claimed that the bills would increase agricultural productivity by reducing restrictions on the purchase and sale of agricultural produce. The main aim was to end the government-controlled wholesale markets (*mandis*) that had guaranteed minimum prices for products to 100 million farmers (Shani, 2021a). Farmers argued that the new laws would create monopolies in the grain markets and that smaller farmers would not be able to survive as corporate buyers will impose their prices. The farm bills, as they were referred to collectively, triggered mass protests, starting in July 2020 in Punjab and resulting in more than 300,000 farmers arriving in Delhi in November 2020. They stayed through the winter, with more than 400 of them dying due to the living conditions in their tractors and carts through the cold winter and hot summer months (Gupta, 2021). The stalemate between the farmers and the government raised some interesting issues about Indian democracy. As one teacher from Chandigarh explained,

'They have passed this farmers bill and they have been protesting, since last six months, they have been protesting there and nothing has been done by the government so according to me this is a failure. If we are a democratic country, and in a democracy, the right is given to the citizens, they should protest, but the government cannot overlook them, they should do something, even if they have made certain laws for the betterment of the society, even if they have made laws for the betterment of the farmers, and if they are unable to understand that it's a duty of government because we have elected the BJP chosen them for a better future. […] Now, what the farmers, they are not feeling safe in their own country because they have a failure that might be their land will be taken by some other people in the coming years, they have a kind of fear that we don't know what the reality is. […]

Students come to you and ask you these questions and they discuss in the classes with you about the amendment and about democracy. They used to, they ask from us, they ask Yes Ma'am, why they are not doing anything?' (PS2 Chandigarh)

Although on the face of it these protests and the issues they address look different from the ones linked to Islamophobia and citizenship, they are nevertheless a hallmark of the neoliberal Hindutva approach that seeks 'to create an entrepreneurial consumer whose behaviour is regulated by the cultural framework of Hindu majoritarianism and is aimed at advancing the Hindu nation' (Chacko, 2019, p.407, cited in Shani, 2021a, p.266). They also reflect Kumar's concept and the Indian government's vision of 'consumer citizenship' (Kumar, 2022), mentioned at the start of this chapter. Giorgio Shani (2021a) argues that the farm laws are part of a larger transformation of Indian society, with neoliberal policies facilitating both marketization as well as social and religious hierarchies. Many of the protesting farmers are Sikhs, and there is (again reflecting the 1980s) a movement across Punjab claiming that Sikhs are not treated equally to Hindus. This is also reflected in the quotes by some Punjab teachers when asked about citizenship. Defining citizens and citizenship some teachers explained:

'Indian citizen's duty is to abide by the Indian Constitution and respect its ideals and institutions, the National Flag and the National Anthem. Every Indian citizen is required to cherish and follow the ideals which inspired our national struggle for freedom. But our PM is not sure of the Indian constitution. See what he is doing to farmers and Kashmiris. This is against the Indian constitution. It is not democratic. […] I can't say anything more. You know what is happening to poor farmers.' (GS8 Chandigarh)

'A citizen of the country should be respected regardless of caste, colour, and creed. I think as Indian citizens, we should respect others. I don't think that is happening. Look at now, Sikhs not respected. I don't feel that I am a citizen of India. I want to move out to a foreign country. […] Sikhs are not respected. They are not at the same level as Hindus. Hindus are the citizens of India.

The constitution has a list of constitutional rights, but my concern is that they are respected. Like Modi doesn't respect the rights of Sikhs. I think our constitutional rights are not respected. Hindus have more rights in the country. There are issues around the caste and religion. See now in the pandemic, the government didn't care of Sikhs' protests. Where is the constitution?' (PS5 Chandigarh)

A number of Hindu teachers based in Chandigarh praised Modi, and some blamed the NRIs for fermenting Sikh separatism:

'Indian citizen believes in democracy and should obey the rights and duties. Someone who respects the government and have faith in it. Situation in Punjab is getting worst day by day. They should pledge to respect India and the government. But you know what is happening here. It is sad to see that the NRIs are helping people to dislike their country' (GS4 Chandigarh).

Hindu teachers spoke with pride and happiness about officials coming to schools and teaching 'about values', and thought this was a good idea given the issues arising in the classroom through the farmers' protest. They implied that the school received extra funds if they allowed officials to visit:

'I think the government officials really help us deal with our issues in the school. A government official once came to the school and helped me how to teach Indian values in the fundamental duties. I really like the idea. Modiji is amazing leader who is a good example of citizen. That's all.' (GS2 Chandigarh)

Some spoke about being asked to use Modi as a role model. Hindu teachers were supportive of this, whilst Sikh teachers remained silent on the issue: 'We show videos of PM and BJP government. Every government is instructed to show the videos of leaders and teach the values by PM. I think this is a good step. Young people should be remembered (*sic*) of their duties and rights' (GS3 Chandigarh). However, some teachers did complain that BJP politics was affecting the Sikh students in the classroom:

'There are a few BJP supporters in my school who have introduced different activities in schools to promote Indian values. Sometimes, they insist students to speak in Hindi as most of our students from the Sikh community.' (GS8 Chandigarh)

'Students don't know much about citizenship. They are still discovering. They have mixed views due to the media and their family. A majority of students are from Sikh families in my class. They do criticize the Modi government and their laws. But I see the influence of their family members on them. Last year, I asked them to write their views about BJP. […] A student shared with me: "Modi chacha [uncle] is not good. He is wrong with farmers. Farmers give us food" [Do you have students from different faiths or views?] Yes, I have students who are Hindu. They are OK but I think they like the BJP because of their family.

They are always quiet. But I read their text. A student said: "Modi uncle is right. I like him so much. He is my hero."' (PS6 Chandigarh)

Conclusion

On 5 August 2020, amidst the COVID-19 pandemic and 28 years after Hindu mobs razed the Babri Masjid to the ground, the foundation ceremony for the Ram Mandir at Ayodhya was held. The 40kg silver foundation stone marked the start of the building of the new temple that is expected to throw open its gates to the public in December 2023. After years of legal wrangling, the land on which the mosque had stood was awarded to a government trust that would allow the Ram temple to be built, fulfilling a key goal of both the BJP and the RSS. The 1,000-page decision did not mention the destruction of the mosque in 1992 (Filkins, 2019). According to Shani, this new Lord Ram temple in Ayodhya will become the central symbol in the Hindu nationalist imaginary (Shani, 2021b, p.274).

One might wonder if the country that was about to go through one of the deadliest waves of the COVID-19 pandemic on the globe did not have better things to do than to inaugurate a structure on grounds that over a 30-year battle had symbolized the deterioration of Hindu–Muslim relations.[52] Yet neither the public not the press seemed to think that much was wrong with what was going on. There were few public dissenting voices – as there have been few dissenting voices regarding the change in Kashmir's status, the effects of the NRC, or the way the government has treated the farmers and their protests. Only the CAA has drawn protests, as described earlier. Those who might have wanted to dissent have certainly learnt to fear the reprisals of the state as well as condemnation by the media and many Indian citizens, who will brand them as leftist lunatics or, worse, as anti-nationals. Chapter 5 described how students and academics were treated when they protested. If those from eminent institutions are beaten in public, who else stands a chance of having their voice heard?

The aim of this chapter has been to show that Hindutva is India's new normal – the hegemonic discourse, accepted by the vast majority of the people. The project that was started in the 1990s has come to a successful conclusion. Hindutva has become the guiding philosophy of India's national identity and its citizenship. Hindutva as propagated by the government is not

---

[52] Officially 500,000 died of COVID-19 in India between 2020 and 2021, yet excess death figures and numbers counted at cremation grounds and cemeteries point to figures ten times at high. People were so desperate that corpses were sometimes not even burnt but just dumped into the rivers. The current accepted death toll is around 4 million (NPR, 2021).

only for Hindus: it is a form of 'cultural nationalism that includes minorities', who are seen as part of an Indian identity that is based on Hindu values, the religion of the majority community (Shani, 2021b, p.264). Anderson and others have proposed the term Neo-Hindutva, which can either be 'hard' or 'soft' (Anderson, 2015, Anderson and Longkumer, 2018).[53] Modi's politics, as described in this book and elsewhere, also shows how the BJP government has moved from a softer approach – where the central government was concerned with the economy and development, leaving Hindutva issues such as the cow slaughter ban and love jihad to local vigilantes – to hardening their stance, with the change of Article 370 on Kashmir and the CAA. The COVID-19 pandemic has made matters worse for dissenting voices, and allowed the Modi government to easily push through legislation that might otherwise have caused more widespread dissent. However, even without COVID-19, protests would most likely have been more muted than a decade or more ago, when such changes could not even be imagined. This is because the new hegemonic discourse is that of Hindutva.

The pandemic has also resulted in more Islamophobia (Lall and Anand, 2020), with Muslims accused of being 'coronavirus terrorists' and launching a 'corona jihad' (Arnold, 2020, p.18). The Tablighi Jamaat were accused of wilfully spreading the virus at a meeting held in Nizamuddin West in Delhi in March 2020. Under the Epidemic Disease Act, criminal charges were filed against the organizer of the gathering (*New York Times*, 2020). However a year later the (Hindu) Kumbh Mela – the largest religious gathering on earth – was allowed to take place, actually one year early on the advice of astrologers. This helped along India's second and very deadly COVID-19 wave, as 9.1 million pilgrims attended and then fanned out back to their localities (Rawat, 2021). Yet even this massive blunder did not result in universal condemnation – as might have been expected. In fact, election rallies were allowed to go ahead as well, with crowds gathering without masks or social distancing, fanning the flames of the virus. The establishment maintained that the Kumbh and the political gatherings were not at fault (*The New India Express*, 2021). This shows that India's majority is now behind the BJP and its Hindutva ethos. The BJP now holds power – either alone or in coalition – in 18 Indian states. Jaffrelot (2017, p.2) suggests that there

---

[53] 'Hard' is openly connected with Hindu nationalism, while 'soft' conceals links with Hindu majoritarian politics (Anderson 2015). Hard would include openly chauvinist groups such as the Hindu Yuva Vahini, the Hindu Janjagruti Samiti, Voice of India, the Forum for Hindu Awakening, and Shri Ram Sena. Soft would include the India Foundation think tank, and various groups serving the diaspora such as the Hindu Forum of Britain, the National Council for Hindu Temples (UK), and the Vedic Foundation in America. They are avoiding overt associations with the Hindutva network.

is a level of political saffronization permeating the wider public sphere that could lead 'toward a Hindu state'.

This book has made the argument that the evolution of contemporary Hindutva, or Neo-Hindutva, is the result of the neoliberal reforms of the 1990s, and that education was the vector that has spread the conception of a Hindutva identity and citizenship. The rise of the middle classes and the benefits they derived from the neoliberal globalization of India's economy led to a return to the roots movement, which resulted in widespread BJP support and a change of national discourse, supported by changes across school textbooks, teacher training, and the rise of Hindutva in HE. Much work points to the media's role, not dealt with in this volume in any detail. An analysis of the media by Bhatia (2020) reveals that the dominant frame projected today is the power and purity of a Hindu nation, defended by a muscular government. However, one needs to remember that the tone of the media has changed gradually over the last two decades, whilst textbooks and teaching changed radically, almost overnight, in 2000. The starting point of India's transformation and the nationwide acceptance of Hindutva is the BJP-led education policy of 2000 under the slogan 'Indianise, nationalise, spiritualise', discussed in Chapters 1 and 2, which also happened long before social media had the kind of reach and power it has today.

This book also presents the evidence for a wider acceptance of Hindutva and neoliberalism across India based on the triangulation of teacher interviews in six states. Whilst speaking to only 225 teachers across six states is a limitation and does not in itself prove the change of national discourse, the government's chosen political priorities and policies as well as the wider public discourse across the media and society bear out the argument made. In particular, the wider news coverage on the Hindutva and neoliberal agendas shows the normalization of the new rhetoric, including on how citizenship and being Indian is viewed. This underscores a shift in citizen–state relations where citizenship practice is mediated through partisan networks in education, thus reshaping the state–citizen relationship (Auerbach and Krucks-Wisner, 2020).

A key part of India's transformation was led by the middle classes. In the same way that education has been a vector to spread the Hindutva discourse across society, they were the happy recipients of increased religiosity as a direct result of the neoliberal reforms. This argument was first made by Meera Nanda in her excellent book – The God Market – in 2011, which shows how the middle classes led to a rising tide of popular Hinduism affecting all social segments and public institutions. Her book charts the rise of popular religiosity across the middle classes since the economic reforms, as rituals became more ostentatious, mega-temples were constructed, God-men/women increased their following, and their political connections and numbers of pilgrimages soared. Nanda's argument looks at the same triangle described in the introduction – the relationship between neoliberalism, Hindu nationalism, and education, but it focuses in particular on how the middle classes became religious and supportive of Hindutva as a result of the neoliberal reforms, and consequently how education changed:

> [T]his religiosity is being cultivated by the emerging state-temple–corporate complex that is replacing the more secular public institutions of the Nehruvian era. In other words, the deregulatory regime put in place to encourage a neo-liberal market economy is also boosting the demand and the supply for religious services in India's God market. […] Given India's growing visibility in the global economy, Hindu religiosity is getting fused with feelings of national pride and dreams of becoming a superpower. the country's economic success is being attributed to the superiority of Hindu values, and India is seen as entitled to the Great Power status because of its ancient Hindu civilization. […] This new culture of political Hinduism is both triumphalist and intolerant in equal measures: while it wants the entire world to admire the superior tolerance and non-violence of the Hindu civilization, it tolerates intolerance and even violence against religious minorities at home. (pp.3–4)

Whilst she argues that there is nothing new with temples and the private sector, their engagement with the state through the neoliberal regime has brought them closer than never before, creating a state–temple–corporate nexus that underpins the Hindutva trajectory the government has taken:

> As the Indian state is withdrawing from its public sector obligations, it is actively seeking partnership with the private sector and the Hindu establishment to run schools, universities, tourist facilities, and other social services. As a result, public funds earmarked for creating public goods are increasingly being diverted into facilitating the work of these private charitable institutions which bear a distinctly Hindu traditionalist bias. (p.5)[54]

Nanda (2011) maintains that the privatization of education, part and parcel of the neoliberal reforms, did not counter saffronization; rather, it helped to inject Hindu traditionalism into modern curricula and textbooks, sometimes

---

[54] She goes on to say: 'This, in turn, is helping to 'modernize' Hinduism: many of the newly minted, English-speaking, and computer-savvy priests, astrologers, vastu shastris, and yoga teachers who service the middle classes' insatiable appetite for religious ritual, are products of this nexus between the state, the corporate sector, and the temples' (p.5).

under the innocuous label of 'value education' at both school and HE levels (p.52). This book has shown that rather than being a result of the state retreating from education, the government actively used education as a vehicle to transmit its ideas. Nevertheless, the increased religiosity of the middle classes engendered through the neoliberal economic reforms was key in helping to propagate the Hindutva message well beyond the school gates and the university campuses across India, making it India's new normal.

Hindutva has transformed Indian national identity and citizenship.[55] It has transformed India as a country from a society driven by inclusive values to one that in effect excludes its largest minority, a key part of its history and society. If we accept that citizenship is a 'meta-public good' (Azad et al, 2020, p.190), then this development points to a spectacular failure of the state, for, as Hannah Arendt (1973) reminds us, when people are stripped of their citizenship, then human dignity is not possible.

---

[55] The idea of citizenship based on Hinduism is not new – Savarkar's vision of nationhood appears in his well-known seminal work *Hindutva: Who is a Hindu*, wherein he makes a clear distinction between those who can and cannot stake a claim to be called Indians. This is reflected in the following text: 'A Hindu is someone who looks upon the land that extends from Sindhu to the Indus to the seas – as the land of his forefathers, hid Fatherland (Pitribhu), who inherits the blood of that race, whose first discernible source could be traced to the Vedic Saptasindhus and which on its onward march, assimilating much that was incorporated and ennobling much that was assimilated, has come to be known as the Hindu people, who has inherited and claims as his own, the culture of that race as expressed chiefly in their common classical language, Sanskrit and represented by a common history, a common literature, art and architecture, law and jurisprudence, rites and rituals, ceremonies and sacraments, fairs and festivals, and who above all, addresses this land, this Sindhustan as his Holyland, as the lands of his prophets and seers, of his godmen and gurus, the land of piety and pilgrimage' (Savarkar, n.d.).

Epilogue: India at 75

As has been established in this volume, education is a deeply political matter in India. Not only have textbooks been rewritten at political convenience, but education has also emerged as critical to political parties' public relations campaigns (Lall, 2008, 2009; Anand and Lall, 2022). Politicians have transmitted Hindu nationalist and neoliberal messages that have transformed the way in which Indians think about their country. This book has shown how politicians have propagated the new neoliberal and Hindu nationalist 'common sense', and how education has been the vehicle to spread and consolidate this message.

The events detailed here that have taken place since the rest of this manuscript was written showcase how anti-minority attitudes have taken hold, underpinning the alienation of Indian Muslims and Christians across society. The BJP has adopted three strategies – undermining the legal framework that protects Muslims, encouraging non-state actors to use violence against Muslims and Christians, and pushing forward an agenda of cultural erasure. This has resulted in attacks both verbal and physical on Muslims and Christians across the BJP-ruled states (Aljazeera, 2021). In the BJP-ruled state of Karnataka, laws were introduced to clamp down on conversion for interfaith marriages. Hindu extremists are carrying out violent attacks in order to reduce or stop interfaith relationships – recently 'a Muslim man was cut into pieces' because of his relationship with a Hindu woman (Peterson and Khan, 2022). In January 2022, a few Muslim students at the government-run college in Karnataka were denied entry into their classes because they wear hijabs (Poddar, 2022). In December 2021, videos leaked showing Hindu religious leaders calling for genocide against Muslims. In Uttarakhand participants called for mass killings and the use of weapons against Muslims (Aljazeera, 2021). Although the Supreme Court has launched an investigation into hate speech against Muslims, the government did not do anything about these calls to violence. These incidents show how the BJP government is normalizing hate speech and violence against Muslims.

There are also increasing attacks on Christians in Madhya Pradesh, Chhattisgarh, Karnataka, and Uttarakhand. These attacks have been perpetrated by mobs led by Hindu right-wing groups, primarily over allegations of religious conversion (Zompa, 2021). Rights groups have listed as many as 300 incidents since October 2021 when churches were vandalized and pastors were beaten up. A report by the Karnataka People's Union for Civil Liberties titled 'Hate crimes on Christians in Karnataka' documents a steady decline in the population of Christians in the last five decades. Christians have also been facing threats from school teachers, who have said they will expel Christian children from school (Ataulla and Sahay, 2021). A mob of around 300 people vandalized a Catholic school in Madhya Pradesh's Vidisha district, alleging that the school was converting its Hindu students to Christianity (Zompa, 2021). In Haryana, members of the Bajrang Dal threatened schools to not dress kids as Santa Claus without consent from their parents. Members of a Hindu right-wing group also disrupted a Christmas programme at a school in Gurugram.[1] The group claimed that the festive event was used as an opportunity to brainwash children into accepting Christianity (Zompa, 2021). On Christmas Day in 2021, Hindutva groups vandalized, attacked, and disrupted Christmas celebrations in BJP-ruled states, including Uttar Pradesh and Karnataka. Bajrang Dal activists captured a church in Silchar, Assam, and protested against Christian schools celebrating Christmas (Thyrniang, 2021). It's not just right-wing mobs: the government has cut off foreign funding to a charity founded by Mother Teresa, giving the reason that the Catholic organization did not meet conditions under local laws (Mihindukulasuriya, 2021). The government even removed Gandhi's favourite song – the Christian hymn 'Abide with me' – from the 2022 Beating the Retreat ceremony that is held a few days after Republic Day in January (Hindustan News Hub, 2022). India's diversity of castes, cultures, ethnicities, languages, and religions is increasingly under attack by mainstream Hindutva (Thyrniang, 2021).

PM Modi has succeeded in acquiring power with a decisive mandate at the centre as well as across several states because of a combination of visible development in the form of big infrastructure projects, a carefully planned network of welfare schemes for the poor, and free market capitalism for the urban elites who support the choice agenda that a neoliberal market structure offers. This is underpinned by nationalist Hindutva rhetoric that appeals to the middle classes. It is, however, incorrect to solely blame the BJP for the success of a Hindu nationalist and Hindu-centric change in identity and education and to simply juxtapose a secular Congress and AAP with the religious nationalism of the BJP. Congress and AAP have bought into the neoliberal model of development, to the point where there is little difference in economic policy between different political parties (Gudavarthy, 2021),

---

[1] Gurugram is a city that used to be known as Gurgaon.

while over the last seven years the BJP has managed to bring a consensus on social imagination to the point where all major parties are vying for space within the limits of a majoritarian cultural nationalism and becoming part of a process of 'competitive Hindutva'. Using similar rhetoric to the BJP, AAP and Congress seem to fancy their chances of winning the trust of the Hindu electorate (Gudavarthy, 2021). This means that the Hindu nationalist agenda is permeating other states through a form of 'soft Hindutva'. Education is often at the heart of this. In Rajasthan, the Congress government is planning a Vedic Education and Sanskar Board to revive the knowledge of ancient Sanskrit scriptures and to connect the learnings of the Vedas with science and yoga (Special Correspondent [The Hindu], 2021). Rajasthan already has about 20 residential Vedic schools, including 'Gurukuls' (seminaries) that adhere to the ancient teacher–disciple tradition; these are run by a trust, and do not follow any regulated curriculum for imparting education (Special Correspondent [The Hindu], 2021).

AAP has started to draw on BJP ideas and ideologies of Hindu supremacy and patriotism via education to expand its mandate beyond Delhi (Aswani, 2021; Sarkar, 2021). Similar to AAP's Deshbhakti Curriculum (see Chapter 2) that has been rolled out in Delhi, the Mumbai government has established Sainik schools to encourage the youth to join the armed forces. The main objective of these schools is to promote qualities such as discipline, self-confidence, bravery, leadership, and patriotism among students (Suryawanshi, 2021). Besides the state governments of Delhi and Mumbai, in Assam the state government also promotes a broader infusion of Hindu culture and national pride through yoga (Sentinel Digital Desk, 2021). Hindutva is now well ingrained across India; even the poor management of COVID-19 did not result in a significant weakening of the BJP government.

India's second COVID-19 wave in May 2021 cost hundreds of thousands of lives and affected millions. Civil society organizations had to step in as hospitals ran out of oxygen and crematoria ran out of space and wood. The distress suffered by so many stained the BJP government and made PM Modi a target of criticism over his government's handling of the pandemic. Despite this, state elections in 2021 and their campaigns in West Bengal, Tamil Nadu, Kerala, and Assam were allowed to go ahead and served to spread the pandemic more widely. The BJP retained power in Assam and its alliance won in Puducherry. The BJP was defeated in both Kerala and Tamil Nadu (Qaisar, 2021); however, Tamil Nadu and Kerala are southern states where the Hindutva message is less pronounced. West Bengal is one of the few states where the BJP does not have a parliamentary majority – but the party still won 77 of 294 seats. Throughout, the BJP continued to motivate its supporters through Hindu nationalist ideology and has used the RSS to consolidate the Hindu voter base. The Elections in Uttar Pradesh confirmed that in the end the BJP did not take a knock due to COVID-19 and the pandemic-induced slump.

Hand in hand with the rise of Hindu nationalist rhetoric has come the discourse of development and market in education. As discussed throughout this volume, the BJP's education vision is in tune with the neoliberal approach that has appealed to Indian voters in recent years. Recent education programmes reflect the government's aim to engage the private sector and offer choice in the name of higher quality. In 2021, the 'CM Rise School' initiative has been implemented initially in five districts of Bhopal to impart 'quality' education, Indian culture, and ethics to state school students. Under this initiative, with the help of the private sector, new schools will be built with modern facilities, including smart classrooms, laboratories, external exposure in the form of school excursions, interschool activities, and career development (Vishwadeepak, 2021). These initiatives are part of a long-term plan designed to increase private sector involvement in education, undermining the role of teachers and their agency in the classroom.

The proposed NEP changes include a number of initiatives that the government claims will usher in an education revolution in India and place India's education system on the global map (HT Correspondent, 2021). In September 2021 PM Modi announced the launch of Vidyanjali 2.0, a portal that will facilitate donations, contributions from corporate social responsibility funds, and volunteering, all aimed at developing and improving schools (HT Correspondent, 2021). The School Quality Assurance and Assessment Framework of the CBSE was launched in 2021 to provide global parameters of attainment in schools affiliated to it. Noting that inclusivity and equitability are required for any country to progress, PM Modi said: 'The National Digital Education Architecture [N-DEAR] is likely to play a major role in eradicating inequality in education and its modernization. N-DEAR will act as a "super-connect" between various academic activities in the same way the UPI interface revolutionised the banking sector' (HT Correspondent, 2021). This is despite the lack of internet access across poorer sections of society (HT Correspondent, 2021; Jain et al, 2021). Digital education was also reflected in the union budget of 2022–2023. The budget is focused on filling the learning gap brought about by COVID-19 induced school closures through schemes that include a digital university and increasing the reach of the PM's EVidya programme – which aims to promote e-learning and digital content for students across the country – and the development of e-content in all Indian languages. The 'One Class One TV channel' scheme will be expanded to provide supplementary education by television – over 200 channels covering multiple regional languages. Teachers will be encouraged to develop quality e-content in different languages and different subjects so that any teacher or student can access the content from anywhere. In contrast, the union budget cut money from the scholarship incentive scheme for girls from STs and rural areas (Chakrabarty, 2022).

In one area Modi's neoliberal reforms were unsuccessful. After 358 days of protests, hundreds of thousands of farmers who had marched on foot and in a convoy of tractors hundreds of miles from the neighbouring states of Punjab and Haryana to the Delhi border with the demand that the farm laws would be repealed were finally able to return home. In November 2021, the government repealed the three bills that would have allowed the free market to dominate agriculture. Despite this setback, neoliberalism has become an India-wide political and economic project that allows political parties and states to pursue their economic interests with the help of the middle classes and the elites (Kochar, 2020). Such a project encompasses all spheres of social, economic political, cultural, and religious life. The neoliberal economic policies pursued by the BJP, Congress, and AAP have helped to create the conditions for the growth and consolidation of 'hard' or 'soft' Hindutva in Indian politics as well as in education. To a superficial observer it can at times seem as if Hindu nationalism is contradictory to neoliberalism. On the ground, however, teachers' voices showcase the organic and reinforcing relationship between Hindutva and neoliberalism in education, exemplified in this volume. Neoliberalism and theocratic politics have started to move together, as they are grounded in the twin ideas of spreading fear and insecurities via education, which promotes the re-emergence of different reactionary religious and regional fault lines in society. This in turn helps Hindutva – hard or soft – to consolidate its power by using security infrastructure via education in the name of the unity and integrity of India and Indian nationalism.

The trajectory described in this volume comes together in the symbolism of India's 75th Independence day – 15 August 2022 – where under the Har Ghar Tiranga campaign all houses and schools have been requested to hoist the Indian flag. Fieldwork in Uttar Pradesh just days before the anniversary also showed that Bharat Mata maps with a 75th independence anniversary logo had been distributed to Central Government schools for public display. The image (see following page) – similar to the one reproduced here, but with the anniversary logo and the lion looking forward – represents India as a Hindu goddess.[2] With this display, India confirms its move away from its Nehruvian and secular roots.

India's current trajectory is well summarized by former vice president Hamid Ansar: 'In recent years, we have experienced the emergence of trends

---

[2] The same image was also displayed in the RSS textbooks reviewed in Chapter 3. Here is a link to the image (without the 75th anniversary logo): https://bvpindia.com/resources/resources-bharatmata-image-2/.

Source: Shutterstock/Photo craze.

and practices that dispute the well-established principle of civic nationalism and interpose a new and imaginary practice of cultural nationalism … It wants to distinguish citizens on the basis of their faith, give vent to intolerance, insinuate otherness, and promote disquiet and insecurity' (Press Trust of India, 2022). The 'new India' thus seems to be a country where under the impact of neoliberalism, the political use of religion in the name of hard or soft Hindutva has abandoned the ideology of the constitution. A 'New India' is being forged through a combination of corporate India and the Hindu Rashtra (Singh, 2022).

APPENDIX 1

Pratab Banu Metha's Article

'India is in the midst of, arguably, the largest student protest since the Emergency.

There is a battle against state authoritarianism, its attempts to exercise pervasive control. But there is also the battle against communalism, the attempt to divide society and unleash passions that relegate minorities to second class citizens. They are two sides of the same coin – the government is fomenting both processes.

The tactical challenge will be that they will once again consolidate majoritarian identities, produce that fog of silence in which the CAA will be excused. The moral challenge will be to find a vocabulary and positions that nudge secularism towards freedom and equality for all individuals rather than one that pits minority and majority identities in competition with each other, as our politics often did. The communal axis will be used to divide society so that it cannot unite against the authoritarian state. So, the fight over CAA cannot be won without ensuring these issues do not divide us.

The communal and institutional fissures that we are dealing with run within our families, often even within us. The streets would not have become necessary if the normal institutional channels of upholding principles had not failed so miserably. Our institutions failed not just because of political forces, but because, few exceptions apart, so many of teachers, university leaders, Supreme Court judges, policemen, bureaucrats, journalists, corporate leaders, etc. often let us down on basic institutional principles. These are the small capillaries that hold any order together. But the people in these institutions, especially amongst the middle classes, are our most intimate acquaintances, whose social esteem is tied to the position they hold not to the principles they espouse.'[1]

---

[1] 'Discrimination, not justice: Hope this generation does a better job of navigating the struggle than the one that came before'. This article first appeared in the print edition on 19 December 2019 under the title 'Discrimination, not justice'. The writer is contributing editor, *The Indian Express*.

Distribution of Teachers and Schools from the Study Areas

Research site/ state	Number of schools from different socio-economic status (middle and low)	Semi-structured interviews (Number of teachers)
Delhi	15 government schools	110 government school teachers
	20 (10 private and 10 government schools)	20 (10 private and 10 government school teachers from different)
Mumbai	20 (10 private and 10 government schools)	20 (10 private and 10 government school teachers from different)
Chandigarh	19 (10 private and 9 government schools)	19 (10 private and 9 government school teachers)
Bengaluru (Karnataka)	17 (10 private and 7 government schools)	17 (10 private and 7 government school teachers)
Jaipur (Rajasthan)	20 (10 private and 10 government schools)	20 (10 private and 10 government school teachers)
Guwahati (Assam)	16 (9 private and 7 government schools)	16 (9 private and 7 government school teachers)
Silchar (Assam)	3 government schools	3 government school teachers

School Education in Delhi, Chandigarh, Mumbai, Bengaluru, Jaipur, and Assam

Delhi

Government schools

	2018–2019	2019–2020
Number of schools	48.8%	48.8%
Enrolment	53.8%	49.5%

Medium of instruction	Number
Hindi	2797
English	1692

Private schools

	2018–2019	2019–2020
Number of schools	46.7%	46.8%
Enrolment	42.6%	37.1%

Medium of instruction	Number
Hindi	157
English	2558

Chandigarh

Government schools

	2018–2019	2019–2020
Number of schools	69.9%	52.8%
Enrolment	58.3%	57.6%

Medium of instruction	Number
Hindi	133
English	107
Punjabi	19

Private schools

	2018–2019	2019–2020
Number of schools	21.1%	32.3%
Enrolment	35.0%	35.5%

Medium of instruction	Number
Hindi	16
English	96
Punjabi	6

Mumbai (Maharashtra)

Government schools

	2018–2019	2019–2020
Number of schools	905	894
Enrolment	813935	797698

Medium of instruction	Number
Hindi	134
English	414
Gujarati	57
Urdu	88
Marathi	389

Private schools

	2018–2019	**2019–2020**
Number of schools	1576	1620
Enrolment	857592	851426

Medium of instruction	**Number**
Hindi	2
English	785
Gujarati	2
Urdu	11
Marathi	16

Bengaluru (Karnataka)

Government schools

	2018–2019	**2019–2020**
Number of schools	2570	3317
Enrolment	420183	370937

Medium of instruction	**Number**
Hindi	728
English	85
Kannada	2021

Private schools

	2018–2019	**2019–2020**
Number of schools	2542	3283
Enrolment	1572426	1671201

Medium of instruction	**Number**
Hindi	255
English	213
Kannada	901

Jaipur (Rajasthan)

Government schools

	2018–2019	2019–2020
Number of schools	1359	2377
Enrolment	416101	423836

Medium of instruction	Number
Hindi	2373
English	476
Sanskrit	402

Private schools

	2018–2019	2019–2020
Number of schools	3088	5145
Enrolment	1195868	1259585

Medium of instruction	Number
Hindi	3949
English	3442
Sanskrit	594

Assam

Government schools

	2018–2019	2019–2020
Number of schools	71.2%	71.6%
Enrolment	68.0%	66.9%

Medium of instruction	Number
Hindi	1427
English	4519
Assamese	40124
Bengali	6886
Bodo	3548
Sanskrit	78

Private schools

	2018–2019	**2019–2020**
Number of schools	9.2%	9.2%
Enrolment	20.4%	21.8%

Medium of instruction	**Number**
Hindi	520
English	2512
Assamese	3718
Bengali	535
Bodo	166
Sanskrit	69

Source: UDISEPLUS: https://udiseplus.gov.in/#/home

References

Adeney, K. (2017) 'Does ethnofederalism explain the success of Indian federalism?', *India Review*, 16(1): 125–48.

Adeney, K. and Lall, M. (2005) 'Institutional attempts to build a "national" identity in India: internal and external dimensions', *India Review*, 4(3–4): 258–86.

Adeney, K. and Sáez, L. (eds) (2007) *Coalition Politics and Hindu Nationalism* (1st edn), Oxford: Routledge.

AFP (2016) 'Indian police arrest Muslim students over beef-cooking rumours', *Yahoo*, [online] 17 March, Available from: https://autos.yahoo.com/indian-police-arrest-muslim-students-over-beef-cooking-090048870.html [Accessed 20 October 2021].

Aggarwal, Y. (2000) 'Public and Private Partnership in Primary Education in India: A Study of Unrecognized Schools in Haryana', New Delhi: National Institute of Educational Planning and Administration.

Agarwal, V. (2002) 'A review of Romila Thapar Ancient India, A Textbook of History for Middle Schools NCERT', b-ok, [online], Available from: https://b-ok.cc/book/3515780/ba43ae?id=3515780&secret=ba43ae [Accessed 20 February 2022].

Agarwal, V. (n.d.) 'Home page of Vishal Agarwal', [online], Available from: http://www.vpmthane.org/Bedekar/bharatvan.htm [Accessed 18 February 2022].

Agarwal, P. (2007) 'Higher education in India: growth, concerns and change agenda', *Higher Education Quarterly*, 61(2): 197–207.

Agarwal, P. (2009) *Indian Higher Education: Envisioning the Future*, New Delhi: Sage Publications India.

Ahmad, S. (2019) 'AAP govt fixed a broken state schooling system, but glitches remain', *Outlook India*, [online] 18 October, Available from: https://www.outlookindia.com/magazine/story/india-news-a-for-aaplause-b-forboos/301297 [Accessed 12 September 2021].

Ahmed, S. (2019) 'Citizenship Amendment Act protest: Delhi Police, protesters clash at Jamia', *India Today*, [online] 13 December, Available from: https://www.indiatoday.in/india/story/citizenship-amendment-bill-cab-protest-delhi-police-jamia-students-1628126-2019-12-13 [Accessed 20 September 2021].

Ahluwalia, M.S. (2000) 'Economic performance of states in post-reforms period', *Economic and Political Weekly*, 14(1): 1637–48.

Ahluwalia, M.S. (2019) 'India's economic reforms: achievements and next steps', *Asian Economic Policy Review*, 14(1): 46–62.

Aiyar, S. (2020) 'Despite Modi, India has not become a Hindu authoritarian state', *Cato Institute, Policy Analysis*, 24(1): 903.

Akaguri, L. (2014) 'Fee-free public or low-fee private basic education in rural Ghana: how does the cost influence the choice of the poor?', *Compare: A Journal of Comparative and International Education*, 44(2): 140–61.

Alam, J. (1998) 'Indispensability of secularism', *Social Scientist*, 10(2): 3–20.

Al-Shammari, N.A.S. and Dali, A.M. (2018) 'Politics of language and linguistic reorganisation before and after independence in India', *Romanian Journal of History and International Studies*, 5(1): 129–59.

Alderman, H., Orazem, P.F., and Paterno, E.M. (2001) 'School quality, school cost, and the public/private school choices of low-income households in Pakistan', *Journal of Human Resources*, 36(2): 304–26.

Alizada, N., Boese, V.A., Lundstedt, M., Morrison, K., Natsika, N., Sato, Y., and Lindberg, S.I. (2022) 'Autocratization changing nature?', V-Dem Working Paper, Available from: https://v-dem.net/media/publications/dr_2022.pdf [Accessed 13 June 2022].

Aljazeera (2021) 'India: Hindu event calling for genocide of Muslims sparks outrage', *Aljazeera*. [online] 24 December, Available from: https://www.aljazeera.com/amp/news/2021/12/24/india-hindu-event-calling-for-genocide-of-muslims-sparks-outrage [Accessed 10 October 2021].

Altbach, P.G. (2009) 'Peripheries and centers: research universities in developing countries', *Asia Pacific Education Review*, 10(1): 15–27.

Aman, S. (2018) 'English-medium in Telangana government schools: more pupils but poor quality', *The New Indian Express*, [online] 1 November, Available from: https://www.newindianexpress.com/cities/hyderabad/2018/nov/01/englishmedium-in-telangana-government-schools-more-pupils-but-poor-quality-1892797.html [Accessed 20 September 2021].

Amnesty International. (n.d.) 'India 2020', *Amnesty*, [online], Available from: https://www.amnesty.org/en/location/asia-and-the-pacific/south-asia/india/report-india/ [Accessed 2 October 2021].

Amnesty International India. (2020) 'Six months since Delhi riots, Delhi police continue to enjoy impunity despite evidence of human rights violations', *Amnesty,* [online], Available from: https://www.amnestyusa.org/press-releases/six-months-since-delhi-riots-delhi-police-continue-to-enjoy-impunity-despite-rights-violations/ [Accessed 20 August 2021].

Amnesty International India (2019) 'Designed to exclude: how India's courts are allowing foreigners tribunals to render people stateless in Assam', *Amnesty*, [online], Available from: https://www.amnesty.be/IMG/pdf/rapport_inde.pdf [Accessed 11 February 2022].

Anand, K. (2019) 'Teaching India and Pakistan relations: teachers' pedagogical responses and strategies', (Doctoral dissertation), UCL (University College London), [online], Available from: https://iris.ucl.ac.uk/iris/publication/1649912/1 [Accessed 10 December 2021].

Anand, K. and Lall, M. (2022) 'The debate between secularism and Hindu nationalism – how India's textbooks have become the government's medium for political communication', *India Review*, 21(1): 77–107.

Anand, K. and Niaz, L. (forthcoming 2022) 'The precarious state of academic freedom and autonomy towards religious minorities in higher education: the case of India and Pakistan', in *Research in the Social Scientific Study of Religion, Volume 32*, Leiden: Brill, pp.281–98.

Anand, K. and Lall, M. (forthcoming 2022) *Delhi Education Revolution: Teachers, Agency and Inclusion*, London: UCL Press.

Anyon, J. (1978) 'Elementary social studies textbooks and legitimating knowledge', *Theory & Research in Social Education*, 6(3): 40–55.

Anyon, J. (2011) *Marx and Education*, New York: Routledge.

Antal, C. (2008) 'Reflections on religious nationalism, conflict and schooling in developing democracies: India and Israel in comparative perspective', *Compare*, 38(1): 87–102.

Andersen, W., and Damle, S. (1987) *The Brotherhood in Saffron: The RSS and the Hindu Revivalism*, New Delhi: Vistaar Publications.

Anderson, E. (2015) 'Neo-Hindutva': the Asia House MF Husain campaign and the mainstreaming of Hindu nationalist rhetoric in Britain, *Contemporary South Asia*, 23(1): 45–66.

Anderson, E., and A. Longkumer. (2018). 'Neo-Hindutva': evolving forms, spaces, and expressions of Hindu nationalism', *Contemporary South Asia*, 26(4): 371–7.

Andersen, W., and Damle, S. (2018) *The RSS: A View to the Inside*, New Delhi: Penguin Random House India Private Limited.

Apple, M. (2004) *Ideology and Curriculum*, New York: Routledge.

Apple, M. and Franklin, B. (2004) 'Curricular history and social control', in M. Apple (ed), *Ideology and Curriculum*, New York: Routledge, pp.89–106.

Apple, M., and Christian-Smith, L. (eds). (2017) *The Politics of the Textbook*, New York: Routledge.

Apple, M.W. (1993) 'The politics of official knowledge: does a national curriculum make sense?', *Discourse*, 14(1): 1–16.

Apple, M.W. (2001) *Educating the Right Way*, New York: Routledge.

Apoorvanand (ed.) (2018) *The Idea of a University: Essays*, Delhi: Context, an imprint of Westland Publications Private Limited.

Appadurai, A. (2019) 'Goodbye citizenship, hello "statizenship."', *The Wire*. [online] 4 September, Available from: https://thewire.in/rights/goodbye-citizenship-hello-statizenship [Accessed 10 September 2021].

Arcand, J.L. and Grin, F. (2013) '11 language in economic development: is English special and is linguistic fragmentation bad?', *Elisabeth Erling et Philip Seargeant, English and development: Policy, pedagogy and globalization*, 17: 243–61.

Arendt, H. (1973) *The Origins of Totalitarianism [1951]*, San Diego and New York: Sage.

Arora, B. (2003) 'Federalisation of India's party system', in A.K. Mehra, D.D. Khanna, and G.W. Kueck (eds), *Political Parties and Party Systems*, New Delhi: Sage, pp.83–99.

Arora, M., Sonali, C., and Prerna, M. (2020) *Delhi Riots 2020: The Untold Story*, Delhi: ATOM Press.

Arora, R. (2020) 'Learning with toys: more fun and creativity', *The New Indian Express*, [online] 4 September, Available from: https://www.newindianexpress.com/cities/delhi/2020/sep/04/learning-with-toys-more-fun-and-creativity-2192148.html [Accessed 11 September 2021].

Arnold, D. (2020) 'Pandemic India: coronavirus and the uses of history', *The Journal of Asian Studies*, 79(3): 569–77.

ASER. (2018) 'Annual Survey of Education Report (Rural)', *ASER*, [online], Available from: https://www.asercentre.org/p/51.html?p=61 [Accessed 16 October 2021].

ASER. (2021)' Annual Status of Education Report (Rural) 2021', *ASER*, [online], Available from: http://img.asercentre.org/docs/aser2021forweb.pdf [Accessed 16 January 2022].

Ashley, L.D., Mcloughlin, C., Aslam, M., Engel, J., Wales, J., Rawal, S., Batley, R., Kingdon, G., Nicolai, S., and Rose, P. (2014) 'The Role and Impact of Private Schools in Developing Countries–Bibliography and Literature Reviews', EPPI-Centre Education Rigorous Literature Review Reference Number 2206, London, UK: DfID, Available from: https://assets.publishing.service.gov.uk/government/uploads/system/uploads/attachment_data/file/439702/private-schools-full-report.pdf. [Accessed 5 October 2021].

Aswani, T. (2021) 'Aam Aadmi Party's Right-Turn', *The Diplomat*, [online] 14 December, Available from: https://thediplomat.com/2021/12/aam-aadmi-partys-right-turn/ [Accessed 10 January 2022].

Ataulla, N. and Sahay, S. (2021) 'Conversion, diversion or distraction? Why attacks on Christians now?', *National Herald India*, [online] 26 December, Available from: https://www.nationalheraldindia.com/amp/story/india/conversion-diversion-or-distraction-why-attacks-on-christians-now [Accessed 11 January 2022].

Athreya, A. and Haaften, L.V. (2020) 'Modi's new education policy: a next step in the saffronisation of India?', *Mondiaal News*, [online] 26 August, Available from: https://www.mo.be/en/analysis/modi-s-new-education-policy-next-step-saffronisation-india [Accessed 10 August 2021].

Atherton, P. and Kingdon, G. (2010) 'The relative effectiveness and costs of contract and regular teachers in India', Institute of Education, University of London, 256–76.

Auerbach, A.M. and Kruks-Wisner, G. (2020) 'The geography of citizenship practice: how the poor engage the state in rural and urban India', *Perspectives on Politics*, 18(4): 1118–34.

Austin, I. and Jones, G.A. (2015) *Governance of Higher Education: Global Perspectives, Theories, and Practices*, New York: Routledge.

Avinah, N. (2017) 'Where do Indian states stand?', *Scroll India*, [online] 26 October, Available from: https://scroll.in/article/1007556/where-do-ind ian-states-stand-in-ensuring-access-to-education-and-healthcare [Accessed 11 August 2021].

Ayyangar, S., Kashyap, S.N., Prasad, P., and Rishikesh, B.S. (2020) 'School choice and implementation: survey evidence across Indian states', *Studies in Indian Politics*, 8(2): 170–85.

Awaaz (2004) *In Bad Faith?: British Charity and Hindu Extremism*, London: Awaaz South Asia Watch Ltd.

Azad, R., Nair, J., Singh, M., and Roy, M.S. (eds). (2016) *What the Nation Really Needs to Know: The JNU Nationalism Lectures*, New Delhi: HarperCollins Publishers.

Azad, K. Azad, M., Mohsin Alam Bhat, and Harsh Mander (2020) 'Citizenship and the Mass Production of Statelessness in Assam', India Exclusion Report, Centre for Equity Studies, pp.189–211.

Bäckman, J. (2020) 'Saffronisation or moderation?: A comparative case study of the Bharatiya Janata Party between two terms', Uppsala University, [online], Available from: https://www.diva-portal.org/smash/get/ diva2:1416811/FULLTEXT01.pdf [Accessed 11 August 2021].

Bagchi, A. (2003) 'Rethinking federalism: changing power relations between the center and the states', *Publius: The Journal of Federalism*, 33(4): 21–42.

Bajpai, N. and Sachs, J.D. (1999) 'The Progress of Policy Reforms and Variations in Performance at the Sub-National Level in India', HIID Development Discussion Paper No. 730', Cambridge, MA: Harvard Institute for International Development, Harvard University.

Baker, T. (2020) 'Hindu group hosts cow urine drinking party in India in belief it will ward off the coronavirus', *Standard*, [online] 14 March, Available from: https://www.standard.co.uk/news/world/cow-urine- drinking-indian-hindu-coronavirus-covid19-a4387386.html [Accessed 22 December 2021].

Bakshi, A. (2020) 'Did Covid-19 become another excuse to rewrite textbooks?', *Mint Lounge*, [online] 11 July, Available from: https://lifest yle.livemint.com/news/talking-point/did-covid-19-become-another- excuse-to-rewrite-textbooks-111634475704644.html [Accessed 12 December 2020].

Ball, J. (2010) 'Educational equity for children from diverse language backgrounds: mother tongue-based bilingual or multilingual education in the early years: summary', Available from: http://dspace.library.uvic.ca/handle/1828/2457 [Accessed 10 October 2021].

Ball, J. (2011) *Enhancing Learning of Children from Diverse Language Backgrounds: Mother Tongue-Based Bilingual or Multilingual Education in the Early Years*, Paris: UNESCO.

Ball, J. (2014). 'Children learn better in their mother tongue: advancing research on mother tongue-based multilingual education', *Global Partnership for Education* [online], Available from: https://www.globalpartnership.org/blog/children-learn-better-their-mother-tongue [Accessed 12 August 2021].

Ball, S.J. (1993) 'What is policy? Texts, trajectories and toolboxes', *The Australian Journal of Education Studies*, 13(2): 10–17.

Ball, S.J. (2003) 'The teacher's soul and the terrors of performativity', *Journal of Education Policy*, 18(2):215–228.

Ball S.J. and Youdell, D. (2008) *Hidden Privatisation in Education*, Brussels: Education International.

Ball, S. J. (2009) 'Privatising education, privatising education policy, privatising educational research: Network governance and the 'competition state'', *Journal of education policy*, 24(1): 83–99.

Ball, S. J. (2012) *Global Education, Inc: New Policy Networks and the Neoliberal Imaginary*, New York: Routledge.

Balagopalan, S. (2009) 'Unity in diversity': social cohesion and the pedagogical project of the Indian state', in M. Nkomo and S. Vandeyar (eds), *Thinking Diversity While Building Cohesion. Transnational Dialogue on Education*, Netherlands: Rozenberg Publishers, pp.133–50.

Bangay, C. (2005) 'Private education: relevant or redundant? Private education, decentralisation and national provision in Indonesia', *Compare: A Journal of Comparative and International Education*, 35(2): 167–79.

Banaji, S. (2018) 'Vigilante publics: orientalism, modernity and Hindutva fascism in India', *Javnost-The Public*, 25(4): 333–50.

Banaji, S. (2005) 'Portrait of an Indian education', *Changing English*, 12(2): 157–166.

Banerjee, B.K. (2007) 'West Bengal history textbooks and the Indian textbook controversy', *Internationale Schulbuchforschung*, 29: 355–74.

Banerjee, B.K. and Stöber, G. (2016) 'The portrayal of "the other" in Pakistani and Indian school textbooks', in J.H. Williams and W.D. Bokhorst-Heng (eds), *(Re) Constructing Memory: Textbooks, Identity, Nation, and State*, Rotterdam: Sense Publishers, pp.143–76.

Bangalore Education (n.d) 'The top/best schools in Bangalore', Bangalore Education, [online], Available from: https://www.bangaloreeducation.com/schools/ [Accessed 19 February 2022].

Barrera-Osorio, F., Guaqueta, J., and Patrinos, H.A. (2012) 'The role and impact of public private partnerships in education', in S.L. Robertson, K. Mundy, A. Verger, and F. Menashy (eds), *Public-Private Partnerships in Education: New Actors and Modes of Governance in a Globalizing World*, Cheltenham/Northampton: Edward Elgar, pp.201–16.

Barrera-Osorio, F. and Raju, D. (2015) 'Evaluating the impact of public student subsidies on low-cost private schools in Pakistan', *The Journal of Development Studies*, 51(7): 808–25.

Baruah, S. (2021) 'Instead of books, teachers asked to rely on discussions'. *Indian Express*, [online] 29 September, Available from: https://indianexpr ess.com/article/cities/delhi/instead-of-books-teachers-asked-to-rely-on-discussions-7540607/ [Accessed 29 October 2021].

Basu, T., Datta, P., Sarkar, S., Sarkar, T., and Sen, S. (1993) *Khaki Shorts and Saffron Flags: A Critique of the Hindu Right* (Vol. 1), India: Orient Blackswan Limited.

Basu, K. (ed.). (2004) *India's Emerging Economy: Performance and Prospects in the 1990s and Beyond*, Cambridge, MA: MIT Press.

Batabyal, S. (2014) *Making News in India: Star News and Star Ananda*, India: Routledge.

Batra, P. (2005) 'Voice and agency of teachers: missing link in national curriculum framework 2005', *Economic and Political Weekly*, 40(40): 4347–56.

Batra, P. (2009) 'Reclaiming the space for teachers to address the UEE teaching–learning quality deficit', *Theme Paper for the Mid-term Review of EFA*, New Delhi: NUEPA.

Batra, R., and Ahmad, S. (2010) 'Academic development and recognition of teachers in higher education', *University News*, 48(34): 1–7.

Batra, P. (2014) Teacher education and classroom practice in India: a critique and propositions', in S. Chunawala and M. Kharatmal (eds), *The Episteme Reviews* (Vol. 4): Research Trends in Science, Technology and Mathematics Education, New Delhi: Narosa, pp.159–86.

Batra, P. (2020) 'Re-imagining curriculum in India: charting a path beyond the pandemic', *Prospects*, 51(1): 407–24.

Baxter, C. (1969) *The Jana Sangh: A Biography of an Indian Political Party*, Philadelphia, PA: University of Pennsylvania Press.

BBC News. (2019) 'Assam NRC: What next for 1.9 million 'stateless' Indians?', *BBC News*, [online] 31 August, Available from: https://www.bbc. co.uk/news/world-asia-india-49520593 [Accessed 30 September 2021].

Beauchamp, C. and Thomas, L. (2009) 'Understanding teacher identity: an overview of issues in the literature and implications for teacher education', *Cambridge Journal of Education*, 39(2): 175–89.

Bellman, E. (2020) 'Hindu nationalism finds outlet in Indian schools', *WSJ*, [online], Available from: https://www.wsj.com/articles/SB101483688987 1316440 [Accessed 30 June 2021].

Bénéï, V. (2005) 'Manufacturing citizenship: confronting public spheres and education in contemporary worlds', in V. Bénéï (ed), *Manufacturing Citizenship*, London: Routledge, pp.1–34.

Benei, V. (2008) *Schooling Passions: Nation, History, and Language in Contemporary Western India*, Stanford, CA: Stanford University Press.

Berry, M. (2014) 'Neoliberalism and the city: or the failure of market fundamentalism', *Housing, Theory and Society*, 31(1): 1–18.

Besley, T. (2019) 'Theorizing teacher responsibility in an age of neoliberal accountability', *Beijing International Review of Education*, 1(1):179–95.

Beteille, A. (2001) 'The Indian Middle Class', *The Hindu*, [online] 5 February, Available from: http://www.hinduonnet.com/2001/02/05/stories/05052 523.htm [Accessed 30 June 2021].

Bhat, D. (2017) 'Harbinger of a New Era? Evaluating the Effect of India's Right to Education Act on Learning Outcomes', M-RCBH Associate Working Paper, 76.

Bharatiya Janata Party. (2014) 'Philosophy', [online], Available from: http://www.bjp.org/en/about-the -party/philosophy [Accessed 11 October 2021].

Bharatiya Janata Party. (2018) 'Hindutva: the great nationalist Ideology', *Bharatiya Janata Party*, [online], Available from: http://www.bjp.org/index. php?option=com_content&view=article&id=369:hindutva-the-great-nationalist-ideology&Itemid=501 [Accessed 13 October 2021].

Bhattacharjee, M. (2016) 'Tracing the emergence and consolidation of Hindutva in Assam', *Economic and Political Weekly*, 80–7.

Bhatty, K. and Sundar, N. (2020) 'Sliding from majoritarianism toward fascism: educating India under the Modi regime', *International Sociology*, 35(6): 632–50.

Bhargava, R. (ed.) (1998) *Secularism and its Critics*, Delhi: Oxford University Press.

Bhargava, R. (2002) 'What is Indian secularism and what is it for?', *India Review*, 1(1): 1–32.

Bharadwaj, A. (2017) 'Dina Nath Batra again: he wants Tagore, Urdu words off school texts', *India Express,* [online] 24 July, Available from: http://indianexpress.com/article/india/dina-nath-batra-again-he-wants-tagore-urdu-words-off-school-texts-4764094/ [Accessed 3 October 2021].

Bhattacharjee, M. (2019) 'The politics of perception and the Citizenship Amendment Act 2019', *Dialogue*, 22(2): 25–32.

Bhatnagar, R. (2003) 'Supreme Court puts ban on capitation fee', *The Times of India,* [online] 14 August, Available from: https://timesofindia.indiati mes.com/india/supreme-court-puts-ban-on-capitation-fee/articleshow/ 130702.cms [Accessed 14 June 2021].

Bhattacharya, N. (2008) 'Predicaments of secular histories', *Public Culture*, 20(1): 57–73.

Bhatia, R. (2017) 'The year of love jihad in India', *New Yorker*, [online] 31 December, Available from: https://www.newyorker.com/culture/2017-in-review/the-year-of-love-jihad-in-india [Accessed 10 December 2021].

Bhatia, A. (2020) 'The 'saffronisation' of India and contemporary political ideology', *World Englishes*, 39(4): 568–80.

Bhatkhande, A. (2019) 'Niti Aayog's school education quality index: Maharashtra slips three positions down despite improving overall score', *Hindustan Times*, [online] 1 October, Available from: https://www.hindustantimes.com/education/niti-aayog-s-school-education-quality-index-maharashtra-slips-three-positions-down-despite-improving-overall-score/story-hOqEcLX1d5E2XTJ7Pwlj7I.html [Accessed 20 February 2022].

Bilgrami, A. (1998) 'Secularism, nationalism and modernity', in R. Bhargava (ed.), *Secularism and Its Critics*, Delhi: Oxford University Press, pp.380–417.

BJP (2004) 'NDA Manifesto 2004. Library BJP' [online], http://library.bjp.org/jspui/handle/123456789/245 [Accessed 5 June 2022].

Bose, M. (1989) *Social History of Assam: Being a Study of the Origins of Ethnic Identity and Social Tension During the British Period, 1905–1947*, New Delhi: Concept Publishing Company.

Bose, J. (2021) 'Deshbhakti curriculum in Delhi govt schools from today in major patriotic push', *Hindustan Times*, [online] 28 September, Available from: https://www.hindustantimes.com/cities/delhi-news/deshbhakti-curriculum-in-delhi-govt-schools-from-today-in-major-patriotic-push-101632788514456.html [Accessed 28 October 2021].

Bourdieu, P. (1971) 'The thinkable and the unthinkable', *Times Literary Supplement*, *15*: 1255–6.

Bourdieu, P. (1973) 'The three forms of theoretical knowledge. *Social Science Information*, 12(1): 53–80.

Bourdieu, P. (1998) *Practical Reason: On the Theory of Action*, Stanford, CA: Stanford University Press.

Boucher, E. (2020) 'Democracy, neoliberalism, and school choice: A comparative analysis of India and the United States', *Journal of Global Education and Research*, 4(2): 96–112.

Brass, P.R. (1994) *The Politics of India since Independence* (Vol. 1), Cambridge: Cambridge University Press.

Brass, P. (2005) 'The body as symbol in the production of Hindu-Muslim violence', in R. Kaur (ed), *Religion, Violence and Political Mobilisation in South Asia*, New Delhi: Sage, pp.46–68.

Brass, P. (2015) *The Politics of India since Independence* (Vol. 2), Cambridge: Cambridge University Press.

Brass, J. and Holloway, J. (2021) 'Re-professionalizing teaching: the new professionalism in the United States', *Critical Studies in Education*, 62(4): 519–36.

Bray, M., Kobakhidze, M.N., Liu, J., and Zhang, W. (2016) 'The internal dynamics of privatised public education: fee-charging supplementary tutoring provided by teachers in Cambodia', *International Journal of Educational Development*, 49: 291–9.

Brenner, N., Peck, J., and Theodore, N. (2010) 'Variegated neoliberalization: geographies, modalities, pathways', *Global Networks*, 10(2): 182–222.

Brooks, J.S., Hughes, R.M., and Brooks, M.C. (2008) 'Fear and trembling in the American high school: educational reform and teacher alienation', *Educational Policy*, 22(1): 45–62.

Brown, J. (2003) *Nehru: A Political Life*, London: Yale University Press.

Bruns, B., Filmer, D., and Patrinos, H.A. (2011). *Making Schools Work: New Evidence on Accountability Reforms*, Washington, DC: World Bank Publications.

Bühmann, D. and Trudel, B. (2008) 'Mother tongue matters: local language as a key to effective learning', [online], (ED.2007/WS/56 REV.). UNESCO. https://unesdoc.unesco.org/ark:/48223/pf0000161 121 [Accessed 10 October 2021]

Buneau, W. (2015) 'Five defences of academic freedom in North American higher education', in P. Zgag, U. Teichler, H. G. Schuetze, and A. Wolter (eds), *Higher Education Reform: Looking Back-Looking Forward*, Frankfurt am Main: Peter Lang Edition, pp.43–8.

Capelos, T. and Basu, I., (2022) 'Who is in the middle: social class, core values, and identities in India', *Political Psychology*, 43(1): 89–109.

Carpentier, V., Chattopadhyay, S., and Pathak, B.K. (2011) 'Globalization, funding and access to higher education: perspectives from India and the UK', in M. Lall and G. Nambissan (eds), *Education and Social Justice: The Era of Globalization in India and the UK*, New Delhi: Routledge, pp.128–60.

Carretero, M. Asensio M., and Rodríguez-Moneo (eds) (2013) 'History education and the construction of national identities', *Heritage & Museography*, 138–40.

Cayla, D. (2021) *Populism and Neoliberalism*, Routledge: London.

Census of India (1921) *Vol I. Part II— Tables*, Delhi: Government of India.

Census of India (1961) *Vol I. Part II—C (ii) Language Tables*, Delhi: Government of India.

Central Square Foundation. (2020) 'State of the Sector Report on Private Schools in India', *Central Square Foundation*, [online], Available from: https://www.centralsquarefoundation.org/state-of-the-sector-rep ort-on-private-schools-in-india/ [Accessed 20 October 2021].

Chacko, P. (2019) 'Marketizing Hindutva: the state, society, and markets in Hindu nationalism', *Modern Asian Studies*, 53(2): 377–410.

Chakrabartty, P. (2019) 'Red flagging universities in IB note is a reminder of growing shadow of government surveillance', *First Post*, [online] 29 January, Available from: www.firstpost.com/india/red-flagging-of-unive rsities-in-ib-note-is-a-reminder-of-growing-shadow-of-governmentsurve illance-5985021.html [Accessed 29 September 2021].

Chakrabarty, R. (2022) 'Education Budget 2022 increases by 11.86%: major areas of union budget allocation, schemes covered, new plans', *India Today*, [online], Available from: https://www.indiatoday.in/business/bud get-2022/story/union-budget-education-budget-2022-increases-by-11- 86-major-areas-of-budget-allocation-education-schemes-education-plans- 1907451-2022-02-01 [Accessed 8 February 2022].

Chakravarty, I. (2018) 'A bureaucrat's report on Assam's NRC takes a more hardline stand on migration than political parties', *Scroll. In*, [online] 30 October, https://scroll.in/article/900024/a-bureaucrats-report-on-ass ams-nrc-takes-a-more-hardline-stand-on-migration-than-political-part ies [Accessed 30 September 2021].

Chakravartty, A. (2019) 'How five people in Assam were killed during anti-citizenship amendment protests', *The Wire*, [online], 16 December, Available from: https://thewire.in/rights/assam-anti-citizenship-amendm ent-act-protest-deaths [Accessed 5 July 2021].

Chandra, Y.U. (2017) 'Higher education student behaviors in spreading fake news on social media: A case of LINE group', *2017 International Conference on Information Management and Technology (ICIMTech)*: IEEE, pp.54–9.

Chandran, M. (2021) 'Teacher accountability and education restructuring: an exploration of teachers' work identities in an urban school for poor in India', *International Studies in Sociology of Education*, 1–20.

Chandhoke, N. (1999) *Beyond Secularism: The Rights of Religious Minorities*, New York: Oxford University Press.

Chaturvedi, M.G. and Mohale, B.V. (1976) *The Position of Languages in School Curriculum in India*, New Delhi: NCERT.

Chattarji, S. (2019) 'Student protests, media and the university in India', *Postcolonial Studies*, 22(1): 79–94.

Chatterjee, P. (1998) 'Secularism and tolerance', in R. Bhargava (ed.), *Secularism and Its Critics*. Delhi: Oxford University Press, pp.10–17.

Chatterji, A.P. (2020) 'Kashmir: a place without rights – just security', *Just Security*, [online] 5 August, Available from: https://www.justsecurity.org/ 71840/kashmir-a-place-without-rights/ [5 August 2021].

Chattopadhyay, S. (2016) 'Neoliberal approach to governance reform in the universities: a critique and a possible alternative', in R. Kumar (ed.), *Neoliberalism and Educational Crisis in South Asia: Alternatives and Possibilities*, Abingdon: Routledge, pp.243–60.

Chattopadhyay, S. (2020) 'Academic freedom, institutional autonomy and institutionalising accountability: a reflection on the National Education Policy 2020', *The JMC Review*, 4(1): 1–23.

Chattopadhyay, S., Simon, M., and Varghese, N.V. (eds) (2022) *Changing Higher Education in India*, London: Bloomsbury.

Chattopadhyay S. and Panigrahi, J. (2022) 'Financing of higher education in India: issues and challenges', in S. Chattopadhyay, S. Marginson, and N.V. Varghese (eds), *Changing Higher Education in India*, London: Bloomsbury, pp.47–67.

Chattopadhay, T. and Roy, M. (2017) 'Low-Fee Private Schools in India: The Emerging Fault Lines', National Center for the Study of Privatization in Education, Working Paper, 233.

Chaudhary, N. (2017) 'RSS textbook visuals', *Proceedings of the Indian History Congress*, 78: 1155–64.

Chaudhury, D. (2020) 'In the 'New India', all the values of the values of the righteous – as enumerated in The Bhagavad Gita – appear to have become penal offences', *Punch Magazine,* [online] 18 April, Available from: http://thepunchmagazine.com/the-byword/non-fiction/about-values-why-hinduism-loving-citizens-tolerate-the-unrighteous-or-the-devilish [Accessed 18 August 2021].

Choudhary, R. (2019) 'Nellie massacre and 'citizenship': When 1,800 Muslims were killed in Assam in just 6 hours', *The Print*, [online] 18 February, Available from: https://theprint.in/india/governance/nellie-massacre-and-citizenship-when-1800-muslims-were-killed-in-assam-in-just-6-hours/193694/ [Accessed 18 June 2021].

Chowdhury, S.R. (2018) 'BJP's major achievement in Rajasthan: rewriting school textbooks to reflect RSS worldview', *Scroll.in,* [online] 14 November, Available from: https://scroll.in/article/901001/bjps-major-achievement-in-rajasthan-rewriting-schools-textbooks-in-the-rss-worldview [Accessed 14 August 2021].

Chris, C. (1994) 'Paradigms regained: towards a historical sociology of the textbook', *Journal of Curriculum Studies*, 26(1): 1–29.

Chopra, P. (1993) *The Crisis of Foreign Policy – Perspectives and Issues*, Allahabad: Wheeler Publishing.

Choudhury, R. (2019) 'India's 1st illegal immigrant detention camp size of 7 football fields', *NDTV*, 12 September, Available from: https://www.ndtv.com/india-news/assam-detention-centre-inside-indias-1st-detention-centre-for-illegal-immigrants-after-nrc-school-ho-2099626 [Accessed 13 February 2022].

Chudgar, A. (2013) 'Teacher labor force and teacher education in India: an analysis of a recent policy change and its potential implications', in M. Akibda (ed), *Teacher Reforms around the World: Implementations and Outcomes*, Bingley: Emerald Group Publishing Limited, pp.55–76.

Chudgar, A. and Quin, E. (2012) 'Relationship between private schooling and achievement: results from rural and urban India', *Economics of Education Review*, 31(4): 376–90.

Conolly, W. (2017) *Aspirational Fascism: The Struggle for Multifaceted Democracy*, Minneapolis: University of Minnesota Press.

Connell, R. (2013) 'The neoliberal cascade and education: an essay on the market agenda and its consequences', *Critical Studies in Education*, 54(2): 99–112.

Connah, L. (2021) 'The Indian northeast: India's shift from colonised to coloniser', *Global Change, Peace & Security*, 33(2): 201–9.

Corbridge, S. and Harriss, J. (2000*) Liberalisation, Hindu Nationalism and Popular Democracy*, Cambridge: Polity Press.

Corbridge, S., Williams, G., Srivastava, M., and Véron, R. (2005) *Seeing the State: Governance and Governmentality in India* (Vol. 10), Cambridge: Cambridge University Press.

Clark, I. (1997) 'Globalization and fragmentation: international relations in the twentieth century', [online], Available from: https://espace.library.uq.edu.au/view/UQ:333514 [Accessed 13 September 2021].

CSDS (Centre for the Study of Developing Societies) (2017) *Attitudes, Anxieties and Aspirations of India's Youth*, New Delhi: CSDS and KAS.

Dahal, M. and Nguyen, Q. (2014) 'Private Non-State Sector Engagement in the Provision of Educational Services at the Primary and Secondary Levels in South Asia: An Analytical Review of its Role in School Enrolment and Student Achievement', Policy Research Working Paper No. 6899, Washington, DC: World Bank, Education Unit, [online], Available from: http://documents1.worldbank.org/curated/en/988021468302502620/pdf/WPS6899.pdf [Accessed 20 September 2021].

Dalrymple, W. (2005) 'India: the war over history', *The New York Review of Books*, [online] 7 April, Available from: https://www.nybooks.com/articles/2005/04/07/india-the-war-over-history/ [Accessed 7 September 2021].

Damle, S.D. and Anderson, W.K. (1987) *Brotherhood in Saffron: The RSS and Hindu Revivalism*, Boulder, CO: Westview Press.

Daniyal, S. (2020) 'Arbitrary arrests of CAA-NRC protesters point to political vendetta under the cover of Covid', *Scroll*, [online] 30 April, Available from: https://scroll.in/article/960619/arbitrary-arrests-of-caa-nrc-protesters-point-to-politicalvendetta-under-the-cover-of-covid [Accessed 30 July 2021].

Dandekar, M. (2019) 'How neoliberalism fragmented our universities and staved off student unrest', *The Wire*, [online] 5 June, Available from: https://thewire.in/education/how-neoliberalism-fragmented-our-universities-and-staved-off-student-unrest [Accessed 5 September 2021].

Darling-Hammond, L. (2004) 'Inequality and the right to learn: access to qualified teachers in California', *Teachers College Record*, 106(10): 1936–66.

Dasra Report. (2019) 'Making the grade: improving Mumbai's public schools', *Education Innovations*, [online], Available from: http://www.educationinnovations.org/sites/default/files/MakingtheGrade_DASRA.pdf [Accessed 20 June 2021].

Das, D.N. and Chattopadhyay, S. (2014) 'Academic performance indicators: straitjacketing higher education', *Economic and Political Weekly*, 49(50): 68–71.

Datta, P.K. (2003) 'Hindutva and its my history in rewriting history', *Seminar*, 522, Available from: www.india-seminar.com.

Davis, K. (1951) *The Population of India and Pakistan* (Vol. 113, No. 2943, p.611), Princeton, NJ: Princeton University Press.

Day Ashley, L., McLoughlin, C., Aslam, M., Engel, J., Wales, J., Rawal, S., Batley, R., Kingdon, G., Nicolai, S., and Rose, P. (2014) *The Role and Impact of Private Schools in Developing Countries*, London: Department for International Development.

De, A., Majumdar, M., Samson, M., and Noronha, C. (2002) 'Private schools and universal elementary education', in R. Govinda (ed), *India Education Report: A Profile of Basic Education*, Delhi: Oxford University Press, pp.131–50.

De, A., Khera, R., Samson, M, and Kumar, A. (2011) *Probe Revisited: A Report on Elementary Education in India*, Oxford: Oxford University Press.

Dearden, J. (2014). *English as a Medium of Instruction – a Growing Global Phenomenon*, London: British Council.

Deb Mukharji, IFS (Retd). & Ors. v. Union of India (2019) W.P. (Civil) no. 1474 of 2019, Supreme Court of India, Available from: https://www.scribd.com/document/449891277/UN-High-Commissioner-for-Human-Rights-Intervention-Application-CAA-SC [Accessed 13 March 2020].

Denning, S. (2011) Why is the world run by bean counters?, *Forbes.com*, [online] 16 July, Available from: https://www.forbes.com/sites/stevedenning/2011/07/16/why-is-the-world-run-by-bean-counters/?sh=1edbfeaa41a8 [Accessed 16 September 2021].

Deshmukh, J. (2021) 'Terrorizing Muslims: communal violence and emergence of Hindutva in India', *Journal of Muslim Minority Affairs*, 41(2): 317–36.

Despande, S. (2003) *The Centrality of the Middle Class -Contemporary India: A Sociological View*, New Delhi: Penguin Books.

DeSena, J. and Ansalone, G. (2009) 'Gentrification, schooling, and social inequality', *Education Research Quarterly,* 33(1): 61–76.

De Saxe, J.G., Bucknovitz, S., and Mahoney-Mosedale, F. (2020) 'The deprofessionalization of educators: an intersectional analysis of neoliberalism and education reform', *Education and Urban Society*, 52(1): 51–69.

Desai, M. (2020) 'CAA–NRC–NPR and its discontents', *Economic and Political Weekly* 25(55): 7.

DH News Service. (2017) 'Governor launches Vidya Veerta Abhiyan', *Deccan Herald,* [online] 10 August, Available from: https://www.decca nherald.com/content/627336/governor-launches-vidya-veerta-abhiyan. html [Accessed 10 July 2021].

Dharmaraj Savicks, A. (2017). 'Democratic participation in education reform: the case of Sarva Shiksha Abhiyan (Campaign for Universal Education) in rural India' (Doctoral dissertation), University of Southampton.

Dhuru, S. and Thapliyal, N. (2021) 'Global Desi?: possibilities and challenges for global citizenship education in India', *Globalisation, Societies and Education,* 19(4): 405–19.

Diamond, L. (2015) 'Facing up to the democratic recession', *Journal of Democracy,* 26(1): 141–55.

Diamond, L., Plattner, M.F., and Walker, C. (eds.). (2015) *Authoritarianism goes Global: The Challenge to Democracy,* Baltimore, MD: Johns Hopkins University Press.

Dieckhoff, A., Jaffrelot, C., and Massicard, E. (2016) *L'Enjeu mondial. Populismes au pouvoir,* Paris: Presses de Sciences Po.

Dinham, A. and Jones, S.H. (2012) 'Religion, public policy, and the academy: brokering public faith in a context of ambivalence?', *Journal of Contemporary Religion,* 27(2): 185–201.

Dixit, K. (2020) 'Muslim students in UP's RSS schools rise 30% in 3 years', *The Times of India,* [online] 21 February, Available from: https://times ofindia.indiatimes.com/city/allahabad/muslim-students-in-ups-rss-schools-rise-30-in-3-years/articleshow/74234292.cms [Accessed 21 June 2021].

Dixon, P. and Tooley, J. (2005) 'The regulation of private schools serving low-income families in Andhra Pradesh, India', *The Review of Austrian Economics,* 18(1): 29–54.

Dixon, P. (2012) 'Why the denial? Low-cost private schools in developing countries and their contributions to education', *Econ Journal Watch,* 9(3): 186–209.

Dixon, P. and Humble, S. (2019) 'How school choice is framed by parental preferences and family characteristics: a study of western area, Sierra Leone', *Journal of School Choice,* 11(1): 95–110.

Diwakar, R. (2017) 'The workings of the single member plurality electoral system in India and the need for reform', *Asian Journal of Comparative Politics,* 4(2): 141–61.

DMC [Delhi Minorities Commission] [Govt of NCT of Delhi]. (2020) 'Report of the Fact-Finding Committee on the North-East Delhi Riots of February 2020', [online], Available from: https://ia801906.us.archive. org/11/items/dmc-delhi-riot-fact-report-2020/-Delhi-riots-Fact-Find ing-2020.pdf [Accessed 13 July 2021].

Draxler, A. (2012) 'International PPPs in education: new potential or privatization of goods?', in S.L. Robertson, K. Mundy, A. Verger, and F. Menashy (eds), *Public-Private Partnerships in Education: New Actors and Modes of Governance in a Globalizing World*, Cheltenham and Northampton, MA: Edward Elgar, pp.43–62.

Dreze, J. and Sen, A. (2013) *An Uncertain Glory: India and its Contradictions*, Princeton, NJ: Princeton University Press.

D'Souza, R. (2017) 'Army tank in JNU: should the sword be mightier than the pen?' *Hindustan Times*, [online] 25 July, Available from: https://www.hindustantimes.com/opinion/army-tank-in-jnu-should-the-sword-be-mightier-than-the-pen/story-Aegre650bne13Ni4KmlM4I.html [Accessed 25 June 2021].

D'Souza, P.M. (2019) 'MHRD okays government's 100 schools plan', *The New Indian Express*, [online] 22 May, Available from: https://www.newindianexpress.com/cities/bengaluru/2019/may/22/mhrd-okays-govts-100-schools-plan-1980227.html [Accessed 22 June 2021].

Dua, S. (2021) 'Abrogation of Article 370 was long overdue. But we must not hurry change in mindset', *The Print*, [online], 5 August, Available from: https://theprint.in/opinion/abrogation-of-article-370-was-long-overdue-but-we-must-not-hurry-change-in-mindset/709647/ [Accessed 19 February 2022].

Duflo, E., Hanna, R., and Ryan, S.P. (2012) 'Incentives work: fetting teachers to come to school', *American Economic Review*, 102(4): 1241–78.

Duhn, I. (2010) 'The centre is my business': neo-liberal politics, privatisation and discourses of professionalism in New Zealand. *Contemporary Issues in Early Childhood*, 11(1): 49–60.

Du Gay, P. (1996) *Consumption and Identity at Work*, London: Sage Publications.

Dyer, C., Choksi, A., Awasty, V., Iyer, U., Moyade, R., Nigam, N., Purohit, N., Shah, S. and Sheth, S. (2004) 'District Institutes of Education and Training: a comparative study in three Indian states', *Department for International Development*, 666: 454–80.

Economic Times [ET] Government. (2020) 'Government to set up e-education unit, National Educational Technology Forum to improve digital infra', *ET Government*, [online] 31 July, Available from: https://government.economictimes.indiatimes.com/news/education/government-to-set-up-e-education-unit-national-educational-technology-forum-to-improve-digital-infra/77276667 [Accessed 30 June 2021].

Edwards Jr, D.B., DeMatthews, D., and Hartley, H. (2017) 'Public-private partnerships, accountability, and competition: theory versus reality in the charter schools of Bogotá, Colombia', *Education Policy Analysis Archives/ Archivos Analíticos de Políticas Educativas*, 25: 1–36.

Educomp (n.d.a) 'EDUREACH', Educomp, [online], available from: http://educomp.com/content/edureach [Accessed 19 February 2022].

Educomp (n.d. b) 'Description', *Educomp,* [online], available from: http://www.educomp.com [Accessed 20 February 2022].

EFSAS [European Foundation for South Asian Studies] (2017) 'Political divisions of the divided state of Jammu & Kashmir', European Foundation for South Asian Studies, [online] https://www.efsas.org/publications/study- papers/political-divisions-of-the-divided-state-of-jammu-and-kashmir/ [Accessed 30 June 2021].

Election Commission of India (2020) 'Order regarding removal of Sh. Anurag Thakur and Sh. Parvesh Sahib Singh from the list of Star Campaigners of BJP', 29 January, Available from: https://www.scconline.com/blog/post/2020/01/29/eci-orders-removal-of-anurag-thakur-parvesh-sahib-singh-from-the-list-of-star-campaigners-of-bjp/ [Accessed 25 February 2022].

Elst, K. (2002) 'The Saffron Wave', book review, [online], Available from: http://koenraadelst.bharatvani.org/reviews/saffronwave.html [Accessed 13 June 2021].

Engineer, A.A. (1991) 'Lok Sabha elections and communalisation of politics', *Economic and Political Weekly*, 26(27/28): 1649–52.

Endow, T. (2019) 'Low cost private schools: how low cost really are these?', *Indian Journal of Human Development*, 13(1): 102–8.

Ericksen, R.P. (2012) *Complicity in the Holocaust: Churches and Universities in Nazi Germany*, Cambridge: Cambridge University Press.

Erling, E.J. (2014) *The Role of English in Skills Development in South Asia: Policies, Interventions and Existing Evidence*, London: British Council.

Erling, E.J., Adinolfi, L., Hultgren, A.K., Buckler, A., and Mukorera, M. (2016) 'Medium of instruction policies in Ghanaian and Indian primary schools: an overview of key issues and recommendations', *Comparative Education*, 52(3): 294–310.

Eryaman, M.Y. (2006) 'Traveling beyond dangerous private and universal discourses: radioactivity of radical hermeneutics and objectivism in educational research', *Qualitative Inquiry*, 12(6): 1198–1219.

Express News Service (2021) 'Delhi: Increase in applicants to govt schools, say officials' [online], Available from: https://indianexpress.com/article/cities/delhi/delhi-increase-in-applicants-to-govt-schools-say-officials-7507012/ [Accessed 5 July 2022].

Express Web Desk [*Indian Express*]. (2019) 'Assam NRC Final List 2019: Over 19 lakh excluded, 3.11 crore included in list', *Indian Express*, [online] 31 August, Available from: https://indianexpress.com/article/india/assam-nrc-final-list-2019-published-19-lakh-left-out-5953202/ [Accessed 23 July 2021].

Fadaee, S. (2014) 'India's new middle class and the critical activist milieu', *Journal of Developing Societies*, 30(4): 441–57.

Farooq, O. (2016) 'Rohith Vemula: the student who died for Dalit rights', BBC UK, [online] 19 January, Available from: https://www.bbc.co.uk/news/world-asia-india-35349790 [Accessed 19 June 2021].

Faust, D. and Nagar, R. (2001) 'Politics of development in postcolonial India: English-medium education and social fracturing', *Economic and Political Weekly*, 36(30): 2878–83.

Fearon, J.D. and Laitin, D.D. (2000) 'Violence and the social construction of ethnic identity', *International Organization*, 54(4): 845–77.

Ferguson, G. (2013) 'English, development and education: charting the tensions', in E.J. Erling and P. Seargeant (eds), *English and Development*, Bristol: Multilingual Matters, pp.21–44. Available from: https://www.degruyter.com/document/doi/10.21832/9781847699473-005/html [Accessed 13 May 2021].

Filkins, D. (2019) 'Blood and soil in Narendra Modi's India', *New Yorker*, [online] 5 April, Available from: https://www.newyorker.com/magazine/2019/12/09/blood-and-soil-in-narendra-modis-indian [Accessed 5 July 2021].

Finnegan, F. (2008) 'Neo-liberalism, Irish society and adult education', The Adult Learner, [online], Available from: http://mural.maynoothuniversity.ie/4780/ [Accessed 10 June 2021].

Financial Express (2019) 'Ghar-wapsi: VHP says reconverted 25,000 Muslims, Christians in 2018', *Financial Express*, [online] 26 October, Available from: https://www.financialexpress.com/india-news/ghar-wapsi-vhp-says-reconverted-25000-muslims-christians-in-2018/1746798/ [Accessed 19 February 2021].

First Post (2019) 'Amit Shah promises to expel all illegal migrants by 2024 but Assam's failed NRC has a lesson or two for Centre', *First Post*, [online] 3 December, Available from: https://www.firstpost.com/india/amit-shah-promises-to-expel-all-illegal-migrants-by-2024-but-assams-failed-nrc-has-a-lesson-or-two-for-centre-7731851.html [Accessed 3 June 2021].

Firstpost (2012) 'India: rescind 'shoot at sight' orders in Assam', Human Rights Watch news release, [online], 27 July, Available from: https://www.hrw.org/news/2012/07/27/india-rescind-shoot-sight-orders-assam [Accessed 11 February 2022].

Flåten, L.T. (2016) *Hindu Nationalism, History and Identity in India: Narrating a Hindu Past under the BJP*, London: Routledge.

Flåten, L.T. (2017) 'Spreading Hindutva through education: still a priority for the BJP?', *India Review*, 16(4): 377–400.

Flåten, L.T. (2019) 'The inclusion-moderation thesis: India's BJP', in *Oxford Research Encyclopedia of Politics*, Available from: https://oxfordre.com/politics/view/10.1093/acrefore/9780190228637.001.0001/acrefore-9780190228637-e-789 [Accessed 31 October 2021].

Forgacs, D. (1988) *Antonio Gramsci Reader,* London: Lawrence & Wishart.

Fraser, N. (1998) 'Social justice in the age of identity politics: redistribution, recognition, participation', *Culture and Economy after the Cultural Turn*, 1: 25–52.

Fraser, N. (1992) 'Rethinking the Public Sphere', in Craig Calhoun (ed), *Habermas and the Public Sphere,* Cambridge, MA: MIT Press.

Freedom House (n.d.) 'Freedom in the world', Freedom House, [online] n.d, Available from: https://freedomhouse.org/country/india/freedom-world/2021 [Accessed 19 February 2021].

Friedman, G.M. (1962) 'On sorting, sorting coefficients, and the lognormality of the grain-size distribution of sandstones', *The Journal of Geology*, 70(6): 737–53.

Freidson, E. (2004) *Professionalism: The Third Logic* (4th edn), Cambridge: Polity Press.

Froerer, P. (2007) 'Disciplining the saffron way: moral education and the Hindu rashtra', *Modern Asian Studies*, 41(5): 1033–71.

Fukuyama, F. (1989) 'The end of history?', *The National Interest*, 16: 3–18.

Fukuyama, F. (1992) 'Capitalism & democracy: the missing link', *Journal of Democracy*, 3(3): 100–10.

Gamarnikow, E. (2009) 'Education in network society: critical reflections', in R. Cowen and A.M. Kazamias (eds), *International Handbook of Comparative Education*, Springer: Dordrecht, pp.619–31.

Gandesha, S. (2018) 'Identifying with the aggressor: From the authoritarian to neo-liberal personality', *Constellations*, 25(1): 147–64.

Ganeshan, B. (2020) 'Bajrang Dal's Valentine's Day plan: round up couples, observe Pulwama Martyr's Day', *The News Minute*, [online] 13 February, Available from: https://www.thenewsminute.com/article/bajrang-dals-val entines-day-plan-round-couples-observe-pulwama-martyrs-day-118102 [Accessed 13 June 2021].

Ganguly, S. (1997) 'India in 1996: a year of upheaval', *Asian Survey*, 37(2): 126–35.

Ganguly, S. (1999) *The Crisis in Kashmir: Portents of War, Hopes of Peace*, Cambridge: Cambridge University Press.

Ganguly, M. (2020) 'India failing on Kashmiri human rights', Human Rights Watch, [online] 17 January, Available from: https://www.hrw.org/news/2020/01/17/india-failing-kashmiri-human-rights [Accessed 17 June 2021].

Ganguly, S. (2020) 'India's democracy is under threat', *Foreign Policy*, [online] 18 September, Available from: https://foreignpolicy.com/2020/09/18/ind ias-democracy-is-under-threat/ [Accessed 19 February 2022].

Ganguly-Scrase, R. and Scrase, T.J. (2008) *Globalisation and the Middle Classes in India: The Social and Cultural Impact of Neoliberal Reforms*, London: Routledge.

Garland, I. and Garland, P. (2012) 'Performative cultures: changing professional roles, responsibilities and relationships of teachers and teaching assistants', in B. Jeffrey and G. Troman (eds), *Performativity in UK Education: Ethnographic Cases of its Effects, Agency and Reconstructions*, Stroud: E&E Publishing, pp.23–33.

Gay, G., (2010) *Culturally Responsive Teaching: Theory Research and Practice*, New York: Teachers College Press.

George, A.M. (2008) 'Learning teacher: Reviewing the narrative of a teacher's journey', *Contemporary Education Dialogue*, 5(2): 292–295.

Geertz, C. (1963) 'The integrative revolution: primordial sentiments and civil politics in new states', in C. Geertz (ed.), *Old Societies and New States: The Quest for Modernity in Asia and Africa*, New York: Free Press, pp.105–19.

Germani, G. (1978) *Authoritarianism, Fascism, and National Populism*, New Brunswick, NJ: Transaction Publishers.

Gethin, R. (2019) 'A lesson in religious tolerance from ancient India', Available from: https://www.theguardian.com/world/2019/apr/24/a-lesson-in-religious-tolerance-from-ancient-india [Accessed 13 June 2022].

Ghas Ghassem-Fachandi, P. (2012) *Pogrom in Gujarat: Hindu Nationalism and Anti-Muslim Violence in India*, Princeton, NJ: Princeton University Press.

Ghosh, P. and Bray, M. (2018) 'Credentialism and demand for private supplementary tutoring: a comparative study of students following two examination boards in India', *International Journal of Comparative Education and Development*, 20(1): 33–50.

Ghosh, J. and Chandrasekhar, C.P. (2003) 'Per capita income growth in the states of India', [online], Available from: http://www. macroscan.com [Accessed 13 July 2021].

Gill, M.K. (2017), 'Globalisation, neoliberalism and the transformation of higher education in Punjab, India', (Doctoral dissertation), SOAS University of London.

Ginsburg, M. (2012) 'Public private partnerships, neoliberal globalization and democratization', in S. Robertson, K. Mundy, and A. Verger (eds), *Public Private Partnerships in Education*, Cheltenham: Edward Elgar Publishing, pp.63–78.

Giroux, H.A. (2004) 'Cultural studies, public pedagogy, and the responsibility of intellectuals', *Communication and Critical/Cultural Studies*, 1(1): 59–79.

Giroux, H. (2011) *On Critical Pedagogy*, New York: Continuum Publishers.

Giroux, H. (2014) 'Henry Giroux on the rise of neoliberalism', *Truthout*, [online] 19 October, Available from: http://www.truthout.org/opinion/item/26885-henry-giroux-on-the-rise-of-neoliberalism [Accessed 19 July 2021].

Giroux, H. (2019) 'Neoliberalism paved the way for authoritarian right-wing populism', *Truthout*, [online] 26 September, Available from: https://truthout.org/articles/neoliberalism-paved-the-way-for-authoritarian-right-wing-populism/ [Accessed 19 February 2022].

Giddens, A. (1991) *Modernity and Self-Identity: Self and Society in the Late Modern Age*, Cambridge: Polity Press.

Gillies, V. (2005) 'Raising the 'meritocracy' parenting and the individualization of social class', *Sociology*, 39(5): 835–53.

Glick, P. and Sahn, D.E. (2006) 'The demand for primary schooling in Madagascar: price, quality, and the choice between public and private providers', *Journal of Development Economics*, 79(1): 118–45.

Global Engagement Monitoring Report (2016) 'Education for people and planet: Creating a Sustainable Futures for all' [online], Available from: https://www.addistaxinitiative.net/sites/default/files/resour ces/2017-ATI-Monitoring-Report-Incl-Annex.pdf [Accessed 13 June 2022].

Goan Connection TV (2020) 'Atishi Marlena shares how she transformed the government schools in Delhi', Goan Connection TV, [online] 6 February, Available from: https://www.youtube.com/watch?v=HIUx7jRk 7qI [Accessed 13 January 2021].

Goel, P. and Malik, N. (2021) 'A study on awareness and usage of E-resource portals among prospective teachers', *Integrated Journal of Social Sciences*, 8(1): 1–8.

Gogoi, D. (ed.) (2016) *Unheeded Hinterland: Identity and Sovereignty in Northeast India*, London: Routledge.

GoI (Government of India) (1953) 'Estimated population by castes (Uttar Pradesh, Delhi, Bombay and Madhya Pradesh)', New Delhi: Office of the Registrar General of India, Ministry of Home Affairs.

GoI (Government of India) (1993) *Learning without Burden: Report of the National Advisory Committee*, New Delhi: Ministry of Human Resources Development.

GoI (Government of India) (1995) *Government Subsidies in India*, New Delhi: Government of India.

GoI (Government of India) (1997) 'Speech of Shri Manmohan Singh, Minister of Finance, introduction the budget for the year 1992–93', *Budget Speeches of Union Finance Ministers*, Vol. 11, New Delhi: Ministry of Finance, 1997.

GoI (Government of India) (2009) *The Right of Children to Free and Compulsory Education Act*, New Delhi: Government Press.

GoI (Government of India) (2010) 'Sarva Shiksha Abhiyan eleventh joint review mission & mid term review – aide memoire', [online], Available from: ssa.nic.in/ssadoc/jrm/AIDE%20MEMOIRE%2011% 20JRM%20 with%20state%20reportss.pdf [Accessed 10 July 2021].

GoI (Government of India) (2011) 'Census of India 2011: Population by religious community [Table C1]', New Delhi: Office of the Registrar General.

GoI (Government of India) (2018) 'Ministry of Human Resource Development UGC (categorisation of universities (only) for grant of graded autonomy) regulations 2018', *The Gazette of India*, [online], 12 February (Part III, Section 4), Available from: https://www.ugc.ac.in/pdfnews/143 5338_182728.pdf [Accessed 18 July 2021].

GoI (Government of India) (2019) 'Annual report-2018–19', University Grants Commission, [online], Available from: https://www.ugc.ac.in/pdfn ews/3060779_UGC-ANNUAL-REPORT--ENGLISH--2018-19.pdf [Accessed 10 June 2021].

GoI (Government of India) (2020a) 'National Education Policy 2020', MHRD, [online], Available from: https://www.mhrd.gov.in/sites/uploa d_files/mhrd/files/NEP_Final_English_0.pdf [Accessed 11 July 2021].

GoI (Government of India) (2020b) 'The Constitution of India', Government of India, [online], Available from: https://legislative.gov.in/sites/default/ files/COI.pdf [Accessed 12 June 2021].

GoI (Government of India) (n.d.) 'OPEN CALL FOR RESEARCH & DEVELOPMENT PROPOSALS', *Government of India*, [online], Available from: https://dst.gov.in/sites/default/files/SUTRA-%20PIC%20Format. pdf [Accessed 18 February 2022].

Gottshalk, P. (2001) 'The Saffron Wave', book review, *The Indian Economic & Social History Review*, 38(3): 333–5, Available from: https://journals.sage pub.com/doi/abs/10.1177/001946460103800309 [Accessed 10 July 2021].

Gooptu, N. (2009) 'Neoliberal subjectivity, enterprise culture and new workplaces: organised retail and shopping malls in India', *Economic and Political Weekly*: 44(22): 45–54.

Gooptu, N. (ed.). (2013) *Enterprise Culture in Neoliberal India: Studies in Youth, Class, Work and Media*, London: Routledge.

Gowda, S. (2020) 'Public-private partnerships in education: a vertical case study of the Right to Education Act (2009), India', (Doctoral dissertation), University of Massachusetts Boston.

Gore, M.S. (1991) 'The rise and fall of Buddhism in India: two perspectives', *Indian Journal of Social Science*, 4: 175–219.

Government of Assam (2012) 'White Paper on foreigners' issue', Government of Assam, [online], Available from: https://cjp.org.in/wp-content/uploads/ 2018/10/White-Paper-On-Foreigners-Issue-20-10-2012.pdf [Accessed 11 February 2022].

Government of Assam (2019) 'Significant Schemes. Secondary Education', Government of Assam, Available from: education.assam.gov.in/schemes/ significant-schemes [Accessed 13 June 2022].

Government of Assam (n.d.) 'List of schools', Government of Assam, [online], Available from: https://education.assam.gov.in/information-servi ces/list-of-schools [Accessed 19 February 2022].

Goswami, N. (2017) *Legitimising Standard Languages: Perspectives from a School in Banaras*, Delhi: SAGE Publications.

Govinda, R. and Josephine, Y. (2004) *Contract Teachers in India: A Review*, Paris: IIEP/UNESCO.

Govinda, R. (2014) 'In search of a new paradigm of schooling', in S.S. Jena and S. Mitra (eds), *Schooling and Beyond*, Delhi: National Institute of Open Schooling.

Govinda, R. and Bandyopadhyay, M. (2012) 'Access to elementary education in India: analytical overview', in R. Govinda (ed.), *Who Goes to School? Exploring Exclusion in Indian Education*, Oxford: Oxford University Press, pp.1–86.

Graham, B.D. (1987) 'The Jana Sangh and bloc politics, 1967–80', *Journal of Commonwealth & Comparative Politics*, 25(3): 248–66.

Gramsci, A. (1971) *Selections from the Prison Notebooks,* London: Lawrence and Wishatr.

Groff, C. (2017) 'Language and language-in-education planning in multilingual India: a minoritized language perspective', *Language Policy*, 16(2): 135–64.

Gudavarthy, A. (2021) 'Spot the difference in what parties vying for India's voters now represent', *The Wire*, [online] 6 December, Available from: https://thewire.in/politics/spot-the-difference-in-what-parties-vying-for-indias-voters-now-represent [Accessed 20 December 2021].

Guichard, S. (2010) *The Construction of History and Nationalism in India: Textbooks, Controversies and Politics*, New York: Routledge.

Guichard, S. (2013) 'The Indian nation and selective amnesia: representing conflicts and violence in Indian history textbooks', *Nations and Nationalism*, 19(1): 68–86.

Guichard, S. (2017) 'Indian populism. Books and ideas', [online], Available from: http://archive-ouverte.unige.ch/unige:97614 [Accessed 23 June 2021].

Gupta, A. (2019) 'Teacher-entrepreneurialism: a case of teacher identity formation in neoliberalizing education space in contemporary India', *Critical Studies in Education*, 62(4): 422–38.

Gupta, A. (2020) 'Heterogeneous middle-class and disparate educational advantage: Parental investment in their children's schooling in Dehradun, India', *British Journal of Sociology of Education*, 41(1): 48–63.

Gupta, L. (2014) 'Making reflective citizens: India's new textbooks for social and political life', in E. Vickers and K. Kumar (eds), *Constructing Modern Asian Citizenship*, London: Routledge, pp.119–38.

Gupta, K.R. (ed.) (1999) *Liberalisation and Globalisation of Indian Economy* (vol. 3), New York: Atlantic Publishers & Dist.

Gupta, R. (2021) 'Farmers in India have been protesting for 6 months, have they made any progress', *The Conversation*, [online], 25 May, Available from: https://theconversation.com/farmers-in-india-have-been-protesting-for-6-months-have-they-made-any-progress-161101 [Accessed 8 February 2022].

Gurney, E. (2017) 'Choosing schools, choosing selves: exploring the influence of parental identity and biography on the school choice process in Delhi, India', *International Studies in Sociology of Education*, 26(1): 19–35.

Habermas, J. (1992) 'Citizenship and national identity: some reflections on the future of Europe', *Praxis International*, 12(1): 1–19.

Hallin, D.C. (2019) 'Mediatisation, neoliberalism and populisms: the case of Trump', *Contemporary Social Science*, 14(1): 14–25.

Hall, R. and Pulsford, M. (2019) 'Neoliberalism and primary education: impacts of neoliberal policy on the lived experiences of primary school communities. *Power and Education*', 11(3): 241–51.

Hallett, T. (2010) 'The myth incarnate: recoupling processes, turmoil, and inhabited institutions in an urban elementary school. *American Sociological Review*', 75(1): 52–74.

Hanson, A.H. (1968) 'Power shifts and regional balances', in P. Streeten and M. Lipton (eds), *The Crisis of Indian Planning*, London: Oxford University Press, pp.43–9.

Hansen, T.B. (1996) 'Recuperating masculinity: Hindu nationalism, violence and the exorcism of the Muslim "other"', *Critique of Anthropology*, 16(2): 137–72.

Hansen, T.B. (1999) *The Saffron Wave: Democracy and Hindu Nationalism in Modern India*, Delhi: Oxford University Press.

Harinath, S. and Gundemeda, N. (2021) 'Dalits and choice of school: a sociological study of private schools in Telangana State', *Sociological Bulletin*, 70(2): 214–31.

Harma, J.C. (2008) 'Are low-fee private primary schools in Uttar Pradesh, India, serving the needs of the poor?', (Doctoral dissertation), University of Sussex.

Härmä, J. and Rose, P. (2012) 'Is low-fee private primary schooling affordable for the poor? Evidence from rural India', in S.L. Robertson, K. Mundy, A. Verger, and F. Menashy (eds), *Public-Private Partnerships in Education*, Cheltenham: Edward Elgar Publishing, pp.243–58.

Härmä, J. (2013) 'Access or quality? Why do families living in slums choose low-cost private schools in Lagos, Nigeria?', *Oxford Review of Education*, 39(4): 548–66.

Härmä, J. (2021) 'Evidence on school choice and the human right to education', In *Realizing the Abidjan Principles on the Right to Education*, Edward Elgar Publishing.

Haq, M.N. (2004) A baseline survey of rural secondary schools: A quest for teaching-learning quality, *Bangladesh Education Journal*, 3(2): 31–54.

Harriss-White, B. (2004) 'India's socially regulated economy', *Indian Journal of Labour Economics*, 47(1): 49–68.

Harriss, J. (2010) 'Is government in India becoming more responsive? Has democratic decentralisation made a difference', working paper, Simons Papers in Security and Development, no. 8, Vancouver: Simon Fraser University.

Hargreaves, A. (1994) *Changing Teachers, Changing Times: Teachers' Work and Culture in the Postmodern Age*, London: Cassell.

Hargreaves, A. (1999) 'Reinventing professionalism: teacher education and teacher development for a changing world', *Asia-Pacific Journal of Teacher Education & Development*, 2(1): 65–74.

Harvey, D. (2005) *A Brief History of Neoliberalism*, New York: Oxford University Press.

Harvey, D. (2006) *Spaces of Global Capitalism*, London: Verso.

Harvey, D. (2007) *A Brief History of Neoliberalism*, Oxford: Oxford University Press.

Hasan, M. (2004) *Will Secular India Survive?*, Gurgaon, India: Imprint One.

Hazarika, S. (2006) 'Illegal migration from Bangladesh: problem and long-term perspective', in B.B. Kumar and A. Bharati (eds), *Illegal Migration from Bangladesh*, New Delhi: Concept Publishing Company, pp.25–34.

Heller, P., Harilal, K.N., and Chaudhuri, S. (2007) 'Building local democracy: evaluating the impact of decentralization in Kerala, India', *World Development*, 35(4): 626–48.

Heller, M. and Duchene, A. (2012) 'Pride and profit: changing discourses of language, capital and nation-state', in A. Duchner and M. Heller (eds), *Language in Late Capitalism: Pride and Profit*, New York: Routledge, pp.1–21.

Held, D. and McGrew, A. (2007) *Globalization/Anti-Globalization: Beyond the Great Divide*, Cambridge: Polity Press.

Herman, E. and Chomsky, N. (2012) 'A propaganda model', in M. Durham and D. Kellner (eds), *Media and Cultural Studies: Key Works* (2nd edn), Malden, MA: Wiley-Blackwell, pp.204–31.

Highlights of New Education Policy (2020) Available from: https://www.mhrd.gov.in/sites/upload_files/mhrd/files/LU19.pdf [Accessed 29 October 2020].

Hill, D. and Rosskam, E. (2009) *The Developing World and State Education: Neoliberal Depredation and Egalitarian Alternatives*, London: Routledge Publishing.

Hill, D. (2004) 'Educational perversion and global neo-liberalism: a Marxist critique', Cultural Logic. 7, [online], Available from: www.clogic.eserver.org [Accessed 22 June 2021].

Hill, E. (2015) 'Expanding the school market in India: parental choice and the reproduction of social inequality', *Economic and Political Weekly* 46(35): 98–105.

Hindustan Times (2018) '2750 Punjab schools to have English-medium from April 1', *Hindustan Times*, [online] 20 April, Available from: https://www.hindustantimes.com/punjab/2-750-%20punjab-schools-%20to-have-%20english-medium-%20from-april-1/storybP7E6yh9yGLWAkLvKjX3pK.html [Accessed 21 September 2021].

Hindustan News Hub (Jan 2022) 'Republic Day 2022: The tune of Mahatma Gandhi's favorite Christian prayer song 'Abide with me' was removed from the 'Beating Retreat' ceremony for the first time', Hindustan News Hub, [online] 22 January, Available from: https://hindustannewshub.com/india-news/republic-day-2022-the-tune-of-mahatma-gandhis-favorite-christian-prayer-song-abide-with-me-was-removed-from-the-beating-retreat-ceremony-for-the-first-time/ [Accessed 2 February 2021].

Hiremath, G.S. and Komalesha, H.S. (2018) 'How IITs turned from Nehru's vision of technology to catering engineers for MNCs', *The Wire* [online], Available from: https://thewire.in/education/iits-nehru-coaching-mhrd [Accessed 4 June 2022].

Horowitz, D. (1985) *Ethnic Groups in Conflict,* Berkeley, CA: University of California Press.

Hossain, A. and Mondal, G.C. (2019) 'History and milestones of higher education in India', *International Journal of Research and Analytical Reviews*, 6(1): 978.

Hoyle, E. and Wallace, M. (2014) 'Organisational studies in an era of educational reform', *Journal of Educational Administration and History*, 46(3): 244–69.

HRW (Human Rights Watch) (2020) '"Shoot the traitors": discrimination against Muslims under India's new citizenship policy', HRW, [online] 9 April, Available from: https://www.hrw.org/report/2020/04/09/shoot-traitors/discrimination-against-muslims-under-indias-new-citizenship-policy [Accessed 10 April 2021].

HRW (Human Rights Watch) (2019) 'India: vigilante "cow protection" groups attack minorities', HRW, [online] 18 February, Available from: https://www.hrw.org/news/2019/02/18/india-vigilante-cow-protection-groups-attack-minorities [Accessed 18 July 2021].

HRW (Human Rights Watch) (n.d.) 'India: Assam's citizen identification can exclude 4 million people', Human Rights Watch, Available from: https://www.hrw.org/news/2018/07/31/india-assams-citizen-identification-can-exclude-4-million-people# [Accessed 15 February 2022].

Hussain, A. and Safiq, I. (2016) 'Teaching intolerance in Pakistan: religious bias in public school textbooks', United States Commission on International Religious Freedom, [online], Available from: https://hsdl.org/?view&did=794028 [Accessed 10 August 2021].

HT Correspondent (2021) 'PM Modi launches key education initiatives for education revolution', *Hindustan Times*, [online] 8 September, Available from: https://www.hindustantimes.com/india-news/pm-modi-launches-key-education-initiatives-for-education-revolution-101631038315626-amp.html [Accessed 8 January 2022].

Hussain, S. and Yunus, R. (2021) 'Right-wing populism and education: introduction to the special section', *British Educational Research Journal*, 47(2): 247–63.

IANS (2006) 'Chattisgarh passes anti-conversion bill'. *Gulf News*, [online] 4 August, Available from: https://gulfnews.com/world/asia/india/chhattisgarh-passes-anti-conversion-bill-1.248514 [Accessed 4 June 2021].

Ibrahim, U. (2019) 'Religious co-existence in South India: role and relevance of Islamic tradition/Güney Hindistan'da Dinsel Biraradalık: İslam Geleneğinin Rolü veİlgisi. *Disiplinlerarası Sosyal Bilimler Dergisi*', 5: 93–122.

Iftikar, F. (2018) 'CBSE: in Delhi region, govt schools drop pass percentage', *Daily News & Analysis*, [online] 30 May, Available from: https://www.dnaindia.com/delhi/report-cbse-class-10th-results-2018-delhi-govt-schools-drop-pass-percentage-2620159 [Accessed 15 July 2021].

Iftikhar, F. (2021) 'Indian universities, 2010–2020: a decade in protest', *Hindustan Times*, [online] 25 March, Available from: https://www.hindustantimes.com/india-news/indian-universities-2010-2020-a-decade-in-protest-101616585103634.html [Accessed 25 June 2021].

Indian Express (2001) 'Texts were rewritten in Nazi Germany Pak', *Indian Express*.

Indiatimes News Network (2005) 'No entry for Modi into US: visa denied', *Times of India*, [online] 18 March, Available from https://timesofindia.indiatimes.com/india/no-entry-for-modi-into-us-visadenied/articleshow/1055543.cms [Accessed 18 July 2021].

India Today (2019) 'NCERT is removing caste conflict chapters from class 9 History textbooks for HRD Ministry exercise', *India Today,* [online] 19 March, Available from: https://www.indiatoday.in/education-today/news/story/ncert-is-removing-caste-conflict-chapters-from-class-9-history-textbooks-1481496-2019-03-19 [Accessed 23 December 2021].

India Today (2020) 'A reality check on NEP 2020: 6 major challenges in implementation', *India Today,* [online] 14 August, Available from: https://www.indiatoday.in/education-today/featurephilia/story/areality-check-on-nep-2020-major-challenges-in-implementation-1711197-2020-08-14 [Accessed 16 July 2021].

India TV News Desk (2020) 'BJP MLA 'warns' anti-CAA protesters, says 'we are 80% and you just 17%', India TV News, Available from: https://www.indiatvnews.com/news/india/bjp-ballari-mla-somashekar-reddy-threatens-anti-caa-protesters-says-we-are-80-percent-576220 [Accessed 17 February 2022].

Iqbal, M. (2020) 'Linguistic minority students deprived of education in mother tongue in Rajasthan', *The Hindu*, [online] 24 September, Available from https://www.thehindu.com/news/national/other-states/linguistic-minority-students-deprived-of-education-in-mother-tongue-in-rajasthan/article32681327.ece [Accessed 13 July 2021].

Islam, M. (2020) 'What the new education policy will mean for universities in India', *The Wire,* [online], 9 August, Available from: https://thewire.in/education/new-education-policy-university [Accessed 15 February 2022].

Indian Kanoon (n.d.) 'Assam Public Works v. Union of India, W.P. (civil) no. 274 of 2009, Supreme Court of India', [online], Available from: https://indiankanoon.org/doc/135202420/ [Accessed 12 February 2022].

Jaffrelot, C. (1996) 'Le multiculturalisme indien à l'épreuve. Le cas des débats constitutionnels', *L'Année sociologique*, 46(1): 187–210.

Jaffrelot, C. (1999) *The Hindu Nationalist Movement and Indian Politics: 1925 to the 1990s: Strategies of Identity-Building, Implantation and Mobilisation (with Special Reference to Central India)*, New Delhi: Penguin Books India.

Jaffrelot, C. (2003) *India's Silent Revolution: The Rise of the Lower Castes in North India*, New York: Columbia University Press.

Jaffrelot, C. (2005) *The Sangh Parivar: A Reader, 445*, New Delhi: Oxford University Press.

Jaffrelot, C. (ed.). (2009) *Hindu Nationalism: A Reader*, Princeton, NJ: Princeton University Press.

Jaffrelot, C. (2015) 'The Modi-centric BJP 2014 election campaign: new techniques and old tactics', *Contemporary South Asia*, 23(2): 151–66.

Jaffrelot, C. (2017) India's democracy at 70: toward a Hindu state?, *Journal of Democracy*, 28(3): 52–63.

Jaffrelot, C. (2019) 'The fate of secularism in India', in Milan Vaishnav (ed.), *The BJP in Power: Indian Democracy and Religious Nationalism*, Washington, DC: *Carnegie Endowment for International Peace*. Available from: https://carnegieendowment.org/2019/04/04/fate-of-secularism-in-india-pub-78689 [Accessed 11 July 2021].

Jaffrelot, C. (2021) *Modi's India: Hindu Nationalism and the Rise of Ethnic Democracy*, Princeton, NJ: Princeton University Press.

Jaffrelot, C. and Therwath, I. (2007) 'The Sangh Parivar and the Hindu diaspora in the West: what kind of "long-distance nationalism"?', *International Political Sociology*, 1(3): 278–95.

Jaffrelot, C. and Verniers, G. (2020) 'A new party system or a new political system?', *Contemporary South Asia*, 28(2): 141–54.

Jaffrelot, C. and Jairam, P. (2020) 'BJP has been effective in transmitting its version of Indian history to next generation of learners', Carnegie Endowment, [online] 16 November, Available from: https://carnegieendowment.org/2019/11/16/bjp-has-been-effective-in-transmitting-its-version-of-indian-history-to-next-generation-of-learners-pub-80373 [Accessed 16 August 2021].

Jafri, A.A. (2020) 'Who were 23 people killed in UP during anti-CAA-NRC protests?' *News Click*, [online], Available from: https://www.newscl ick.in/who-were-23-people-killed-during-anti-caa-nrc-protests [Accessed 20 February 2022].

Jain, M. (2004) 'Elementary school civics after independence: a content analysis of textbooks', (Unpublished M.Ed. dissertation), Department of Education: University of Delhi.

Jain, M. (2005) 'Past and present in the curriculum', *Economic and Political Weekly*, 40: 1939–42.

Jain, P.S. and Dholakia, R.H. (2010) 'Right to education act and public-private partnership', *Economic and Political Weekly*, 44(25): 38–43.

Jain, P., Dhawan, A., and Ishwaran, G. (2014) *Private Sector's Contribution to K-12 Education in India*, New Delhi: FICCI and Ernst and Young.

Jain, M., Mehendale, A., Mukhopadhyay, R., Sarangapani, P.M. and Winch, C. (eds.). (2018) *School Education in India: Market, State and Quality*, New Delhi: Taylor & Francis.

Jain, R. and Lasseter, T. (2018) 'By rewriting history, Hindu nationalists aim to assert their dominance over India', *Reuters*, [online] 6 March, Available from: https://www.reuters.com/investigates/special-report/india-modi-culture/ [Accessed 10 January 2022].

Jain, S. (2020) 'Rajasthan to have only one third language in schools, minorities fear Sanskrit imposition', *The Wire*, [online] 12 October, Available from: https://thewire.in/education/rajasthan-schools-third-langu age [Accessed 18 February 2022].

Jain, S., Lall, M., and Singh, A. (2021) 'Teachers' voices on the impact of COVID-19 on school education: are ed-tech companies really the panacea?', *Contemporary Education Dialogue*, 18(1): 58–89.

Jairam, P. (2021) 'Hinduising the idea of India: the BJP and the writing of school history textbooks in Rajasthan', (unpublished thesis), King's College London.

Janyala, S. (2016) 'As Ambedkar association grew, so did its assertiveness', *The Indian Express*, [online], Available from: https://indianexpress.com/article/india/india-news-india/as-ambedkar-association-grew-so-did-its-assertiveness/ [Accessed 10 January 2021].

Jason, Z. (2017) 'The battle over charter schools', Harvard Graduate School of Education, [online], Available from: https://www.gse.harvard.edu/news/ed/17/05/battle-over-charter-schools [Accessed 10 August 2021].

Jayadeva, S. (2019) 'English-medium: schooling, social mobility, and inequality in Bangalore, India', *Anthropology & Education Quarterly*, 50(2): 151–69.

Jayapalan, N. (2005) *Problems of Indian Education*, Delhi: Atlantic Publishers.

Jayaram, N. (2015) *Sociology of Education in India*, Jaipur: Rawat Publication.

Jayal, N. (2019) 'Fear and desire: crippling the public university', in N. Jayal (ed), *Reforming India: The Nation Today*, New Delhi: Penguin Viking, pp.475–92.

Jeffrey, B. and Troman, G. (2004) 'Time for ethnography', *British Educational Research Journal*, 30(4): 535–48.

Jeffery, R., Jeffery, P., Jeffrey, C., and Chopra, R. (2005) *Educational Regimes in India*, New Delhi: Sage Publications.

Jenkins, R. (1999) *Democratic Politics and Economic Reform in India*, Cambridge: Cambridge University Press.

Jenkins, R. (2004) 'Labor policy and the second generation of economic reform in India', *India Review*, 3(4): 333–63.

Jena, M. (2016) *Introduce English Education from Primary Level in All Schools*, Bhubneshwar: The Pioneer.

Jha, D.K. (2014) 'RSS sets up panel to supervise saffronisation of education', *Scroll*, [online], 2 August, Available from: https://scroll.in/article/672545/rss-sets-up-panel-to-supervise-saffronisation-of-education [Accessed 2 December 2021].

Jha, D.N. (2002) *The Myth of the Holy Cow*, London: Verso Books.

Jha, P.K. (2020) 'From barter to partner in the Russia–India arms trade', East Asia Forum, [online], 18 April, Available from: https://www.eastasiaforum.org/2020/04/18/from-barter-to-partner-in-the-russia-india-arms-trade/#:~:text=During%20the%201970s%20the%20weapons,located%20in%20Eastern%20European%20countries [Accessed 20 February 2022].

John, K. and Raju, S. (2019) 'Embracing modernity: RSS schools increasingly adopting English medium education technology', *Hindustan Times*, [online] 17 September, Available from: https://www.hindustanti mes.com/cities/embracing-modernity-rss-schools-increasingly-adopting-english-medium-education-technology/story-cAyNAFBrLSWikLGIPYH HMK.html [Accessed 17 July 2021].

Joshi, V. and Little, D. (1996) *I.M.D. India's Economic Reforms 1991–2001*, New Delhi: Oxford University Press.

Jolad, S. and Doshi, I. (2021) 'Colonial legacy of language politics and medium of instruction policy in India', [online], Available from: https://osf.io/preprints/socarxiv/w9j7x/download [Accessed 13 June 2021].

Joppke, C. (2007) 'Transformation of citizenship: status, rights, identity', *Citizenship Studies*, 11(1): 37–48.

Kabir, N.A. (2020) 'Identity politics in India: Gujarat and Delhi riots', *Journal of Muslim Minority Affairs*, 40(3): 395–409.

Kadiwal, L. and Jain, M. (2020) 'Civics and citizenship education in India and Pakistan', in P.M. Sarangapani and R. Pappu (eds), *Handbook of Education Systems in South Asia*, Singapore: Springer, pp.1–27.

Kailash, K.K. (2014) 'Regional parties in the 16th Lok Sabha elections: who survived and why?', *Economic and Political Weekly*, XLIX(39): 64–71.

Kamat, S. (2011) 'Neoliberalism, urbanism and the education economy: producing Hyderabad as a 'global city'', *Discourse: Studies in the Cultural Politics of Education*, 32(2): 187–202.

Kamat, S., Spreen, C., and Jonnalagadda, I. (2018) 'Profiting from the poor: the emergence of multinational edu-businesses in Hyderabad, India', report, Brussels: Education International. Available from: https://www.unite4education.org/resources/india/profiting-from-the-poor-the-emergenceof-multinational-edu-businesses-in-hyderabad-india/ [Accessed 18 July 2022].

Kanungo, P. (2019) 'Sangh and Sarkar: the RSS power centre shifts from Nagpur to New Delhi', in A.P. Chatterji, T.B. Hansen, and C. Jaffrelot (eds), *Majoritarian State*, London: Hurst and Company, pp.133–50.

Karthikeyan, D. (2011) 'Suicide by Dalit students in 4 years', *The Hindu*, [online] 5 September, Available from: https://www.thehindu.com/news/cities/Madurai/suicide-by-dalit-students-in-4-years/article2425965.ece [Accessed 5 July 2021].

Karopady, D.D. (2014) 'Does school choice help rural children from disadvantaged sections? Evidence from longitudinal research in Andhra Pradesh', *Economic and Political Weekly*, XLIX(51): 46–52.

Karwan-e-Mohabbat, Anhad and Muslim Women's Forum (2020) 'Sifting evidence – the untold story of the Delhi Riots book, September 18th 2022', [online], Available from: https://karwanemohabbat.in/wp-content/uploads/2020/09/SIFTING-EVIDENCE-SEPT-18-2020.pdf [Accessed 13 June 2022].

Katju, M. (2003) *Vishva Hindu Parishad and Indian Politics*, Hyderabad: Orient Blackswan.

Katsambekis, G. (2017) 'The populist surge in post-democratic times: theoretical and political challenges', *The Political Quarterly*, 88(2): 202–10.

Kaur, N. (2019) 'Draft National Education Policy 2019: An Overview', *Voices of Teachers and Teacher Educators, VIII*(I): 90–101. Available from: https://ncert.nic.in/pdf/publication/journalsandperiodicals/vtte/vtte_July_2019.pdf [Accessed 18 July 2022].

Kaushik, H. (2017) 'Private is passé: Gujarat villagers go old school', *Times of India*, [online] 4 June, Available from: https://timesofindia.indiatimes.com/city/ahmedabad/private-is-passe-villagers-go-old-school/articleshow/58980743.cms [Accessed 4 July 2021].

Kazmin, A. (2018) 'India's north-south fissures deepen over national budgeting', *Financial Times*, [online], Available from: https://www.ft.com/content/cd5efba4-6d9f-11e8-852d-d8b934ff5ffa [Accessed 20 October 2021].

Keating, J., Preston, R., Burke, P., Heertum, R., and Arnove, R. (2013) 'Institutionalizing international influence', in R. Arnove, C. Torres, and S. Franz (eds), *Comparative Education: Dialectics of the Global and the Local*, Lanham, MD: Rowman and Littlefield, pp.247–92.

Kennedy, L. (2004) 'The political determinants of reform packaging: contrasting responses to economic liberalization in Andhra Pradesh and Tamil Nadu', in R. Jenkins (ed), *Regional Reflections: Comparing Politics across India's States*, Delhi: Oxford University Press, pp.29–65.

Kennedy, L. (2007) 'Regional industrial policies driving peri-urban dynamics in Hyderabad, India', *Cities*, 24(2): 95–109.

Kennedy, L., Robin, K., and Zamuner, D. (2013) 'Comparing state-level policy responses to economic reforms in India. a subnational political economy perspective', *Revue de la régulation. Capitalisme, institutions, pouvoirs*, 13: 1.

Kerawalla, R. (2020) 'NEP 2020: challenges that govt must address to expedite education reforms', *Hindustan Times*, [online] 12 February, Available from: https://www.hindustantimes.com/education/nep-2020-challenges-that-govt-mustaddress-to-expedite-education-reforms/story-GBNZVBj0Zt1fzTLk33m0LI.html [Accessed 12 January 2022].

Khan, M. and Lutful, B.R. (2021) 'Equality to Second Class: India's Governance of its Muslim Minority', International Institute of Islamic Thought (IIIT), [online] Available from: https://iiit.org/en/equality-to-second-class-indias-governance-of-its-muslim-minority/ [Accessed 18 February 2022].

Khaitan, T. (2020) 'Killing a constitution with a thousand cuts: executive aggrandizement and party-state fusion in India', *The Law & Ethics of Human Rights*, 14(1): 49–95.

Kheera, R. (2019) 'Aadhaar failures: a tragedy of errors' [online], Available from: https://www.epw.in/engage/article/aadhaar-failures-food-services-welfare [Accessed 14 February 2022].

Khilnani, S. (1997) 'India's theaters of independence', *Wilson Quarterly*. [online], Available from: http://archive.wilsonquarterly.com/sites/default/files/articles/WQ_VOL21_A_1997_Article_01.pdf [Accessed 10 January 2022].

Khilnani, S. (1999) *The Idea of India*, New Delhi: Penguin Books.

Khubchandani, L.M. (1981) *Multilingual Education in India*, Pune: Center for Communication Studies.

Kidwai, H., Burnette, D., Rao, S., Nath, S., Bajaj, M., and Bajpai, N. (2013) 'In-service teacher training for public primary schools in rural India findings from district Morigaon (Assam) and district Medak (Andhra Pradesh)', [online], Available from: https://repository.usfca.edu/cgi/viewcontent.cgi?article=1014&context=soe_fac [Accessed 11 January 2022].

Kim, H., Talreja, V., and Ravindranath, S. (2019) 'How do you measure happiness? Exploring the happiness curriculum in Delhi schools', *Education Plus Development. Brookings*, [online] 13 November, Available from: https://www.brookings.edu/blog/education-plus-development/2019/11/13/how-do-you-measure-happiness-exploring-the-happiness-curriculum-in-delhi-schools/ [Accessed 13 January 2022].

Kingdon, G. (1996) 'The quality and efficiency of private and public education: a case-study of urban India', *Oxford Bulletin of Economics and Statistics*, 58(1): 57–82.

Kingdon, G.G. (2005) 'Private and public schooling: the Indian experience', prepared for the conference 'Mobilizing the Private Sector for Public Education', Co-sponsored by the World Bank Kennedy School of Government, Harvard University, working paper, pp.5–6.

Kingdon, G.G. (2007) 'The progress of school education in India', *Oxford Review of Economic Policy*, 23(2): 168–95.

Kingdon, G.G. (2015) 'Indian schools are failing their students', *The New York Times*, [online] 16 December, Available from: http://www.nytimes.com/2015/12/16/opinion/indian-schools-are-failing-their-students.html [Accessed 16 January 2022].

Kingdon, G.G., (2017) 'The emptying of public schools and growth of private schools in India', *Budget Private*, 12: 12–31.

Kingdon, G.G. and Sipahimalani-Rao, V. (2010) 'Para-teachers in India: status and impact', *Economic and Political Weekly*, XLV: 59–67.

Kingdon, G.G. and Muzammil, M. (2013) 'The school governance environment in Uttar Pradesh, India: implications for teacher accountability and effort', *The Journal of Development Studies*, 49(2): 251–69.

Kingdon, G.G. and Pal, S. (2014) 'Can private school growth foster 'education for all': Tracing the aggregate effects at the district level', Available from: http://dx.doi.org/10.2139/ssrn.2327001 [Accessed 22 June 2021].

Kinnvall, C. (2004) 'Globalization and religious nationalism: self, identity and the search for ontological security', *Political Psychology*, 25(5): 741–68.

Kivisto, P. and Thomas F. (2007) *Citizenship – Discourse, Theory and Transnational Prospects*, Oxford: Blackwell.

Kirkpatrick, A. and A.J. Liddicoat (eds). (2019) *The Routledge Handbook of Language Education Policy in Asia*, Abingdon: Routledge.

Klees, S.J. (2008) 'A quarter century of neoliberal thinking in education: misleading analyses and failed policies', *Globalisation, Societies and Education*, 6(4): 311–48.

Klees, S. (2017) 'Beyond neoliberalism: reflections on capitalism and education', *Policy Futures in Education*, 18(1): 9–29.

Kochar, R. (2020) 'Promoting exclusion to make education inclusive?', *Education South Asia*, [online] 7 August, Available from: https://educationso uthasia.web.ox.ac.uk/article/thinkpiece7 [Accessed 17 February 2022].

Kohli, A. (1990) *Democracy and Discontent: India's Growing Crisis of Governability*, Cambridge: Cambridge University Press.

Kosonen, K. (2017) 'Language of Instruction in Southeast Asia. Paper Commissioned for the 2017/8 Global Education Monitoring Report, Accountability in Education: Meeting Our Commitments', Paris: UNESCO, Available from: http://unesdoc.unesco.org/images/0025/002595/259576e.pdf [Accessed 10 June 2022].

Koshy, J. (2021) 'Science ministry funds trial on effect of Gayatri mantra in treating COVID-19', *The Hindu*, [online] 20 March, Available from: https://www.thehindu.com/news/national/science-ministry-funds-trial-on-effect-of-gayatri-mantra-in-treating-covid-19/article34111676.ece [Accessed 19 February 2022].

Krastev, I. and Holmes, S. (2019) *The Light that Failed: A Reckoning*, London: Penguin UK.

Krishna, A. (2021) 'Assam, Bihar, Jharkhand have worst retention rate in schools: Education Ministry', *News Careers 360*, [online] 29 November, Available from: https://news.careers360.com/educat ion-ministry-assam-jharkhand-bihar-school-dropout-rate-rajasthan-uttar-pradesh-retention-parliament-lok-sabha-news-udise [Accessed 29 July 2021].

Kulandaiswamy, V.C. (2006) *Reconstruction of Higher Education in India*, Hyderabad: The ICFAI University Press.

Kuchay, B. (2019) 'What you should know about India's 'anti-Muslim' citizenship law', *Aljazeera,* [online], 16 December, Available from: https://www.aljazeera.com/news/2019/12/16/what-you-should-know-about-indias-anti-muslim-citizenship-law/?utm_source=website%2526utm_medium=article_page%2526utm_campaign=read_more_links [Accessed 18 February 2022].

Kumar, K. (1986) 'Textbooks and educational culture', *Economic and Political Weekly*, 21(30): 1309–11.

Kumar, K. (1988) 'Origins of India's textbook culture', *Comparative Education Review*, 32(4): 452–64.

Kumar, K. (2001) *Prejudice and Pride*, New Delhi: Viking by Penguin.

Kumar, K. (2005) *Political Agenda of Education: A Study of Colonialist and Nationalist Ideas*, New Delhi: SAGE Publications India.

Kumar, V.A. (2009) 'Federalism and Decentralisation in India: Andhra Pradesh and Tamil Nadu. Institute for Social and Economic Change', Working Paper, [online], Available from: https://www.researchgate.net/profile/Anil-Vaddiraju-2/publication/314096479_FEDERALISM_AND_DECENTRALISATION_IN_INDIA_ANDHRA_PRADESH_AND_TAMIL_NADU/links/58b565d0aca272b99390f5e3/FEDERALISM-AND-DECENTRALISATION-IN-INDIA-ANDHRA-PRADESH-AND-TAMIL-NADU.pdf [Accessed 10 June 2022].

Kumar, A. (2019) 'Cultures of learning in developing education systems: government and NGO classrooms in India', *International Journal of Educational Research*, 95(2): 76–89.

Kumar, A. (2022) Between criticality and conformism: citizenship and education in post-independent India, *Journal of Human Values*, 28(1): 57–69.

Kumar, D. and Choudhury, P. K. (2020) 'Determinants of private school choice in India: all about the family backgrounds?', *Journal of School Choice*, 15(4): 576–602.

Kumar, K. (2010) 'Quality in education: competing concepts', *Contemporary Education Dialogue*, 7(1): 7–18.

Kundu, P., Rout, S., Singh, G., Mobeen, K., and Rehman, R. (2016) 'Public financing of school education in India: a fact sheet', Centre for Budget and Governance Accountability.

Kurian, N.J. (2000) 'Widening regional disparities in India: some indicators', *Indian Journal of Medical Research*, 126: 374–80.

Kymlicka, W. and Wayne, N (eds) (2000) *Citizenship in Diverse Societies*, Oxford: University Press.

Laclau, E. (2005) *On Populist Reason*, London, Verso.

LaDousa, C. (2014) *Hindi is our Ground, English is our Sky: Education, Language, and Social Class in Contemporary India*, New York: Berghahn Books.

Ladson-Billings, G. (2006) 'From the achievement gap to the education debt: understanding achievement in US schools', *Educational Researcher*, 35(7): 3–12.

Lafleur, M. and Srivastava, P. (2020) 'Children's accounts of labelling and stigmatization in private schools in Delhi, India and the Right to Education Act', *Education Policy Analysis Archives*, 27(135): 33.

Lall, M. (2007) 'Indian education policy under the NDA government', in K. Adeney and L Saez, *Coalition Politics and Hindu Nationalism*, London: Routledge, 169–86.

Lall, M. (2008) 'Educate to hate: the use of education in the creation of antagonistic national identities in India and Pakistan', *Compare*, 38(1): 103–19.

Lall, M. (2009) 'Globalization and the fundamentalization of curricula: lessons from India', in M. Lall and E. Vickers (eds), *Education as a Political Tool in Asia*, London and New York: Routledge, pp.171–92.

Lall, M. and Vickers, E. (eds.) (2009) *Education as a Political Tool in Asia*, London: Routledge.

Lall, M. and Nambissan, G. (eds.) (2011) *Education and Social Justice in the Era of Globalisation – India and the UK*, New Delhi: Routledge.

Lall, M. (2012) 'India's education crisis – the withdrawal of the Indian middle classes from government education', in A. Rachid and I. Muzaffar (eds), *Educational Crisis and Reform: Perspectives from South Asia*, Karachi: Oxford University Press, pp.31–55.

Lall, M. (2013) 'National identity, citizenship and the role of education in India', in S. Mitra, (ed.), *Citizenship as Cultural Flow, Structure, Agency and Power*, Berlin: Springer, 151–66.

Lall, M. (2021a) *Myanmar's Education Reform – A Pathway to Social Justice?*, London: UCL Press.

Lall, M. (2021b) 'The value of Bama-saga: minorities within minorities' views in Shan and Rakhine States', *Language and Education*, 35(3): 204–25.

Lall, M. and Saeed, T. (2019) *Youth and the National Narrative: Education, Terrorism and the Security State in Pakistan*, London: Bloomsbury Publishing.

Lall, M. and Anand K. (2020) 'How the Covid 19 crisis is exacerbating and embedding communal inequalities in India and Pakistan', *UCL Blogs*, [online] 27 April, Available from: https://blogs.ucl.ac.uk/ceid/2020/04/27/lall-anand/ [Accessed 27 June 2021].

Lall, M., Anand, K., Bali, M., Banerji, A., Jain, S., Khan, F., and Singh, A. (2020) 'What works and why in Indian government schools – teachers' voices in Delhi NCR', *IRDSE*, [online], Available from: https://www.irdse.org/front/Final-Report.pdf [Accessed 10 June 2021].

Lall, M.C. (2001) *India's Missed Opportunity*, Aldershot: Ashgate, Reprinted by Routledge 2019.

Lahoti, R. and Mukhopadhyay, R. (2019) 'School choice in rural India: perceptions and realities in four states', *Economic and Political Weekly*, 54(49): 51–7.

Languille, S. (2017) 'Public private partnerships in education and health in the global south: a literature review', *Journal of International and Comparative Social Policy*, 33(2): 142–65.

LaRocque, N. (2008) *Public-Private Partnerships in Basic Education: An International Review*, Reading: CfBT Education Trust.

Lasky, S. (2000) 'The cultural and emotional politics of teacher–parent interactions', *Teaching and Teacher Education*, 16(8): 843–60.

Lawrence III, C.R. (2004) 'Forbidden conversations: on race, privacy, and community (a continuing conversation with John Ely on racism and democracy)', *Yale Law Journal*, 114: 1353.

Leaton Gray, S.H. (2006) 'What does it mean to be a teacher? Three tensions within contemporary teacher professionalism examined in terms of government policy and the knowledge economy', *Forum*, 48(3): 305–16.

Leathwood, C. (2004) 'A critique of institutional inequalities in higher education: (or an alternative to hypocrisy for higher educational policy)', *Theory and Research in Education*, 2(1): 31–48.

Lee, J. (2018) 'Understanding site selection of for-profit educational management organization charter schools', *Education Policy Analysis Archives*, 26(77): 1–26.

Levitsky, S. and Ziblatt, D. (2018) *How Democracies Die*, London: Penguin Books.

Lightfoot, A., Balasubramanian, A., Tsimpli, I., Mukhopadhyay, L., and Treffers-Daller, J. (2021) 'Measuring the multilingual reality: lessons from classrooms in Delhi and Hyderabad', *International Journal of Bilingual Education and Bilingualism*, 25(6): 2208–28.

Lipman, P. (2004) 'Education accountability and repression of democracy post-9/11', *Journal for Critical Education Policy Studies*, 2(1): 52–72.

Lipman, P. (2011) 'Neoliberal education restructuring dangers and opportunities of the present crisis', *Monthly Review*, 63(3).

Lok Jumbish Parishad Jaipur. (1992) 'Lok Jumbish: The First Report (Nov. 1992)', Available from: http://14.139.60.153/bitstream/123456789/8983/1/Lok%20Jumbish%20The%20first%20Report%20Nov.%201992%20D7336.pdf [Accessed 13 June 2022].

Longkumer, A. (2020) *The Greater India Experiment: Hindutva and the Northeast*, Stanford, CA: Stanford University Press.

Lüde Rolf von. (2015) 'Academic freedom under pressure: from collegial governance to new managerialism', In P. Zgag, U. Teichler, H.G. Schuetze, and A. Wolter (eds), *Higher Education Reform: Looking Back-Looking Forward*, Frankfurt am Main: Peter Lang Edition.

Macedo, D. (2000) *Chomsky on Miseducation*, Lanham, MD: Rowman & Littlefield Publishers.

MacKenzie, P.J. (2009) 'Mother tongue first multilingual education among the tribal communities in India', *International Journal of Bilingual Education and Bilingualism*, 12(4): 369–85.

MacPherson, I., Robertson, S., and Walford, G. (eds). (2014) *Education, Privatisation and Social Justice: Case Studies from Africa, South Asia and South East Asia*, Oxford: Symposium Books Ltd.

Madan, T.N. (1998) 'Secularism in its place', in R. Bhargava (ed.), *Secularism and its Critics*, Delhi: Oxford University Press.

Mahajan, G. and Jodhka, S.S. (eds). (2010) *Religion, Community and Development: Changing Contours of Politics and Policy in India*, New Delhi: Routledge.

Mahajan, G. (2020) 'In India: secularism or multiculturalism?', Open Democracy, [online] 3 February, Available from: https://www.opende mocracy.net/en/global-extremes/india-secularism-or-multiculturalism/ [Accessed 3 January 2022].

Mallapur, C. (2018) 'Communal violence up 28% under Modi govt but short of UPA's decadal high', *Business Standard*, [online] 9 February, Available from: https://www.business-standard.com/article/current-affairs/commu nal-violence-increases-28-under-modi-govt-yet-short-of-upa-high-118 020900128_1.html [Accessed 9 January 2022].

Manjrekar, N. (2013) 'Women school teachers in new times: some preliminary reflections', *Indian Journal of Gender Studies*, 20(2): 335–56.

Manor, R. (1998) 'Democracy, participation, and public policy: the politics of institutional design', in M. Robinson and G. White (eds), *The Democratic Developmental State: Politics and Institutional Design*, pp.150–86.

Manor, J. (1995) 'India's chief ministers and the problem of governability', in P. Oldenburg and P. Armonk (eds), *India Briefing: Staying the Course*, New York: M.E. Sharpe, pp.47–73.

Mander, H. (2018) 'The dark side of humanity and legality: a glimpse inside Assam's detention centres for 'foreigners', *Scroll.in*, 26 June, Available from: http//scroll.in/article/883936/assam-citizens-register-detention-cent res-for-foreigners-offer-a- glimpse-of-the-looming-tragedy [Accessed 14 February 2022].

Mangaldas, C.A. (2020) 'NEP 2020: an interplay of education and technology', *Bloomberg Quint*, [online], Available from: https://www.blo ombergquint.com/opinion/nep-2020-aninterplay-of-education-and-tec hnology [Accessed 10 January 2022].

Manor, J., (2010) 'Local governance', in N. Gopal Jayal and P. Bhanu Mehta (eds), The *Oxford Companion to Politics in India*, Delhi: Oxford University Press, pp.55–65.

Marik, P. (2020) 'How India is silencing its students'. *The Diplomat*. [online] 14 October, Available from: https://thediplomat.com/2020/10/how-india-is-silencing-its-students/ [Accessed 14 January 2021].

Mathew, A. (2016) 'Reforms in higher education in India: a review of recommendations of commissions and committees on education', CPRHE Research Paper, 2.

Mathrubhumi (2018) 'UP's anti-Romeo squads: sobering reminder of how far moral policing has gone in India', *Mathrubumi*, [online] 28 February, Available from: https://english.mathrubhumi.com/features/social-issues/ up-s-anti-romeo-squads-sobering-reminder-of-how-far-moral-policing-has-gone-in-india-1.2636673 [Accessed 28 January 2021].

Mathur, N. (2018) 'The low politics of higher education: saffron branded neoliberalism and the assault on Indian universities', *Critical Policy Studies*, 12(1): 121–125.

Matthan, T., Anusha, C., and Thapan, M. (2014) 'Being Muslims, becoming citizens: a Muslim girls' school in post-riot Ahmedabad', in M. Thapan (ed.), *Ethnographies of Schooling in Contemporary India*, New Delhi: Sage Publications, pp.225–70.

Mediavigil (2019) 'Contested citizenship in Assam: people's tribunal on constitutional processes and human cost', interim jury report, 7–8 September, Available from: https://www.mediavigil.com/wp-content/uploads/2019/09/Assam-NRC-Peoples-Tribunal-Interim-Jury-Report.pdf [Accessed 12 September 2019].

Mehta, A. (2021) 'NCERT: the saffronising of academica', Education For All In India, [online] 11 April, Available from: https://educationforallinindia.com/ncert-the-saffronising-of-academica/ [Accessed 10 January 2022].

Mehrotra, S. and Panchamukhi, P.R. (2006) 'Private provision of elementary education in India: findings of a survey in eight states', *Compare*, 36(4): 421–42.

Mehta, D., Gardia, A., and Rathore, H.C.S. (2010) 'Teacher participation in the decision-making process: reality and repercussions in Indian higher education', *Compare*, 40(5): 659–71.

Mehta, A.K. and Otto, C. (1996) *Global Trading Practices and Poverty Alleviation in South Asia: A Gender Perspective*, New York: UNIFEM.

Menon, N. (2020) 'Sifting evidence – a review of Delhi riots 2020: the untold story'. Karwan-E-Mohabbat, Anhad and Muslim Women's Forum. Kafila Online. [online], Available from: https://kafila.online/2020/09/19/sifting-evidence-a-review-of-delhi-riots-2020-the-untold-story-karwan-e-mohabbat-anhad-and-muslim-womens-forum/ [Accessed 10 July 2021].

Menon, S., Viswanatha, V., and Sahi, J. (2014) 'Teaching in two tongues: rethinking the role of language (s) in teacher education in India', *Contemporary Education Dialogue*, 11(1): 41–65.

Menashy, F. (2016) 'Understanding the roles of non-state actors in global governance: evidence from the Global Partnership for Education', *Journal of Education Policy*, 31(1): 98–118.

Metcalf, T. (1994) *Ideologies of the Raj*, Cambridge: Cambridge University Press.

Mettler, S. and Lieberman, R.C. (2020) *Four Threats: The Recurring Crises of American Democracy*, New York: St. Martin's Press.

MHRD [Ministry of Human Resource Development] (1999), (2000), (2001) *Selected Educational Statistics 1997–98, 1998–99 and 1999–2000*, New Delhi: Government of India.

MHRD [Ministry of Human Resource Development] (2004) 'Report of the Panel of Historians', *MHRD*, [online], Available from: www.ncert.nic.in [Accessed 8 September 2020].

MHRD [Ministry of Human Resource Development]. (2019) *Draft National Education Policy*, New Delhi: Ministry of Human Resource Development.

Mihindukulasuriya, R. (2021) 'Twitter calls IIT Kharagpur 2022 calendar mumbo-jumbo, creator says it's colonial hangover', *The Print*, [online] 26 December, Available from: https://theprint.in/tech/twitter-calls-iit-kharag pur-2022-calendar-mumbo-jumbo-creator-says-its-colonial-hangover/788 447/?amp [Accessed 5 January 2022].

Miller, D. (1988) 'The ethical significance of nationality', *Ethics*, 98(4): 647–62.

Miller, S. (2005) 'Language in education: are we meeting the needs of linguistic minorities in cities', in R. Banerji and S. Surianarian (eds), *City Children, City Schools: Challenges of Universalising Elementary Education in Urban India*, Pratham Resource Centre Working Paper (in collaboration with UNESCO).

Milligan, L.O. and Tikly, L. (2016) 'English as a medium of instruction in postcolonial contexts: moving the debate forward', *Comparative Education*, 52(3): 277–80.

Milner, H.R. and Laughter, J.C. (2015) 'But good intentions are not enough: preparing teachers to center race and poverty', *The Urban Review*, 47(2): 341–63.

Ministry of Education (n.d.) 'Article 350A - facilities for instruction in mother-tongue at primary stage' [online], Available from: https://www. education.gov.in/en/article-350a [Accessed 5 June 2022].

Ministry of External Affairs (1972) 'Treaty of Peace and Friendship between the Government of India and the Government of the People's Republic of Bangladesh', 19 March, Available from: https://www.mea.gov.in/bilateral-documents.htm?dtl/5621/Treaty+of+Peace+and+Friendship [Accessed 25 February 2022].

Ministry of Finance (Government of Finance). (n.d.) 'Economic Survey 1996–1997', *Union and Exonomic Survey*, [online], Available from: https:// www.indiabudget.gov.in/budget_archive/es96-97/esmain.htm [Accessed 20 February 2022].

Ministry of Law and Justice (2019) The Citizenship Amendment Act, 2019 No. 47 of 2019, *The Gazette of India Extraordinary*, 47: 4–6.

Ministry of Law and Justice (n.d.) 'The Gazette of India' [online], Available from: https://egazette.nic.in/WriteReadData/2019/214646.pdf [Accessed 11 February 2022].

Mishra, A. (2020) 'JNU a centre of excellence, but it must get rid of the anti-national forces', *Outlook India*, [online], Available from: https://www. outlookindia.com/website/story/opinion-jnu-must-get-rid-of-anti-natio nal-forces-to-transform-into-centre-of-educational-excellence/354797 [Accessed 10 January 2022].

Mishra, P. (2012) 'The Gujarat massacre: New India's blood rite', *The Guardian*, [online] 14 March, Available from: https://www.theguardian.com/commen tisfree/2012/mar/14/new-india-gujarat-massacre [Accessed 14 June 2021].

Misra, S. (2019a) 'Controversy over Hindi language; an attempt to divert attention from important issues?', *ORF*, [online] 30 September, Available from: https://www.orfonline.org/expert-speak/controversy-over-hindi-language-an-attempt-to-divert-attention-from-important-issues-55964/ [Accessed 30 September 2021].

Misra, D. (2019b) 'Universities and regions—the role of regional engagement in the development of new universities in India', (Doctoral dissertation), London: University College London).

Mitra, S.K. (2001) 'Panchayati raj and governance in India', in A. Kohli (ed), *The Success of India's Democracy*, Cambridge: Cambridge University Press, pp.103–26.

Mitra, S.K. (ed.). (2013) *Citizenship as Cultural Flow: Structure, Agency and Power*, Springer Science & Business Media.

Mitra, Y. and Singh, D. (2020) 'NEP 2020: an interplay of education and technology', *India Corporate Law*, [online], Available from: https://corporate.cyrilamarchandblogs.com/2020/08/nep-2020-an-interplay-ofeducation-and-technology/#_ftn6 [Accessed 20 October 2021].

Mody, N.B. (1987) 'The press in India: the Shah Bano judgment and its aftermath, *Asian Survey*, 27(8): 935–53.

Modi, S. and Postaria, R. (2020) 'How COVID-19 deepens the digital education divide in India', *Weforum,* [online] 5 October, Available from: https://www.weforum.org/agenda/2020/10/how-covid-19-deepens-the-digital-education-divide-in-india/ [Accessed 5 January 2022].

Mohammad-Arif, A. (2012) 'Muslims in Bangalore: a minority at ease?', in L. Gayer and C. Jaffrelot (eds), *Muslims in Indian Cities: Trajectories of Marginalisation*, London: Hurst and Co., pp.287–310.

Mohan, R. (2016) 'Indianise, nationalise, spiritualise: The RSS education project is in expansion mode', *Scroll India*, [online] 30 August, Available from: https://scroll.in/article/815049/indianise-nationalise-spiritualise-the-rss-education-project-is-in-for-the-long-haul [Accessed 30 September 2021].

Mohan, G. (2020) 'UN human rights body moves Supreme Court over CAA, India hits back saying citizenship law internal matter', *India Today,* 3 March, Available from https://www.indiatoday.in/india/story/now-un-human-rights-body-moves-supreme- court-over-caa-1651950-2020-03-03 [Accessed 13 March 2020].

Mond, H. and Prakash, P. (2019) 'Motivations to set up and manage low-fee private schools in India', *Education Policy Analysis Archives*, 27: 134.

Mondal, P. (n.d.) 'Top 4 projects initiated by government on rural education in India', Available from: http://www.yourarticlelibrary.com/sociology/top-4-projects-initiated-by-government-on-rural-education-in-india/34978 [Accessed 13 June 2021].

Monbiot, G. (2019) 'Neoliberalism promised freedom- instead it delivers stifling control', *The Guardian*, [online] 10 April, Available from: https://www.theguardian.com/commentisfree/2019/apr/10/neoliberalism-freedom-control-privatisation-state [Accessed 10 June 2021].

Mok, K.H. (2003) 'Similar trends, diverse agendas: higher education reforms in East Asia', *Globalisation, Societies and Education*, 1(2): 201–21.

Morris, A.K. and Hiebert, J. (2011) 'Creating shared instructional products: an alternative approach to improving teaching', *Educational Researcher*, 40(1): 5–14.

Mohan, G. (2020) 'UN human rights body moves Supreme Court over CAA, India hits back saying citizenship law internal matter', *India Today*, 3 March, Available from https://www.indiatoday.in/india/story/now-un-human-rights-body-moves-supreme- court-over-caa-1651950-2020-03-03 [Accessed 13 March 2020].

Mohanty, D. (2018) 'Tea seller who runs school for slum kids can't believe praise', *Times of India*, [online] 27 January, Available from: https://www.indiatimes.com/news/india/padma-shri-tea-seller-who-runs-school-for-80-slum-kids-with-his-meagre-earnings-is-an-inspiration-for-all-361120.html [Accessed 27 July 2021].

Mohanty, A.K. (2008) 'Multilingual Education for Indigenous Children: Escaping the Vicious Cycle of Language Disadvantage in India', NESCO-UNU International Conference on Globalization and Languages, 27–8 August, Tokyo.

Moore, A. and Clarke, M. (2016) 'Cruel optimism': teacher attachment to professionalism in an era of performativity, *Journal of Education Policy*, 31(5): 666–77.

Mouffe, C. (2018) *For a Left Populism*, London: Verso.

Mousumi, M.A. and Kusakabe, T. (2019) 'The dilemmas of school choice: do parents really 'choose' low-fee private schools in Delhi, India?', *Compare: A Journal of Comparative and International Education*, 49(2): 230–48.

Mujahid, A.M. (2020) 'Hindu nationalists are using COVID-19 to fuel a humanitarian disaster in India', *Washington Monthly*, [online] 18 April, Available from: https://washingtonmonthly.com/2020/04/18/hindu-nationalists-are-using-covid-19-to-fuel-a-humanitarian-disaster-in-india/ [Accessed 18 July 2021].

Mukerji, S. and Walton, M. (2012, 2016) 'Learning the right lessons: measurement, experimentation and the need to turn India's right to education act upside-down', *India Infrastructure Report 2012*, Delhi: Routledge India, pp.109–26.

Mukherjee, M. and Mukherjee, A. (2001) 'Communalisation of education, the history textbook controversy: an overview', Available from: http://www.sacw.net/HateEducation/MridulaAditya122001.html [Accessed 1 June 2021].

Mukherjee, R. (Director) (1960) Hum Hindustani [film]. Motion Picture. Available from: https://www.youtube.com/watch?v=t31XUGHYmdM [Accessed 18 July 2022].

Mukhopadhyay, R. and Sriprakash, A. (2011) 'Global frameworks, local contingencies: policy translations and education development in India', *Compare*, 41(3): 311–26.

Mukhopadhyay, R. and Sarangapani, P.M. (2018) 'Introduction: Education in India between the state and market – concepts framing the new discourse: quality, efficiency, accountability', in M. Jain, A. Mehendale, R. Mukhopadhyay, P. M. Sarangapani, and C. Winch (eds), *School Education in India*, Delhi: Routledge India, pp.1–27.

Müller, J.W. (2017) 'Qu'est-ce que le populisme? Définir enfin la menace', *Apres-demain*, 3: 5–7.

Mundy, K. and Menashy, F. (2012) 'The role of the international finance corporation in the promotion of public private partnerships for educational development', in A. Verger, F. Menashy, K. Mundy and S. Robertson (eds), *Public Private Partnerships in Education*, Cheltenham: Edward Elgar Publishing, pp.81–103.

Muralidharan, K. and Kremer, M. (2006) *Public and Private Schools in Rural India*, Cambridge, MA: Harvard University, Department of Economics.

Muralidharan, K. and Kremer, M. (2009) 'Public-private schools in rural India', in R. Chakrabarti and P.E. Peterson (eds), *School Choice International: Exploring Public-Private Partnerships*, (pp. 91–110), Cambridge, MA: The MIT Press.

Muralidharan, K. and Sundararaman, V. (2011) 'Teacher performance pay: experimental evidence from India', *Journal of Political Economy*, 119(1): 39–77.

Muralidharan, K. and Sundararaman, V. (2013) *Contract teachers: Experimental evidence from India* (No. w19440). National Bureau of Economic Research.

Muralidharan, K. and Sundararaman, V. (2015) 'The aggregate effect of school choice: evidence from a two-stage experiment in India', *The Quarterly Journal of Economics*, 130(3): 1011–66.

Nair, P. (2009) 'Religious political parties and their welfare work: relations between the RSS, the Bharatiya Janata Party and the Vidya Bharati Schools in India', Working Paper, Birmingham, UK: University of Birmingham.

Nair, J. (2017) 'The provocations of the public university', *Economic and Political Weekly*, 52(37): 34–41.

Nair, S. (2019) 'Why is the northeast on the boil?', *The Hindu,* [online] 15 December, Available from: https://www.thehindu.com/news/natio nal/why-is-the-northeast-on-the-boil/article30307359.ece [Accessed 15 July 2021].

Nair, R. (2020) 'The Citizenship (Amendment) Act, 2019 – a constitutional defence', *NLIU Law Review*.

Nambissan, G.B. (2006) 'Terms of inclusion: Dalits and the right to education', in R. Kumar, *The Crisis of Elementary Education in India*, New Delhi: Sage Publications, pp.225–65.

Nambissan, G.B. (2012) 'Private schools for the poor: business as usual?', *Economic and Political Weekly*, 47(41): 51–8.

Nambissan, G.B. (2013) 'Opening up the black box? Sociologists and the study of schooling in India', in G.B. Nambissan and S.S. Rao (eds). *Sociology of Education in India: Changing Contours and Emerging Concerns*, Oxford: Oxford University Press, pp.83–102.

Nambissan, G.B. (2014) 'Sociology of school education in India: a review of research 2000– 2010', *Indian Sociology*, 2: 66–101.

Nambissan, G.B. and Rao, S.S. (eds) (2013) *Sociology of Education in India: Changing Contours and Emerging Concerns*, Oxford: Oxford University Press.

Nambissan, G. and Ball, S. (2011) 'Advocacy networks, choice and schooling of the poor in India', *Global Networks*, 10(3): 324–43.

Nambissan, G.B. and Ball, S.J. (2010) 'Advocacy networks, choice and private schooling of the poor in India', *Global Networks*, 10(3): 324–43.

Nanda, M. (2005) *Postmodernism, Hindu Nationalism and 'Vedic Science'*, Oxford: Oxford University Press, pp.221–36.

Nanda, M. (2011) *The God Market: How Globalization is Making India More Hindu*, New York: New York University Press.

Nanda, M. (2004) *Prophets Facing Backwards: Postmodernism, Science and Hindu Nationalism*, New Delhi: Permanent Black.

Nandy, A. (1998) 'The politics of secularism and the recovery of religious toleration', in Rajeev Bhargava (ed.), *Secularism and Its Critics*, Delhi: Oxford University Press, pp.177–94.

Narula, A. and Kalra, M.B. (2019) 'Exploring in-service teachers' beliefs about happiness', *International E-Journal of Advances in Education*, 5(14): 146–59.

Narwana, K. (2019) 'Hierarchies of access in schooling: an exploration of parental school choice in Haryana', *Millennial Asia*, 10(2): 183–203.

Naseem, M.A. and Stöber, G. (2014) 'Textbooks, identity politics, and lines of conflict in South Asia', *Journal of Educational Media, Memory, and Society*, 6(2): 1–9.

National Council of Educational Research and Training (India). (2005) *National Curriculum Framework 2005*, New Delhi: National Council of Educational Research and Training.

Nawani, D. (2013) 'Continuously and comprehensively evaluating children', *Economic and Political Weekly*, 48(2): 33–40.

NCERT [National Council of Educational Research and Training] (1992) 'Fifth All-India Educational Survey', New Delhi: NCERT.

NCERT [National Council of Educational Research and Training] (1997–1998) *Sixth All-India Educational Survey: National Tables*, vols. I to VI, New Delhi: NCERT

NCERT [National Council of Educational Research and Training] (2004) *Learning History without Burden, A Note to School Teachers*, [online], Available from: www.ncert.nic.in [Accessed 9 October 2021].

NCERT [National Council of Educational Research and Training] (2005) *National Curriculum Framework*. New Delhi: NCERT, [online] Available from:http://www.ncert.nic.in/html/framework2005.htm [Accessed 10 October 2021].

NCERT [National Council of Educational Research and Training] (2006) 'Position Paper: National Focus Group on Curriculum, Syllabus and Textbooks', [online], Available from: http://www.ncert.nic.in/new_nc ert/ncert/rightside/links/pdf/focus_group/cst_final.pdf [Accessed 20 June 2021].

NCERT [National Council of Educational Research and Training] (2007) National Curriculum Framework 2005 (No. id: 1138), Available from: https://ideas.repec.org/p/ess/wpaper/id1138.html [Accessed 12 June 2021].

NCERT [National Council of Educational Research and Training] (2000) National Curriculum Framework (NCF) Available from: http://www.ncert.nic.in/oth_anoun/NCF_2000_Eng.pdf [Accessed 2 October 2021].

NCTE [National Council for Teacher Education] (2009) *National Curriculum for Teacher Education (NCFTE): Towards a Humane and Professional Teacher*, New Delhi: NCTE.

NCTE [National Council for Teacher Education] (2010) *National Curriculum Framework for Teacher Education: Towards Preparing Professional and Humane Teacher*, New Delhi: National Council for Teacher Education.

Nehru, J. (1946) *The Discovery of India*, London: Meridian Books Ltd.

NEP [National Education Policy] (2020) 'Ministry of Human Resource Development', Government of India, [online] Available from: https://www.mhrd.gov.in/sites/upload_files/mhrd/files/NEP_Final_English_0.pdf [Accessed 20 July 2021].

Nichols, J.R. (2020) 'What kind of (citizen)? Civic orientations in Indian education policy', *Citizenship Teaching & Learning*, 15(2): 239–54.

Niti Aayog (2019) *School Education Quality Index (SEQI)*. [online], Available from: https://www.educationforallinindia.com/SEQI_MHRD_30Sept2 019.pdf [Accessed 13 July 2021].

NPR (2021) 'India's pandemic death toll estimated at about 4 million: 10 times the official count', 20 July, Available from: https://www.npr.org/sections/goatsandsoda/2021/07/20/1018438334/indias-pandemic-death-toll-estimated-at-about-4-million-10-times-the-official-co?t=1633608513 701 [Accessed 25 February 2022].

Ohara, Y. (2012) 'Examining the legitimacy of unrecognized low-fee private schools in India: comparing different perspective', *Compare: A Journal of Comparative & International Education*, 42(1): 69–90.

Oommen, T.K. (2005) *Crisis and Contention in Indian Society*, Delhi: Sage.

Olsen, B. (2008) *Teaching What They Learn, Learning What They Live*, Boulder, CO: Paradigm Publishers.

Olssen, M. and Peters, M.A. (2005) 'Neoliberalism, higher education and the knowledge economy: from the free market to knowledge capitalism', *Journal of Education Policy*, 20(3): 313–45.

Osgood, J. (2006) 'Deconstructing professionalism in early childhood education: resisting the regulatory gaze', *Contemporary Issues in Early Childhood*, 7(1): 5–14.

O'Sullivan, M. (2006) 'Lesson observation and quality in primary education as contextual teaching and learning processes', *International Journal of Educational Development*, 26(3): 246–60.

Outlook India (2017) 'New Rajasthan textbooks make way for RSS ideologue Savarkar, remove Nehru and give passing mention to Gandhi', *Outlook India*, [online] 9 June, Available from: https://www.outlookindia.com/website/story/new-rajasthan-textbooks-make-way-for-rss-ideologue-sarvarkar-remove-nehru-and-gi/299267 [Accessed 14 December 2021].

Oza, R. (2006) *The Making of Neoliberal India: Nationalism, Gender, and the Paradoxes of Globalization*, New York: Routledge.

Padwad, A. and Dixit, K. (2018) 'Coping with curricular change with limited support: an Indian English teacher's perspective', in M. Wedell and L. Grassick (eds), *International Perspectives on Teachers Living with Curriculum Change*, London: Palgrave Macmillan, pp.103–24.

Padma, V. (2019) 'Intolerance and funding concern Indian scientists ahead of elections', *Nature*, [online] 10 May, Available from: www.nature.com/articles/d41586-019-01465-3 [Accessed 11 July 2021].

Paik, S. (2020) 'Educational policies and practices: a critical perspective', *Learning Curve*, 6: 63–6.

Palshikar, S. (2013) 'Regional and caste parties', in A. Kohli and P. Singh (eds), *Routledge Handbook of Indian Politics*, Abingdon: Routledge, pp.91–104.

Palshikar, S. (2015) 'The BJP and Hindu nationalism: centrist politics and majoritarian impulses', *South Asia: Journal of South Asian Studies*, 38(4): 719–735.

Palshikar, S. (2019) 'Toward hegemony: the BJP beyond electoral dominance', *Economic and Political Weekly*, 53(33): 36–42.

Panda, A. (2020a) 'US religious freedom watchdog highlights "campaigns of harassment and violence" against minorities in India', *The Diplomat*, [online] 29 April, Available from: https://thediplomat.com/2020/04/us-religious-freedom-watchdog-highlights-campaigns-of-harassment-and-violence-against-minorities-in-india/ [Accessed 19 September 2021].

Panda, V. (2020b) 'NEP 2020: implementation challenges', *Education World*, [online], Available from: https://www.educationworld.in/nep-2020-implementation-challenges/ [Accessed 23 September 2021].

Pandey, G. (1991) 'In defence of the fragment: writing about Hindu–Muslim riots in India today', *Economic and Political Weekly*, 26(11–12): 559–73.

Pandey, S. (2006) 'Para-teacher scheme and quality education for all in India: policy perspectives and challenges for school effectiveness', *Journal of Education for Teaching*, 32(3): 319–34.

Pandey, N. (2018) 'Class 12 NCERT book drops "anti-Muslim" from 2002 Gujarat Riots', *Hindustan Times*, [online] 25 March, Available from: https://www.hindustantimes.com/education/class-12-ncert-book-on-political-science-drops-anti-muslim-from-2002-gujarat-riots/story-EIakJGVf4EIYiueHz2y3YI.html [Accessed 10 January 2022].

Pandey, N. and Arnimesh, S. (2020) 'RSS in Modi govt in numbers- 3 of 4 ministers are rooted in the Sangh', *The Print,* [online] 27 January, Available from: https://theprint.in/politics/rss-in-modi-govt-in-numbers-3-of-4-ministers-are-rooted-in-the-sangh/353942/ [Accessed 22 August 2021].

Pandey, K. (2020) 'COVID-19 lockdown highlights India's great digital divide', *Down To Earth*, [online] 30 July, Available from: https://www.downtoearth.org.in/news/governance/covid-19-lockdown-highlights-india-s-great-digital-divide-72514 [Accessed 30 August 2021].

Pandey, A. (2020) 'Keeping India's universities for the rich', *Jacobinmag,* [online], 27 January, Available from: https://jacobinmag.com/2020/01/jawaharlal-nehru-university-india-fee-hike [Accessed 4 September 2021].

Pandey, G. (2021) 'Beaten and humiliated by Hindu mobs for being a Muslim in India', *BBC News*, [online] 2 September, Available from: https://www.bbc.co.uk/news/world-asia-india-58406194 [Accessed 4 September 2021].

Panigrahi, S. (n.d.) 'Higher education fee hikes: affordability vs. sustainability'. *RGICS*, [online]. Available from: https://www.rgics.org/wp-content/uploads/Higher-Education-Fee-Hikes-Affordability-vs-Sustainability.pdf [Accessed 15 June 2021].

Park, J.S.Y. and Wee, L. (2013) *Markets of English: Linguistic Capital and Language Policy in a Globalizing World*, New York: Routledge.

Parliament of India, Lok Sabha (2016) 'Report of the Joint Committee on the Citizenship (Amendment) Bill, 2016, [online], Available from: http://prsindia.org/sites/default/files/bill_files/Joint%20committee%20report%20on%20citizenship%20(A)%20bill.pdf [Accessed 14 January 2020].

Patrinos, H.A., Osorio, F.B., and Guáqueta, J. (2009) *The Role and Impact of Public-Private Partnerships in Education*, Washington, DC: World Bank Publications.

Pattanaik, D. (2015) 'Holy cow unholy violence', *The Hindu*, [online] 6 October, Available from: https://www.thehindu.com/opinion/op-ed/holy-cow-unholy-violence/article7727157.ece [Accessed 15 July 2021].

Patel, I.G. (1992) 'New economic policies: a historical perspective', in D.K. Das (ed.), *Structural Adjustment in the Indian Economy*, New Delhi: Deep & Deep Publications, pp.113–33.

Peck, J. (2010) *Constructions of Neoliberal Reason*, Oxford: Oxford University Press.

Peck, J. and Tickell, A. (2002) 'Neoliberalizing space', *Antipode*, *34*(3): 380–404.

Perrigo, B. (2021) 'It is dangerous to speak up in India today. what the resignations of 2 academics show about freedom of expression under Modi', *Time*. [online] 19 March, Available from: https://time.com/5948112/acade mic-freedom-india-mehta/ [Accessed 13 January 2022].

Petersen, H. and Khan, A. (2022) 'They cut him into pieces': India's 'love jihad' conspiracy theory turns lethal', *The Guardian*, [online] 21 January, Available from: https://www.theguardian.com/world/2022/jan/21/ they-cut-him-into-pieces-indias-love-jihad-conspiracy-theory-turns-let hal [Accessed 2 February 2022].

Phillipson, R. (2017) 'Myths and realities of global English', *Language Policy*, 16(3): 313–31.

Pisharoty, S.B. (2021) 'Explainer: what do the MHA's changes to 1964 foreigners tribunals order mean?', [online], Available from https:// parichayblog.org/2021/07/10/foreigners-tribunal/ [Accessed 19 February 2022].

Planning Commission (2002) *Tenth Five Year Plan 2002–2007 Volume II. Social Sector Policies and Programs*. New Delhi: Planning Commission, Government of India.

Planning Commission Government of India (2013) *Twelfth Five Year Plan: Social Sectors* (Vol. 3), Delhi: Sage.

Poddar, U. (2022) 'Why a Karnataka college's hijab ban is an assault on the fundamental right to religion', *Scroll*, [online] 19 January, Available from: https://scroll.in/article/1015333/why-a-karnataka-colleges-hijab-ban-is-an-assault-on-the-fundamental-right-to-religion [Accessed 11 June 2022].

Prakash, P. (2019) 'No improvement in school education: NITI ranking', *Tribune India*, [online] 2 October, Available from: https://www.tribunein dia.com/news/archive/punjab/no-improvement-in-school-education-niti-ranking-841254 [Accessed 19 February 2022].

Prakke, B., van Peet, A., and van der Wolf, K. (2007) 'Challenging parents, teacher occupational stress and health in Dutch primary schools', *International Journal about Parents in Education*, 1: 36–44.

Pratt, N. (2018) 'Playing the levelling field: teachers' management of assessment in English primary schools', *Assessment in Education: Principles, Policy & Practice*, 25(5): 504–18.

Press Trust of India (2017) 'Kairana 'exodus', love jihad key issues for BJP in UP polls: Adityanath'. *Business Standard*, [online] 11 February, Available from: https://www.business-standard.com/article/politics/kairana-exodus-love-jihad-key-issues-for-bjp-in-up-polls-adityanath-117020400330_1.html [Accessed 10 September 2021].

Press Trust of India (2018) 'Campaign on "ills of love jihad" to be launched by VHP in Bengal schools', *NDTV*, [online], 4 September, Available from: https://www.ndtv.com/kolkata-news/campaign-on-ills-of-love-jihad-to-be-launched-by-vishwa-hindu-parishad-in-bengal-schools-1911309 [Accessed 10 August 2021].

Press Trust of India (2019) 'It will reduce India to Hindutva version Of Pakistan: Shashi Tharoor on CAB', *Outlook*, [online], Available from: https://www.indiatvnews.com/news/india/bjp-ballari-mla-somashekar-reddy-threatens-anti-caa-protesters-says-we-are-80-percent-576220 [Accessed 10 January 2022].

Press Trust of India (2020) 'Days after Parvesh Verma's 'terrorist' dig at Arvind Kejriwal, Prakash Javadekar says not much difference between anarchist and terrorist', *First Post*, Available from: https://www.firstpost.com/politics/days-after-parvesh-vermas-terrorist-dig-at-arvind-kejriwal-prakash-javadekar-says-not-much-difference-between-anarchist-and-terrorist-7996671.html [Accessed 10 February 2022].

PTI (Press Trust of India) (2020a) 'RSS, BJP trying to do away with reservation: Maharashtra Congress chief', *Business Standard,* [online] 13 February, Available from: https://www.business-standard.com/article/pti-stories/rss-bjp-trying-to-do-away-with-reservation-thorat-120021202053_1.html [Accessed 13 December 2021].

PTI (Press Trust of India) (2020b) 'Won't sit quiet till each oppressed Pakistani refugee gets Indian citizenship: Amit Shah', *NDTV*, [online] 12 January, Available from: https://www.ndtv.com/india-news/wont-sit-quiet-till-each-oppressed-pakistani-refugee-gets-indian-citizenship-amit-shah-2162862 [Accessed 10 July 2021].

PTI (Press Trust of India) (2020c) 'Anti-national sloganeers at JNU deserve jail: Amit Shah; slams Rahul, Kejriwal', *EconomicTimes*, [online] 12 January. Available from: https://economictimes.indiatimes.com/news/politics-and-nation/anti-national-sloganeers-at-jnu-deserve-jail-amit-shah-slams-rahul-kejriwal/articleshow/73217651.cms?from=mdr [Accessed 12 August 2021].

PTI (Press Trust of India) [Business Standard] (2022) 'India vibrant democracy, don't need certificate from others: MEA to Hamid', *Business Standard*, [online] 28 January, Available from: https://www.business-standard.com/article/current-affairs/india-vibrant-democracy-don-t-need-certificate-from-others-mea-to-hamid-122012801811_1.html [Accessed 2 February 2022].

Probe Report (1999) *Public Report on Basic Education in India*, New Delhi: Oxford University Press.

PRS, Legislative Research (2020) 'Rajasthan budget analysis 2020–21', *PRS India*, [online], Available from: https://www.prsindia.org/parliamenttr ack/budgets/rajasthan-budget-analysis-2020-21 [Accessed 10 June 2021].

Puniyani, R. (2017) 'What is the RSS agenda in education?', *Mainstream Weekly*, [online] 9 October, Available from: http://www.mainstreamwee kly.net/article7504.html [Accessed 9 July 2021].

Purohit, B. C. (2008) 'Health and human development at sub-state level in India', *The Journal of Socio-Economics*, 37(6): 2248–60.

Qaisar, A. (2021) 'Will India's COVID-19 crisis impact Modi's chances in the 2024 general elections?', *PGI* [online], 19 May, Available from: https:// www.pgitl.com/blog/india-covid-19-crisis-impact-modis-chances-2024- general-elections/ [Accessed 19 May 2022].

Qureshi, A. (2015) 'Public–private partnerships and bureaucratic culture in Pakistan', *The Cambridge Journal of Anthropology*, 33(1): 35–48.

Rajagopal, A. (2001) *Politics after Television: Hindu Nationalism and the Reshaping of the Public in India*, Cambridge: Cambridge University Press.

Rajaraman, I. and Sinha, D. (2007) 'Functional devolution to rural local bodies in four states', *Economic and Political Weekly*, 16 June: 2275–83.

Rahman, T. (2005) 'Passports to privilege: the English-medium schools in Pakistan', [online], Available from: https://www.repository.cam.ac.uk/bitstr eam/handle/1810/229190/pdsa_01_01_04.pdf?sequence=2 [Accessed 10 August 2021].

Rai, A. (2020) 'Bloomsbury says it won't publish book on Delhi riots after social media backlash', *Hindustan Times,* [online] 22 August, Available from: https://www.hindustantimes.com/india-news/bloomsbury-says-it- won-t-publish-book-on-delhi-riots-after-social-media-backlash/story-KsE s4hLXrRfxCj3X0vimyN.html [Accessed 20 July 2021].

Raina, J. (2020) 'Policy shifts in school education: where do we stand?', [online], Available from: https://www.jmc.ac.in/uploads/staticfiles/jmcrev iew/vol4/Jyoti%20Raina%20The%20JMC%20Review%202020.pdf [Accessed 11 August 2021].

Ram, A. and Sharma, K.D. (1995) *National Policy on Education: an Overview*, Delhi: Vikas Publishing House.

Ramachandran, V. and Harish, S. (2000) 'Rajasthan Shiksha Karmi Project an overall appraisal', Available from: http://www.eruindia.org/files/Shik sha%20Karmi%202000.pdf [Accessed 5 July 2022].

Ramachandran, V. (ed.). (2003a) *Getting Children Back to School: Case Studies in Primary Education*, India: Sage.

Ramachandran, V. (2003b) 'Backward and forward linkages that strengthen primary education', *Economic and Political Weekly*, 8 March: 959–68.

Ramachandran, V., S. Bhattacharjea, and K. Sheshagiri. (2008) *Primary School Teachers: the Twist and Turns of Everyday Practice: A Project Supported by Azim Premji Foundation, Bangalore*, New Delhi: Educational Resource Unit.

Ramachandran, V. (2009) *The Elementary Education System in India: Exploring Institutional Structures, Processes and Dynamics*, Cambridge: Routledge.

Ramachandran, S. (2017) 'Hindutva terrorism in India', *The Diplomat*, [online] 7 July, Available from: https://thediplomat.com/2017/07/hindu tva-terrorism-in-india/ [Accessed 11 September 2021].

Ramachandran, S. (2020) 'Hindutva violence in India', *Counter Terrorist Trends and Analyses*, 12(4): 15–20.

Rampal, N. (2018) 'Muslims' enrolment in higher education rises by 37%, gender parity also improves', *The Print*, [online] 29 July, Available from: https://theprint.in/india/governance/muslims-enrolment-in-hig her-education-rises-by-37-gender-parity-also-improves/90152/ [Accessed 15 July 2021].

Rao, A. (2014) '6 worst communal riots under UPA government'. *DNA India,* [online] 3 May, Available from: https://www.dnaindia.com/india/rep ort-6-worst-communal-riots-under-upa-government-1984678n [Accessed 20 September 2021].

Rao, S.S. (2008) 'India's language debates and education of linguistic minorities', *Economic and Political Weekly*, 43(36): 63–9.

Rao, S.S. (2013) 'Structural exclusion in everyday institutional life: labelling of stigmatized groups in an IIT', in G. Nambican and S.S. Rao (eds), *Sociology of Education in India: Changing Contours and Emerging Concerns*, New Delhi: Oxford University Press, pp.199–223.

Rao, S. (2020) 'Keep campus under watch, monitor Whatsapp', *Indian Express*, [online], 10 February, Available from: https://indianexpress.com/ article/india/conference-of-dgp-ifp-pm-modi-pune-6259539/ [Accessed 10 September 2021].

Rao, S., Ganguly, S., Singh, J., and Dash, R.R. (2017) 'School closures and mergers: a multi-state study of policy and its impact on public education system in Telengana, Odisha and Rajasthan', Gurgaon: Save the Children.

Rao, U. (2019) 'Mixed reaction to government's English-medium schools move', *Times of India*, [online] 7 November, Available from: https://times ofindia.indiatimes.com/city/visakhapatnam/mixed-reaction-to-govts- eng-medium-schools-move/articleshow/71945188.cms [Accessed 11 September 2021].

Rashid, S. and Yadav, S.S. (2020) 'Impact of Covid-19 pandemic on higher education and research', *Indian Journal of Human Development*, 14(2): 340–3.

Rashid, O. (2020) 'Ayodhya awaits Modi's launch of Ram temple construction', *The Hindu*, [online] 4 August, Available from: https://www. thehindu.com/news/national/ayodhya-awaits-modis-launch-of-ram-tem ple-construction/article32271388.ece [Accessed 4 September 2021].

Raveendhren, R.S. (2020) 'New education policy and erosion of states' powers', *The Times of India*, [online] 19 August, Available from: https://timesofindia.indiatimes.com/city/chennai/new-education-policy-and-erosion-of-states-powers/articleshow/77624663.cms [Accessed 30 January 2022].

Ravitch, D. (2010) *The Death and Life of the Great American School System: How Testing and Choice are Undermining Education*, New York: Basic Books.

Rawat, S. (2021) '9.1 million thronged Mahakumbh despite Covid-19 surge: govt data', *Hindustan Times*, [online] 30 April, Available from: https://www.hindustantimes.com/cities/dehradun-news/91-million-thronged-mahakumbh-despite-covid-19-surge-govt-data-101619729096750.html [Accessed 30 May 2021].

Reay, D. (2004) 'It's all becoming a habitus': beyond the habitual use of habitus in educational research', *British Journal of Sociology of Education*, 25(4): 431–44.

Reay, D., David, M.E., and Ball, S.J. (2005) *Degrees of Choice: Class, Race, Gender and Higher Education*, London: Trentham Books.

Reddy, D.S. (2006) *Religious Identity and Political Destiny: Hindutva in the Culture of Ethnicism* (Vol. 3), Lanham, MD: AltaMira Press.

Rekhi, S. (1998) 'Taskforce on IT lays out plans to wire up India, propel it into the Information Age', *India Today*, [online] 20 July, Available from: https://www.indiatoday.in/magazine/economy/story/19980720-task-force-on-it-lays-out-plans-to-wire-up-india-propel-it-into-the-information-age-826748-1998-07-20 [Accessed 20 September 2021].

Reich, W. (1970) *The Mass Psychology of Fascism*, ed. M. Higgins and C.M. Raphael, New York: Farrar, Strauss & Giroux.

Robert, S.L. (2000) *A Class Art: Changing Teachers' Work, the State, and Globalisation*, New York: Falmer Press.

Right to Education Act (2009) 'The Right of Children to Free and Compulsory Education Act 2009', Ministry of Law and Justice, New Delhi: Government of India.

Robinson, N. and Gauri, V. (2010) 'Education, labor rights, and incentives: contract teacher cases in the Indian courts', Policy Research Working Paper 5365. World Bank.

Rodriguez, V. (2005) 'Citizenship and the Indian Constitution', in R. Bhargava and H. Reifeld (eds), *Civil Society, Public Sphere and Citizenship: Dialogues and Perceptions*, New Delhi: Sage Publications, pp.209–35.

Roy, A.K. (1992) 'Destruction of Babri Masjid'. *Economic and Political Weekly*, 49–50: 2618–40.

Roy, I. (2020a) 'India: a year after Narendra Modi's re-election the country's democracy is developing fascistic undertones', *The Conversation*, [online] 22 May, Available from: https://theconversation.com/india-a-year-after-narendra-modis-re-election-the-countrys-democracy-is-developing- fascistic-undertones-135604 [Accessed 22 September 2021].

Roy, K. (2002) 'National textbooks for the future?', *Economic and Political Weekly*, 37(51): 5083–5.

Roy, K. (2020b) 'A pandemic and a policy: contextualizing the National Education Policy 2020', *The Leaflet*, [online], Available from: https://www.theleaflet.in/a-pandemic-and-a-policycontextualizing-the-national-education-policy-2020/ [Accessed 20 July 2021].

Roy, S., Mukherjee, M., Sinha, P., Das, S., Bandopadhyay, S., and Mukherjee, A. (2021) 'Exploring the dynamics of protest against National Register of Citizens & Citizenship Amendment Act through online social media: the Indian experience', arXiv:2102.10531 Cornell University.

Rudolph, L.I. and Rudolph, S.H. (2001) 'Iconisation of Chandrababu: sharing sovereignty in India's federal market economy', *Economic and Political Weekly*, 36: 1546–60.

Runciman, D. (2018) *How Democracy Ends*, London: Basic Books.

Ruparelia, S., Reddy, S., Harriss, J., and Corbridge, S. (eds). (2011) *Understanding India's New Political Economy: A Great Transformation?*, Abingdon: Routledge.

Sabharwal, N.S. and Malish, C.M. (2017) 'Student diversity and challenges of inclusion in higher education in India', *International Higher Education*, 91: 25–27.

Sachar, R., Hamid, S., Oommen, T.K., Basith, M.A., Basant, R., Majeed, A., and Shariff, A. (2006) 'Social, economic and educational status of the Muslim community of India', 22136. East Asian Bureau of Economic Research.

Sachs, J. (2005) 'Teacher education and the development of professional identity: learning to be a teacher', in P. Denicolo and M. Kompf (eds), *Connecting Policy and Practice: Challenges for Teaching and Learning in Schools and Universities*, Oxford: Routledge, pp.5–21.

Sachs, J. (2016) 'Teacher professionalism: Why are we still talking about it?', *Teachers and Teaching*, 22(4): 413–425.

Sadgopal, A. (2008) 'Common school system: do we have an option?', *Janata Magazine*, 63: 19.

Sadgopal, A. (2016) 'Common classrooms, common playgrounds', in M. Prasad (ed), *Newsletter*, New Delhi: All India Forum for Right to Education.

Sah, P.K. (2021) 'Reproduction of nationalist and neoliberal ideologies in Nepal's language and literacy policies', *Asia Pacific Journal of Education*, 41(2): 238–52.

Sah, P.K. and Li, G. (2018) 'English medium instruction (EMI) as linguistic capital in Nepal: promises and realities', *International Multilingual Research Journal*, 12(2): 109–23.

Saha, A. (2019) 'Across Assam, chorus rises among MLAs: NRC is faulty, many genuine citizens out', *The Indian Express*, [online] 2 September, Available from: https://indianexpress.com/article/north-east-india/assam-nrc-mlas-faulty-genuine-citizens-out-5957268/ [Accessed 2 June 2021].

Saha, A. (2020) 'Explained: in Assam, new regional party Assam Jatiya Parishad sets up new equations', *The Indian Express*, [online] 17 September, Available from: https://indianexpress.com/article/explained/in-assam-new-regional-party-assam-jatiya-parishad-sets-up-new-equations-6598482/ [Accessed 10 July 2021].

Sahoo, N. (2021) 'Five challenges that would shape the outcome of NEP 2020', *ORFOnline*, [online] 26 November, Available from: https://www.orfonline.org/expert-speak/five-challenges-that-would-shape-the-outcome-of-nep-2020/?amp [Accessed 10 February 2021].

Sahoo, S. (2017) 'Intra-household gender disparity in school choice: evidence from private schooling in India', *The Journal of Development Studies*, 53(10): 1714–30.

Sahu, B., Jeffery, P., and Nakkeeran, N. (2017) 'Barriers to higher education: commonalities and contrasts in the experiences of Hindu and Muslim young women in urban Bengaluru', *Compare: A Journal of Comparative and International Education*, 47(2): 177–91.

Saikia, N., Joe, W., Saha, A., and Chutia, U. (2016) 'Cross border migration in Assam during 1951–2011: process, magnitude and socio-economic consequences', Major Project for ICSSR, India.

Saikia, S. (2020) 'Saffronizing the periphery: explaining the rise of the Bharatiya Janata Party in contemporary Assam', *Studies in Indian Politics*, 8(1): 69–84.

Samaddar, R. and Sen, S.K. (eds). (2020) *Political Transition and Development Imperatives in India*, New Delhi: Taylor & Francis.

Sammy, S. (2002) 'The model of ethnic democracy: Israel as a Jewish and democratic state', *Nations and Nationalism*, 8(4): 475–503.

Samoff, J. (2013) 'Institutionalizing international influence', in R. Arnove, C. Torres, and S. Franz (eds), *Comparative Education: Dialectics of the Global and the Local*, Lanham, MD: Rowman and Littlefield, pp.55–87.

Sancho, D. (2015) *Youth, Class and Education in Urban India: The Year that Can Break or Make You*, London: Routledge.

Sandhu, A.H. (2009) 'Reality of 'divide and rule' in British India'. *Pakistan Journal of History & Culture*, 30(1): 61–80.

Sandhu, S. (2021) 'Teachers within neoliberal educational reforms: a case study of Delhi', in A.W. Wiseman and P. Kumar (eds), *Building Teacher Quality in India: Examining Policy Frameworks and Implementation Outcomes*, Bingley: Emerald Publishing Limited, pp.159–87.

Sangeetha, G. (2020). 'Online higher education tipped to grow ten-fold post-Covid, NEP,. *Deccan Chronicle*, [online], Available from: https://www.deccanchronicle.com/business/companies/230820/online-highereducation-tipped-to-grow-ten-fold-post-covid-nep.html [Accessed 10 July 2021].

Santoro, D.A. (2011) 'Good teaching in difficult times: demoralization in the pursuit of good work', *American Journal of Education*, 118(1): 1–23.

Sanu, V.P. (2020) 'A battle for India's soul', *Jacobin,* [online], Available from: https://jacobinmag.com/2020/03/india-student-university-protesters-movement-citizenship-amendment-act-muslims [Accessed 10 May 2021].

Sarangapani, P.M. (2009) 'Quality, feasibility and desirability of low cost private schooling', *Economic and Political Weekly*, 44(43): 67–9.

Sarangapani, P.M. and Winch, C. (2010) 'Tooley, Dixon and Gomathi on private education in Hyderabad: a reply', *Oxford Review of Education*, 36(4): 499–515.

Saravanakumar, A.R. and Padmini Devi, K.R. (2020) 'Indian higher education: issues and opportunities', *Journal of Critical Reviews*, 7(2): 542–5.

Sarkar, S. (2005) 'In memoriam: Ernst Mayr (1904–2005)', *Journal of Biosciences*, 30(4): 415–18.

Sarkar, N. (2020) 'Has the Covid-19 pandemic accentuated inequality in the higher education sector? Evidence from India', Webinar presentation for the ESRC/OFSRE Centre for Global Higher Education, [online], Available from: https://www.researchcghe.org/events/cghe-seminar/has-the-covid-19-pandemic-accentuated-inequality-in-the-higher-education-sector-evidence-from-india/ [Accessed 20 July 2021].

Saraswathy, M. (2020) 'Explained | How toys will be made part of National Education Policy 2020', Money Control, [online] https://www.moneycontrol.com/news/business/economy/explained-how-toys-will-be-made-part-of-national-education-policy-2020-5751311.html [Accessed 5 September 2021].

Savarkar, V.D. (2021) 'Essentials of Hindutva', Savarkar.org, [online], Available from: http://savarkar.org/en/encyc/2017/5/23/2_12_12_04_essentials_of_hindutva.v001.pdf_1.pdf [Accessed 15 February 2022].

Sarkar, T. (2021) 'History as patriotism: lessons from India', *Journal of Genocide Research*, 24(2): 171–81.

School Search List (n.d) 'List of Schools', *Schoolsearchlist,* [online], Available from: https://schoolsearchlist.com [Accessed 19 February 2022].

Schools.org.in (n.d.) 'Schools in Assam', *schools.org.in,* [online], Available from: https://schools.org.in/assam [Accessed 19 February 2022].

School Education (n.d) 'Blockwise high schools list', *schooleducation.kac.nic.in,* [online], Available from: http://www.schooleducation.kar.nic.in/SchoolSearch/hsschlist.asp [Accessed 19 February 2022].

Schweisfurth, M. (2015) 'Learner-centred pedagogy: towards a post-2015 agenda for teaching and learning', *International Journal of Educational Development*, 40: 259–66.

SDSA (State of Democracy in South Asia) (1998), New Delhi: Oxford University Press.

Seargeant, P., and E. J. Erling. (2013) 'Introduction: English and development', in E. J. Erling and P. Seargeant (eds), *English and Development: Policy, Pedagogy and Globalization*, Bristol: Multilingual Matters, pp.1–20.

Sen, A. (2002) 'NGO says Gujarat riots were planned', *BBC News*, [online] 19 March, Available from: http://news.bbc.co.uk/1/hi/world/south_asia/1881497.stm [Accessed 19 September 2021].

Setalvad, T. (2005) 'Comments on National Curriculum Framework 2005', *The South Asian*, [online], Available from: http://www.thesouthasian.org/archives/2005/comments_on_national_curriculu.html [Accessed 6 September 2021].

Sethi, R. (2017) *The Last Battle of Saraighat: The Story of the BJP's Rise in the North-east*, New Delhi: Penguin Random House India Private Limited.

Sentinel Digital Desk (2021) 'Awareness campaign on yoga and Ayush practices held in Silchar', *Sentinel Assam*, [online], 10 September, Available from: https://www.sentinelassam.com/north-east-india-news/assam-news/awareness-campaign-on-yoga-and-ayush-practices-held-in-silchar-554192 [Accessed 15 September 2021].

Shamika, R., Gupta, N., and Nagaraj, P. (2019) 'Reviving higher education in India', Brookings India Research Paper, No. 11–01.

Shani, G. (2005) 'Indigenous modernities: nationalism and communalism in colonial India', *Ritsumeikan Annual Review of International Studies*, 4: 87–112.

Shani, G. (2008) *Sikh Nationalism and Identity in a Global Age*, London and New York: Routledge.

Shani, G. (2014) *Religion, Identity and Human Security*, London and New York: Routledge.

Shani, G. (2016) 'Spectres of partition: religious nationalism in post-colonial South Asia', In J. Kingston (ed.), *Asian Nationalism Reconsidered*, London and New York: Routledge, pp.35–47.

Shani, G. (2017) 'Human security as ontological security: a post-colonial approach', *Postcolonial Studies,* 20(3): 275–93.

Shani, G. (2019). 'Midnight's children: religion and nationalism in South Asia', in G. Shani and T. Kibe (eds), *Religion and Nationalism in Asia*, London: Routledge, pp.32–47.

Shani, G. (2020) 'Securitizing 'bare life'? Human security and coronavirus', *E-International Relations*, [online], Available from: https://www.e-ir.info/2020/04/03/securitizing-bare- life-human-security-and-coronavirus/ [Accessed 10 October 2021].

Shani, G. (2021a) 'Farmer protests warrant Modi's concern', *The Japan Times*, [online], 10 February, Available from: https://www.japantimes.co.jp/opinion/2021/02/10/commentary/world- commentary/india-farmers-narendra-modi-agriculture/ [Accessed 14 October 2021].

Shani, G. (2021b) 'Towards a Hindu Rashtra: Hindutva, religion, and nationalism in India', *Religion, State & Society*, 49(3): 264–80.

Shani, O. (2011) 'Gandhi, citizenship and the resilience of Indian nationhood', *Citizenship Studies*, 15(6–7): 659–78.

Sharma, A. (2016) 'Communal riots up 17% in 2015 under NDA', *Economic Times*, [online], 25 February, Available from: https://economictimes.indiatimes.com/news/politics-and-nation/communal-riots-up-17-in-2015-under-nda/articleshow/51130192.cms?from=mdr [Accessed 11 October 2021].

Sharma, A. (2017) 'Economically weaker sections', parental involvement and private schools: An exploratory study in Delhi', Unpublished MPhil dissertation, ZHCES-JNU.

Sharma, A. (2018) 'Accountability and academic freedom of faculty: a study of select public universities in India', PhD thesis, Jawaharlal Nehru University, New Delhi.

Sharma, A. Chishti, V., and Pathak, B.K. (2022) 'Teachers and students as political actors in Indian higher education', in S. Chattopadhyay, S. Marginson, and N.V. Varghese (eds) *Changing Higher Education in India*, Bloomsbury, London, pp.211–40.

Sharma, K. (2016b) 'State and politicisation of education in India: a comparative study between NDA and UPA regime', [online], Available from: https://docplayer.net/64965625-State-and-politicisation-of-education-in-india-a-comparative-study-between-nda-and-upa-regime-kangkana-sharma.html [Accessed 3 October 2021].

Sharma, K. (2020a) 'Indian colleges see spurt in applications as Covid forces students to ditch foreign plans', *The Print*, [online], 11 August, Available from: https://theprint.in/india/education/indian-colleges-see-spurt-in-applications-as-covidforces-students-to-ditch-foreign-plans/478856/ [Accessed 4 October 2021].

Sharma, M. (2016a) 'Narendra Modi and the new education policy: retrospection, reform and reality', *Journal of Asian Public Policy*, 9(2): 140–53.

Sharma, R.N. (2002) *Indian Education at the Crossroads*, Delhi: Shubhi Publications.

Sharma, S. (2020b) 'JNU violence: Indian university's radical history has long scared country's rulers', *The Conversation*, [online], 13 January, Available from: https://theconversation.com/jnu-violence-indian-universitys-radical-history-has-long-scared-countrys-rulers-129488 [Accessed 10 October 2021].

Shaw, G.R. (2012) 'India opens a door to private education', *New York Times*, [online], Available from: https://www.nytimes.com/2012/08/20/world/asia/india-opens-a-door-to-private-education.html [Accessed 10 September 2021].

Sherman, J. (2020) 'Kashmir internet shutdown continues, despite Supreme Court ruling', *The Diplomat*, [online], Available from: https://thediplomat.com/2020/08/kashmir-internet-shutdown-continues-despite-supreme-court-ruling/ [Accessed 19 February 2022].

Shukla, P.D. (1988) *The New Education Policy,* Delhi: Sterling Publishers Private Ltd.

Siddique, N. (2020) 'Inside Assam's detention camps: how the current citizenship crisis disenfranchises Indians', *Economic and Political Weekly*, 55: 7.

Singh, A. (2019) 'Policy brief: study on teacher time allocation and work perceptions', New Delhi: Accountability Initiative, Centre for Policy Research.

Singh, A.P. (2008) 'Globalization and its impact on national politics with reference to India: an overview of different dimensions', *The Indian Journal of Political Science*, 69(4): 801–14.

Singh, K. (2020) 'COVID-19 has pushed the Indian economy into a tailspin. But there's a way out', *The Wire*, [online], Available from: https://thewire.in/economy/covid-19-india-economicrecovery [Accessed 10 July 2021].

Singh, P. (2022) 'Blunting Constitution? 'Secular' parties using communalism to compete with BJP', *Counterview* [online], 27 January, Available from: https://www.counterview.net/2022/01/blunting-constitution-secular-parties.html [Accessed 19 May 2022].

Singh, R. (2013) 'Culturally inclusive pedagogies of care: a narrative inquiry', *Journal of Pedagogy*, 10(2): 87–99.

Singh, R. and Bangay, C. (2014) 'Low fee private schooling in India – more questions than answers? Observations from the Young Lives longitudinal research in Andhra Pradesh', *International Journal of Educational Development*, 39: 132–40.

Singh, S. (2018) 'Education for peace through transformative dialogue: perspectives from Kashmir', *International Review of Education*, 64(1): 43–63.

Skeggs, B. (2004) 'Context and background: Pierre Bourdieu's analysis of class, gender and sexuality', *The Sociological Review*, 52(2_suppl): 19–33.

Sleeter, C.E. (2002) 'State curriculum standards and the shaping of student consciousness', *Social Justice*, 29(490): 8–25.

Smail, A. (2014) 'Rediscovering the teacher within Indian child-centred pedagogy: implications for the global Child-Centred Approach', *Compare: A Journal of Comparative and International Education*, 44(4): 613–33.

Smith, A.D. (1999) *Myths and Memories of the Nation*, Oxford: Oxford University Press.

Smyth, J. (1995) 'Teachers' work and the labor process of teaching: central problematics in professional development', in: T.R. Guskey and M. Huberman (eds), *Professional Development in Education: New Paradigms & Practices,* New York: Teacher College Press, pp.69–91.

Smyth, J., Dow, A., Hattam, R., et al. (2000) *Teacher's Work in a Globalizing Economy*, London: The Falmer Press.

Smooha, S. (2002) 'The model of ethnic democracy: Israel as a Jewish and democratic state', *Nations and Nationalism*, 8(4): 475–503.

Sodhi, J. (2021) 'The Article 370 Amendments on Jammu and Kashmir: explaining the global silence', Observer Research Foundation Occasional Paper, Issue 318.

Sohal, K. (2020) 'Should it only be about development? Education at the 2019 Indian General Election' Think Pieces Series No. 5, Education. SouthAsia. Available from: https://educationsouthasia.web.ox.ac.uk/ [Accessed 2 October 2021].

Solomon, S. (2019) 'The false scientific claims made during Modi's first term', *Caravan Magazine*, [online], 26 June, Available from: https://caravanmagazine.in/science/false-scientific-claims-modi-first-term [Accessed 26 September 2021].

Special Correspondent [The Hindu]. (2021) 'SFI for incentive to bring back dropouts to schools', *The Hindu*, [online], 6 December, Available from: https://www.thehindu.com/news/cities/Madurai/sfi-for-incentive-to-bring-back-dropouts-to-schools/article37871778.ece [Accessed 6 October 2021].

Special Correspondent [The Hindu]. (2014) 'Historian Bipan Chandra passes away', *The Hindu*, [online] 30 August, Available from: https://www.thehindu.com/news/national/historian-bipan-chandra-passes-away/article6364874.ece [Accessed 30 September 2021].

Spring, J. (2015) 'Globalization of education: an introduction', *Journal of Global Education and Research,* 4 (2) [2020], Art. 1:96–112.

Sridharan, E. and Varshney, A. (2001) *Toward Moderate Pluralism: Political Parties in India*, Baltimore, MD, and London: Political Parties and Democracy.

Sridhar, K.K. (1991) 'Bilingual education in India', *Studies in Second Language Acquisition*, 14(4): 484, doi:10.1017/S0272263100011505.

Sriprakash, A. (2009) 'Joyful Learning in rural Indian primary schools: an analysis of social control in the context of child-centred discourses', *Compare*, 39(5): 629–41.

Sriprakash, A. (2012) *Pedagogies for Development: The Politics and Practice of Child-Centred Education in India*, (Vol. 16), New York: Springer Science & Business Media.

Srivastava, A. K. (2013) 'Leaders of slum dwellers: a study based on slums of Jaipur city', *IOSR Journal of Humanities and Social Sciences,* 8(2): 18–24.

Srivastava, P. (2008) 'Private schooling and mental models about girls' schooling in India', *Compare: A Journal of Comparative and International Education*, 36(4): 497–514.

Srivastava, P. (2016) 'Questioning the global scaling up of low-fee private schooling: the nexus between business, philanthropy, and PPPs', in A. Verger, C. Lubienski, and G. Steiner-Khamsi (eds), *World Yearbook of Education 2016: The Global Education Industry*, New York: Routledge, pp.248–63.

Srivastava, P. and Noronha, C. (2014) 'India's Right to Education Act: household experiences and private school responses', [online], Available from: https://ir.lib.uwo.ca/edupub/112/ [Accessed 10 October 2021].

Srivastava, P. and Noronha, C. (2016) 'The myth of free and barrier-free access: India's Right to Education Act — private schooling costs and household experiences', *Oxford Review of Education*, 42(5): 561–78.

Srivastava, R. (2020) 'The RSS impact on New Education Policy'. *India Today*, [online], 31 July, Available from: https://www.indiatoday.in/india/story/new-education-policy-rss-sangh-parivar-impact-sanskrit-1706340-2020-07-31 [Accessed 20 October 2021].

Stanley, J. (2018) *How Fascism Works: The Politics of Us and Them*, New York: Random House.

Starnawski, M. and Gawlicz, K. (2021) 'Parental choice, collective identity and neoliberalism in alternative education: new free democratic schools in Poland', *British Journal of Sociology of Education*, 42(8): 1172–91.

Subramaniam, C.N. (2003) NCERT's National Curriculum Framework: a review, *Revolutionary Democracy*, 9(2), Available from: http://www.revolutionarydemocracy.org/rdv9n2/ncert.htm [Accessed 13 June 2022].

Subramanian, V. (2019) 'Parallel partnerships: Teach for India and new institutional regimes in municipal schools in New Delhi', *International Studies in Sociology of Education*, 1–20.

Subramanian, V.K. (2018) 'From government to governance: Teach For India and new networks of reform in school education', *Contemporary Education Dialogue*, 15(1): 21–50.

Sukumar, N. (2008) 'Living a concept: semiotics of everyday exclusion', *Economic and Political Weekly*, 43(46): 14–17.

Sundar, N. (2005) 'Teaching to hate', in T. Ewing (ed), *Revolution and Pedagogy*, New York: Palgrave Macmillan, pp. 195–218.

Sundar, N. (2018) 'Academic freedom and Indian universities', *Economic and Political Weekly*, 53(24): 48–56.

Sundar, N. (2021) 'When universities become objects of counterinsurgency', *The Wire*, [online], 26 March, Available from: https://thewire.in/education/when-universities-become-objects-of-counterinsurgency [Accessed 10 January 2021].

Sundar, N. and Fazili, G. (2020) 'Academic freedom in India. A status report, 2020', In *The India Forum,* [online], 28 August, Available from: https://www.theindiaforum.in/article/academic-freedom-india [Accessed 29 August 2021].

Suraiya, J. (2013) '"Dented, painted" holy cows: RSS chief says rearing gau mata will prevent attacks on women', *Times of India* [online], Available from: https://timesofindia.indiatimes.com/edit-page/dented-painted-holy-cows-rss-chief-says-rearing-gau-mata-will-prevent-attacks-on-women/articleshow/17800024.cms [Accessed 29 December 2013].

Sutherland, L. A. (2016) 'Right to education – from policy to practice: social exclusion and gender in Delhi's primary education system', (Doctoral dissertation), Université d'Ottawa/University of Ottawa.

Suryawanshi, S. (2021) 'Congress pitch for Muslim quota could hurt Shiv Sena', *The New India Express*, [online], 25 February, Available from: https://www.newindianexpress.com/nation/2021/feb/25/congress-pitch-for-muslim-quota-could-hurt-shiv-sena-2268703.html [Accessed 15 October 2021].

Swain, M., Swain, M., and Das, D.K. (2009) 'Regional disparity in agricultural development in Orissa in the pre and post-reform period', *Social Change*, 39(2): 195–215.

Syed, A.R. (2019) 'Saffronised India', *Daily Times,* [online], 26 July, Available from: https://dailytimes.com.pk/437525/saffronised-india/ [Accessed 26 June 2020].

Tabulawa, R. (2003) 'International aid agencies, learner-centred pedagogy and political democratisation: a critique', *Comparative Education*, 39(1): 7–26.

Takwale, R. (2003) 'Challenges and opportunities of globalization for higher education in India – alternatives through e-education. *UGC*', [online], Available from: https://www.ugc.ac.in/oldpdf/pub/lectures/ugc_pro2.pdf [Accessed 20 October 2021].

Taneja, N. (n.d.) 'BJP assault on education and educational institutions', *CPIML*, [online], Available from: www.cpiml.org/liberation/year_2001/september/saffronimp.htm [Accessed 21 October 2021].

Target Study (n.d) 'Schools in India', *Target Study*, [online], Available from: https://targetstudy.com/school/ [Accessed 19 February 2021].

Thamarasseri, I. (2008) *Education in the Emerging Indian Society*, New Delhi: Kanishka Publishers.

Tharoor, S. (1997) *India from Midnight to the Millennium*, New Delhi: Viking Penguin India.

Thapar, R. (2009) 'The history debate and school textbooks in India: a personal memoir', *History Workshop Journal*, 67(1): 87–98.

Thapar, R. (2014) *The Past as Present: Forging Contemporary Identities through History*, New Delhi: Aleph Book Company.

The Companion (2018) 'Educational status of Muslims in India: problems & prospects', *The Companion*, [online], 9 October, Available from: https://thecompanion.in/educational-status-of-muslims-in-india-problems-prospects/ [Accessed 13 August 2021].

The Economist (2020) 'Narendra Modi threatens to turn India into a one-party state', *Economist*, [online], 28 November, Available from: https://www.economist.com/briefing/2020/11/28/narendra-modi-threatens-to-turn-india-into-a-one-party-state [Accessed 19 February 2022].

The Federal (2020) 'Chargesheet refers to Sharjeel's M.Phil on partition, attempts to divide Hindus', *The Federal,* [online] 25 September, Available from: https://thefederal.com/states/north/delhi/police-chargesheet-ref ers-to-sharjeels-m-phil-on-partition-attempts-to-divide-hindus/ [Accessed 10 August 2021].

The Guardian (2014) 'Dozens of Muslims killed in ethnic violence in north-east India', *The Guardian,* [online], 3 May, Available from: https://www.theg uardian.com/world/2014/may/03/dozens-muslims-killed-ethnic-viole nce-north-east-india-assam [Accessed 13 February 2022].

The Guardian (2020) 'A violent attack on academic freedom', Letters, *The Guardian,* [online], 9 January, Available from: https://www.theguard ian.com/world/2020/jan/09/a-violent-attack-on-academic-freedom [Accessed 9 January 2022].

The New India Express (2021) 'Don't blame Kumbh Mela for spread of COVID-19: Ravi Kishan to opposition', *The New India Express,* [online], Available from: https://www.newindianexpress.com/nation/2021/may/ 20/dont-blame-kumbh-mela-for-spread-of-covid-19-ravi-kishan-to-opp osition-2304841.html [Accessed 13 February 2022].

The Telegraph (2019) 'Partha Chatterjee promises 1000 English-medium schools Across Bengal', *The Telegraph,* [online], 8 July, Available from: https://www.telegraphindia.com/states/west-bengal/partha-chatter jee-promises-1000-englishmedium- schools-across-bengal/cid/1694087 [Accessed 10 July 2021].

The Times of India (2021) 'Two years since Article 370 abrogation: what has changed in Jammu and Kashmir?', *Times of India,* [online], 5 August, Available from: https://timesofindia.indiatimes.com/india/two-years-since-article-370-abrogation-what-has-changed-in-jammu-kashmir/arti cleshow/85057707.cms [Accessed 20 February 2021].

The Wire Staff (2018) 'Hindutva politics in command at DU, complaints mount of teacher (dis)orientation', *The Wire,* [online], 19 February, Available from: https://thewire.in/education/hindutva-politics-command-du-com plaints-mount-disorientation-teachers [Accessed 11 February 2021].

The Wire Staff (2020a) 'India registers low "Academic Freedom Index" score in new international report', *The Wire,* [online], 7 June, Available from: https://thewire.in/rights/india-registers-low-academic-freedom-index-score-in-new-international-report [Accessed 10 August 2021].

The Wire Staff (2020b) 'JNU Academic community slams VC's decision to host retd Armyman for Saraswati civilisation talk', *The Wire,* [online], 11 June, Available from: https://thewire.in/education/jnu-vc-major-gene ral-gd-bakshi-saraswati-webinar [Accessed 10 September 2021].

Therwath, I. (2011) 'The Indian state and the Diaspora: towards a new political model', in Eric Leclerc (ed.), *Political Models and Actors of the Indian Diaspora,* New Delhi: Manohar, pp.45–63.

Therwath, I. (2012) 'Cyber-hindutva: Hindu nationalism, the diaspora and the Web', *Social Science Information*, 51(4): 551–77.

Thyrniang, A. (2021) 'Christmas, Christ and the Indian situation', *The Shillong Times*, [online], 21 December, Available from: https://theshillo ngtimes.com/2021/12/22/christmas-christ-and-the-indian-situation/ [Accessed 10 January 2022].

Tickner, A. (2003) 'Seeing IR differently: notes from the Third World', *Millennium*, 32(2): 295–324.

Tierney, W.G. and Sabharwal, N.S. (2016) 'Academic freedom in the world's largest democracy', *International Higher Education*, 86: 15–16.

Tierney, W. and Sabharwal, N.S. (2017) 'Academic corruption: culture and trust in Indian higher education', *International Journal of Educational Development*, 55(1): 30–40.

Tilak, J.B. (1994) 'South Asian perspectives', *International Journal of Educational Research*, 21(8): 791–8.

Tilak, J.B. (1996) 'How free is' free'primary education in India?', *Economic and Political Weekly*, 31(5–6): 355–66.

Tilak, J.B. (1999) 'National human development initiative: education in the union budget', *Economic and Political Weekly*, 34(10–11): 614–20.

Tilak, J.B. (2002) 'Privatization of higher education in India', *International Higher Education*, Fall: 11–13.

Tilak, J.B. (2004) 'Public subsidies in education in India', *Economic and Political Weekly*, 39(4): 343–59.

Tilak, J.B. (2008) 'Higher education: a public good or a commodity for trade?' *Prospects*, 38(4), 449–66.

Tilak, J.B. (2011) 'What matters for outcomes in elementary education in India?', *Indian Journal of Human Development*, 5(1): 29–60.

Tilak, J.B. (2018) 'Education poverty in India', *Review of Development and Change*, 7(1): 1–44.

Tilak, J.B. (2021) 'COVID-19 and education in India: a new education crisis in the making', *Social Change*, 51(4): 493–513.

Tilak, J.B. and Sudarshan, R.M. (2001) *Private Schooling in Rural India* (No. 76), New Delhi: National Council of Applied Economic Research.

Tillin, L. (2015) 'Regional resilience and national party system change: India's 2014 general elections in context', *Contemporary South Asia*, 23(2): 181–97.

Tiwary, D. (2016) 'Section 124A: Jharkhand tops sedition cases, J&K has none', *Indian Express*, [online], 19 February, Available from: https://indian express.com/article/india/india-news-india/kanhaiya-kumar-jnu-sect ion-124a-2014-jharkhand-tops-sedition-cases-jk-has-none/ [Accessed 3 July 2021].

Tooley, J. (2001) 'The enterprise of education: opportunities and challenges for India', Liberty Institute Occasional Paper #6, New Delhi: Liberty Institute.

Tooley, J. (2009) *The Beautiful Tree*, Washington, DC: The Cato Institute.

Tooley, J. (2018) 'A chain of low-cost private schools for England', *Policy: A Journal of Public Policy and Ideas*, 34(2): 13–17.

Tooley, J. and Dixon, P. (2002) 'The private sector serving the educational needs of the poor: a case study from India: a case study from the Philippines', Available from: http://www.nc.ac.uk/egwest/research/India [Accessed 7 July 2021].

Tooley, J. and Stanfield, J. (2003) 'Government failure: EG West on education', IEA Occasional Paper No. 130, Available from: https://ssrn.com/abstract=676684 [Accessed 13 June 2022].

Tooley, J. and Dixon, P. (2005) 'An inspector calls: the regulation of "budget" private schools in Hyderabad, Andhra Pradesh, India', *International Journal of Educational Development*, 25(3): 269–85.

Tooley, J. and Dixon, P. (2006) 'De facto'privatisation of education and the poor: implications of a study from sub-Saharan Africa and India', *Compare*, 36(4): 443–62.

Tooley, J. and Dixon, P. (2007) 'Private schooling for low-income families: a census and comparative survey in East Delhi, India', *International Journal of Educational Development*, 27(2): 205–19.

Tooley, J. and Longfield, D. (2015) *Countries: A Response to the DFID-Commissioned Rigorous Literature Review*, London: Pearson.

Tooley, J. and Longfield, D. (2015) 'Affordability of private schools: exploration of a conundrum and towards a definition of "low-cost"', *Oxford Review of Education*, 42(4): 444–59.

Tooley, J., Bao, Y., Dixon, P., and Merrifield, J. (2011) 'School choice and academic performance: some evidence from developing countries', *Journal of School Choice*, 5(1): 1–39.

Traub, A. (2018) 'India's dangerous new curriculum', *The New York Review of Books*, [online] 6 December, Available from: https://www.nybooks.com/articles/2018/12/06/indias-dangerous-new-curriculum/ [Accessed 6 January 2022].

Tripathi, S. (2016) 'JNU has always been a 'hub of anti-national activities', says internal dossier', *Firstpost*, [online], 28 August, Available from: https://www.firstpost.com/india/jnu-dossier-kanhaiya-kumar-administrator-kashmir-umar-khalid-anti-national-sedition-2753874.html [Accessed 28 October 2021].

Tukdeo, S. (2019) 'Towards reconstruction: education in postcolonial India', in S. Tukdeo (ed), *India Goes to School*, New Delhi: Springer, pp.43–56.

Tummers, L., Bekkers, V., and Steijn, B. (2009) 'Policy alienation of public professionals: application in a new public management context', *Public Management Review*, 11(5): 685–706.

UCG (University Grants Commission) (2019) Annual Report 2018–2019, New Delhi: UGC.

UDISE (Unified District Information System for Education) (2019) https://udiseplus.gov.in/#/home.

UDISE (Unified District Information System for Education Plus) (n.d.) 'School Education Dashboard', *UDISE Plus,* Available from: https://dashboard.udiseplus.gov.in/#/reportDashboard/state [Accessed 20 February 2022].

Umarji, V. (2021) 'Enrolment shifts from private to govt schools in rural India: ASER 2021', *Business Standard*, [online] 17 November, Available from: https://www.business-standard.com/article/education/enrollment-shifts-from-private-to-govt-schools-in-rural-india-aser-2021-121111700520_1.html [Accessed 19 February 2022].

UNESCO (United Nations Educational, Scientific and Cultural Organization) (1990) *World Declaration on Education for All and Framework for Action to Meet Basic Learning Need*, Paris: United Nations Educational, Scientific and Cultural Organization.

UNESCO (United Nations Educational, Scientific and Cultural Organization) (2016) 'Road Map for Arts Education: The World Conference on Arts Education: Building Creative Capacity for the 21st Century', 6–9 March, Lisbon: United Nations Educational, Scientific and Cultural Organization.

United Liberation Front of Assam (n.d.) 'South Asia terrorism portal', [online], Available from: https://www.satp.org/satporgtp/countries/india/states/assam/terrorist_outfits/Ulfa.html.

United Nations (1948) 'Security Council Resolution 47, The India–Pakistan Question, S/RES/47', 21 April 1948, Available from: https://digitallibrary.un.org/record/111955/?ln=en, p.16 [Accessed 13 June 2021].

Vaish, V. (2008) 'Language attitudes of urban disadvantaged female students in India: an ethnographic approach', *Journal of Multilingual and Multicultural Development*, 29(3): 198–215.

Vaishnav, M. (2021) 'The decay of Indian democracy', *Foreign Affairs*, [online] 18 March, Available from: https://www.foreignaffairs.com/articles/india/2021-03-18/decay-indian-democracy [Accessed 19 February 2022].

Vajpeyi, A. (2017) *India Dissents*, New Delhi: Speaking Tiger.

Valenzuela, A. (1999). *Subtractive Schooling: US Mexican Youth and the Politics of Caring*. Albany: State University of New York Press.

Valli, L. and Buese, D. (2007) 'The changing roles of teachers in an era of high-stakes accountability', *American Educational Research Journal*, 44(3): 519–58.

Vanaik, A. (1997) *The Furies of Indian Communalism: Religion, Modernity, and Secularization*, New York: Verso.

Vanaik, A. (2006) 'Communalization of Indian polity', in P. R. Desouza and E. Sridharan (eds), *India's Political Parties*, New Delhi: Sage Publications, pp.173–98.

Vanaik, A. (2020) 'As the Hindu Rashtra project rolls on, it's time to consider what the end goal is', *The Wire*, [online] 11 June, Available from: https://thewire.in/politics/hindu-rashtra-project-end- goal [Accessed 13 September 2021].

Varghese, N.V. (n.d) 'Reforming education financing', India Seminar, [online], Available from: https://www.india-seminar.com/2000/494/494%20n.v.%20varghese.htm [Accessed 14 September 2021].

Varghese, N.V. (2022) 'Directions of change in higher education in India: from massification to universalization', in S. Chattopadhyay, S. Marginson, and N.V. Varghese (eds) *Changing Higher Education in India*, London: Bloomsbury, pp.23–46.

Varghese, N.V. and Sarkar, N. (2022) 'Privatization versus private sector in higher education in India', in S. Chattopadhyay, S. Marginson, and N.V. Varghese, (eds), *Changing Higher Education in India*, London: Bloomsbury, pp.95–120.

Vasavi, A.R. (2020) 'NEP 2020 ignores crisis in education among the marginalised majority in rural India', *Indian Express*, [online] 15 September, Available from: https://indianexpress.com/article/opinion/columns/national-education-policy-rural-education-schools-6596233/ [Accessed 28 September 2021].

Venkatanarayanan, S. (2015) 'Economic liberalization in 1991 and its impact on elementary education in India', *SAGE Open*, 5(2): 215824401557951.

Venkatesh, V. and Ahmad, F. (2020) 'Rewriting India: the construction of the "Hindutva" citizen in the Indian state', *Third World Approaches to International Law Review, Reflections*, 22.

Venugopal, V. (2018) 'Remove colonial influences in courses on social work: RSS to tell universities', *Economic Times*, [online] 14 June, Available from: https://economictimes.indiatimes.com/news/politics-and-nation/remove-colonial-influences-in-courses-on-social-work-rss-to-tell-universities/articleshow/64581978.cms?from=mdr [Accessed 20 September 2021].

Verger, A. (2012) 'Framing and selling global education policy: the promotion of public- private partnerships for education in low-income contexts', *Journal of Education Policy*, 27(1): 109–30.

Verger, A. and VanderKaaij, S. (2012) 'The national politics of global policies: public-private partnerships in Indian Education', in A. Verger, M. Novelli, and H.K. Altinyelken (eds), *Global Education Policy and International Development: New Agendas, Issues, and Policies*, London/New York: Bloomsbury Academic, pp.245–66.

Verger, A., Altinyelken, H., and De Koning, M. (2013) 'Global managerial education reforms and teachers', *Education International Research Institute IS Academic Program*.

Verger, A., Fontdevila, C., and Zancajo, A. (2016) *The privatization of education: A political of global education reform*, New York: Teachers College Press.

Verger, A., Fontdevila, C., Rogan, R., and Gurney, T. (2018) 'Manufacturing an illusory consensus? A bibliometric analysis of the international debate on education privatisation', *International Journal of Educational Development*, 64:81–95.

Verma, P. (2004) 'The terror of POTA and other security legislation in India', New Delhi: Human Rights Law Network and People's Watch, Madurai.

Verniers, G., Basim-u-Nissa, Kumarm, M., and Agrawal, N. (2021) 'Assam verdict: 29 charts that show just how polarised the election was', *Scroll India*, [online] 7 May, Available from: https://scroll.in/article/994249/assam-verdict-29-charts-that-show-just-how-polarised-the-election-was [Accessed 10 July 2021].

Vernoff, E.J. (1992) 'History in Indian schools: a study of textbooks produced by the central government and the state governments of Maharashtra, Gujarat, West Bengal, Andhra Pradesh, Kerala and Tamilnadu', Doctoral dissertation, New York University.

Vickers, E. and Jones, A. (2005) *History Education and National Identity in East Asia*, New York: Routledge.

Vidya Bharati (n.d.) 'Formal Schools', *Vidya Bharati*, [online], Available from: https://vidyabharti.net/formal-schools [Accessed 20 February 2022].

Vijan, D. (Producer) and Choudhary, S. (Director). (2017) '*Hindi Medium*', [Motion picture] [Film]. India: AA Films.

Vincent, C. and Menon, R. (2020) 'The educational strategies of the middle classes in England and India', in M. Lall and G. Nambissan, *Education and Social Justice in the Era of Globalisation*, India: Routledge, pp.56–80.

Vishwadeepak (2021) 'BJP govt's move to merge schools in MP will shut down 90% state-run schools, render one lack teachers jobless', *National Hearld India,* [online] 16 September, Available from: https://www.nationalheraldindia.com/india/bjp-govts-move-to-merge-schools-in-mp-will-shut-down-90-state-run-schools-render-one-lakh-teachers-jobless [Accessed 11 October 2021].

Wadhwa, W. (2014) 'Government vs private schools: Have things changed', *Annual Status of Education Report (Rural),* New Delhi: ASER centre.

Wahab, P. (2020) 'A War of Narratives: Understanding 2020 Delhi Violence in India', *A War of Narratives: Understanding*, [online], Available from: https://papers.ssrn.com/sol3/papers.cfm?abstract_id=3821421 [Accessed 20 July 2021].

Waikar, P. (2018) 'Reading Islamophobia in Hindutva: An Analysis of Narendra Modi's Political Discourse', *Islamophobia Studies Journal*, 4(2): 161–180.

Wen, C. (2020) 'Educating rural migrant children in interior China: The promise and pitfall of low-fee private schools', *International Journal of Educational Development*, 79: 102–276.

Westerfield, C. (2019) 'The Saffronization of Indian Textbooks', *Caitlin Westerfield*, [online], Available from: http://caitlinwesterfield.com/writing_samples/RLST375.pdf [Accessed 22 August 2021].

Widmalm, S. (2016) *Political Tolerance in the Global South: Images of India, Pakistan and Uganda*, London: Routledge.

Widmalm, S. (2020) 'Democratic virtues and educational institutions in India–black swans in conflict-ridden Jammu and Kashmir', *Journal of Peace Education*, 17(1): 61–82.

Windschitl, M. (2002) 'Framing constructivism in practice as the negotiation of dilemmas: An analysis of the conceptual, pedagogical, cultural, and political challenges facing teachers', *Review of educational research*, 72(2): 131–75.

Wirsing, R.G. (1998) *India, Pakistan and the Kashmir Dispute; On Regional Conflict and Its Resolution*, The MacMillan Press. Ltd.

Wolf, P.J., Egalite, A.J., and Dixon, P. (2015) 'Private school choice in developing countries: Experimental results from Delhi, India', in P. Dixon, S. Humble, and C. Counihan (eds), *Handbook of International Development and Education*, Cheltenham: Edward Elgar Publishing, pp.456–71.

Woodhead, M., Frost, M., and James, Z. (2013) 'Does growth in private schooling contribute to Education for All? Evidence from a longitudinal, two cohort study in Andhra Pradesh, India', *International Journal of Educational Development*, 33(1): 65–73.

World Bank (1991) 'India 1991 country economic memorandum vol 1 policies for adjustment with growth', 23 August 1991, *Country Operations Division, Asia Region*.

World Bank (1994) *Higher Education: The Lessons of Experience*, Washington: The World Bank.

World Bank (2021) *Indicators*. Available at: https://data.worldbank.org/indicator.

World Happiness Report (n.d.) Available at: https://worldhappiness.report.

Wrigley, T.E. (2007) 'Wayne Ross and Rich Gibson', in *Neoliberalism and Education Reform*, Creskill, NJ: Hampton Press.

Wrigley, T. (2011) 'Rethinking Education in the Era of Globalization', in *Contesting Neoliberal Education*, London: Routledge, pp.79–100.

Wyatt, A. (2009) *Party System Change in South India: Political Entrepreneurs, Patterns and Processes*, Abingdon, UK: Routledge.

Wyatt, A. (2015) 'Arvind Kejriwal's leadership of the Aam Aadmi party', *Contemporary South Asia*, 23(2): 167–80.

Wyatt, A. (2017) 'Paradiplomacy of India's chief ministers', *India Review*, 16(1): 106–24.

Wyatt, A. (2019) 'Small parties and the federal structure of the Indian state', *Contemporary South Asia*, 27(1): 66–72.

Youth for Human Rights Documentation (2020) 'An account of fear and impunity', *Human Rights Foundation*, Available from: https://www.hrfn. org/wp-content/uploads/2020/03/An-Account-of-Fear-Impunity.pdf [Accessed 10 October 2021].

Zavos, J. (2000) *The Emergence of Hindu Nationalism in India* (Vol. 42), New Delhi: Oxford University Press.

Zembylas, M. (2003) 'Interrogating "teacher identity": emotion, resistance, and self-formation', *Educational Theory*, 53(1): 107–27.

Zhang, W. (2014) 'The demand for shadow education in China: mainstream teachers and power relations', *Asia Pacific Journal of Education*, 34(4): 436–54.

Ziegfeld, A. (2016) *Why Regional Parties?*, Cambridge: Cambridge University Press.

Zimmer, O. (2003) 'Boundary mechanisms and symbolic resources: towards a process-oriented approach to national identity', *Nations and Nationalism*, 9(2): 173–93.

Zompa, T. (2021) 'Church vandalised, school stormed, Xmas disrupted: these are 8 attacks on Christians since Oct', *The Print*, [online], 30 December, Available from: https://theprint.in/theprint-essential/church-vandalised-school-stormed-xmas-disrupted-these-are-8-attacks-on-christians-since-oct/790764/ [Accessed 12 August 2021].

Textbooks

Bhattacharya, N. (2006) Class XII *Themes in Indian History-I, II, and III*, NCERT: New Delhi.

Lal, M. (2002) *India and the World: Social Sciences Book for Class VI*, Delhi: NCERT, p.58.

Jain, M. (2002) Class XI *Medieval India*, New Delhi: NCERT.

Om, H. (2002) Class IX *Contemporary India*, New Delhi: NCERT.

Mittal, S.C. (2003) Class XII *Modern India*, New Delhi: NCERT.

Saraswati Shishu Mandir Prakashan (2016a) Class XI *Themes in World History*, NCERT: New Delhi.

Saraswati Shishu Mandir Prakashan (2016b) Class III *Saraswati English Reader*, Mathura: Saraswati Shishu Mandir Prakashan.

Saraswati Shishu Mandir Prakashan (2016c) Class I–V *Personality Development Textbook, Vyaktigat Vikas Bhag 1–5*, Mathura: Saraswati Shishu Mandir Prakashan.

Saraswati Shishu Mandir Prakashan (2016d) Vyaktigat Vikas Bhag 1–5, Class 1 to 5, Mathura: Saraswati Shishu Mandir Prakashan.

Shiksha Mandir Prakashan (2016e) Vandana, Uttar Pradesh: Shiksha Mandir Prakashak.

Index